D0662460

BUDDHA OF
LOVE

Awarded the

Edward Cameron Dimock, Jr. Prize
in the Indian Humanities

by the American Institute of Indian Studies and
published with the Institute's generous support.

AIIS Publication Committee:

Susan S. Wadley, Co-Chair
Brian A. Hatcher, Co-Chair
Joyce B. Flueckiger
Pika Ghosh
Nytheli Sreenivas
Ramnarayan S. Rawat

BATTLING THE BUDDHA OF LOVE

A CULTURAL BIOGRAPHY OF THE GREATEST STATUE NEVER BUILT

JESSICA MARIE FALCONE

CORNELL UNIVERSITY PRESS

Ithaca and London

Copyright © 2018 by Cornell University

All rights reserved. Except for brief quotations in a review, this book, or parts thereof, must not be reproduced in any form without permission in writing from the publisher. For information, address Cornell University Press, Sage House, 512 East State Street, Ithaca, New York 14850. Visit our website at cornellpress.cornell.edu.

First published 2018 by Cornell University Press

Printed in the United States of America

Library of Congress Cataloging-in-Publication Data

Names: Falcone, Jessica Marie, 1976– author.
Title: Battling the Buddha of love : a cultural biography of
    the greatest statue never built / Jessica Marie Falcone.
Description: Ithaca : Cornell University Press, 2018. |
    Includes bibliographical references and index.
Identifiers: LCCN 2018008239 (print) | LCCN 2018009939
    (ebook) | ISBN 9781501723476 (pdf) |
    ISBN 9781501723490 (ret) | ISBN 9781501723469 |
    ISBN 9781501723469 (cloth ; alk. paper) |
    ISBN 9781501723483 (pbk. ; alk. paper)
Subjects: LCSH: Foundation for the Preservation of the
    Mahayana Tradition. | Mahayana Buddhism—Relations.
    | Buddhist converts. | Mahayana Buddhism—India—
    Kushinagar (District) | Maitreya (Buddhist deity)—
    Cult—India—Kushinagar (District) | Ethnology—
    India—Kushinagar (District)
Classification: LCC BQ7310 (ebook) | LCC BQ7310 .F35
    2018 (print) | DDC 294.3/437—dc23
LC record available at https://lccn.loc.gov/2018008239

To my family

❧ Contents

✒ NOTE ON CONVENTIONS

I wrote this book primarily for scholars and students of anthropology and Buddhist studies, but I can well imagine that it will find its way into the hands of people who have predisposed stances about the Maitreya Project one way or the other. In an effort to get all my readers on the same page from the outset about exactly what I am writing about, where that information is coming from, and how I have chosen to represent that data, I have moved a few notes on my research and writing conventions out of the footnotes and here into the foreground.

This book is about a giant statue project planned in India by the transnational Buddhist group FPMT, or the Foundation for the Preservation of the Mahayana Tradition. Initially, the giant Maitreya statue project envisioned by FPMT's Maitreya Project International (MPI) group was slated to be built in Bodh Gaya (in the state of Bihar), but for a number of reasons FPMT officially moved their plan to Kushinagar (in the state of Uttar Pradesh) in 2003. This book is about the version of the statue that was heralded in 2003 but summarily canceled in 2012. In 2012, it seemed that MPI's "greatest statue in the world" had passed away into the ether. A year later, with little warning, MPI representatives were in Kushinagar for a ground-breaking ceremony attended by Lama Zopa Rinpoche and the chief minister of the state of Uttar Pradesh. A giant statue looms in Kushinagar once more, but it appears to be a scaled-back, less ambitious avatar of the project. Even as plans and hopes suffuse the present, so too do past dreams and nightmares haunt the future; the battle against the statue by the local community is a part of Kushinagar's history and a part of FPMT/MPI's history, and thus the pre-2012 iteration's tale ought to be remembered, in part to help contextualize what happens next.

I define my MPI statue retronyms as follows: the initial pre-2003 period in Bodh Gaya is Maitreya Project 1.0; the period in Kushinagar (from 2003 to 2012) is Maitreya Project 2.0; the period following the explosive 2012 rupture, shake-up, and reboot of the organization led to two fundamentally altered Maitreya Project statue plans: one in Kushinagar (Maitreya Project 3.0) and one in Bodh Gaya (Maitreya Project 3.1). This book, then, is about Maitreya Project 2.0, the earliest version of the Kushinagar statue, one that was never built.

The core ethnographic field research for this book was done while living in India from roughly late 2005 through spring 2007. In addition, for a few months before and after the India stint, I did research work in the United States, mostly attending Relic Tour events, visiting FPMT centers, and soliciting interviews. I also did a handful of follow-up visits to several of these field sites in subsequent years, so the ethnographic present for this book is probably best captured by a time frame spanning the mid- to late aughts. That is, I wrote this book during the Maitreya Project 2.0 era, even though readers of this note know from the outset that that time has since passed.

As is the convention in my discipline, I am committed to protecting the confidentiality of my informants. I have given pseudonyms to my informants, even those who indicated that they would not mind if I shared their names in my work. Given the particular and continuing sensitivity of the situation in Kushinagar proper at the time of publication, whenever it seemed prudent to do so, I also altered some of the identifying details about selected informants from the Kushinagar locale in order to try to more effectively protect their privacy. Aside from their names, I have not changed significant identifying details about my FPMT informants, including MPI officials that I interviewed on the record.

As one might expect, the conventions for public figures require additional clarifications. I have not changed the names of public figures that I interviewed who are already widely known in either the Indian worlds of social justice work (e.g., Sandeep Pandey) or Buddhism (e.g., the late Kirti Rinpoche or Christopher Titmuss); these individuals were not promised confidentiality in the process of interviewing. I have not given pseudonyms to the public faces of MP 2.0 whose perspectives will be related only through archival material: Peter Kedge, Linda Gatter, Tony Simmons, and Lama Zopa Rinpoche.

I tried to organize my chapters under Sanskrit headings—as an acknowledgement of the shared linguistic vein that would be understood by most of my informants, whether Buddhist practitioners in California or villagers in rural India—such as "The Teachings/DHARMA" and "Faith/SHRADDHA," that are themselves meaningful concepts in many Indic religions in general, including FPMT's Buddhism. Every Sanskrit word used in these chapter headings can be found in FPMT discourse and practice and would also be understood by many Kushinagari activists, except perhaps tirtha, meaning "holy place" or "crossing place," which is used more in Hindu and Jain circles and not widely utilized in Buddhist subcultures. I learned the word tirtha from Hindu informants in Kushinagar, and thus I use it self-consciously as a word that itself extends added meaning to the chapter on the interreligious social life of a contested Buddhist pilgrimage site.

Less familiar non-English words are italicized, but I have decided to eschew diacritical marks for two main reasons: readability and ethnographic accuracy. First, this book was written to be accessible to scholars and non-specialists alike. Second, it would be a scholarly imposition to force diacritical markings on FPMT's brand of Tibetan Buddhism, which is already circulating widely in English largely without the use of these markings. Since this book is focused on a specific brand of Tibetan Buddhism that is already in translation, in both the literal and figurative senses, I have made the choice that more accurately represents the subculture in its own terms.

❧ Acknowledgments

First and foremost, I would like to thank each and every one of my informants from Delhi to Kushinagar to California; my interlocutors gave me the precious gift of their time and their stories, and in exchange I have endeavored to represent their opinions and narratives with care and precision. Every ethnography is a collaboration between an anthropologist and those who gave them grist for the mill—it is not enough just to be there, and not one of us could do it alone.

I would particularly like to extend my gratitude to all of the farmers in Kushinagar who trusted me with their perspectives, anxieties, and hopes. My informants in Kushinagar, especially those who saw fit to place their confidence in me in a time of acute local crisis, were welcoming and gracious. I wish for my Kushinagari interlocutors all the calm and stability that they crave—and of course, the bright futures for their children that they long for.

I would also like to thank the FPMT center directors who gave me permission to conduct my research in their midst. I cannot express to my FPMT informants how much I valued their candor, time, and companionship. I know that a handful of my FPMT interlocutors will be disappointed that this book critiques the rollout of an institutional pet project, but I hope that all of my FPMT friends and informants can be generous, open-minded readers and trust that I conducted my research and writing with professionalism and integrity. I tried to infuse my methodology with the values of loving-kindness and compassion so revered in the Tibetan Buddhist literature that we diligently read together in FPMT settings.

This research was generously funded by a Junior Fellowship awarded by the American Institute of Indian Studies (AIIS); I am grateful for their largesse, as well as the excellent in-country support provided by the Delhi office. I was allocated twelve months of research funding from AIIS, but stretched it to over fourteen months of fieldwork in India proper between December 2005 and April 2007. In addition, I was awarded several Lambert and Sharp awards from the Cornell Department of Anthropology for the parts of this research that were conducted in the United States, such as my work with FPMT centers and the Relic Tour in California in the summer of 2007. The Cornell Graduate School also supported my work with a research travel grant, as well as several conference grants. Furthermore, the Telluride Association was a generous supporter of my graduate education and research, as they awarded me Full Preferment (a Room and Board Scholarship) at the Cornell Branch of the Telluride Association for a full five semesters, including the academic year in which I began writing up my fieldwork. I also thank the handful of short-term field assistants and translators who helped at various points during the years I worked on this project.

My mentors from New College of Florida, John Newman, Maria Vesperi, and Sarah Hernandez, should see themselves and the deeply engrained lessons they taught me reflected back at them in this book; together they set me on the winding path that led me to Kushinagar, and I could not have hoped for better role models in careful, ethical research and writing. I owe hearty thanks to many at Cornell University, especially Andrew Willford, Anne Blackburn, and Hiro Miyazaki, as well as Dominic Boyer at Rice University; they have been tireless advocates for my advancement. I thank them for their advice, guidance, and intellectual engagements. With the help of National Science Foundation–funded and university-awarded ADVANCE grants, I received mentorship in the book-writing process from Kirin Narayan and Joyce Flueckiger, two incomparable scholars of South Asian studies. Thus, with the help and loving-kindness of many mentors, peers, and interlocutors, I crafted this book manuscript, an earlier draft of which won an AIIS book prize in 2014: the Edward C. Dimock Book Prize in the Indian Humanities. More recently, the careful readings of anonymous peer reviewers, beta readers, and the editors at Cornell University Press have gone a long way toward polishing this final book manuscript even further.

I have a wealth of friends and family who supported me as I wrote this book and kept me going when I considered walking away. I offer very sincere thanks to my friends scattered across the world, but I owe more specific acknowledgement to Cornell University, New College, and Telluride Association friends who were thoughtful sounding boards for the earliest versions of this project, and also to those very dear friends in Manhattan, Kansas, who were there urging me forward as I labored toward the finish line.

I have such gratitude for my family members, both affinal and fictive—kin-of-the-heart, not the imagination!—as they have all contributed to this book with their unending support, but this book simply would not be if not for the extraordinary kindness of the Parashar family. There are not sufficient superlatives extant to adequately describe my gratitude to the Parashar family, my *muboli* family—my Indian parents, sisters, and extended kin—who have graciously welcomed me into their fold for nearly two decades. They gifted me with a home away from home in the Delhi area, adopting me as an oddball, wayward American who was just happy to bask in their harmonious, constant, centering warmth. I smile even now while recalling hilarious lessons in dirty Hindi *gaalis* whose purpose was surely to heartily entertain them at least as much as it was to make the streets a bit safer for a foreign woman traveling India alone. Of course, there was that one time that I infamously raised Vatsala Parashar's blood pressure when I jumped aboard a slowly moving train—the wrong train as it turned out—while trying to get to Dharamsala in 2000 (again, I'm so sorry!), but the good times were so lovely and so abundant that I trust they outweighed any such headaches I brought to their doorstep. I will always cherish the lessons I learned from the Parashars about loving-kindness, generosity, and family. Living and teaching in Kansas as I do now, I do not get to see as much of the Parashars these days as I once did, but they should never doubt that I count them among my very favorite people on the planet.

My parents, Connie and David Falcone, as well as my brother, Dylan Falcone, have each in their own way been staunch supporters of my studies, this research, and my overall health and happiness. Over the years, the Falcones have been my most enthusiastic cheerleaders. They were the rapt e-mail audience for my early reports from the field. They were the loved ones on the other end of the phone, listening attentively as I wrestled with my conscience, and later with the anxieties of book writing. While I worked through the unique challenges of this research project, they offered valuable, sage advice that I very often followed. As I traveled across Asia and back, my parents, and my brother, were the constellation that helped me locate myself; I knew where, and who, I was primarily in relation to them.

Thanks, finally, to my wonderful, loving husband, George Wame Matthews, who has given me the support and encouragement I needed to complete work on this book project, as well many compelling and marvelous reasons to emerge from behind the computer screen and back out into the world. I will endeavor to keep writing books, and George has promised to keep crafting beautiful bookshelves to rest them on.

❧ Abbreviations

ASI	Archaeological Survey of India
BBSS	Bhoomi Bachao Sangharsh Samiti (the Save the Land Association/Council for the Struggle to Save the Land)
BJP	Bharatiya Janata Party
BSP	Bahujan Samaj Party
BUPC	Bhumi Ucched Pratirodh Committee (the Committee to Resist Eviction from the Land)
CPI-M	Communist Party of India-Marxist
CPMT	Council for the Preservation of the Mahayana Tradition
FPMT	Foundation for the Preservation of the Mahayana Tradition
GDI	Gender Development Index
GDP	Gross Domestic Product
HDI	Human Development Index
KSDA	Kushinagar Special Development Area
LAA	Land Acquisition Act
MoU	Memorandum of Understanding
MLA	member of the legislative assembly
Maitreya Project 1.0	retronym referring to the early, pre-2003 period of the Maitreya Project, when the main statue was to be located in Bihar
Maitreya Project 2.0	retronym referring to the period during which the singular five-hundred-foot Maitreya Project statue was to be built in Kushinagar, specifically from 2003 to 2012 (the period focused on in this book)
Maitreya Project 3.0	retronym referring to the reworked, scaled-down Maitreya Project plan in Kushinagar that was touted to FPMTers after the ground-breaking ceremony there in 2013

Maitreya Project 3.1	retronym referring to the 2012 onward Maitreya Project statue plan at Bodh Gaya, a more modest proposal
MPI	Maitreya Project International
NAPM	National Alliance of People's Movements
SEZ	special economic zone
SP	Samajwadi Party

BATTLING THE
BUDDHA OF
LOVE

Meditation / DHYANA

Focusing on the Maitreya Project

Lama Thubten Zopa Rinpoche, the current spiritual director of the Foundation for the Preservation of the Mahayana Tradition (FPMT), has dozens of ambitious Buddhist construction projects underway at any given time, but a colossal Maitreya Project statue slated to be the biggest statue in the world is known to be Rinpoche's most cherished dream. The statue plan to build a five-hundred-foot Maitreya Buddha (inclusive of pedestal) would have made it not only the tallest Buddha in the world, but indeed the tallest statue in the world at the time.[1] Just for comparison, five hundred feet is greater than three times the size of the Statue of Liberty (sans pedestal). The idea to repay India for sheltering Tibetan refugees from the Chinese occupation of their homeland with the gift of a grand Maitreya statue was the wish of Lama Zopa Rinpoche's deceased guru, Lama Thubten Yeshe.

When I first heard about the giant Buddha statue project being planned in India by the transnational Tibetan Buddhist religious community, I found the idea immediately appealing. I had already spent a little time in India, and I had already found myself personally drawn to Buddhism. At the time, in the late 1990s, I was living in Florida, home of giant Disney structures; in lieu of another corporate amusement park, the notion of a gigantic Buddha actually seemed like a reasonable course correction for modern society. The statue was slated to be the biggest in the world, and at that point it was supposed to be built in Bodh Gaya, in the state of Bihar. I was intrigued straightaway.

Almost a decade later, in 2006, I had just settled into my spare room at the rundown Tibetan monastery in Kushinagar, India, where the plan for the statue had fairly recently been relocated, when I welcomed my first visitor in the field. My friend, Abe, another anthropologist with an interest in global Tibetan Buddhism, wanted to see the site where the Maitreya Project International (MPI) would build their monumental statue (also known as "the Maitreya Project"), so we piled into the back seat of his rented car, and his driver spirited us away from the pilgrimage spots of Kushinagar and deeper out into the countryside. I was excited and anxious. My nascent research project—my whole reason for moving to a sleepy, little town in rural Uttar Pradesh—hinged on studying the plan to build a five-hundred-foot statue of the Maitreya Buddha right here. I had returned to Kushinagar a week before; I had not left town and ventured into the countryside since my short preliminary trip to the area more than two years prior. And now, we were headed straight for the heart of the contested land. Eventually, I directed my friend's driver to stop on a small cement bridge overlooking a flushed green river valley. The riverbed bisected farmland, and I could see houses, sheds, and irrigated farmland on either side.

"This is it," I told my friend. "This is the land."

I had been shown this land by Nathu, a local informant, two years before, during my first brief visit to Kushinagar. Nathu was an Indian staffer at a nearby Buddhist temple, and he had swelled with enthusiasm as he discussed the plans he had heard about in the newspaper and through the grapevine. During that visit, Nathu had waxed poetic about the Maitreya Project as a dream come true. But Nathu and other pro-MPI locals were precisely the people who gave me my first indication of the controversy surrounding the plan. Nathu had told me that disgruntled farmers were "making problems" and impeding the process. He acknowledged that the farmers had reason to fear for their livelihoods, but he wished aloud that they would put their personal considerations behind the economic well-being of the region in general.

On the Maitreya Project's website at the time, in 2006, there was only one single photo of Kushinagar, and it was taken at around this spot; it was a picture of a vast green expanse—utterly empty of farms and people, not a bullock cart or fence in sight.

"Right there," I pointed.[2]

But MPI's photo had strategically omitted, or cropped out, the farms on the edge of that parcel of the larger expanse of coveted land, and thus they had certainly not given their devotees an accurate sense of how many people lived in the affected area. The Maitreya Project photo seemed carefully framed to fabricate an air of local calm: as if the region was an uninhabited blank slate, as if the land itself was waiting for Maitreya.

As we surveyed the spot with our eyes, I wondered which way the giant statue would eventually face. I took a photo.

Foreigners were uncommon this far from the pilgrimage sites, so we were an anomaly. A crowd of passersby began to gather around us. My friend, Abe, and I, both curious anthropologists, proceeded to pepper the crowd with questions.

"The giant Buddha statue is coming here, right?" We pointed to the land. The response was as unambiguous as it was hostile.

"No, it won't come here. It is bad."

"Are you a farmer?," we asked.

The man was emotional and his voice was raised: "Yes I'm a farmer. Where will we go? Where will our *chapati-roti* come from? The government is giving a very low price. It is a very bad thing. I will fight them. I will not sell no matter what the price."

Another farmer told us that they would not permit the statue to come. "We will not let this thing happen here."

The crowd pressed forward. They wanted to know what were we doing there and who we were. The farmers seemed to be trying to discern if Abe and I were in favor of the Maitreya Project or, worse, if we were agents of MPI itself.

During that early exchange on the bridge, a businessman from nearby Kasia noted that the farmers were not taking into consideration the economic development that would come with the project. Four farmers angrily replied in turn that the rate of compensation was pitifully low. One said, "If they come to take the land, we will fight. I will kill anyone who comes." A teacher from a nearby intermediate college also countered the businessman's desire for "development" (Hindi: *vikas*) by confirming that the compensation rate was far too low and that the farmers had every reason to mistrust government promises on compensation anyway. My friend and I asked question after question about the statue plan and its potential effects here in Kushinagar.

I was not prepared for the angry, dark looks or the frustrated, raised voices of some of the men on the bridge that day. One man in particular scowled at me angrily and then threatened violence against any minions of the Maitreya Project; he was the first to imply that I was allied to the Maitreya Project, but he was nowhere near the last.

But I was not an enemy, and I said so. I reiterated the fact that I was an anthropologist, which I rendered in Hindi as "a student of culture." I told them that I wanted to understand their side, their story, and their cultural views.

The intermediate college instructor said that if we were really interested in learning more about the anti–Maitreya Project movement, then we should return that afternoon for a protest in the community commons in the nearby village of Siswa Mahant. He explained that the land that I had just photographed was only a small parcel of the land being acquired for the project. Further afield, prime arable land under cultivation, as well as many houses and village neighborhoods, would have to make way for Maitreya.

By now it was apparent that local tensions about this issue ran very deep, and the men on the bridge were still trying to decide if we were friends or foes. "Do they believe us?," I wondered. The Kushinagari farmers talking to us that day were probably wondering the very same thing.

The crowd continued to grow, so Abe's driver anxiously packed us back into his car. The bridge receded behind us as we drove off toward a chai stall in the bustling town of Kasia where Abe and I both sat and scribbled down our notes about the encounter. Later, I wondered what our interlocutors would have thought if I had told them that I had come to Buddhism through FPMT and taken refuge as a Buddhist at one of their events with one of their lamas,[3] or if I had confessed to them that I had donated money to the Maitreya Project at one of their Relic Tour stops in upstate New York just a few months before. I did not lie to my Kushinagari interlocutors that day, but I did not tell them everything. Those personal tidbits were shared with some of my village informants much later, but the extent to which my allegiances were stretched was probably not crystal clear to my informants on either side of the rift.

That day in Kushinagar in 2006, I tucked my personal fondness for FPMT away and reminded myself to set aside my preconceptions. I was here to listen and learn. Just a few hours after the emotional flurry on the bridge, I attended my very first anti–Maitreya Project protest. The first of many to come.

A Cultural Biography of a Dream

FPMT was founded in the 1960s by a Tibetan refugee, Lama Yeshe, and his Nepali-born disciple, Lama Zopa Rinpoche, when they began teaching Westerners in Nepal about Tibetan Buddhism.[4] At a time of great uncertainty about the future of Tibet, the two lamas began teaching non-Tibetan devotees from America, Europe, and elsewhere to ostensibly preserve Gelugpa

Tibetan Buddhist religious conventions.[5] Today, the devotees, monastics, and administrators worshipping at FPMT's global network of over 150 centers are as likely to hail from Canada or Switzerland as Malaysia or Taiwan. Thus, it is worth noting that while FPMT teaches a form of Tibetan Buddhism, the large majority of practitioners in FPMT are not ethnically Tibetan; most FPMTers have embraced Buddhism in adulthood and are thus what I call nonheritage Buddhists.

Why a Maitreya statue? Proponents from MPI, the FPMT affiliate responsible for seeing the statue project through to fruition, claim that the statue will establish a direct karmic connection between Maitreya himself, the long-awaited Buddha of Loving-Kindness, and the donors (and worshippers) of the statue. The Tibetan Buddhist ritual and practice surrounding Maitreya emphasizes the significance of making karmic connections to Maitreya in this life, by building and worshiping a Maitreya statue for example, in order to be in a good karmic position to be reborn during his lifetime. Aside from the religious goal of constructing a statue in order to establish a link to the Maitreya Buddha, MPI boasted a secondary motivation for their plans in Kushinagar: humanitarianism. MPI literature of all kinds noted that the statue will be flanked by a host of charitable, Engaged Buddhist projects, such as a school and a hospital, so as to provide immediate socioeconomic benefits to complement long-term karmic advantages.

MPI's statue project was once slated to be built in Bodh Gaya, Bihar, but for a myriad of reasons, they moved the plan to Kushinagar in 2003. This book is primarily focused on the second major imagining of the Maitreya Project and the period during which the agricultural fields of Kushinagar were MPI's contested, embattled hinterland. Some Kushinagaris rejected MPI's plan and fought vigorously against it, even establishing groups dedicated to defeating the giant statue project. Yet, during the Maitreya Project 2.0 era, MPI had no office, Buddhist center, or staffer in Kushinagar. Statue planners and supporters had no presence on the land; it was coveted from a distance.

Throughout the Maitreya Project 2.0 period, Kushinagar remained a completely unknown space to the Buddhist devotees and staffers of FPMT and MPI—as if it were a new frontier. In the anthropologist Vincent Crapanzano's discussions of the notion of "hinterland," he perceives it as a boundary that cannot be transgressed literally or figuratively: Frontiers "mark a change in the ontological register" (2004, 14). Thus, the hinterland is an ambiguous beyond that manifests as plans, dreams, images, desires, but even as it is approached, it recedes ever further into the distance. There is another horizon beyond every horizon, ad infinitum. The "imaginative horizon," in

Crapanzano's view, can never be reached, even though it pulls us forward. He writes, "It is a land of pure possibility, of desire, and fear" (2004, 16). For MPI's distant fundraisers and public relations experts, Kushinagar was perceived as empty wilderness, the frontier, and the hinterland on which their dream could be made tangible. Like Joseph Masco's "fantasy playground," the Nevada desert "wasteland" (2005), and Anna Tsing's notion of the constructed Indonesian resource "frontier" (2005), the vision of the empty, barren lands of Kushinagar are a myth, a dream woven by those who have something to gain from spinning the yarn. I view their hinterland, the frontier that FPMTers had failed to occupy for the duration of my time in the field, as primarily a failure of the imagination, not a confirmation that the wilderness was really and truly too wild. As Tsing knowingly writes, "Frontiers are not just discovered at the edges; they are projects in making geographic and temporal experience" (2005, 28). Kushinagar was viewed by MPI agents as so much a hinterland that it could only be visited incognito. An MPI staffer told me that in the fall of 2008, Lama Zopa Rinpoche and some statue supporters traveled to the disputed Kushinagar land without alerting the local people to their identities or purpose. In secret, they conducted a *puja* to rid the land of evil spirits and overcome the myriad obstacles to the project.

The Kushinagari Resistance

From a Kushinagari perspective, the most formidable obstacles in MPI's way were desperate Indian farmers, not wrathful spirits. Kushinagar, a Buddhist pilgrimage town in rural India where the historical Buddha, Siddhartha Gautama, is thought to have breathed his last, is surrounded by arable farmland and several villages of local Indians who have farmed and worked that land for generations. When the MPI plan to acquire nearly 750 acres of land on the outskirts of the pilgrimage areas for their statue project was announced in the early aughts,[6] the plan quickly ran afoul of the local farming families (many of whom farmed very small subsistence plots) who understandably worried that their futures were being placed at risk.

There was a swift and strong local Kushinagari backlash against the project, especially by the thousands of locals who stood to lose their farmland, homes, or livelihoods. Incensed farmers established an anti–Maitreya Project group called the Bhoomi Bachao Sangharsh Samiti (BBSS), which can be translated as the Council for the Struggle to Save the Land, or more simply, the Save the Land Association. In the years that followed, the anti-MPI resistance spent countless precious hours and resources fighting against the statue project. Since MPI did not have a local office in Kushinagar, nor did

FPMT have a Buddhist center there, most local Kushinagari activists never met a single FPMT devotee in person in the decade they spent fighting FP-MT's heart project.

Global Buddhism today is inextricably linked to the phenomenon of globalization, in all of its cultural, economic, and media forms, as elucidated by social scientists such as Appadurai (1996, 2001), Harvey (1989), and others. Buddhism has long been transnational, but the global Buddhism of the technological, jet-set age of neoliberal globalization has created new challenges and opportunities for Buddhist practitioners. The Maitreya Project and the controversy it has garnered are manifestations, or symptoms, of the occasional dissonances extant in global Buddhism. Appadurai warned that globalization entails the "disjunctive flows" that are wont to "produce problems that manifest themselves in intensely local forms but have contexts that are anything but local" (2001, 6). Moreover, Anna Lowenhaupt Tsing writes that in the context of globalization, the motion of various ideas, communities, and institutions often produces unforeseen "friction": "the awkward, unequal, unstable, and creative qualities of interconnection across difference" (2005, 4). The story of the Maitreya Project, one in which a transnational Buddhist group blithely undermines the socioeconomic stability of the poorest inhabitants of a poor region in India, tragically and perfectly illustrates the disjunctive flows and frictions of neoliberal globalization.

Circumambulating the Maitreya Project

I did *kora* (Tibetan: circumambulated, ritually circled) around countless *stupas* and holy objects in India during my research tenure, but to write this book I essentially had to do *kora* around a statue that did not exist. I came to see my research trajectory as a sustained circumambulation of the Maitreya Project.[7] I circled the project in small tight rings and wandered further out on longer, lengthier cycles around the heart of the matter. My object of study was technically a statue on the drawing board, but I found that its future presence permeated my field sites with various manifestations of hope and anxiety.

For many years, I have concentrated deeply on the Maitreya Project 2.0 statue—meditated on it, if you will. The anthropologist Stephen Tyler has deemed ethnographic research a kind of meditation itself: "I call ethnography a meditative vehicle because we come to it neither as a map of knowledge nor as a guide to action, nor even for entertainment. We come to it as the start of a different kind of journey" (Tyler 1986, 140). Ethnographic work, even on nonreligious topics, is always a kind of pilgrimage; we go there—to a place that someone finds sacrosanct—and we pay homage in our way. I have a complex relationship with the statue project—equal parts faithful and faithless—but few people in the world outside of the FPMT-MPI staff rosters can claim to have been as ardently fixated on it as I have been for as long a time.

When I moved to India in late 2005, I asked MPI if I could volunteer with the Maitreya Project's remote officer in Gorakhpur (a little over an hour away from Kushinagar), but the officer himself quickly rejected that request (probably to our mutual benefit given what later transpired). I was barred from the inner sanctum, so I was denied the primary data that I had hoped to collect: meeting minutes and memos, MPI maps, interviews with staff about working through logistical and moral dilemmas, etc.[8] I decided to instead focus on the Kushinagar locale, as well as the fundraising and support-generation activities conducted for the Maitreya Project in FPMT centers.[9] Circling the project from the outside meant spending my two years of full-time research shuttling between very disparate field sites: (1) in Indian FPMT centers in Dharamsala, Bodh Gaya, and Delhi, as well as in American FPMT centers in California and elsewhere; (2) with Maitreya Project side projects, that is, the Relic Tour in various American towns and the Maitreya Project school in India; (3) in Kushinagar with both the potential winners and losers of the land acquisition plan; and (4) in Lucknow acquiring the Maitreya Project paperwork, legislation, and plans from Uttar Pradeshi state government partners.[10]

My research trajectory reflects a transnational pull that led me in small concentric circles in both India and the United States (and in far wider circles between the two nations). If I had spent two years shuttling the fifty-five kilometers between Gorakhpur and Kushinagar as initially planned, this book would have been more of a story of local Indian politics and their effects on a transnational organization, rather than a "history of the future" (Rosenberg and Harding 2005) of the nascent Maitreya Project itself. Multi-sited ethnography is increasingly ubiquitous (Finn 1998; Marcus 1995), and it is especially useful as means for understanding how globalization haunts localities and vice versa. During nearly two years of concentrated fieldwork, I traveled often, usually never staying in one place for more than a few months at one stretch. Like many of the MPI administrators, staff, and FPMT devotees that I met along the way, I was in constant motion, but I returned to many of the same places again and again. Sometimes you can get somewhere by going in circles.

I used standard participant observation techniques; I was a hunter and gatherer of interviews, written information, experiences, interactions, and diverse perspectives and viewpoints. I collected everything possible that was directly, or even peripherally, related to the Maitreya Project, transnational Buddhism, Uttar Pradeshi politics, the Land Acquisition Act, and dispossession in rural India: newspaper articles, pamphlets, blog postings, maps, plans, advertisements, and more. I collected many government documents about the Maitreya Project, including official maps, the Memorandum of Understanding (a draft and the final version), and the Kushinagar Master Plan 2021. Some documents were in Hindi, and some were in English; I translated some of the Hindi materials I collected myself, but I also hired translators to help with some of the documents and articles. I gathered books, pamphlets, *puja* booklets, schedules, listserv e-mails, and other documents from the FPMT centers where I did research. I solicited interviews from all levels of FPMT: staff, students, monastics, and volunteers. I attended several dozen FPMT courses, lectures, meditation sessions, and discussions; some required fees or payment, while other events requested donations, all of which I duly provided.

In the Kushinagar area, I interviewed businesspeople, monastics, students, teachers, factory workers, day laborers, and farmers.[11] I spent my days collecting interviews, both formal and informal, with nearly everyone who crossed my path. I was as interested in the perspectives of the local sweeper at the Tibetan monastery as I was in the Thai abbot's viewpoints. I visited and took notes at Buddhist pilgrimage sites on a regular basis. I also spent a good deal of time in the villages affected by the MPI plan, especially Siswa Mahant, Anirudhwa, and Dumari. I conducted a survey of affected areas—going compound to compound, neighborhood to neighborhood, village to village—interviewing people about their families, their socioeconomic situation, their views on the Maitreya Project, the potential effects of the proposed land acquisition, and their hopes and anxieties about the future. I also organized several dozen extended-family group interviews in local homes, as well as many group interviews in public village spaces. I became particularly attached to a specific elementary school in the village of Siswa Mahant and visited regularly, both to support their educational work and to do interviews with the staff and parents connected to the school. Finally, I attended dozens of anti–Maitreya Project protests. Later, toward the end of my research, I often acceded to requests from the BBSS to give short speeches during protests and sit-ins.

I was not a passive researcher. After some time, when I recognized that the proposed forcible land acquisition could be disastrous for the local farming villages, I began approaching FPMT insiders with connections to the project: I talked to an FPMT center leader whose group had recently hosted the Relic

FIGURE 1. BBSS collaborators in Greater Kushinagar pose with the author during a village visit. From the author's photo collection.

Tour; I arranged to meet a Maitreya Project board member; I talked to an FPMT nun who was not a statue advocate and asked her to help me reach someone in the organization who might have some pull. I sent e-mails and letters to MPI representatives. Roughly midway through my work I began giving interviews to FPMTers and MPI associates, instead of just taking their perspectives one-directionally. In the end, for better or worse, I engaged in a form of advocacy anthropology work that made my research itself a factor in the Maitreya Project story. In chapter nine, I will discuss this personal aspect of the story, since it would be disingenuous to disregard it; however, this book is primarily about the beliefs and practices of my informants, both those in FPMT/MPI and those in Kushinagar, and how those two communities persistently frustrated one another in their attempts to model the future of Kushinagar in their own terms.

The Bridge Revisited

The debate on the bridge that I narrated at the beginning of this chapter was the moment that my fieldwork in India on the Maitreya Project 2.0 statue began in earnest. The episode was a raucous confirmation of the dark, tender underbelly of MPI's ambitious endeavor. It was also a loud and volatile refutation of a popular notion floating around FPMT at the time, the idea that nothing was happening in Kushinagar and that the Maitreya Project was simply a harmless plan on paper making no ripples (or *karma*) in the world. The interlocutors talking on the bridge that day evoked themes of anxiety, stress, and hope regarding their community's now uncertain future, and the echoes of that moment reverberate through this work.

This book will explore both sides straddling the Kushinagar controversy: the would-be statue makers versus the statue antagonists. The statue, which could have served as a bridge between transnational Buddhists and Kushinagar-area villagers if all had gone differently, is instead better represented as the gap itself. The book's very structure mimics the chasm between communities; in this way, I replicate the disconnect between these competing groups as they tried and failed to make sense of one another across a gaping geographical, linguistic, and cultural divide. Since the statue cheerleaders at FPMT and the statue naysayers of Kushinagar railed against each other from a distance, and across troubled waters, the bridge between them—the connecting point, that is, this study itself (and to some extent, my role as an advocacy anthropologist)[12]—has also become a part of the story.

Part 1, inclusive of chapters 1 through 5, is largely concerned with understanding the statue makers: who they are, why they wanted to build a statue, and how they went about it. This portion handles the Maitreya Project's statue itself, a potential bridge between two communities that instead ended up as a divisive wedge that made the gap between the two sides deeper and wider, perhaps even untraversable.

In chapter 1, I tell the story of how FPMT emerged in the 1960s as a conduit for Western Buddhism and discuss how we might situate FPMT's new brand of Tibetan Buddhism in the context of the phenomenon of global Buddhism today. Chapter 1 focuses on the people of FPMT and how we might understand disparate backgrounds and levels of faith.

In chapter 2, I explore the institution of FPMT in more depth by discussing what it teaches, how it is structured, and what kinds of activities it sponsors around the world. I look at FPMT conventions and religious practices in general terms and offer a ritual case study to provide ethnographic depth toward better understanding FPMT as an institution.

In the first two chapters, I also introduce the notion of the heritage spectrum. One of the challenges facing scholars of global Buddhism is that with the increasing flow of ideas and people across national borders, it is hard, yet critical, to carefully acknowledge differences between and within communities of practice. FPMT as an institution itself promotes a type of Tibetan Buddhism that has diverged somewhat from its antecedents, and thus I label it a relatively nonheritage Buddhist group that is mostly peopled with nonheritage practitioners. This book defines distinct heritage spectrums for both practitioners (chapter 1) and institutions (chapter 2) and makes a case that anthropologically these differences matter (see appendix). At the same time, while my typology can assist scholars in the task of representing disparate Buddhisms and Buddhists, I uphold the conventional anthropological perspective that no one type of practice or practitioner is more authentic or real than any other. I argue that attention to the heritage of practices and practitioners is the most useful way for scholars to delineate the significant distinctions between global Buddhisms and the Buddhists therein.

The third chapter focuses on MPI, FPMT's giant statue makers, by examining how the dream took shape over time. I introduce the people, finances, and institutional structures of MPI. I look at how aesthetics and politics meet in artist and prototype renderings. I examine the industrial, technological, and bureaucratic aspects of building the colossus. Finally, I trace the early history of MPI's work in India and the circumstances that led them to shift their plans from Bodh Gaya to Kushinagar.

In chapter 4, I discuss one of the main public aspects of MPI's work during my research period, the traveling Relic Tour that served to spread the message about the statue project and raise money for it. The Relic Tour carried and displayed various Buddhist relics across many continents for the Maitreya Project for many years, functioning as a kind of global ambassador for Maitreya Project 2.0.[13]

In chapter 5, I take a closer look at the medium of futurity that runs through MPI's project—a future statue of the future Buddha. I examine the beliefs surrounding the coming of the Maitreya Buddha and other relevant principles that govern future-thinking in the Buddhist milieu. I also look to the current of futurity that runs through the ethnographic present by looking at the actual details of planning and prophesying the MPI statue; here I also do a detailed analysis of the prospective momentum established through the use of publicly circulated progress reports and the way that the yawning gap between possible outcomes can manifest in the anxious discourse of the future tense.

Part 2—chapters 6 through 9—is primarily focused on local Kushinagari perspectives and social realities, as well as the MPI land controversy. In this section, I illustrate the ways that the plan both compelled and repelled various subgroups and communities in Greater Kushinagar. I tell the story of the grassroots resistance movement that formed in Kushinagar to combat the colossal statue plan. I detail how the BBSS, the Save the Land activists, worked to organize farmers and landowners into a cohesive anti-statue effort and what kind of futures these activists were advocating for instead.

Chapter 6 provides an exposition of the Kushinagari social world, in order to provide context for the resistance movement against Maitreya Project 2.0. I describe the Greater Kushinagar region in detail to show how the Buddhist pilgrimage place is co-constituted by pilgrims, temporary residents, transplants, and locals. In this sense, Kushinagar, like many other pilgrimage sites, is itself a "realm of competing discourses" (Eade and Sallnow 1991, 5).

In chapter 7, I lay out the activist work undertaken by the BBSS, which claims to represent and be inclusive of all the farmers of the project-affected villages. For example, BBSS has organized countless hunger strikes, fasting relays, protests, highway blockades, and strikes. I discuss my interviews with affected farmers and explain why they were so vehemently opposed to the Maitreya Project plan. To contextualize the farmers' views, I also look at how politicians weighed in on Maitreya Project 2.0, as well as how some local people cheered the possibility of a tourism boom.

In chapter 8, I continue discussing the grassroots resistance movement against Maitreya Project 2.0 by asking what values are really being espoused by MPI. Is the project to build a monument to *maitri* actually practicing *maitri* as it moves forward? I handle the issue of contested values by putting two sets of values at the heart of the controversy side by side: spiritual values and economic values. I look at how global Buddhist ethical practice has taken the form of Engaged Buddhism. I explore the intractability of ethical practice, generosity, and charitable works in the context of a neoliberal, globalized era that presumes that economic development is a good way forward. I discuss the type of top-down development being embraced by MPI, the ambivalence of Kushinagaris' farmer-activists to the form that FPMT's vaunted charitable project has taken thus far, and the dissonance between competing notions of progress. Develop-mentality, the passion for progress in purely socioeconomic terms, has played a key role in the planning of Maitreya Project 2.0 and its troubled reception in Kushinagar.

In the ninth chapter, I discuss the rough terrain of engaged ethnographic fieldwork, especially when it involves such a contested object of analysis. Specifically, I address the particular ethical challenges of this research project, including my advocacy and media interventions on behalf of MPI-affected Kushinagaris. Was I able to do ethnographic research with *karuna* (Sanskrit: compassion), as I sought to do? Finally, as it follows from my advocacy work, I narrate the final piece of the Maitreya Project 2.0 controversy here; I look at the media blowup and how MPI sought to manage it. This chapter is a reflexive space for the interrogation of authorial anxiety and hope.

In the conclusion, I address a number of questions: What led to this improbable imbroglio? How could a transnational Buddhist organization callously create so much suffering for impoverished rural Indians? What were the cultural logics at work that led to such an unbridgeable gulf between advocates and opponents of the statue? I argue that the key is faith: both faith in neoliberal development, but also the particular type of faith taught in FPMT subculture, one that stresses unquestioning guru devotion. In this final chapter, I show how guru devotion provided the foundation for the desire to build the colossal statue in India in the first place and how, in the end, it also created many of the conditions that led directly to the intractable problems faced by the Maitreya Project in India.

A History of the Future of a Statue

In sum, this book is essentially an ethnography of the Maitreya Project's future past. Like so many other "histories of the future" (Rosenberg and Harding 2005), though the actual object of my research, the statue itself, was not yet extant, I could productively study the futurity saturation of the past (through archival work) and the present (through participant observation). As an anthropologist studying futurity, I observed the acts of mediation in the present through which my informants work toward and create their futures.

Not unlike Walter Benjamin's (1968) angel of history who rushes forward facing backward into the past, the angel of futurity rushes forward into ever new present moments, but never gets where s/he sought to go. The angel of futurity is, and has always been, stuck in the here and now. When I envision the angel of futurity, I think about the Sri Lankan men charged with painting on the eyes of the Buddha statue without looking straight at it,[14] as the angel also faces the opposite direction of its object and can only intuit where it is going through dull reflections and images of images. Just as no human eye can look directly in the face of the creation of Buddha without mediation, reflection, and artifice, none of us, not even the angel of futurity, can look straight into the face of the future. By looking at the ways that FPMTers, MPI staff, and the Kushinagari interlocutors have framed their futures, I trace the Maitreya Project's origins, its progress and setbacks, and its forward momentum past and present.

Celebrated work written over the past thirty years in material culture studies, the anthropology of materiality, and the anthropology of art (Appadurai 1986; Geary 1986; Gell 1998; Kopytoff 1986; Miller 2005; Myers 2001) teaches us that social scientists must be attentive to the life trajectory or "cultural biography" (Kopytoff 1986) of an object. As Appadurai notes, "commodities, like persons, have social lives" (1986, 3). The real and imputed effects of holy objects give them a special place in the discussion of the agency of objects. Alfred Gell (1998) has written of the "secondary" agency of objects in which the objects that humans create have the ability to significantly shape human lives.[15] Similarly, Daniel Miller, a materiality studies scholar, puts the agency of the object into sharp relief, writing, "In short, we need to show how the things that people make, make people" (2005, 38).

Holy objects, like Maitreya Buddha statues, can be understood as representations, simulations, signs, or "simulacra" (Baudrillard 1994), and so too can the rituals of creating them, worshiping them, and making offerings to them. It is tempting to read the Maitreya statue as a third-order simulacra, as wholly "hyperreal" (Baudrillard 1994), because literally and figuratively the map is all we ever had, and the territory was always forthcoming. And in truth, there is something hauntingly, achingly hyperreal about the way that the model of the Maitreya Project statue sits in a place of honor as the centerpiece of the Relic Tour's traveling altars of ancient Buddhist artifacts.

This book is a study of a statue, an object, a thing, which has frustrated anticipations, not wholly unlike Bruno Latour's (1996) exploration of the rise and fall of the idea of Aramis. Aramis, a technological innovation in public transportation that was supposed to be built in Paris, France, was cancelled in 1987. Latour's "scientifiction" whodunnit asks: Who killed Aramis? To answer that question, the scholar lays out the cultural biography of the object as it weaves its way from idea(s), to prototype, to models, and then back to idea/text. Latour argues that the line between human and machine (object) is blurrier than is immediately obvious, since objects such as Aramis have their own life and death, just like their creators. Although Aramis is no more, for some twenty years Aramis was in the process of becoming, so much so that Latour rather eccentrically gives the machine a voice; with that voice, Aramis expresses a will to live, frustration at the reticence of his ersatz makers, and despair at having been loved too little. By arguing that objects must be seen as co-constituting agents of sociality, Latour asserts the agency of the object, even one that never manifested.

Like Aramis, the giant Maitreya Project 2.0 statue is a "fiction seeking to come true" (Latour 1996, 18). Also like Aramis, the Maitreya statue hit stumbling block after obstacle after rough patch, and it is incumbent on us to understand the context and complexity behind both the project in and of itself and the social environments that have resisted and welcomed it (sometimes doing both simultaneously). This book is a history of the future of the Maitreya Project 2.0, a non-existent statue that nonetheless has touched many lives around the world, for better and for worse.

✍ PART 1

The Transnational Buddhist Statue Makers

🐌 CHAPTER 1

Community / *SANGHA*

FPMT's Transnational Buddhists

Wallace, a Canadian yoga teacher, was traveling in India with his girlfriend when I met him at an FPMT center in Dharamsala in 2006. Wallace was an FPMT student, a newcomer who had taken just a few courses in the organization, who identified himself as "hooked" but not yet "a devotee." Previously, he had taken meditation courses with a Hindu teacher in Canada, and then he had found a second meditation instructor, a Buddhist; still, Wallace felt that much of his early knowledge about Buddhism had come from books, which is why he had been moved to seek out FPMT courses during his trip to India.

Wallace told me that the teachers in the FPMT courses he had recently taken had helpfully broken down complex Buddhist ideas and practices and put them into a more comprehensible register. Yet Wallace explained that he felt welcome to further translate some of what he had learned into forms that would be the most personally satisfying to him. For example, Wallace told me that while an FPMT nun led a visualization on Chenrezig, the bodhisattva of compassion, at an FPMT retreat, she first directed the practitioners to look at the Chenrezig statue on the altar in front of them; she told them to fix the image of the statue in their minds to help them focus, but then told them that they could choose another image of compassion if they found it helpful to do so. Wallace told me that he preferred the latter option: "I created a creature for visualization. The statues are all cartoon pictures anyway, so I tried to take the human Jesus, Buddha, Krishna, Zoroaster, Sita, Mahavir, Rumi, Ram, Guru Nanak, Kabir, Superman, Moses, and Lao-tzu. It was during a Chenrezig visualization. She said you could visualize anyone who inspires you, so I thought of them all together. It was all heads, a lot of arms. I made Jesus Iranian looking. It was hard to visualize!" For Wallace, the statues themselves did not provide the most viable model or template for his visualization on compassion; like many nonheritage Buddhists, Wallace felt comfortable massaging a traditional ritual into something that worked better for him.

In the context of exploring the significance of statues in practice, I later repeated the gist of Wallace's visualization story to a few FPMT monks and nuns teaching at centers in India. One monk, a nonheritage Buddhist from Europe, roared with appreciation.

"Jesus, Buddha, and Superman?! I love it," he said. He then proceeded to discuss his own self-proclaimed "ambivalence" toward holy objects.

On a separate occasion, when I told an FPMT monk from Australia about Wallace's hybrid visualization, he was less than enthusiastic.

"He doesn't get it," he said, and then after a pause, "I don't think you get it either."

Wallace's practice was indeed unique, but his willingness to tailor a traditional practice to fit his needs is actually quite a common phenomenon in FPMT. The very different reactions to Wallace's thinking by other FPMTers tells us less about visualization conventions in Tibetan Buddhism and more about the extent of variation in practices, beliefs, and backgrounds in a Buddhist organization that is primarily peopled by nonheritage practitioners.

In this chapter I will discuss the people who comprise the body of FPMT. This chapter is about the FPMT *sangha* in the most general sense of "Buddhist spiritual community."[1] Since FPMT is a transnational organization, I work to delineate and understand some of the different kinds of Buddhist practitioners in FPMT centers around the world. In doing so, I answer the question, Who is the community working to build the Maitreya Project statue?

The Princess and the Lamas

Lama Thubten Yeshe was born in 1935 in the U-Tsang area of Tibet (Landaw 1982). He was soon recognized as the reincarnation of the abbess of a small Gelugpa nunnery in his natal region. With the financial assistance of the nuns, young Lama Yeshe was enabled to join the Sera Je Monastery at the age of six. Lama Yeshe stayed at Sera Je until he was twenty-five years old, when the Chinese occupation of Tibet caused him to flee to India with many of his peers and teachers. In Buxa, India, at a Tibetan resettlement camp, he continued his studies for a few years and finally took his full ordination in exile at the age of twenty-eight.

Lama Thubten Zopa Rinpoche was born to a Sherpa family in the Khumbu area of Nepal in 1945 and was called Dawa Chotar (Wangmo 2005). Dawa Chotar was recognized as the reincarnation of the Lawudo Lama Kunzang Yeshe although the boy was born two months before the old Lawudo Lama passed away.[2] As a reincarnated lama, Dawa Chotar had many opportunities to study in his childhood: he studied at the Thangme Monastery and in Rolwaling as a Nyingmapa Tibetan Buddhist. On a pilgrimage to Tibet in 1957 with his uncles, Dawa Chotar became a student at a Gelugpa monastery where he stayed, took novice vows, and was given the name Thubten Zopa. In 1959, as the Chinese occupation of Tibet grew increasingly violent and repressive, Lama Zopa Rinpoche and some of his peers at the monastery in Tibet fled together to India.

Since monastic exiles were being sent to Buxa by Indian authorities, Lama Zopa Rinpoche joined his comrades there and began study with a series of different Gelugpa teachers, including Geshe Rabten (Wangmo 2005). For a time he traveled to Delhi and Dalhousie to study at a special educational institution founded to educate Tibetan *tulkus* (Tibetan for "reincarnate lamas"), but eventually he returned to Buxa.[3] Back in Buxa, he was ultimately directed to Lama Thubten Yeshe. Lama Yeshe took full responsibility for the education of the teenaged Lama Zopa Rinpoche. The two traveled to Darjeeling to visit a colleague at the Ghoom Monastery, and while staying there in 1965 they met Zina Rachevsky (Landaw 1982).

Zina Rachevsky was from a Russian royal family that had settled in France to escape the Communist revolution; Zina had immigrated to the United States, married a film financier, and had children, but eventually began a process of spiritual exploration that led her to India in the mid-1960s (Wangmo 2005). In Wangmo's book, Lama Zopa Rinpoche describes Zina's entrance into his life like this: "Her life had been very interesting. I think she did everything one can possibly do in the West (Hollywood star, fashion model, can-can dancer in Paris, and so forth), except being a president or prime minister. Zina believed herself to be an incarnation of H. P. Blavatsky and came to the Himalayas looking for a Tibetan lama" (Wangmo 2005, 203). Zina Rachevsky proceeded to seek out lamas and teachers in the Darjeeling area, sitting with them and asking questions.

Zina wanted to meet a particular learned *geshe* who she had heard about, but given that his name was almost identical to Lama Thubten Zopa's nickname, Dromo Rinpoche, she was misdirected and was instead taken to meet

Lama Zopa Rinpoche and his mentor, Lama Yeshe (Landaw 1982). After getting over her initial surprise at the mix-up, she was reputedly quite taken with Lama Yeshe and returned often to meet the monks. Eventually Lama Yeshe and Lama Zopa Rinpoche were invited to stay with her in Darjeeling, where Lama Yeshe would give her informal teachings and Lama Zopa Rinpoche would translate as best he could from Tibetan to English (Wangmo 2005). Zina Rachevsky became their benefactor, and in return they traveled with her to Kathmandu when her Indian visa expired in 1968. In Kathmandu, Lama Yeshe began taking English lessons.

Lama Zopa Rinpoche has described how inappropriate and informal Zina was with them at the outset, but he notes that their patience with her was worth it, since she provided the connections and means to make FPMT a reality (Wangmo 2005). He said in an interview:

> We had to use the same toilet, and on the way we had to pass her, sitting in her underpants in front of the mirror. She would spend about two hours every morning putting creams and make-up on her face. . . . After Zina's toilette was finished, we would join her for breakfast. Then she would come to receive teachings from Lama Yeshe and I would translate. She usually brought a book with her to leaf through, sat with her legs up or stretched out because she did not know that this is considered disrespectful, and would nibble on biscuits, chocolate, or *pakoras* (a popular fried Indian snack). Most of the time it was not a formal teaching, and we would just talk about cause and effect and the things she had done in her life. (Wangmo 2005, 204–205)

In her autobiography, Dr. Jan Willis, an early nonheritage FPMTer, candidly talked about how Zina had a reputation for trying to keep other seekers away from the lamas, and indeed she tried to keep Dr. Willis and her friends from meeting the lamas; Lama Yeshe then told her, "Zina . . . Mommy . . . is sometimes . . . how you say? . . . too much protective" (Willis 2001, 154). Although the two lamas were sometimes frustrated with Zina, they clearly also had an effect on her, since after a few years with them, she took novice vows in the Gelugpa sect and began wearing Tibetan Buddhist nun's robes, becoming the first known Westerner to do so (Mackenzie 1995).

In Kathmandu, Zina rented a house on a hill—the nascent Kopan Monastery—where "her Tibetan lamas" (Wangmo 2005, 209) could begin teaching her and her friends about meditation and Buddhist thought. Kopan was a difficult and piecemeal undertaking at first; according to Lama Zopa Rinpoche it was an exercise in patience: "The house was full of Zina's friends—hippies taking drugs and playing music with guitars and so forth.

We were given the smallest room with space for only two beds and a very small table in between. Lozang Nyima had to sleep on the floor. Actually during the years we were with Zina we really had to practice thought training. One evening she got very upset about something and threw the bamboo tray with bowls of thugpa all over us. We just laughed and cleaned it up, and the next day she apologized" (Wangmo 2005, 233). In the same vein, Lama Zopa Rinpoche has reminisced about the way in which Zina underfed the lamas, or fed them insubstantial meals such as peanut butter and bread, so that occasionally they would go hungry (Wangmo 2005). Despite such notorious behavior, Zina would eventually become a celebrated figure within FPMT, as she funded the edifice of what would become the FPMT empire.

When Zina first asked Lama Yeshe to begin teaching meditation courses at Kopan for Western students he refused, so Lama Zopa Rinpoche volunteered in his stead (Wangmo 2005). According to Lama Zopa Rinpoche, Lama Yeshe's hesitation stemmed from the fact that at Sera Je and other monasteries there is no "meditation" in the classic sense until after many years of study and Tantric initiations (Wangmo 2005, 241).[4] Despite his guru's reticence, and perhaps because he had not been enculturated into a huge scholastic monastery like Sera Je, Lama Zopa Rinpoche began teaching meditation courses at Kopan in 1971. Eventually Lama Yeshe capitulated and began teaching groups of foreign searchers as well. By the time of the seventh month-long course in 1974, attendance had grown to two hundred persons, which stretched the capacity of the newly built *gompa* (Tibetan for "temple") facilities (Landaw 1982). In 1975, Lama Yeshe officially founded the Foundation for the Preservation of the Mahayana Tradition. Lama Zopa Rinpoche also began planning to build a monastery, the Mount Everest Center, in his home region of Khumbu, so he started working on raising money toward that end.

Lama Zopa Rinpoche and Lama Yeshe simultaneously cultivated their foreign devotee community and completed their work on the Mount Everest Center. After a handful of years, the monastery at Lawudo was transformed back into a retreat hermitage, and the young monks of the center were transferred to a new monastery for them at Kopan. The seventies saw several shifts in the FPMT world: the growth of the Kopan meditation courses that are now famous among foreigners studying Tibetan Buddhist in South Asia, a steady influx of Western devotees, and Zina's untimely death.[5]

FPMT grew quickly and expansively, as compared to the organizations of many other Tibetan lamas who boast a much smaller number of centers and instead cultivate more intensive relationships with fewer committed devotees.[6] The FPMT lamas seized their opportunity to establish and teach at centers all over the world. Monastic travel is not a completely new, modern, postexile phenomenon among Tibetan Buddhist lamas,[7] but the extent of FPMT's religious empire is fairly unique in scope and size, especially since the devotees are mostly non-Tibetans.[8] While FPMT's influence spread into the Americas, Europe, Australia, and South and Southeast Asia from the seventies onward, FPMT does not consider itself a proselytizing tradition; FPMTers argue that it provides a religious service for those who seek it, as opposed to aggressively working to recruit members. My FPMT informants tell me that Lama Yeshe's smile and laugh alone won converts by the hundreds.

According to most reports from longtime FPMT devotees whom I interviewed, Lama Yeshe was charming, friendly, and prone to exploration and curiosity. A devotee wrote about his adventures, saying, "on a trip to America, he astonished not a few by playing the tables at Las Vegas! He then dragged a reluctant Lama Zopa (who by inclination would much prefer meditating in his room), not only to Disneyland, where he tried most of the rides and wore a Mickey Mouse hat—but also to a strip joint, where they both sat eating ice-cream, not at all shocked by the antics of the lady on the stage. Lama was certainly never a prude" (Mackenzie 1988, 26). There is remarkable consensus among my informants with decades-long involvement in FPMT that the organization was primarily built on the strength of Lama Yeshe's considerable charisma.

Much to the sorrow of his devotees, Lama Yeshe passed away on March 3, 1984. His health had declined rapidly, and he was only forty-nine years old when he died.[9] After Lama Yeshe's death, Lama Zopa Rinpoche took on the work of running and expanding the FPMT empire. By the late eighties, there were fifty FPMT centers worldwide (Mackenzie 1988). Devotees who had committed to Lama Yeshe had to decide whether to stay with FPMT: some of these individuals receded quietly out of the organization, while others transitioned to accept Lama Zopa Rinpoche as the new head of the organization.

After a few years, Lama Zopa Rinpoche found and recognized Lama Osel Hita Torres (born to Spanish parents in February 1985) as the reincarnation of Lama Yeshe; the Dalai Lama confirmed this identification in 1986 (Wangmo 2005).[10] Shortly thereafter, Lama Zopa Rinpoche articulated his plans to have Osel educated at a heritage Tibetan monastery as befits a reincarnate lama, and his parents conceded, sending their son to a heritage Tibetan monastery in India as a young boy. Osel lived at Sera Je Monastery in India for many years before leaving the monastery early and distancing himself from FPMT (Fuchs 2009; Jenkins 2012; Pontones 2009). Although he was outside of the FPMT fold during the bulk of my fieldwork period, many

FPMT informants articulated their hopes that he would return to the organization someday. Years later, Osel did return and he began making short films for FPMT, giving talks at their centers, and serving as a social media influencer in his own right.[11]

FPMT's early history layers individual and institutional tales of globalization, exile, translation and transformation. FPMT's story is about the transgression of borders. An exiled, cosmopolitan royal who wants to be a better person endows a charismatic Tibetan lama with a penchant for belly laughs and living life to the fullest (and his student) with the means to spread the Buddhist word to a new constituency. Later, the lama's favorite student, a reincarnation of a Nepali monk famous for solitary meditation, finds his own teacher's reincarnation with a European family who are members of the community he cofounded. As a boy, the white lama straddled two worlds: a classical Tibetan monastery in exile, and a transnational Buddhism empire. He stepped away from both, for a time, to get a Western education, film school training, and to see the world on his own terms. The first few decades of FPMT history demonstrate that it is a product of, and a producer of, global Buddhism. While FPMT is a relatively nonheritage institution founded by heritage Tibetan Buddhist monks primarily for the benefit of nonheritage practitioners, it is no less authentically Buddhist than its antecedent institutions.

Buddhism in the Age of Neoliberal Globalization

To various practitioners, at various times, and in various places, Buddhism has been experienced as philosophy, worldview, cultural inheritance, commodity, magic, spiritual path, aesthetic world, and religious practice.[12] The historical Buddha lived about 2,500 years ago and may have taught some of the lessons that are popularly attributed to him, but scholastic work in Buddhism has taught us nothing if not the fact that Buddhism has been changing and continually becoming over the course of millennia (Williams and Tribe 2000). The movement of Buddhism from the Gangetic plains of the subcontinent across Central, Southeast, and East Asia and beyond leaves us in no doubt that the tradition is flexible, ambulatory, and always already transnational.[13]

In their edited volume, Nalini Bhushan and Abraham Zablocki define contemporary Buddhism as "TransBuddhism," which essentially asserts that globalization is changing the nature of Buddhism worldwide. They write, "These intersections of the real and the imagined, and of the Asian and the Western, generate what we refer to as *TransBuddhism*" (2009, 4). Indeed, there is a unique speed and character to the changes of the age of globalization, and these changes have impacted Buddhism and created the conditions for the emergence of an organization like FPMT. Taking my cue from David Harvey (1989), I would argue that it is precisely the character and speed of change that is actually changing, and not the fact of change itself.[14] The editors of the volume define TransBuddhism as the emergence of a "new Buddhism" (Bhushan and Zablocki 2009, 4). Even though I entirely agree that there is something important happening now, something that scholars of Buddhism have a responsibility to research and name, and we could call it "TransBuddhism,"[15] I prefer the use of the moniker "global Buddhism."[16]

In their work, Bhushan and Zablocki rightly observed that it is not just immigrants and new converts that are experiencing a flux and transformation in practice, as there have been substantive changes in conventions in Asia as well. However, they define the transition as hinging on contact between the "Asian and Western"—"TransBuddhism involves a bidirectional flow of ideas, texts, and sensibilities between Asia and the West" (2009, 8)—and this may gloss the complexities and changes happening in intra-Asian and intra-Western contexts. To be crystal clear, global Buddhism does not simply refer to nonheritage Buddhisms, since there are new, globalizing shifts occurring in the East, the West, and everywhere in between, but one significant aspect of global Buddhism today is the robust presence of Buddhism in the West.

Western Buddhism, as delineated in opposition to Buddhisms located in Asia, has two interrelated components: (1) the movement of Asian Buddhists into the West, and the innovations and transformations in practice within their communities; and (2) the development of new transnational Buddhist communities that were either founded by or mostly populated with Westerners who found and embraced aspects of Buddhism in adulthood. As such, James William Coleman delineates two different Western Buddhisms: the "ethnic Buddhism" of immigrants to the West and the "new Buddhism" of Western converts (2001, 7). Coleman's formulation reverberates with the "two Buddhisms" approach to American Buddhisms as established by Charles Prebish, which notes the distinction between "ethnic Asian-American Buddhist groups" and those of "European derived ancestry" (1993, 189). The limitations of the two Buddhisms approach (Pierce 2000, Rocha 2006, e.g.) have been explored before, and I echo those critiques here: it can oversimplify the complexity of the Buddhist practitioners in the West. My frustration primarily extends from the fact that the terminology favored as an expression of these binaries often makes ethnicity the sole distinguishing criterion between the two, an approach that has obvious shortcomings.[17]

The two Buddhisms approach can be read as an effort to avoid defining American Buddhism exclusively as the domain of converts, which would indeed be an egregious way of thinking. Such a troubling misrepresentation of American Buddhism is precisely what got Helen Tworkov into trouble when she infamously suggested that "American Buddhism" be seen as an innovation that had taken place almost entirely in convert Buddhist communities (1991, 4). Quite rightly Jodo Shinshu priest Ryo Imamura quickly countered this position to assert that Asian American Buddhisms must be included in the realm of innovative and creative American Buddhist practices (Nattier 1998). I take the perspective that both "American Buddhism" and "Buddhism in America" should be all-inclusive.

The two Buddhisms notion often explicitly recognizes two very different ideal types of practice simply on the basis of race. In an epilogue on a tome dedicated to the scholarly exploration of American Buddhism, Kenneth K. Tanaka put race and ethnicity front and center. Tanaka writes that "the two groups are referred to by several appellations, for example, ethnic, immigrant, Asian and Asian-American for the former, and white, Caucasian, Western, Anglo, and Euro-American or European American for the latter" (1998, 287); for the rest of the chapter he proceeds to use the terms "ethnic" and "Asian-American," in contrast to "Euro-American." He goes on to write that this delineation is useful as it identifies different patterns of practice (e.g., he says that Asian American Buddhist immigrant temples often merge Buddhist spirituality with community and other cultural affairs and festivals). I agree that there are significant differences in practices in American Buddhisms, but the statement that "ethnicity determines not only the composition of the members but also the members of the group" (Tanaka 1998, 287) overdetermines ethnicity as the sole distinguishing characteristic between these groups. Tanaka qualified his perspective somewhat when he noted that this racial distinction is sometimes overemphasized to the point that it sometimes masks overlap and cooperation between "the two camps" (1998, 288), but again this presupposes the binary. Rick Fields, in trying to draw attention to the prevalence of white privilege in the convert group, overcorrects and divides the groups into "ethnic Buddhists" and "white Buddhists" (explicitly suggesting that the category of "white Buddhists" includes Americans of many races) (1998, 197). But although "white Buddhist" as an oppositional binary works in certain very specific contexts, such as when he was focusing solely on particular white theosophists, such as Madame Blavatsky and Henry Olcott (Fields 1992), it is problematic to broaden that category into one in opposition to Buddhist Asian Americans more generally.

The Buddhist studies scholar Jan Nattier, as frustrated with the use of race as the sole categorical determiner as I am—"How would one classify, for example, a Chinese American who meditates with a predominantly Caucasian group, or a Latino adherent of Sōka Gakkai?" (Nattier 1998, 188)—took the common bifurcation of Buddhist types one step further in her typology of American Buddhists: (1) "Elite" Buddhists (189) practice the "demand-driven" Buddhism of the privileged, which is assumed to be dominated largely by the upper-middle class because it can require outlays of money for meditation and philosophy opportunities at centers here and abroad; (2) "Evangelical" Buddhists (190), on the other hand, practice an exported, proselytizing Buddhism (Sōka Gakkai, for example), which often aggressively touts the spiritual benefits available through Buddhist prayer; (3) "Ethnic" Buddhists (190) are Buddhist immigrants from Asia and their progeny who congregate in temples that primarily function on behalf of a sole ethnic group (Nattier 1998). Thus, Nattier's terminology continues the trend of articulating terms according to ethnicity, but it also brings socioeconomic status and proselytization practices to bear. While more complex than its predecessors, Nattier's system still fall short: the term "ethnic" overstates ethnicity, while the term "elite" overdetermines economic class.

Under Nattier's rubric, most FPMTers (all but the relatively few Tibetan heritage teachers and practitioners) would be considered elite Buddhists as opposed to ethnic Buddhists. This terminology makes for awkward and potentially problematic inferences and glossing. Since ethnicity is a constructed cultural category that is as often linked to race and skin color as it is to language and other shared cultural ideas, the term "ethnic Buddhism" indicates that only Asian-American Buddhists are ethnic Buddhists. The category implies a problematic classification of nonethnic Buddhists. But, arguably, all people are ethnic in their own way, so to make it a category here seems to restore a racial significance that is unhelpful and unintended. The categories of ethnic or nonethnic Buddhists are wont to be read as literal descriptors of the particular Buddhist adherent rather than as descriptors of the origins of Buddhist belief for a particular Buddhist. Ethnicity is not just under the purview of people of color, and defining one group as "ethnic" exposes the privilege of a white majority society. Given the racial hierarchy of American and European societies, it behooves scholars to make sure they are not uncritically erasing the ethnic and racial differences that people labor under; for example, in our white dominated society, it would be problematic to implicitly indicate that FPMTers of color are nonethnic (or necessarily elite) Buddhists.

Under Nattier's typological regime, nonheritage FPMTers would explicitly be considered elite Buddhists. The use of the word "elite" carries its own baggage that glosses the class diversity of the devotees who worship in relatively nonheritage Buddhist communities like FPMT. "Elite" can refer to a higher socioeconomic class status or a superior, cream of the crop, status. I do not think that Nattier meant to imply that one Buddhist group is superior to the others, but the fact that it can be misinterpreted as such makes it a poor word choice.[18] Furthermore, it is problematic to define one group according to a single, higher class status. There are low-income, lower-class FPMTers. There are FPMTers who have not earned university degrees, or who rely on some form of government assistance. There are people who have adopted Buddhism who would bristle at the suggestion that they are being categorized in a way that implies that they are part of a social or economic elite. Conversely, there are many well-educated, upper- and middle-class (in other words, "elite") people in all of the various types of American Buddhist communities, including the Asian heritage communities that Nattier's "elite" category defines itself against. "Elite," like "ethnic," carries problematic linguistic baggage that makes Nattier's typology less than ideal in practice.

Angela, a black American woman who became a Tibetan Buddhist devotee with FPMT, told me that she would be very uncomfortable being called a nonethnic or an elite Buddhist, since she was from a working-class, Southern, African American background. Sasha, a white FPMT student I met in Dharamsala, was from a rural farming family, so the idea of being called an elite Buddhist grated on her. Jan Willis (2001), a celebrated black female professor of religious studies—who had grown up in a poor family in Alabama—wrote a book that includes detailed memories of Lama Yeshe's mentorship and guidance as one of her first Buddhist gurus. While reading her story (and when meeting her at a visit to our shared alma mater), it struck me that calling her an elite Buddhist might be appropriate now (because she is a celebrated professor of Buddhism at a private university), but I would have balked at using that terminology throughout her entire life as a Buddhist. I would prefer to call Angela, Sasha, and Dr. Willis nonheritage Buddhists. I submit that it is more accurate and useful to use the term "heritage" rather than "ethnic," and "nonheritage" instead of "elite," and to stretch those terms across a spectrum that makes room for "semiheritage" Buddhists who may fall in between categories (see appendix).

The Heritage Spectrum of Practitioners

Who is a Buddhist, and how can we talk about distinctive types of Buddhists in a meaningful way? The religious studies scholar Thomas Tweed was perfectly right when he wrote, "For our purposes as scholars, Buddhists are those who say they are" (2002, 24). As far as processing the distinctions, I argue that focusing on the heritage of a practitioner makes upbringing and enculturation, rather than skin color, class, or ethnicity, the defining characteristic of the category. However, lest the reader think that further discussion is moot, I cannot emphasize enough how important it is for social scientists studying these communities to recognize that there are important differences between Buddhists that must be acknowledged. Thomas Tweed noted astutely that those who choose Buddhism do not practice in the same ways as those raised as Buddhists (Tweed 2002). He wrote, "Religious identity also can be complex for converts. Conversion involves a more or less (often less) complete shift of beliefs and practices. . . . Some celebrate conversion; others conceal it. Either way, the converts' self-understanding and everyday practice are complex" (Tweed 2002, 19). It would be problematic just to deem everyone a "Tibetan Buddhist practitioner" full stop, as if Geshe Lama Konchog (a heritage Buddhist), a beloved FPMT teacher born in Tibet—whose *tulku*, Tenzin Phuntsok Rinpoche (heritage Buddhist), was recently discovered in a Nepali village—had the same enculturation that Osel (a semiheritage Buddhist) had as a child of Western converts; or, as if Osel, identified as a *tulku* as a child and enculturated in a monastery for many years, should be put in the same category as Hollywood actor Steven Seagal (a nonheritage Buddhist), who embraced Buddhism and was identified a Tibetan Buddhist *tulku* in adulthood.

I would advocate for specific, case-by-case definitions of "heritage,"[19] but as a default definition, I would suggest that heritage practitioners have been actively enculturated by at least one side of the family who raised them—a family whose connection to the traditions extends back at least a few generations.[20] Most ethnically-Tibetan Tibetan Buddhists are heritage Buddhists, with several generations on both sides going back as far as the families can remember. Most FPMTers are nonheritage practitioners, because they were not enculturated into Buddhism by their families; they chose Buddhism later in life.

Some interlocutors may not neatly fit in one category or the other, and thus a "semiheritage" category with all manner of other enculturated possibilities can be enumerated: for example, my friend Stefanie was raised in a household of nonheritage Buddhists who embraced Geshe Sopa's teachings at Deer Park in Wisconsin. I would suggest that since my friend embraced Buddhism and was raised as such, she could be deemed a semiheritage Tibetan Buddhist. In contrast to one another, the people in this story can be arrayed across a spectrum based on their enculturation: Geshe Sopa (a heritage Tibetan Buddhist); Stefanie (semiheritage); Stefanie's parents (nonheritage Tibetan

Buddhists). Thus I endeavor to make room in my typology for semiheritage Buddhists such as the slowly growing ranks of second-generation FPMTers. Even Osel Hita, the Spanish-born FPMT *tulku,* a second-generation FPMTer who was so uniquely enculturated in nonheritage *and* heritage Tibetan Buddhist contexts, would best be understood sociologically as a semiheritage Buddhist himself.[21] Enculturation and practitioner status do not tell us anything about degree of faith; however, these appellations do help us to get a better sense of the relationship someone has with Buddhism.

Another popular qualifier used by my FPMT informants was "convert"; while it is tempting to use the term "convert" Buddhist interchangeably with "nonheritage" Buddhist, the term "convert" must be used with care.[22] In discussing American Buddhism, Peter Gregory acknowledges the difficulty of using the term "convert," saying that he does so "for lack of anything better," and that "many American Buddhist practitioners who would fit into this category would not recognize themselves in this label" (2001, 242). Indeed, while some of my nonheritage Buddhist informants embraced the qualifier "convert," others found it extremely vexing. One reason for the hesitation is that some informants have embraced Buddhism but simultaneously continue to hold some of the religio-cultural beliefs or practices from their heritage religion, and the term "convert" could be interpreted to preclude that connection. Many new Buddhists do give up old religious affiliations, but some do not.[23] To the latter, it is perfectly acceptable to be both Buddhist and Jewish, or Buddhist and Christian. Natalie, a Brazilian nun who was living at Tushita Dharamsala, told me that she felt that although her Buddhism had helped her to nurture her simultaneous belief in Catholicism, her parents still worried that she would go to hell. During an interview, Natalie said the following:

> In Brazil, it is rare to believe in nothing. It is easier there, since Brazilians are so spiritual. I'm much more open to Catholicism than before. I see Jesus as a bodhisattva. But it is the practice in daily life in Buddhism that is so attractive to me. I talked to a Buddhist friend that is very into Mary. He lived in a Franciscan monastery. I see the Ten Commandments in the same way as the virtues and nonvirtues in Buddhism, but in Buddhism it is practiced better. In church it is not said often that one should not just focus on Jesus and God, but one should act like Jesus. I say to my mom, if you try to act like Jesus then it will be better than praying. There's a book by a Buddhist monk and a Benedictine monk—I read it, my mom (who is a psychologist) read it. It said that death for Catholics means heaven, hell, and purgatory. I asked my

mom about it and she said that most of us go to purgatory until we're ready to meet God. But how do you get ready? Do you purify there? She didn't know, though she had studied some. I think that purgatory is like *samsara*. The book was saying that you go to heaven when you are ready meet God, but it didn't say that you have to be active now, to purify. . . . I think that different minds need different religions.

Natalie reconciled her Catholicism and her Buddhism, and thus calling her a "Buddhist convert" would be a misnomer.

Abby, an American FPMT nun, told me that when she first took refuge in 1988 she tried juggling two spiritual paths but found the experience very difficult. Eventually Abby chose Buddhism as a religious path and Judaism as a cultural path: "In the beginning, I was doing both, and then Lama Zopa Rinpoche said that the path would become clear. For me I still feel Jewish. I'm still culturally Jewish, but not an observant Jew." Still, Abby bristled at the notion that she had "converted to Buddhism," rejecting that turn of phrase utterly.

In Jan Willis's book (2001), she calls herself a "Baptist Buddhist," since she recognizes that she has deep connections to her heritage tradition (Baptist) and her adopted tradition (Buddhism). In her memoir, she relates a story of an experience in which, fearing imminent death on an airplane that was have landing issues, she prayed to both Lama Yeshe and Jesus. The term "convert" has a closed quality that suggests finality—a total and complete break with past religious beliefs or religious identities—but that is not the nature of all nonheritage Buddhists' relationships with their former religious cultures. Certainly, given the pains Dr. Willis takes to emphasize that she has retained aspects of her Baptist heritage even as a practicing Buddhist, the moniker of "Buddhist convert" does not feel appropriate to impose on her.

Many devotees and monastics (and even many students) in FPMT, unlike Natalie and Abby and others, do consider themselves Buddhists to the exclusion of other spiritual traditions but say that they still engage in religio-cultural practices with their families: choosing Christian rituals in marriage ceremonies; occasionally singing or chanting prayers from one's natal religion; celebrating holidays, such as Christmas, Hanukkah, or Eid. That is, not everyone who participates in the religio-cultural world of their heritage traditions still holds those beliefs, but some do, and therefore, to gloss all nonheritage Buddhist practitioners as converts is an unappealing terminological option. As a more general category of nonheritage Buddhists, "converts" also fails because there are many nonheritage Buddhists with children who have been brought up as Buddhists; as second-generation

Buddhists they cannot be sensibly lumped into the pool of converts proper. Thus, I argue that children of nonheritage Buddhists—if the former have indeed grown up with Buddhism strongly permeating aspects of their enculturation—would best be categorized as semiheritage Buddhists.

The heritage spectrum typology works well enough, as long as one recognizes the nuances within each category, and that it functions best according to a particular context. That context can be wide (Buddhism) or narrow (Tibetan Buddhism) or even narrower (Gelugpa Tibetan Buddhism), whatever is most useful as a scholarly frame for a particular study. By using the term "heritage," one makes the case for generations of exposure according to a particular tradition, but this means that heritage Buddhists are necessarily heritage Buddhist of one (or more) tradition, but not a heritage Buddhist in other types of Buddhist traditions. My friend Tsering, for example, is a heritage Buddhist. She is also a heritage Tibetan Buddhist and, to be even more specific, a heritage Gelugpa Buddhist. Hypothetically, if she were to embrace a type of Buddhism that was completely alien to her upbringing (e.g., Japanese Zen Buddhism), then she remains a heritage Buddhist, but at the same time she would be a nonheritage practitioner of Zen. In FPMT centers in East Asia—in Singapore, Taiwan, and elsewhere—the laity may or may not have grown up with Buddhism, but few, if any, grew up as Tibetan Buddhist practitioners. For example, in a Taiwanese FPMT context, a devotee who grew up practicing Taiwanese Buddhism is a heritage Buddhist and a heritage Taiwanese Buddhist, but if she found and embraced FPMT later in life, then she is simultaneously a nonheritage practitioner of FPMT's Tibetan Buddhist tradition by virtue of the fact that she is choosing to practice in an unfamiliar context, language, and subculture.[24]

In sum, the rash of typologies regarding various Buddhists demonstrates that to understand global Buddhism, many Buddhists, Buddhist scholars, and social scientists have recognized the need to contrast the Buddhists who have been brought up to believe in certain notions with those who embraced these ideas later in life. Not wholly unlike a missionized subject's decision to believe or not (Asad 1993), and with due respect to the significance of a person's unconsciously perpetuated *habitus* (Bourdieu 1977), nonheritage Buddhists generally have a different relationship to Buddhism than heritage Buddhists do, and their approaches and perspectives cannot be anthropologically collapsed. While the heritage spectrum for practitioners that I have proposed must be used with care in its application—and once again, "heritage" carries no value judgment regarding the authenticity, validity, or enthusiasm of one's practice—I would argue that it is a crucial aspect of social analysis, particularly in the study of a community like FPMT, which boasts heritage

Tibetan Buddhist lamas as cofounders, but a *sangha* of mostly nonheritage Buddhists.

The Faith Continuum from Searchers to Monastics

The literary genre of popular Buddhist books is a part of the story of many nonheritage Buddhists. Millions of readers from around the world, from the Americas to Asia, have embraced the books of respected Buddhist masters, and even many solidly non-Buddhist families have a book or two by the Dalai Lama sitting on their bookshelves. Almost every single non-heritage FPMTer I interviewed about their religious trajectory told me that their first contact with Buddhism had been through books. Many FPMT practitioners found their first Buddhist books (by the Dalai Lama, Chögyam Trungpa Rinpoche, and others) in New Age bookstores or in a spirituality section in mainstream bookstores, although some encountered Buddhism through readings assigned in college courses. For example, Carl, a British FPMT student, told me that Sogyal Rinpoche's *The Tibetan Book of Living and Dying* had made a huge impact on him and propelled his visit to FPMT's Tushita Center in Dharamsala. Some nonheritage Buddhists even admit that readings about other Asian religions, such as Hinduism, paved the way for their subsequent interest in Buddhism.[25]

For some readers, these popular Buddhist books serve as a gateway toward the further exploration of Buddhist doctrine and practice. Those inspired by Buddhist books to seek out more direct Buddhist experiences often found themselves on their first visit to a meditation session at an FPMT center (or some other Buddhist center), or on their first trip to Asia to travel through pilgrimage places. FPMT appeals to many nonheritage Buddhists traveling in South Asia, since they have centers in some of the major Buddhist-affiliated pilgrimage stops in India and Nepal that maintain a very good reputation among travelers for their food and sanitation standards and their Westerner-targeted curriculums in English.

FPMT has set up various formal and informal mechanisms for membership, but since it is an oft-shifting concept in FPMT, in this book I do not differentiate between or identify "members" and "friends" of FPMT.[26] Instead, I have identified patterns in order to establish some broad distinctions between nonheritage FPMT practitioners—searchers, students, devotees, and monastics—à la Weberian ideal types.[27] I have found it useful to identify an individual's particular commitments to institutional practices. This requires looking at faith in a particular temporal moment or time span, such as my ethnographic present (and acknowledging a person could move back and forth along the spectrum over time). At one end, there are the wholly uncommitted searchers, and on the opposite end there is the firmly committed monastic *sangha*. In between, I find two subsets: the students and the devotees.

I would categorize searchers as those whose connection to an institution is simply mediated through literature, video, or objects. "Buddhist sympathizers" or "nightstand Buddhists" (Tweed 1999, 2002), "inquirers" (Layman 1976), or bookstore Buddhists, searchers are those who have a general affinity for Buddhist ideas as they have seen them represented in popular culture or the books that they have read.[28] Buddhist searchers, in general, might be people who have a few books by the Dalai Lama, Lama Yeshe, and Pema Chödrön on their shelves, shop for a smiling Buddha statue for their garden and a wheel-of-life tapestry for their kitchen, and stream Buddhist documentaries to their devices. Either because a book or statue is aesthetically pleasing or spiritually engaging, or because they are commodities that help them to publicly self-identify as something in particular (e.g., philosophical, deep, Tibetan-freedom supporter), essentially these objects alone represent forays into, and not commitment to, Buddhism. A searcher in FPMT is a person who has been reading FPMT books, downloading their materials online for personal spiritual edification, or buying incense from the online FPMT store, but is not an active participant in the institution. I see searchers as a peripheral, passive part of the larger FPMT network, but like Tweed, I think these outliers ought not be ignored. Some searchers are still a part of the Maitreya Project 2.0 story, as they might have attended a Relic Tour event in their city, made donations to MPI, or read updates and media reports about the project with interest.

A "student" has engaged with Buddhism in more active ways that are being guided by contact with a Buddhist *sangha* (or multiple communities), though the student may self-identity as a Buddhist or not. FPMT students have taken courses or done meditation sessions at FPMT centers but have yet to commit to FPMT, its prescribed practices, or the lamas in a serious manner. Some of these students are neophytes to Buddhism or newcomers to the organization, but others came to FPMT long ago yet have settled in at this stage; they may be interested and active learners but have not felt moved to commit to the organization and its gurus.

I consider devotees to be those who have committed to a guru within an organization. FPMT devotees are those who consider a high-ranking FPMT lama as a root guru (or among their primary vow-administering gurus),[29] and who see themselves as firmly embedded in the FPMT world as Buddhist lay practitioners in FPMT. Devotees are not dabbling; they have determined to accept the truth of FPMT discourse, although not necessarily to the exclusion of all other worldviews. Aside from being dedicated practitioners and continuing learners, many devotees also participate in the organization in more committed ways than the average student: serving as FPMT staff, working as center staffers, joining the Council for the Preservation of the Mahayana Tradition (CPMT), becoming meditation leaders or teachers, or doing some of the heavy-lifting as volunteers.

Finally, on the most committed end of the faith continuum, one will find the ultimate devotees, the monastic *sangha*: renunciant monks and nuns. Monks and nuns have taken their vows within the tradition. Like heritage Gelugpa Tibetan monastics, FPMT's monastic vows ideally represent a lifelong commitment, and these adherents are expected to remain celibate. There are several types of FPMT monastic *sangha*: (1) FPMT's founding lamas, Lama Yeshe and Lama Zopa Rinpoche (and perhaps young Osel Hita by extension); (2) nonheritage monks and nuns, some of whom are also teachers; (3) heritage Tibetan Buddhist monastics who are either teachers from outside FPMT (many of whom were first trained at Sera Je or other formal teaching monasteries within the Gelugpa tradition, and then hired by FPMT), or the

FIGURE 2. Nonheritage FPMT monks and nuns at a multidenominational relic processional sponsored by Sinhalese Buddhists in Bodh Gaya in 2007.
Photo by the author.

monks and nuns who are enrolled as the rank and file in FPMT's few heritage Tibetan monasteries.[30]

From an FPMT perspective, ideally people will move through searcher or student phases to become a devotee (or even a monastic). These categories are not necessarily a progression (someone could skip the searcher step, for example) nor necessarily linear (as the same person can move back and forth between them over time). I have known FPMT searchers and students who have never met the definition of devotee and yet stay loosely connected to the organization for years. I have interviewed others who have slid from devotee back to student or searcher again after a crisis of faith, or after slipping out of tune with the organization or its teachers. These differentiations—this faith continuum—are made to some extent within FPMT discourse, that is, various levels of commitment by practitioners are recognized, but the terminology laid out here is not strictly used within the institution itself. The FPMT sangha is comprised of those with some connection to the community, that is, it is inclusive of students, devotees, and monastics.

The People of FPMT

FPMT is an organization composed of countless small communities that are networked together by common literature, practices, and gurus. At any given center, there is a fluid network of people who work with, study with, and meditate with one another. Fresh off an "Introduction to Buddhism" course at Tushita Dharamsala, a thirty-five-year-old German man, Julius, described the community at the course this way:

> It's such a good group dynamic. I mean you do this meditation on compassion with sixty people. It was like a big family. It was so peaceful. Only sometimes the mind would throw a tantrum because it was too peaceful and it got bored. It's amazing to see people from all over: from Southern India, Japan, a nun from Korea (from a Theravadin school), all kinds of people, businessmen, former drug addicts. People from seventeen to sixty years old. The age spectrum was also diverse. From complete newbies to people who studied with Lama Yeshe thirty years ago. People from New Zealand, Australia, Argentina, Germany, Poland, Holland, Switzerland, Scotland, Ireland, Vietnam, all over the place . . . Spain, France, Canada . . . and Germany!

FPMT is an extremely amorphous institution with affiliated community members across the globe.

Various centers have their own local emphases and specialties, which often depend on the locale, the needs of the local community, and the teachers at hand. I did research (and often lived) at a handful of Indian and American FPMT centers for weeks, and sometimes months, at a time. One advantage of studying FPMT in those two countries is that I was able to contrast a more fluid, mobile constituency with a more permanent, local one. For example, certain centers were geared primarily toward housing and teaching travelers and pilgrims, such as the Indian centers in Dharamsala and Bodh Gaya, while other centers were more geared toward serving the needs of local practitioners, such as the centers in San Francisco, California, and Raleigh-Durham, North Carolina. Most FPMT centers, as one might expect, attract a more settled, local, commuter *sangha*. In Indian pilgrimage places, the community is mostly comprised of an ever-changing mix of international FPMTers. While the national and regional differences of individual FPMTers do not melt away, the character of FPMT centers in India is singularly cosmopolitan, and thus a unique place to study global Buddhism. Some places both cater to a local *sangha* and provide for travelers (or short-term transplants), such as the Land of the Medicine Buddha Center in Soquel, California, and the Tushita Center in Delhi, India. Some centers have specialties such as long-term retreat, hospice care, while others generally maintain a schedule of teachings and meditation sessions based on FPMT texts and by relying on FPMT approved teachers.

Several FPMT informants told me that there are substantive differences between devotees from various world regions, which accords with Jeff Wilson's (2012) observation that when it comes to studying Buddhism, regional differences matter. Certainly, there are observable differences between FPMTers from different places: Asian devotees versus European devotees versus North American devotees, and so on.[31] One can discern general cultural and linguistic variations between British devotees as compared to Swiss devotees, just as one could contrast FPMT's Californian devotees with their counterparts in Massachusetts or North Carolina.

Diversity, at least according to nationality, is especially evident at many of FPMT's pilgrim-focused South Asian centers. At any given time, FPMT's Root Institute in Bodh Gaya may be hosting devotees and students from various countries and ethnic backgrounds. At a Buddhist course on "Death and Dying" at FPMT's Tushita in Dharamsala in April 2006, the approximately fifty practitioners enrolled in the course hailed from Sweden, Hungary, the Czech Republic, Venezuela, Peru, Israel, France, the United States, Switzerland, Canada, Australia, Mexico, England, Germany, Ireland, and other nations. Although we were in India, there was but one enrolled student from

India (an upper-middle-class Keralan man), but he dropped the course after the first hour-long session. The FPMTers at that course were almost all white, except for some people of color from Latin America.[32] That particular course boasted participation of roughly half below the age of thirty and half above, and it seemed about even gender-wise. This rough sketch is not inconsistent with the normative composition of FPMT courses in pilgrimage centers in India, although "Introduction to Buddhism" courses tend to have slightly more young pilgrims (and slightly more participants, especially at high seasonal points) than the particular course that I have just described.

Early in FPMT's history, most FPMTers' first contact with the organization was in South Asia, and almost all of the very longtime devotees started their practices with Lama Zopa Rinpoche or Lama Yeshe at pilgrimage centers in Nepal or India. Like Zina before them, many find FPMT while on pilgrimage or vacation in South Asia, since many are attracted to India in the first place by its spiritual traditions. Over time, the proliferation of centers around the world has provided a multiplicity of alternative FPMT entry points. Nowadays, it is not uncommon to meet many FPMTers whose first contact with FPMT came when they attended a talk, *puja*, or meditation session at the FPMT center closest to their home.

Leslie, a Western volunteer at Tushita Dharamsala, shared her story about the long, circuitous route she followed that ultimately led to her embrace of FPMT:

My first contact with Buddhism was as college student. It was a meditation group that met once a week. It was affiliated with the FWBO [Friends of the Western Buddhist Order], which is very big in the UK, but not so much elsewhere. I don't know if you've ever heard of it. [I nodded "yes."] The group was called the Buddhist Meditation Society. It was a very superficial interest at the time, and I was bad at meditation at first.

I went to China during school. I went back later to finish a degree in modern Chinese studies, but altogether I've spent the last nine years in Asia. Mostly in China, Taiwan, and India. In China and Taiwan I was exposed to the environment of Buddhism, but I never considered Buddhism there and I didn't meditate much. I found the philosophy of life useful, but for a long time I didn't want to be an -ist. Like the way that I was a Christian in my youth—I rebelled. I thought that religions are in conflict and they all claim a monopoly on the truth. I was agnostic.

I really discovered Buddhism in India. I came by accident. I was here for a year the first time. I was studying yoga for four months in

Rishikesh. I was in an eclectic group that drew from Sufism, Buddhism, Hinduism, and other things. It showed me that all paths could be on the path to the same goal. It was the stereotypical spiritual quest in India. I hadn't intended it; it was quite unexpected.

It was in Spiti and Ladakh that I started gravitating toward Tibetan Buddhism. Then I went back to China for a few years. I started working for a nonprofit in Kham called Kham Aid. It worked on nonreligious projects—there were just so many problems there to work on. In between our work we would go and visit monasteries, and I met a lot of Rinpoches. I worked with some of them to set up schools and clinics. I couldn't quite find my way in at that point. I met a lot of Chinese Buddhists studying Tibetan Buddhism. I wrote a piece about the Chinese Buddhists in a Chinese paper. I began to start to consider myself Buddhist. I wanted to take refuge, but I wanted to find a teacher I was committed to. I thought that's what you have to do.

In India, I had done Vipassana. I was and I am attracted to different traditions. After two years I went back to India. That was two and a half years ago. I spent some time in Nepal, in Boudha; there were mostly Tibetans there. It was again hard. It was like a secret society. Westerners were getting initiations. I ended up at Kopan; I walked up one day. I got the schedules, and I just liked the FPMT style, the helpfulness, everything is right out there. So I did one of the ten-day courses. I was familiar with the material by then, quite [missing word], but it was great to be there. Lama Lhundrup was teaching. I took refuge with him—he was the abbot of Kopan. Taking refuge was a powerful step for me. Finally I'd committed myself to this path. It was a great relief to me. From there I came straight here [to Tushita Dharamsala]. I knew I wanted to stay here and do work, so I asked to be a volunteer.

Leslie's story is not atypical. Many FPMTers find that they have an interest in Buddhism that slowly grows over time, and FPMT happens to be there at the right place at the right time with opportunities for more sustained learning and practice. There are many elements to her story that run parallel with most of my other informants' "finding FPMT" stories: she rebelled against her ancestral religion; she learned about Buddhism first in college; she traveled and lived in Asia; she did yoga and meditation; she shopped around with various spiritual communities; she eventually felt a connection with Tibetan Buddhism; she was looking for a guru; she found FPMT to be a convenient way to engage with the world of Tibetan Buddhism that seemed somewhat enigmatic and exclusive at the outset.

Many people choose FPMT over other Buddhist groups or other religious groups, because they like the feel of the community. One woman at a California center talked about her fellow volunteers, saying that she felt that FPMT provides a very caring community: "a very supportive and loving *sangha* that keeps us all connected to what's really important." In FPMT centers in Bodh Gaya and Dharamsala, which cater to pilgrims and tourists who were constantly coming and going, FPMTers still indicated that they had a lot in common with one another. A devotee in Bodh Gaya told me something to the effect of, "we were all thrown into the deep end here [in India], so we keep each other afloat with the *dharma*."

Even a ten-day course conducted in silence for the majority of the participants can be an enormously social experience, as people relate to one another and communicate in subtler ways. After such a course, Carl, a British FPMT student, told me, "At Tushita my favorite thing was offering lights at the *stupa*. It was very moving. There was a real feeling of a collective. I lost myself in it. I lost my comparative isolation." After a similar silent FPMT course, a woman approached a stranger from the course and said, "Thank you. You smiled at me a few times, at really important moments."

In FPMT circles, there are often more women practitioners than men, although arguably there is overrepresentation of men in positions of authority. The gender dynamics in FPMT deserve their own dedicated study perhaps, but allow me to make just a few observations on the issue. One of the truisms about nonheritage Buddhisms is that they tend to be more egalitarian and gender inclusive than the practicing heritage communities from which their traditions have been adapted. This is certainly true in FPMT as there are arguably more opportunities for upward mobility accorded to women in FPMT than one would find in most heritage Tibetan religious enclaves, whether preexile (Sopa 1983) or postexile (Dreyfus 2003). In FPMT institutions, women often account for the majority of practitioners, and the volunteers in any given center are more likely to be women than men. The FPMT monastic *sangha* has welcomed many men and women, and many of these monastics from both genders are important teachers, especially those who teach "Introduction to Buddhism" courses in centers in South Asia. One famed FPMT female teacher even had a long life prayer composed for her by her devotees—a rare honor accorded to a nonheritage monastic of either gender.

Despite the fact that the FPMT gender relations were more equal than one might find in heritage Tibetan Buddhist institutions, one could argue that there is less equality than one might expect in a nonheritage Tibetan

Buddhist context. There is not as much respect and equality as many FPMT women would like, since power brokers, and leadership in general, are more likely to be male than female.[33] I have heard a surprising number of FPMT women call the organization "patriarchal" or an "old boys club" and hypothesize that this was a result of the Tibetan patriarchy as well as Western ones. I have also observed that with the exception of a few notable standouts, female teachers are often relegated to beginner courses, while the more advanced teachings are often done by male teachers. Thus, the gender-equity issue for FPMT is a work in progress, and informants discussing bias either emphasize the work needed or the progress made.

In terms of age, FPMT centers run the gamut, although in most places older, middle-aged practitioners are in the majority.[34] Centers in pilgrimage areas tend to attract younger communities than those in the domestic centers back in FPMTers' homelands, since the pilgrims themselves are often young people traveling Asia or the world in college, after the bar exam, or after Israeli military service, for example.

In terms of ethnicity, nonheritage FPMTers are a diverse group if one takes a global view. The majority of practitioners at Indian FPMT centers are white American and European pilgrims, but there are almost always some practitioners of color in and out of the pilgrimage centers as well. The majority of practitioners in American FPMT centers are white, but again, not exclusively so. In Latin American FPMT centers, the racial dynamics are not so clear, since whiteness itself is such a complex category.[35] The FPMT center in Delhi has a small community of highly educated older Indians, mostly of Hindu and Sikh backgrounds, with a smattering of white expatriates. While I never visited those FPMT centers in East Asia, interviewees told me that the FPMTers in East Asian locales are mostly of Asian ethnicities with some ethnic variation due to Western expatriate participation. The wide ethnic diversity of FPMTers across the globe is one of the reasons that I find it most useful to describe FPMTers across a heritage spectrum, rather than through a terminological model that takes race and ethnicity as strident determining factors.

This chapter provided an introduction to the actors involved in FPMT and its Maitreya Project. I have argued that in order to understand and represent global Buddhisms today, one might trace the differences between Buddhists across a heritage spectrum of practitioners. In addition, I have found that a faith continuum helps build a deeper understanding of the disparate ways that FPMTers engage with their Buddhism: searchers, students, devotees,

and monastics. I have introduced the reader to the demograph
Ters in very broad strokes, and discussed some common "find
stories. By discussing the community of people praying for, pla
donating to FPMT's religious projects, I have laid the groundwo
derstanding the community's institutional and theological support for the
Maitreya Project

CHAPTER 2

The Teachings / *DHARMA*

Religious Practice in a Global Buddhist Institution

FPMT is a transnational federation of local organizations that spans the globe and has a changing cast of characters, visions, and projects. Just a few decades old, FPMT is an institution in the process of constructing itself. This chapter will provide a brief overview of global Buddhist trajectories and movements and discuss where FPMT as an institution fits into the contemporary Buddhist landscape. I suggest that FPMT's borrowings and transformations from Tibetan Buddhism have simultaneously created something new out of the old and also followed in a timeless Buddhist tradition of doing just that. This is a crucial part of the story of the Maitreya Project, as one must understand FPMT's religious beliefs and practices in order to understand why they would undertake such a distinctive statue project in the first place.

FPMT Inc.

According to the documentary attached to its website, FPMT's message is at the same time personal and global: "World peace through inner peace. Inner peace through helping others" (FPMT 2017a). FPMT's international headquarters, or international office, is located in Portland, Oregon.[1] The international office is FPMT's central administrative operation, and FPMT's board of directors guides their work. Lama Zopa Rinpoche was the spiritual director of FPMT during my fieldwork period. Rinpoche's attendant, Roger Kunsang, a nonheritage Buddhist monk, became the president/CEO of FPMT Inc. in 2005 and remained so during my research period and well beyond.

While diffuse legal and economic responsibilities fall to individual centers, FPMT has a fairly centralized mission and platform that requires center directors and spiritual directors to follow specific institutional rules and guidelines. One way of keeping everyone on the same page is to hold regular meetings of the CPMT, which loosely consists of center directors, spiritual directors, board members, and certain administrators and teachers. CPMT meets periodically to discuss the organization's trajectory and the nuts and bolts of running FPMT projects. While CPMT can make recommendations to the FPMT Inc. board of directors, the latter have absolute authority.

Each center has its own board of directors, but the local centers must obtain permission from the international board of directors to appoint center directors. In effect, while the centers are legally and economically independent from FPMT Inc., FPMT is a very centralized bureaucracy that has control over high-level personnel and teachers (center directors, high-level staff, teachers, etc.), educational policies and programs, and defining program outcomes. Kay puts it this way: "Lama Yeshe's project of defining and implementing an efficient organizational and administrative structure within the FPMT created the potential for friction at a local level. The organization's affiliate centers had initially been largely autonomous and self-regulating, but towards the late-1970's were increasingly subject to central management and control" (2004, 61–62). The board of directors guides the international office and CPMT, who then have authority over the staff and volunteers at FPMT's various centers, projects, and services.

Lama Zopa Rinpoche and his designees appoint resident *geshes* to the centers that can support them. FPMT has asked lamas to sign a "Geshe agreement," which makes FPMT's expectations of them explicit and functions to ensure that FPMT centers remain under their institutional purview and control. Centers are only supposed to invite Gelugpa teachers and instructors; the international office is expected to give permission to centers in advance of their extending invitations to speakers and teachers. The centralization of authority in FPMT to some extent complicates claims that new Western Buddhisms tend to be highly democratic (Tanaka 1998).

In March 2010, FPMT's website (www.fpmt.org) advertised that FPMT had "156 centers, projects and services" and that there were meditation centers in thirty-three countries. Each center is required to be financially self-sufficient, although there are occasionally monies available to the centers from the international office of FPMT. FPMT's center services director wrote: "If a center, project, or service is affiliated with FPMT, it means that it follows the spiritual direction of Lama Zopa Rinpoche. It means that the centers and study groups use FPMT's educational programs and material, created in the unique lineage of Lama Yeshe and Lama Zopa Rinpoche" (FPMT 2009a).

FPMT centers come and go. Cumbria, England, had one. Asheville, North Carolina, had one. These centers and many others either switched religious affiliations within the Buddhist community or simply fizzled out and became defunct. On the other hand, centers in the making are currently called study groups. Study groups must have permission from FPMT to start, and they are expected to eventually submit plans to become a permanent center (FPMT 2009a). In its monthly e-mail updates, FPMT includes a section called "Impermanence at Work," which details the comings and goings of the center directors and high-level staffers, as well as openings and closings of various centers and study groups.

FPMT's manicured spaces are also part of their attraction, especially in South Asian pilgrimage areas. I cannot overstate the importance of the social comfort factor at FPMT centers in India and Nepal, according to informants; aesthetically, functionally, and especially socially, the centers excel at making pilgrims from around the world feel comfortable. For example, after a long journey by train from Delhi to Gaya, and a sometimes harrowing auto rickshaw ride to Bodh Gaya, the clean rooms, comforting food, hot showers, peaceful ambiance, and security inside FPMT's Root Institute complex serve as a balm for the anxious international traveler. The high razor-wire-topped walls, the police presence at the gates, and the late-night Sherpa patrol project to guests a feeling of being safely ensconced in a protective bubble, even as it alerts those outside the gates that they are not welcome. These are not luxury hotels, but my FPMT informants emphasized that the manicured gardens in full bloom give the Root Institute a calm, quiet, oasis-like quality in a crowded, dusty, loud, sensorially overstimulating place like Bodh Gaya.

FPMT students and devotees at the Root Institute gushed about the "clean," "sanitized," and "safe" food at the Root Institute, which was nourishing but implicitly set apart from the Indian food at dhabas outside the gates. During an extended stay in the early aughts, I was not the only person who felt that the Root Institute's breakfast staple—warm homemade puffed breads served with fruit jam and orange marmalade—was almost as comforting as a phone call home. At the Tushita Meditation Center in Bodh Gaya, there was similar feeling expressed that the food was healthy and that the cooks had been taught to cook for foreign palates (and stomachs).

Most FPMT centers work to create a particular aesthetic and environment that stands in contrast to the world outside its doors. This spiritual space is created through a particular material culture (holy objects in gift shops, holy objects in chapels) and also by constructing "docile bodies" (Foucault 1979) that require that FPMTers use the space in particular ways. Whether in California or Bihar, centers ask people to behave in certain prescribed manners: taking off shoes before entering a *gompa*, bowing to high lamas as they enter a room, and refraining from inappropriately risqué dress. For example, many FPMT centers require some version of the Buddhist lay precepts to be respected. At the Root Institute, guests and staff at a center must refrain from sexual misdemeanors (like adultery), killing (even mosquitoes), and lying, for example. The rules at FPMT centers are enforced through signs, through social repetition, and through informal and formal disciplining. I learned informally at the Root Institute in 2001 how to behave inside an FPMT *gompa*: when and how to rise, bow, pray, sit, and arrange myself and the objects around me. I learned, along with others, how to do these things like everyone else. I learned that one way to guess if someone on the cushion next to you was a neophyte or an established devotee was the speed and confidence with which they could make a "mandala offering" by knotting together their ten fingers in the proper way. FPMT, as an institution, does regulate the bodies of those inside its centers, sometimes by expelling those who brazenly defy precepts or by using peer pressure and soft power to motivate behavioral changes.

The operating budget of FPMT Inc. supports numerous *dharma* and charity projects. FPMT has affiliated hospices (mostly in developed nations) and a handful of healthcare projects (in developing nations). FPMT financially supports animal liberation events, which entail devotees rescuing doomed animals or insects and then circumambulating the rescued beings around holy objects in order that the nonhumans receive good merit for a better rebirth.[2]

FPMT has developed several educational programs and services. They have an intensive Tibetan language program, in which students get subsidized education in return for eventually working for FPMT centers as a translator for Tibetan teachers without English fluency. The headquarters also supports a Western teacher training program, a fund for supporting FPMT *sangha*. FPMT supports publishing efforts in the forms of Wisdom Publications and also the Lama Yeshe Wisdom Archives. FPMT also raises money to sponsor the translation of *dharma* texts into various languages, including English, French, Spanish, German, Chinese, Mongolian, and Vietnamese.

In the aughts, educational materials were being produced for several different lay practitioner programs that could be practiced at FPMT centers carrying the program or independently as home-study or correspondence courses: (1) "Discovering Buddhism," a two-year introductory course that covers fourteen modules of Tibetan Buddhist Mahayana theory and practice; (2) "Foundations of Buddhist Thought," a two-year intermediate course that covers six modules and includes papers and exams; (3) "the Basic Program," a more advanced intermediate course that is meant to span five years and challenge students to keep the precepts, ritual practices, meditation, and retreats during the course of the progression. In the midaughts, FPMT founded a Buddhist college in Portland, Oregon, Maitripa College, which grants an MA in Buddhist studies. Daniel Cozort (2003) also wrote about a "Master's Program" at an Italian FPMT center that was meant to take seven years of intense study and graduate advanced teachers.

FPMT also makes contributions to some non-FPMT institutions, notably to some heritage Tibetan Buddhist institutions. For example, FPMT pays for daily meals at the Sera Je Monastery in exile in India. In 1991, there were about 1,300 monks at Sera Je in India, and this offering was made in perpetuity as part of the ritual acceptance of Lama Osel into the monastic community (though he was to live in a separate dwelling at Sera Je). As of 2007, the approximate doubling of the size of the Sera Je Food Fund makes it a contribution of $270,000 per annum (FPMT 2008e). FPMT has also sponsored some of the monks from Sera Je to attend the revived tradition of Jang winter debate sessions of the three most celebrated monastic colleges.[3]

On the auspicious days of the Tibetan Buddhist calendar, FPMT also donates money as offerings to some of Lama Zopa Rinpoche's gurus and to various heritage Tibetan *sanghas*. The website notes, "On these days, virtuous karma is increased by as much as 100 million times, so Rinpoche has put in place permanent arrangements to have *pujas* and other activities performed by various Gelug monasteries in Nepal and India by tens of thousands of monks" (FPMT 2008c). Merit from these offerings is dedicated to the long life of His Holiness the Dalai Lama as well as to removing obstacles from all of FPMT's projects; merit is also dedicated to all FPMT practitioners and benefactors. The FPMT Puja Fund also supports the cleaning and decoration of the famous Boudhanath Stupa in Kathmandu once a month.

The extension of funds outside the FPMT community to more traditional, heritage Tibetan institutions can be read as a way to stay connected to its institutional predecessors and establish some prestige in Tibetan-in-exile circles, as well as a way to demonstrate authenticity of practice to its non-Tibetan followers. Maintaining the connections that FPMT has to Sera Je as the monastic college that trained Lama Yeshe (in Tibet) and Lama Osel (in India) is considered very meritorious by FPMTers. These donations have enhanced FPMT's reputation in the ethnically Tibetan communities in Tibet and in exile. According to most heritage Tibetan Buddhist informants, the FPMT cofounders fortuitously amassed fame and fortune with nonheritage devotees; before FPMT, Lama Yeshe was not a particularly important teacher in Tibetan circles, never having earned a *geshe* degree nor having been the reincarnation of an important lama, and Lama Zopa Rinpoche was only revered in local circles in his home region of Nepal. That is, FPMT's Lama Zopa Rinpoche has ambiguous religious standing in Tibetan exile circles, but the financial power gleaned from helping to spread Buddha *dharma* to the West and the ability to spread those dollars back to some heritage Tibetan monasteries has resulted in increased social status with the Tibetan community in exile.

Holy objects are important to FPMT, which in the aughts was supporting several large-scale holy object development projects: (1) the "Padmasambhava Project for Peace" that aims to build one hundred thousand large Padmasambhava statues around the globe; (2) the "Prayer Wheel Fund" that aims to build one hundred thousand large prayer wheels around the world; (3) the "Stupa Fund" that aims to build one hundred thousand *stupas* worldwide.[4] Many of these holy objects will be located at the site of a currently extant center. Centers are expected to raise the money for the projects but can apply to these FPMT funds for assistance. For example, in 2007, when I was in residence at the Root Institute, the preparations were being made to build a giant prayer wheel as per Lama Zopa Rinpoche's explicit request; the expenses were substantial, so in addition to raising money through the Festival of Lights and Merit and direct donations, the Root Institute was granted several thousand dollars from an FPMT fund to help pay for the construction of their wheel.

The Maitreya Project—the plan to build a giant Maitreya Buddha statue in Kushinagar—has a place of special prominence in FPMT as the "heart project" of Lama Zopa Rinpoche.[5] By all accounts, it is the most ambitious holy object project that the group has conceived to date.

FPMT's Religious Life

In the Foundation for the Preservation of the Mahayana Tradition, "preservation" is literally a part of how they define their organization's mission.[6] FPMT presents itself as an extension of the old, as part of an ancient lineage, and as a force for the conservation of, rather than the reinvention of, Gelugpa Mahayana practices. I argue that both the reinvention and preservation at work in FPMT are two forces in dialectical play with one another, in tension with one another and yet co-constituting, and that this entanglement is at the heart of FPMT as an Buddhist institution.

Are all of FPMT's activities "preservation" in the strictest sense of the term? Preservation suggests a tradition frozen in time, as well as the absence of change, a stillness that would make it familiar to those of past generations. But FPMT is not considered conservative or even normative by the standards of contemporary heritage Tibetan Buddhists. Many aspects of FPMT culture and practice would be considered markedly different in contrast to both Lama Yeshe's educational experiences inside Sera Je in pre-occupation Tibet and the dynamic between Tibetan lay people and monastics at that time. Perhaps Tibetan Buddhism is being preserved, but that preservation has taken the form of adaptation, transformation, and innovation. Just to identify a few of the many changes: a pedagogy that allows lay people to fast forward past the decades of philosophical training that is supposed to precede meditation practice;[7] practitioners who have different notions of decorum and authority (e.g., Westerners wearing short shorts or revealing clothing during courses); completely new gender dynamics (for example, coed courses and religious spaces, the high status of certain women teachers); abandoning certain heritage Tibetan pedagogies, in favor of some new, nonheritage pedagogies;[8] super-sized ambitions and projects (such as the Maitreya Project); a Spanish-born lineage-holding *tulku*, Lama Osel, temporarily questioning his faith and leaving the fold (Falcone 2017); and the global empire-building of jet-set lamas.

Within FPMT it is known that some Buddhist practices have diverged from their antecedents; for example, there were tensions about teaching meditation and giving empowerments, etc., to those who have not been prepared in the traditional monastic program. Still, FPMT has been adamant that it is preserving the Mahayana tradition in the lineage of Je Tsongkhapa. Lineage is significant in many Buddhisms, Tibetan and otherwise; "kinship" in Buddhist monasticism is focused most specifically on the transmissions of monastic lineages (see Blackburn 2003, for example). In Tibetan Buddhism, the lineage transmissions are one thing, but specific direct person-to-person empowerments (Tibetan: *wang*) provide a different way of establishing links to the past. In relatively nonheritage Tibetan Buddhisms, questions of appropriation of theological and cultural ideas are often solved with the answer that the teacher, the guru, or the lineage lama has allowed it, so the appropriation has been vetted, mediated, and facilitated. Nonheritage FPMTers are considered Tibetan Buddhists by virtue of ideological genealogy; for example: they are devotees of Ani Rachel, who is the disciple of Lama Zopa Rinpoche, who is himself the disciple of Lama Yeshe, who was in turn empowered by X, Y, or Z at Sera Je Monastery in Tibet. That said, FPMT's leadership, and its clientele base, have expressed occasional anxieties about trying to maintain the pure teachings in the face of translation and cultural differences.

Not only has FPMT translated certain older forms and practices into new iterations, they have literally translated countless prayers and ritual texts from Tibetan into English (and other languages, such as French, German, Portuguese, Chinese, and Vietnamese). Some of this work has been done in house by FPMT staff and volunteers, and these books are published by FPMT Inc. and primarily distributed to centers. Other work has been published by FPMT's Wisdom Publications by independent scholars or writers who may or may not be FPMT affiliated. The Lama Yeshe Wisdom Archive, an FPMT affiliate, collects and publishes the works of Lama Yeshe and Lama Zopa Rinpoche. Many of the prayer books produced by FPMT Inc. have the transliterated Tibetan on one side and the English translation on the other. Few of these books, if any, have the Tibetan script anywhere on its pages. Tibetan language learning is not discouraged, but in practice it is also not specifically encouraged or required for lay or monastic persons in FPMT. Daniel Cozort (2003) writes that for FPMT *dharma* learners, the emphasis is on philosophy and meditation, so Tibetan is not taught in centers nor does it need to be.

There seem to be divergences between centers about when to chant particular verses in Tibetan versus English. Since nonmonastic staff or volunteers often lead them, on any given day, at any given center, even if one is doing a familiar *puja* (such as a Guru *puja*, or a Medicine Buddha *puja*), there are many ways that it might be done. Almost every Guru *puja* that I did over my many years studying in a half dozen FPMT centers was different than the time before. For example, there is skipping around in the prayer books, new addendums that are sometimes ignored, various levels of training in how to pronounce words or in which cadences one should chant them, or whether one should do a shorter or longer version of disparate components of the prayer. Should one do multiplying mantras after the Long Life Prayer for the Dalai Lama or just before it? I have seen it both ways and multiple times at that. Which set of dedications should be read, and from which book? At the outset of most FPMT *pujas* that I participated in, the leader handed out several pamphlets and books, as different parts of the *puja* were located in various publications. FPMT practitioners tend to try to go with the flow. Admittedly, ritual consistency is probably more common at centers catering to fixed practitioner communities as opposed to the transient, pilgrimage centers where I studied in India.

There is institutional resistance to anything that would dilute the perceived authenticity of the teachings. FPMT is Gelugpa Tibetan Buddhist and generally will not allow people from other Buddhist denominations to teach courses or give talks at their centers. For example, Robbie, a longtime volunteer at the Root Institute, complained to me that his primary guru, Thich Nhat Hanh, would never be allowed to teach or lead a meditation session at the FPMT center where he worked, nor would many other revered and respected Tibetan lamas from other sects. Robbie told me, "Here at Root, it is the Gelugpa tradition, and there is a resistance to letting anyone outside of the Gelugpa school teach. It seems attached. . . . We can't get too attached or we'll experience spiritual slavery. . . . Thich Nhat Hanh is my root teacher, but I read others. Thich Nhat Hanh doesn't have a monopoly on the *dharma*." Robbie went on to say that neither did Gelugpa teachers have sole claim on the truth, so it made no sense to him that FPMT was so narrowly focused ideologically. While I have come across occasional exceptions to this rule at some centers, FPMT Inc. has articulated a rigorous emphasis on purely Gelugpa teachings, even as they stretch the category itself.

Some of my informants, devotees who have been around for a while, can remember times when FPMT center directors and administrators were asked by the head office to distance themselves explicitly from the fuzzy New Age spirituality that tends toward pastiche,[9] and instead work to maintain the Tibetanness of the institution. Also, having various heritage Tibetan Buddhist contexts meant that there was sometimes disagreement about what kinds of Tibetan Buddhist practices should be institutionalized. The centralization of the centers under the auspices of the international office in the late seventies and early eighties was done in some part to ensure that FPMTers and their teachers stayed on (FPMT-approved) message. Not all of the Tibetan *geshes* recruited from various heritage Tibetan Buddhist monastic centers to teach at FPMT centers were amiable about taking strong direction from the international office. For example, in Australia, much to FPMT's consternation, the resident *geshe* of FPMT's Chenrezig Institute, Geshe Loden, broke away from FPMT to start his own Buddhist institution (Kay 2004). In a more famous case, the Manjushri Institute was an FPMT center in Britain whose core members and FPMT-recruited *geshe* eventually resisted the centralized spiritual direction of Lama Yeshe and Lama Zopa Rinpoche, finally splitting from their parent organization and founding the controversial New Kadampa Tradition (Kay 2004).[10]

Inclusiveness and multidenominationalism are sensitive issues within the FPMT institution. Although the Dalai Lama often diplomatically counsels followers to retain whatever religious identity they were born into, and simply to add certain Buddhist meditation and mindfulness practices as a philosophical and practical complement, if so desired, there is also an underlying understanding in his work that one can only go so far along the Buddhist path without adopting the full program outlined in Gelugpa Tibetan Buddhism. FPMT teachers are fairly amiable about students maintaining connections to other traditions—up to a point.

Many students and devotees shop around for a while and maintain connections to multiple communities, Buddhist and otherwise. However, as one advances in the organization, especially in becoming ordained, one is ideally supposed to shed one's alternative religious connections.[11] Laura, a longtime European FPMT devotee whom I met at Tushita Dharamsala, told me that she tried to balance both Tibetan and Goenka communities, but that there are substantial "*dharma* politics" and tensions that muddled her attempt at being involved in both of the traditions at once:

> There hasn't been that thunderbolt from the sky saying, "this is my lama." Right now I'd say that His Holiness the Dalai Lama is my root lama. I still do some other practices. I spent six weeks in Lumbini doing a Vipassana retreat—it's a Burmese style tradition. The simplicity of it appeals to me. I have done Goenka but that was just . . . (I have to stay clear of *dharma* politics. It's all more mischief by our minds.) There is a fantastic lack of understanding between Mahayana-ists and Theravadins. The Mahayana says that Theravadins are selfish. The Theravadins say that the Mahayana has corrupted the *dharma*—they're referring to the sex and ritual in the Vajrayana. His Holiness says that the difference between Mahayana and Theravada has nothing to do with the color of your robes or your particular practice; it has to do with your motivation to practice. Some Tibetan lay people don't even have a Hinayana motivation to achieve enlightenment. It's about your personal motivation. Doing retreat at a Theravadin center—I want to maintain my connection to that. It's a lonely endeavor trying to do it by yourself. At the Goenkan Vipassana centers they say, no other practices while you're there. They say that no other commitments can be fulfilled or practices done, even if you've promised. One Vipassana monk was a German, he was disapproving about Mahayana and the Tibetan tradition, but he let people maintain their commitments. In Tibetan meditation you have to do a lot of work manipulating the energies in your body. In Vipassana it's just the absence of everything.

Laura and I had several conversations about how she felt pressured by FPMT teachers and administrators to focus and choose one practice over the other.

Since she had become a volunteer living at Tushita, she now felt extra pressure to finally choose FPMT. During the last conversation I had with Laura, she remained committed to trying to continue in both Goenka and FPMT communities, although she noted that both institutions would have preferred her to settle on their style of practice and abandon the other.

A Norwegian FPMT nun whom I interviewed in Delhi in 2006 also began her meditation practices with Goenka but finally decided that her fellow practitioners were too competitive with one another. "It had a sharper edge than Tibetan Buddhism," she told me. Many FPMT teachers say that they see Goenka's Vipassana meditations as a viable Buddhist path, but not the best possible one, and that FPMT helps one move onto the most potent practices for the benefit of oneself and others. This emphasis on committing to help others towards enlightenment is one of the key distinctions that FPMT and other Mahayana groups articulate about their practice in opposition to Theravadin groups.[12]

Appropriation and recontextualization of ideas is not unlike the movement of objects from one social context to another. One could discuss the "social life" (Appadurai 1986) of Buddhist ideas, rather than people (and objects). For example, Nicholas Thomas (1991) has extensively written about how objects are "promiscuous." By demonstrating that the identity of things is never fixed, but rather that objects pass through social transformations through different phases of their history, Thomas specifically works to undermine the former essentialist notion that a particular object was, essentially, either a "commodity" or a "gift." While Thomas specifically discussed the promiscuity of objects vis-à-vis their fluid identities—which is also relevant in terms of the movement of Tibetan statues, art, and décor through the capitalist milieu of Buddhist center gift shops, for example—I would also use his insights to refer to the promiscuity of notions and ideas: Buddhist traditions, mantras, rituals, etc. The notion of *karma*, for example, is arguably as promiscuous, mobile, and global as the now-ubiquitous Tibetan prayer flags.

Appropriation as borrowing can be seen as a positive adaptation when a less powerful group subverts a dominant or dominating discourse by transforming it themselves (Comaroff 1985; Wolf 2002). The appropriation of cultural elements from the less powerful by a dominant regime, however, can also be considered exploitation, even stealing (Deloria 1969; Goonatilake 1999; Sardar 1999; Stephen 1980). Where the obvious problems of postcolonial appropriation are less apparent, there are more ambivalent, multilayered spaces in which there can be something created that is both an extension of the old as well as the creation of the new. The line between preservation and appropriation is muddled at FPMT because of the diversity of *sangha* across the heritage spectrum, as well by the fact that the religious leaders of FPMT are ethnically Tibetan. Any charge of appropriation would certainly be mitigated by the fact that ethnic Tibetans overwhelmingly seem to welcome the interest of nonheritage practitioners in their religious traditions. The increasing number of nonheritage Tibetan Buddhists has been profitable to ethnic Tibetan refugees—the romantic notions of "Tibetophilia," Western appreciation for Tibetanness (Diehl 2002, 151), has fed Western tourism, charity, and donations to refugee communities.

The dialogue between appreciation, tradition and translation is constantly at work in FPMT practice. To illustrate FPMT's singular practices and practitioners, I share a narration of one ritual event with an FPMT *sangha* in Bodh Gaya, India.

Making Ritual Offerings in FPMT

Offertory rituals are a key practice in Tibetan Buddhism, including FPMT's brand of relatively nonheritage Buddhism. Lama Zopa Rinpoche is known to prescribe these rituals both for centers looking to thrive and for individuals who meet him to ask for personal guidance with a spiritual program. Many nonheritage practitioners demonstrate a strong interest in Tibetan ritual practices such as robe and light offerings, regular guru devotion *pujas*, and merit multiplication recitations, although some of these adherents struggle to believe in the efficacy of these ritual practices.

On February 2, 2007, I joined nearly twenty FPMTers, including a few Root Institute volunteers and two nonheritage Buddhist nuns, at a full-moon day ritual: a robe offering at the Mahabodhi Temple in Bodh Gaya. We could not fit inside the temple's tiny chapel for the duration of the approximately half-hour long *puja*, so the *dharma* program director of the Root Institute spread out mats brought from the center in the walkway around the temple; the FPMT chanters faced the Mahabodhi Temple's front right corner, and the two nuns leading the *puja* sat to our right, facing us.

One of the nuns, a German nun, called Ani Tsering, began the *puja* by noting that the temple was "unfortunately" bedecked in exotic, expensive flowers, such as orchids, that had been flown in by a Sri Lankan community for a relic enshrinement procession earlier that day; she said that we should not be dismayed by the fact that so much money had been spent on the floral arrangements, even though they stood in such extreme contrast to the beggars who sat just outside the Mahabodhi Stupa gates. Ani Tsering told us not to allow our feelings of consternation at this waste of money, nor her present crankiness about it, to disrupt the solemnity and heart of the robe offerings we were about to undertake.

The FPMT nuns passed around Xerox copies from FPMT prayer booklets—"The Extensive Offering Practice" (Z. Rinpoche 2006b), "Dedication Prayers for Special Occasions" (Z. Rinpoche 2004), and "Selection of Verses for Offering Robes" (FPMT n.d.)—and then Ani Tsering led the congregation in chanting from the texts. During the chanting, most devotees from other Buddhist communities continued to circumambulate the *stupa*, but a few ethnic Tibetan pilgrims stopped to listen to the FPMT devotees, especially in the short interludes when we chanted in Tibetan. We first chanted *The Extensive Offering Practice* itself, which was composed of the following sections: "Motivation," "Blessing the Offerings," "Making Charity to the Beings of the Six Realms," "Offering to the Merit Field," "Offering Cloud Mantra," "Extensive Power of Truth," the "Actual (Light) Offering Practice," and "Dedications."

First, devotees were instructed to set our motivation toward achieving enlightenment to help others, and this offering would allow us to generate merit toward that goal. We performed the "Blessing the Offerings" section

FIGURE 3. FPMTers make a ritual offering at the Mahabodhi Temple in Bodh Gaya in 2007.
Photo by the author.

and read to ourselves that this keeps the offerings from being possessed by spirits. As the FPMT assembly recited the "Making Charity to the Beings of the Six Realms," we were told to think that the offerings are not ours, and rather that we were giving them to others to offer. "Think that you are making these offerings on their behalf—you and all other beings are going to make offerings to the Buddhas together. Generate great happiness at having accumulated infinite merit by thinking this way," read Ani Tsering.

Devotees then chanted the next section, "Offering to the Merit Field," in order to make the actual modest offerings into imaginary offerings that pervade the whole sky; the "Offering Cloud Mantra" was then chanted in Tibetan to empower the multiplication of offerings. After chanting the "Extensive Power of Truth," we were instructed to visualize ourselves making the offerings by prostrating, giving a whole sky full of offerings, and generating great bliss by the thought that these offerings have been received. Offerings are made step-by-step to holy objects, holy places, and then to Buddhas: "Make offerings to all holy objects, visualizing them as manifestations of your own root guru, who is one with all other virtuous friends. Since the virtuous friend is the most powerful object in the merit field, by offering like this, you accumulate the most extensive merit" (Z. Rinpoche 2006b, 11). While presenting the visualized offering, we were instructed to pause as the offering was mentally made and ostensibly received. The FPMTers then chanted from a loose handout titled the "Selection of Verses for Offering Robes," (FPMT n.d.) in which there were several offering verses from Tibetan sources such as the Tibetan *lama chopa* (guru devotional practice), and even one unsourced passage from a Theravadin text.

Afterward, we returned to the FPMT book on "extensive offerings" to chant the selection on the "Actual (Light) Offering Prayers" three times. The robe offerings were now officially made, and the devotees accumulated merit: "I have accumulated infinite merit by having generated *bodhichitta*, having made charity to the sentient beings, and having made actual (light) offerings to the gurus, Triple Gem, and to all holy objects of the ten directions" (Z. Rinpoche 2006b, 14). The devotees then chanted a reading which had us ask that this merit be used to purify the bad *karma* of all sentient beings.

The ritual offering ceremony ended with a series of dedications, each of which multiplied the merit already created by the offering.[13] The dedication, which we chanted in Tibetan, translates thusly: "Due to the merits of these virtuous actions / May I quickly attain the state of a Guru-buddha, and lead all living beings, without exception / Into that enlightened state. May the supreme jewel bodhichitta / That has not arisen, arise and grow / and may that which has arisen not diminish / But increase more and more" (Z. Rinpoche

2006b, 15). In English, the chant continued, "Due to these infinite merits, may whatever sufferings sentient beings have ripen on me right now. May whatever happiness and virtue I have accumulated, including all the realizations of the path and the highest goal enlightenment, be received by each hell being, preta, animal, human, asura, and sura right now. Having dedicated in this way, you have accumulated infinite merit, so rejoice" (Z. Rinpoche 2006b, 15). Here the devotees were told again that we had increased the size of our return gift by trying to give away the merit over and over, and thus in the process our merit had increased all the more.

The gathered FPMTers were then instructed to chant the "Abbreviated Dedication Prayers for Special Occasions" from another pamphlet created and distributed by FPMT Inc. (Z. Rinpoche 2004). These dedication prayers were explicitly geared toward promoting the success of all FPMT centers and projects. It began with a dedication toward the swift achievement of the Maitreya Project statue:

> We dedicate all these merits for immediate success in getting all the funding needed for the Maitreya Project, for the statue to be completed quickly, and for it to be most beneficial for sentient beings to purify their minds, collect extensive merits, and generate faith in Buddha, Dharma, and Sangha. May the statue generate compassion, loving-kindness, and bodhichitta in the hearts of all living beings, particularly, in this world—particularly in the hearts of all the leaders of the world and all the terrorists, those who cause so much violence to others in this world. May it be the cause for perfect enjoyments and peace, as well as inner prosperity, generating the complete path to enlightenment in their hearts as quickly as possible.

The dedication then continued on to wish success for other FPMT causes and projects, but with far greater brevity; in this dedication, there is as much written about the Maitreya statue as all other FPMT projects put together.[14] The center's individual list of dedications had already been silently read by the spiritual program director of the Root Institute; these were short prayers for the well-being of specific donors, and also dedications for the success of specific Root Institute projects, such as the health care center and the giant *stupa* wheel project.

The group then chanted "Multiplying Mantras" in Tibetan, which Ani Tsering told us would increase the merit one hundred thousand times, and which we followed with a quick mantra that guarantees that the prayers made will come to pass. Finally, as is customary in Gelugpa traditions, the final dedication prayers were made to Lama Tsongkhapa and to the long life of His Holiness the Dalai Lama.

After the event, I talked to several of the participants about the robe offerings, and there were rather divergent views on the matter. Most informants told me that they were glad that they had participated in a service at the Mahabodhi temple, because it had a certain spiritual gravitas that they would never forget. A few of us discussed whether there had been any real robes offered; we had not seen any at the site. Ani Tsering was prevailed on later to settle this question, and she said that there had been an actual offering in the temple to go with our visualized offerings outside. I followed up with several robe-offering participants about merit-making at a Root Institute meal soon afterwards, and two of the FPMTers began passionately debating the issue from opposing sides: one believed that by giving merit one would make more merit, while another felt that this system was somehow "cheating." The former, Gertie, a longtime FPMTer from Germany, felt strongly that ritual offerings were "win-win" and that the karmic calculus was just "inherently good" and would benefit all people primarily because of the dedications. The latter, Dean, an American who had just gotten out of his first FPMT course, said that he just went to the robe-offering event to "see what the fuss was about." He said, "I am a Buddhist, but I don't believe in all the merit-making mumbo jumbo. It's just a way to make us feel good about giving stuff away to monks!"

This conversation grew quite heated, and each of the two FPMTers seemed to feel that the other was quite wrong and were both a bit curt with each other as they said their goodnights. Still, they drank their tea and sat together at meals for the next few days, until finally Gertie left Bodh Gaya a little while later. In recalling this exchange a few days later during a formal interview, Dean said that he had conversations like that all the time at the Root Institute. "I like that in FPMT there is room for debate like that. Of course, only up to a point! I have been told that I am not a real Buddhist even by FPMT standards unless I believe in *karma*, merit, guru devotion—all that stuff. Whatever. I have two words for you. Write this down. Two words: merit multiplication." He went on to say that the whole concept of mathematically multiplying merit through mantras was simply too much for him to believe. "If I could believe stuff like that then I'd still be a Catholic. I came to Buddhism to transcend all that faith crap."

Ritual offerings are an important part of FPMT's *dharma* practice, but the practice of karmic merit multiplications was seen as a theological stretch for some informants in FPMT. But for every Dean, there were at least a few

Gerties. It is useful to note that Gertie was a devotee, and Dean was not; those with more commitment to FPMT tended to show more faith in the efficacy of merit-making and merit-multiplication. In fact, there are many FPMT devotees around the world who believe so strongly in the concept of merit that they will give substantive donations to FPMT to sponsor merit-making activities.

The Heritage Spectrum for Institutions

In Dharamsala in 2006, I interviewed Jon, a young white American monk who had taken vows in a heritage Gelugpa Tibetan lineage. Jon had immersed himself in the Tibetan language and studied in monasteries in India populated almost entirely by ethnic Tibetans for the better part of a decade. Much to my surprise, Jon expressed deep ambivalence about relatively non-heritage Buddhist institutions like FPMT, saying that they adapt and modify Tibetan traditions so much that they are creating something new, untested, and probably defective:

> Westerners are still pretty stupid. They don't know how to treat *geshes*, lamas, and monks. The highly realized monks understand that these are degenerate humans and so these *geshes* run back to India. . . . These [Westerners] are insane. The first two hundred or three hundred years of Buddhism in Tibet was a debacle. Mahasiddhas were invited to dissipate the evil, and eventually lineages started. There were several degenerations, and then Je Tsongkhapa started . . . all that. But there are no lineages in America. It's all hippie cool. Buddhism in America is all secondhand. You can't just make up Buddhism. How can you do it without a base? You have to light the butter lamp from the currently existing butter lamps, or it won't light.[15]

FPMT wrestles internally with the problem of transformation and authenticity, but Jon's critique would have been seen as extreme by most of my FPMT interlocutors. Still, there is a strong debate within the organization about how to mitigate claims of misappropriation or mishandling of Buddhist doctrine. FPMTers see their brand of Buddhism as a direct translation of Tibetan Buddhist practice. Jon's criticism of organizations like FPMT, which translate and alter Tibetan Buddhist practice to make it palatable to non-Tibetan practitioners, hinges on the view that this new form is inherently flawed, nonauthentic, or lesser than its antecedents in some essential way.

Buddhist studies scholars working to understand Buddhist institutions today have found it productive to differentiate between the Buddhists that embrace the overt cultural aspects of the traditions and, conversely, the Buddhists who work to erase particular cultural aspects of their Buddhism. The latter perspective, also known as the "modernist perspective," is generally more prevalent with nonheritage believers. Buddhists who advocate for an acultural (or more strictly philosophical) engagement with Buddhist traditions have also been called "neobuddhists" (Faure 2004), "Protestant" Buddhists (Gombrich and Obeyesekere 1988; Zablocki 2008), and "modernist" Buddhists (Bechert 1984). While the differences are not irrelevant, I argue that assessing the degree to which institutions are innovating or preserving will have more value if arrayed across a spectrum according to a more culturally and historically robust context (see appendix). In his work, Martin Baumann (2001) writes that in both types of American Buddhism, there are "traditionalist" elements and "modernist" elements, and goes on to report that heritage Buddhists rely more heavily on the former, while nonheritage Buddhists are keener on the latter. I submit that on both of the far ends of the spectrum of Buddhist institutions—I choose to call them "relatively heritage" and "relatively nonheritage"—there are adherents to more traditional/cultural practices and advocates for more modern/rational practices.[16] I am interested in degrees of maintenance on the one hand and innovation on the other, but I would also like to work to perceive the degrees of divergence between institutional generations. Which institutions are considered mainstream by the standards of the entire religious community? Which institutions have diverged most spectacularly from their antecedents? From a scholarly, sociocultural, historical perspective, is a particular institution a preserver of practices or an innovator of practices?

This book is focused on a transnational Tibetan Buddhist community that is primarily an innovator and transformer of religious practice. Relatively nonheritage Tibetan Buddhist communities of practice, such as Shambhala International and FPMT, have been creating new traditions from a pastiche of antecedents, additions, and translations.[17] In the United States, there are heritage Tibetan Buddhist communities as well, and those that are diverse enough that they serve more than one community. For example, it is important to recognize that many Tibetan Buddhist religious communities, such as the Drepung Loseling Monastery in Atlanta, Georgia, work to some degree with both nonheritage and heritage Tibetan Buddhists. In Ithaca, New York, the Namgyal Institute is a satellite center of the Namgyal Monastery in Dharamsala, India. The Namgyal Institute in India sends monks to teach classes, lead meditations, and do rituals for the nonheritage students, as well as for the robust heritage immigrant community. As the home to these two "parallel congregations" (Numrich 1996, 63), Namgyal Institute in Ithaca is not just a replicated version of its Indian iteration, where the Dalai Lama lives.[18] The events, classes, spaces, languages spoken, rituals, and proxemics are locally unique.[19] As such, it might be most appropriate to express the current character of the Namgyal Institute in Ithaca as a relatively semiheritage institution.

These institutional distinctions are as relevant in Asia as they are in the West. In drawing a global Tibetan Buddhism spectrum of institutions one would need to focus on degree of rupture from the past. In India, for example, there are countless Tibetan Buddhist temples of different denominations and sects, which serve the varying religious needs of heritage Tibetan Buddhists. I hate to gloss over the difference between Tibetan Buddhist institutions in Chinese-occupied Tibet and Tibetan Buddhist institutions in India in exile, as their practices are necessarily different (Diehl 2002), but in broad strokes Sera Je Monastery is viewed as an important and legitimate mainstream Gelugpa institution in both its iterations, and thus, from a macro point of view, they are both relatively heritage institutions.

If we array these various institutions of global Buddhism across a heritage spectrum: Sera Je Monastery and Namgyal Monastery (both in Tibet and in India) would be relatively heritage institutions; Drepung Loseling Monastery (in Atlanta, Georgia) and the Namgyal Institute (in Ithaca, New York) would be relatively semiheritage institutions; FPMT and Shambhala's centers in Massachusetts would be relatively nonheritage Tibetan Buddhist institutions.

FPMT's centers in Europe and the United States (and even in Asian countries like Singapore and Taiwan) generally serve a nonheritage Buddhist clientele, but they are careful to celebrate the Tibetan cultural aspects of their practices, so you may wonder, why is FPMT relatively nonheritage? It is because FPMT is a nascent, innovative institution and its practices diverge substantially from its antecedents, that I consider it a relatively nonheritage transnational Tibetan Buddhist organization.[20]

FPMT's lineage is Tibetan Buddhist, specifically Gelugpa Tibetan Buddhist. However, FPMT has developed a teaching method, program, and institutional culture that would be altogether unfamiliar to their Gelugpa Tibetan Buddhist forebears. FPMT's Kopan Monastery is different from Sera Je Monastery (either the one in Tibet or its reproduction in exile in India). Adaptation is regarded as a necessary evil, and therefore it is a fraught issue for relatively semiheritage and nonheritage religious groups that want to maintain their commitment to their traditional antecedents. Although the gurus at the top tend to be perceived as irreproachable, the mid- and lower-level teachers and staff (who do most of the actual work to transform the original teachings into programs that work for various levels of nonheritage Buddhist students) often field criticism for changing and adapting traditions too much. There is a constant underlying tension and anxiety among FPMTers that they have strayed too far from the original that sometimes manifests as a strong undercurrent but occasionally seems a much more explosive and dominant concern.

Notably, the large Tibetan-in-exile community in Delhi does not attend teachings or rituals at this FPMT center but prefers the heritage Tibetan Buddhist practices in the Tibetan settlement of Majnu-ka-tilla, which are entirely conducted in the Tibetan language, for and by ethnic Tibetans. I once took Dechen, a Tibetan-in-exile friend living long-term in Delhi, with me to the FPMT center there. Like most second-generation exiles in India, Dechen spoke perfect English, and given that FPMT's center in Delhi was much more convenient to her apartment than the heritage temples in Majnu-ka-tilla, I thought she might enjoy the services there. But Dechen was ambivalent about the meditation, uncomfortable with the proxemics, and discomfited by the fact that the service was led by a single Norwegian nun (rather than a heritage Tibetan monastic), and she never went back. In general, my ethnic Tibetan informants (in Delhi, Bodh Gaya and Dharamsala, and in California, all of whom lived near FPMT centers) told me that they do not feel comfortable practicing in FPMT.

Aside from differences in religious practice, the proxemics of FPMT are quite distinct from the typical heritage Tibetan Buddhist space. That is, the ways that FPMTers lay out, occupy, and use Tibetan Buddhist ritual space is not identical to the ways in which heritage Tibetan Buddhists generally occupy equivalent spaces. My heritage Tibetan Buddhist lay informants tend to circumambulate, prostrate, and make offerings. On the other hand, FPMTers meditate, sometimes in groups and sometimes alone, and they sit on cushions while chanting lengthy rituals (some with faith, some just going through the motions); many Tibetans associate these practices with monastic religious work, not the purview of lay Buddhists. This may be one reason that on Tibetan pilgrimage tours of Indian Buddhist places, FPMT centers are rarely, if ever, a stop along the way. Tibetan Buddhist pilgrims, regardless of sect, visit the heritage Gelugpa, Nyingmapa, and Kagyu monasteries in Bodh Gaya, but rarely an FPMT center. Transnational, nonheritage Tibetan Buddhist spaces—the way that they are set up, and the way that they are moved through—feel quite exotic to heritage Tibetan Buddhists. This cultural disconnect may hold some clues to why the Maitreya Project has thus far operated almost entirely outside of the sphere of heritage Tibetan Buddhist communities. Overall, my Tibetan-in-exile friends in India seem

somewhat nonplussed by FPMTers, but also grateful for the Western love affair with Buddhism that has been so good for their community in particular.[21]

I have made a case for why it is scholastically useful to characterize FPMT
as a relatively nonheritage Tibetan Buddhist institution from a macro perspective, but it could also be useful to zoom in. The organization generally
serves a nonheritage Buddhist consumer base, and its practices are thereby
often unconventional in contrast to conventional heritage Tibetan Buddhist
perspectives, but FPMT also works to support some heritage Tibetan Buddhist groups for good measure (financially supporting a handful of heritage
Tibetan Buddhist monasteries, nunneries, and projects in Nepal, Mongo-
lia, and India, for example). From a more nuanced perspective, one could
also look at various projects and centers in FPMT and array them across
a more internal spectrum in relation to one another: the Dharmarakshita
study group in Mauritius (relatively nonheritage); Tong-Nyi Nying-Je Ling
center in Denmark (relatively nonheritage); Kopan as a space that has both
a traditional monastery for hundreds of Tibetan and Nepali monks, as well
a famous nonheritage Buddhist educational program for visitors (relatively
semiheritage); and Mu Monastery (a *gompa* founded in 1936 that is now financially sponsored by and loosely affiliated with FPMT)[22] in the Tsum valley in Nepal (relatively heritage).

On balance, FPMT is a tradition in the making, a Buddhism in the process of translation and transition. What, if anything, is being lost in translation? Benjamin (1968) argues that translation should not be literal; rather
the translation should transcend the literal to capture the essence of the
original. Is FPMT constructing good translations that capture the aura of
the original, or are they being too careful, too true to word-for-word translations? I ask this question in terms of literal translations—that is, the work
of turning Tibetan text to English text—but also in terms of more figurative translations, such as ways that the inculcated behaviors, beliefs, values,
and ritual forms are being constructed for FPMTers over time. Latour (1996)
writes that translation is always ambiguous. If nothing else, the use of the
word "preservation" as a key appellation and motivation of the Foundation
for the Preservation of the Mahayana Tradition denotes a conceit, or perhaps an ideological statement of intent. Whether for better or worse, the
translations of tradition seem to indicate flexibility and transformation, not
a frozen or inert-in-formaldehyde type of preservation. Therefore, although
it is hidden and fraught, it is precisely the creative, processual nature of their
engagement with their antecedents that has made FPMT a workable and
successful institution.

Ultimately, there is no essential Buddhism, no essential Tibetan Buddhism, no one authentic way of doing things, and therefore FPMT's new transnational Buddhism is no more or less real than any other form of Buddhism. FPMTers are constructing their Buddhist traditions more or less like everyone else. From a more conventional anthropological perspective, claims of appropriation, preservation, and authenticity must be seen in terms of their sociohistorical context. In FPMT, a relatively nonheritage Tibetan Buddhist institution, the work of innovation and translation is being glossed over as a means to capitalize on a veneer of ancient wisdom.

In this chapter, I discussed the nature of FPMT as an institution. I looked at its leadership and organizational structures and the work that it does around the world. This chapter illustrates the heart of the transnational Buddhist experience by showing what Buddhist practice in FPMT looks like to its adherents, what the institution does around the world, and how FPMT governs its constitutive parts and relates to its antecedent communities.

The key to understanding the way that FPMTers dealt with the Maitreya Project controversy is very tightly linked to the religious tradition as it is taught and reinforced in the organization. FPMT purports to follow a Gelugpa Tibetan Buddhist lineage and tradition, but in fact the practices of lay FPMTers are quite different than those of most heritage lay Gelugpa Tibetan Buddhists of both today and yesterday. FPMT's Buddhisms are different from their forbearers' Buddhisms, yet the similarities are significant as well; to contextualize these gaps and bridges, I have given an accounting of FPMT's brand of transnational Buddhism through a discussion of its place in the landscape of global Buddhism.

Do FPMT's divergences from tradition make it less authentic? There are many Westerners who have argued that the converse is true, that newer Buddhist forms take the tradition back to a purer, more authentic past. From an anthropological perspective, relatively nonheritage Buddhist institutions are just as valid as relatively heritage forms, yet they are different in ways that scholars have struggled to name and theorize. I offer a corrective in the form of a heritage spectrum for institutions that differentiates by way of examining ruptures with past traditions—including creative, new ways of practicing within the tradition—as well as institutional trends that tend toward sustaining recently innovated conventions.

✆ CHAPTER 3

The Statue / *MURTI*

Planning a Colossal Maitreya

By all accounts, the Maitreya Project was originally conceived by Lama Yeshe, who desired that a Maitreya statue be built in India as a way to give back to the nation that had offered refuge to the Tibetan refugee community. The statue itself was conceived of as a gift to India, a return gift of kindness for kindness. Lama Yeshe did not detail the specific height or breadth of the statue project; he only expressed his desire that it be built in Bodh Gaya, the place of the Shakyamuni Buddha's enlightenment. Although the statue was originally supposed to be built in Bodh Gaya, it was shifted to Kushinagar, which marks the shift from Maitreya Project 1.0 to 2.0, and the beginning of the statue version that is the main character of this book.[1] Given that the statue was the wish of his guru, Lama Zopa Rinpoche has described the MPI statue as his "heart project"; he has made it clear that the statue is a profoundly important personal dream.

Why would FPMT want to build a giant statue of Maitreya? Maitreya is the Buddha of Loving-Kindness (Sanskrit: *maitri*) and the future Buddha. In Tibetan Buddhist institutions, especially in the Gelugpa tradition, there is ample precedent for constructing Maitreya statues, but usually they are housed inside temples and monastery chapels (Tibetan: *lha-khang*), and none has come close to the staggering size of the statue proposed in Maitreya Project 2.0.

In the summer of 2005, I visited over a dozen monasteries in Tibet with large Maitreya statues. I did a pilgrimage to the largest Maitreya Buddha statue in Tibet proper, which is in the Tashilhunpo Monastery in Shigatse. The seated giant of Shigatse is an eighty-six-foot Maitreya housed in a specially designed *lha-khang*. There are many large Maitreya statues in Tibet and in Tibetan Buddhist sites in India (mostly concentrated in Ladakh), but none dwarves the Shigatse Maitreya Buddha. Thus, when it announced that it would build a five-hundred-foot Maitreya statue, MPI took the tradition of Maitreya statue building to a previously unknown degree of gigantism.[2] MPI's statue design would make it the first Maitreya statue that would itself house chapels inside the body of Maitreya. That is, MPI would build the first Maitreya statue that practitioners, pilgrims, and tourists could enter and walk through. The symbolic significance of Maitreya himself, as the future Buddha, will be taken up in greater detail in the following chapters. This chapter will detail the institutional culture, personalities, and history of MPI.

Of Gifting Statues

Holy objects have a special place of prominence in Tibetan Buddhism, and they are highly valued in FPMT (Z. Rinpoche 2006). Tibetan Buddhist philosophy emphasizes the emptiness of all things, including holy objects, but this fact does not diminish their spiritual power in the eyes of devout practitioners. In "Different Ways of Looking at Things," a chapter of a book taken from talks given in 1990, Lama Zopa Rinpoche (2008) discusses the fundamental emptiness of all things: objects, people, etc. He writes, "Everything—what is called 'I,' 'action,' and 'object,' the names that we say and hear—is labeled. When we talk, we talk by labeling on a base. From morning to night, everything we think, talk, or hear about is labeled. We think things that we have labeled. We talk about things that we have labeled. We hear things that we have labeled. Everything, every word, shows that it is empty of existing from its own side. Everything, every word, shows that it is a dependent arising, merely imputed by the mind in dependence upon its base" (Z. Rinpoche 2008, 85–86). The emptiness of all things is a cornerstone of Buddhist belief, and Tibetan Buddhists do not consider emptiness of objects to be at odds with the sacralization and worship of holy objects, which are ultimately empty, but still have special attributes at the conventional level of perception.

Making offerings directly to statues, and indeed the act of funding and constructing the statues themselves, is considered an important aspect of

FIGURE 4.   A Maitreya statue at Ganden Monastery in Tibet in 2005.
Photo by the author.

practice. In the summer of 2007, I spent time at FPMT's Tsatsa Studio in Richmond, California, to learn more about the importance of holy objects in FPMT practice. According to a quote on the Tsatsa Studio website, Lama Zopa Rinpoche wrote, "To have the scriptural understanding and realizations of the teachings is not easy. For these, you need to have a lot of merit.

The most powerful merit that one can accumulate, and accumulate so easily, is in relation to holy objects. By making statues of Buddha and making offerings to statues of Buddha, one accumulates infinite, inconceivable merit that immediately becomes the cause for enlightenment" ("Tsatsa Studio" 2017). The studio, located in an industrial park, was no *gompa*, but it was a place that nonheritage Buddhists came to practice Buddhism by making Green Taras, Chenrezigs, Manjushris, Maitreyas, etc. As we worked on making *tsatsas* together, the director of the studio told me that she produced her art as spiritual practice for the benefit of herself and all sentient beings.[3]

Generosity is needed to become more accomplished on the Buddhist path. According to the Dalai Lama, while altruism is necessary toward developing the motivation to attain Buddhahood, it must be cultivated in steps, beginning with charitable acts (Gyatso 2000). In order to attain Buddhahood, wisdom is not enough, a direct experience of emptiness is not enough; a bodhisattva must attain extreme levels of altruism and generosity in order to purify negative *karma* and create positive *karma*. Generosity takes many forms in Tibetan Buddhism. Patrul Rinpoche teaches three ways of giving: "material giving, giving Dharma, and giving protection from fear" (1994, 234).

On their website, MPI statements encourage devotees to give generously so that they will be rewarded by a future rebirth in the era of the Maitreya Buddha: "May the beings who contribute to the creation of images of Maitreya, Buddha of Love, experience the dharma of the great way in the presence of Maitreya himself" (MPI 2005). The Maitreya Buddha statue is meant to give devotees an opportunity to create a karmic connection to Maitreya that will ripen in the Maitreya's future lifetime on earth, and thus it is meant to bring benefits now and later (Z. Rinpoche 2014). According to FPMT, the benefits of the statue will accrue to all sentient beings, but especially to those whose proximity will enable them to be inspired by the Maitreya, thus creating karmic links with him. At the heart of the project lies the motivation that the statue is a gift to the Indian people—those who will see the statue and receive blessings and inspiration from it.

Maitreya Project director Peter Kedge has written that the merit created in assisting with the project is "indescribable" and quoted Lama Zopa Rinpoche as having said, "Those who work, sponsor, or help build this statue in any way will be the first disciples of Maitreya Buddha when he comes to this world" (Kedge 1998, 40). The penchant to link one's future self to the future Maitreya Buddha complicates the notion that Buddhist practitioners give disinterestedly, purely, or without reciprocity, because the benefits accrue to future selves (Klima 2002; Ohnuma 2005).[4] Those of my FPMT informants who believe in *karma* (mostly devotees and monastics) are deeply self-interested about their karmic balance, and much of their present practice hinges on nurturing the well-being of their karmic futures. I call this type of merit-based gifting "karmic reciprocity"; it may not appear that social ties are being made, but when karmic intent in merit is present, it motivates social actions, and thus is crucial to understanding Buddhist gifting and attendant social practices. Karmic reciprocity means that while donors who believe in *karma* may not expect a return from the receiver, they do expect a return in the form of karmic reward.

Lama Zopa Rinpoche has given many talks about the benefits that accrue to the donors of statues. He is known for his focus on the creation and worship of holy objects—and much more than his guru Lama Yeshe. Lama Zopa Rinpoche has said,

> We are not aware of the limitless skies of benefits we achieve from the practice of offering, what we achieve and can enjoy from life to life. Even while we are in samsara, we will enjoy good rebirths, wealth, and every happiness. . . . Offering to a statue of the Buddha and offering to the actual living Buddha is exactly the same. . . . And there is no difference between offering to a statue of the Buddha or a visualized Buddha. . . . Therefore, offering, making prostrations, circumambulating, service, and so forth—all these things related to the Buddha—creates inexhaustible merit. (Z. Rinpoche 2006b, 6)

An FPMT nun from Germany, who has taught Westerners the basics of Buddhism for the past fifteen plus years, told me that "bowing in front of the Maitreya Project statue will give us a huge benefit, but maybe not in this life. The seeds are in midstream. The practicing of the past is what leads us to now, and now our merit is developing for the future. With no faith there is no interest. Merit has come from making prostrations and offerings to holy objects in the past. . . . People making offerings to the giant statue, or even just seeing it—it will help those people." She went on to say, "It is not just the *sangha* who think about the project and dedicate merit; all the students of Rinpoche do so. And there are representatives in every country to help collect money—if not in every country, then every region."

A European FPMT devotee living in Delhi named Helena once told me that Lama Zopa Rinpoche dreams of making holy objects for our benefit. In discussing the MPI statue project, Helena said, "That is how compassionate he is. The statue isn't for him, it's for us, so that we can make merit." This may be, but it is also the case that the karmic calculus of this gift will necessarily shower Lama Zopa Rinpoche and MPI donors with merit as well.

FPMT informants run the gamut on whether they wholly agree with the current institutional emphasis on holy objects. While many FPMT students and devotees believed strongly in the value of the Maitreya Project, for example, many did not. Dozens of students articulated dissatisfaction that so much money would be spent on the construction—money that could be used for helping the poor, for example. What is notable is that most, although not all, of those who criticized the idea of the statue were those who had less faith in the karmic cosmology of Buddhism that Lama Zopa Rinpoche espouses, or evinced no faith in *karma* or rebirth.

In the midaughts, the Maitreya Project statue came up often in casual conversations at FPMT's centers in India, and FPMTers who believed in *karma* were far more likely to say that they supported it and had donated to it. The statue project remains the primary recipient of transferred merit from the ritual offerings at the Root Institute, for example. While most of the actual dollars donated to Root Institute programs go straight back into the running of the center and its own local programs, during ritual offerings at Root the Maitreya Project got more specific and sustained attention during the merit dedications than any other FPMT project in the world.

In chapter 2, I narrated a robe-offering ceremony to illustrate a typical FPMT *dharma* practice. Participants in that robe-offering ceremony were mostly volunteers at the Root Institute or students enrolled in courses there. In interviews I did in the following days, I learned that the devotees who believed in FPMT's articulation of karma were motivated to do the offerings because of both the positive *karma* created for themselves and others, as well as the promise that negative *karma* is burned away from oneself and others. In my discussions, the benefits were couched in these terms: "for myself and others"; further probing for the motivations behind the offering were often met with resistance. "Yes, of course, by taking bodhisattva vows or giving our merit away we are also making merit for ourselves, but you shouldn't think about it that way—it defeats the purpose," one Root Institute devotee told me.

In this ritual example, the offerings were done toward the creation of merit for the Maitreya Projects statue and other FPMT projects and persons, but the actual participants, despite the discomfort it seemed to provoke, spoke more often of creating good *karma* and burning off bad *karma* themselves. The two are not mutually exclusive, of course, but we see here that devotees seem to explicitly buy into the implicit karmic calculus that sees the return of the gift in the creation of karmic merit for oneself even as one also gives the gift of merit to others.

Imag(in)ing Maitreya

Lama Yeshe first discussed his desire to build a Maitreya statue in Bodh Gaya, the place of the historical Buddha's enlightenment, in 1982 (Colony 1998, 38), but the size, scope, and contours of the project evolved for many years after that. In this section, I trace the development of the form of the Maitreya statue itself, from artistic and technological perspectives, since this provides a text for understanding the hopes and anticipations of the project. For, as Crapanzano writes, "As with the dream, so do our constructions—and our evocations—of that which lies beyond the imaginative frontier translate experience into text. . . . Our constructions situate it within understanding" (2004, 22).

Bruno Latour's work on Aramis—a French transport technology that never made it out of the planning and drafting stages—provides a useful frame for the innovations of the Maitreya Project, since he focuses on how the innovation and the innovators co-constitute one another, and how they shape and change one another over time and space. Latour (1996) writes that Aramis, in the making, is a text, a fiction to be realized or not, made manifest or not. Latour understood that there was not just one Aramis, there were many, and that projects drift through various identities. There are also multiple giant Maitreya Project statues. The colossus, although it does not exist at present, has taken many preliminary forms already.

After Lama Yeshe's death, the statue project grew exponentially—not only in terms of momentum, but in terms of the prospective size of the statue. Lama Yeshe never specified that the Maitreya statue of his dreams needed to have a certain height or dimension. For many years the statue was just an idea floating around the corridors of FPMT centers called "Maitreya for World Peace"; initially, it was conceived of by many devotees as an "ambitious plan to build a sixty-foot statue of Maitreya, the Buddha to come, in Bodhgaya, the place where Buddha attained enlightenment" (Mackenzie 1995, 207).

Lama Zopa Rinpoche had even more ambitious plans for the statue, and the size and scope of the project increased gradually until in 1996 the height of the statue jumped from 421 feet to 500 feet ("News India/Nepal" 1996, 26), where it stayed through the Maitreya Project 1.0 and Maitreya Project 2.0 iterations. Peter Kedge says that the final size was determined in collaboration with Taiwanese experts: "'The very idea to make the image so big came from an architect in Taiwan,' Kedge said, adding that they settled on the round number of 500 feet (152.4m) during a visit by Lama Thubten Zopa Rinpoche to Taiwan five years ago" (Bartholomew 2001).

According to FPMT lore, as a young boy, Lama Yeshe's Spanish-born re-incarnation, Lama Osel, described his preference that the statue would be a giant transparent statue with lights blinking inside at the chakra points. Over the past twenty plus years, MPI has published various images and representations of the statue as they have developed and altered over time, although none quite as fanciful as the one envisaged by Lama Yeshe's young *tulku*. In each version of MPI's statue, Maitreya is seated aloft on a pedestal in the classic *bhadrasana* pose, but the qualities and details of some of the faces are quite distinct, and according to public reports from the project, it is the face that has received the most attention. Early images were two-dimensional pictures painted or drawn as artists' renderings of the project, while later renderings were three-dimensional prototype statues (or 3-D representations of the prototype).

In an article, an MPI administrator detailed the commissioning of an early prototype of the statue from a factory owner (to whom Lama Zopa Rinpoche had given a portfolio of both Maitreya and Shakyamuni Buddhas to draw inspiration from) (Bertels 1996). In the piece, Bertels described how for six hours Lama Zopa Rinpoche worked tirelessly on the five-foot proto-type: "Using little wooden tools and occasionally his finger, Rinpoche caringly again and again would return to the area of Maitreya's mouth to get just the right loving smile. As the day wore on, our initial disappointment started to disappear and a sense of wonder and joy replaced it as Rinpoche put his magic to work. At the end of the day, there was a very happy and smiling Maitreya Buddha. Rinpoche declared that 'if the face of the Maitreya Statue in Bodhgaya would look like this, I would be very happy'" (Bertels 1996, 11). In an interview with another MPI-networked FPMT monk, I was told that the face was indeed paramount: "For the face of the Maitreya Project statue, it has to be just right. Lama Zopa Rinpoche has gone to great lengths to make sure that it is just right."

In 1997, Denise Griffin, a British sculptor and an FPMTer, accepted a commission to create the next prototype of the statue ("Peter Kedge International Director of Maitreya Project" 1997, 12). Denise was eventually joined in the artistic undertaking by her husband, Peter Griffin. Once the Griffins had finished a prototype in 1998, they disassembled it, packed it up, and sent it to Kathmandu, where they received hands-on assistance from a Tibetan sculptor and guidance from Rinpoche. The Griffin prototype produced in 1998—accounting for some minor adjustments to the right hand and forearm in 2001—is essentially the image of the Maitreya that has been reproduced and globally circulated since then.

The first architects chosen were TCC Architects and Associates from Taiwan, and during this period the Maitreya Project Taiwan National Office was opened at the FPMT Taipei center, which served as both a technical and fundraising base ("Maitreya Project Moves Ahead" 1996, 11). However, the years following the subsequent appointment of Peter Kedge to the CEO position showed a marked shift toward Western project experts instead of Taiwanese ones, and the onus of the technical operations was moved to the United Kingdom. A team from Whinney Mackey Lewis, the Maitreya Project's architects in 2000, formed AROS in 2001 and has continued to provide architectural advice for the project.

In 2001, there was a great deal of excitement in FPMT periodicals and MPI ads over the computer generation of the schematics created by scanning the original prototype. The life-size, five-to-six-foot prototype, finished by the Griffins in Kathmandu with help from a master Tibetan sculptor, was shipped to Salt Lake City, Utah, for scanning. The scanned images were then to be used to control for artist error. Also, this "rapid prototyping" process was supposed to aid in the computer generation of statues; computer-guided lasers were reputed to work an epoxy into an exact replica of the image within just a few hours. The computer-generated images were also billed as fundamental in eventually creating the giant bronze pieces that would eventually be assembled into the giant statue on site. The Maitreya Project's literature on planning in 2001 emphasized the significance of the new technologies being used and developed for the statue process. The technology in Salt Lake City was used to make two twenty-four-foot fiberglass-coated Styrofoam models, one that was installed at an FPMT center in California in 1999, and the other that was delivered to a hangar on the Maitreya Project land in Bodh Gaya soon after.

The new technologies being reported by the Maitreya Project in 2007 emphasized that Delcam, a UK-based company, would be engaging in a process of "reverse engineering." The "non-contact" scanning of the prototype statue with software designed to capture "millions of points describing the shape of the statue" would guide the creation of a "triangle model" (MPI 2007b). Delcam software would then create a smooth model from the triangle model to ensure that no anomalies exist in the final computerized "CAD model." The computer model would be used to crop out four thousand plus individual panels, which could then be modified with engineering features, such as joints. Another partner, the Casting Development Center, was slated to make more than four thousand molds from Delcam's computer panels, probably out of "solid blocks of 'green sand,'" which would be shipped to

FIGURE 5.   The large, twenty-four-foot MPI prototype statue in a hangar on the MPI land in Bodh Gaya in 2007, flanked by a Maitreya *thangka* (L) and a Medicine Buddha *thangka* (R).
Photo by the author.

India, so that each two-meter-square bronze panel could be cast on-site in Kushinagar (MPI 2007b). Thus, the process by which the statue would be built required several technologically mediated steps between the visionary, the artist(s), and the finished product.

The Maitreya Project 2.0 version of the Maitreya statue that was slated to be built in Kushinagar was expected be a mechanical reproduction of an original small statue handcrafted by the Griffins and their teachers. In his seminal writing on "The Work of Art in the Age of Mechanical Reproduction," Benjamin tackles the ineffability of a reproduction by showing that it ultimately destabilizes the notion of traditional art: "that which withers in the age of mechanical reproduction is the aura of the work of art" (1968, 221). Benjamin seemed to indicate that within the destabilization of aura there was an opportunity for liberation, and so too the technology being used to build the colossus could be read as an opportunity rather than a lack.[5] However, according to many of my informants, there is something about the creation of the Maitreya statue by new technologies that makes it more prone to doubt regarding its spiritual efficacy: indeed, its aura was circumspect.

Molds are not an uncommon technique in traditional Tibetan art, but the perceived gap between traditional craft and modern technology had some devotees whispering that the authenticity of the statue was in doubt. One FPMTer told me, "The statue won't even be Tibetan." Another said, "It won't be authentic, but maybe that's okay." A third joked, "They should program the computers to run mantras at the same time as they are running the graphics software! That would be better." The casting of statues in Tibet is often done mindfully, as part of a prescribed religious practice, and so the idea that a giant statue would be made by machines and non-Buddhist workers has led some Buddhists (including some FPMTers and heritage Tibetan Buddhists) to wonder if spiritual ends justify unspiritual means.

Even if the machine-made, completed statue of Maitreya would retain its aura in the eyes of its beholders, there is another level of reproduction in the offing, which evokes tension between art and commodity. Images of the proposed statue, in the forms of posters, postcards, *tsatsas*, etc., have long been widely circulated among FPMT supporters, and these images are even found among peripheral Buddhist communities whose members often frequent the Relic Tour events. The five-hundred-foot Maitreya Project 2.0 statue has had quite a celebrated prelife. It is a recognizable image, a commodified image, at times bordering on fetishized. I found small versions of MPI's specific images all over the world from the United States to India to Tibet.

At the FPMT e-store, one could buy a set of postcards with images of the relics and the statue. On the MPI website, one could purchase a six-inch replica of the statue made in white resin for $150. Outside every Relic Tour event, there was a table where one could buy souvenirs like Maitreya Project posters, DVDs, CDs, etc. MPI postcards often sat propped up on FPMI devotees' home altars. In that context, the smiling visage of the Maitreya Project's prototype can be experienced as a conduit toward spiritual liberation for some, but for others it was a sign of a karmic or social vision that they had bought into.

Even as a representation of a plan, it was a real image with substantial cultural currency—the image was a plan of action, an advertisement, a call to donate, a charming ambassador for their ambitions in Kushinagar, and as Benjamin prophesized, "instead of being based on ritual, it begins to be based on another practice—politics" (1968, 224). To the extent that Benjamin felt that political liberation could ensue from replication, there certainly is a sense here that the replication of images would help to create a positive momentum for the future. This echoes social scientist Kirk Junker's approach to the image of a drafted object, in which the graphic becomes an activating and motivating prescription for the future (1999, 23).

Some of my FPMT informants think that the Maitreya Project statue visage is beautiful, perfect even. Other Tibetan Buddhists, FPMTers and others, contend that Lama Zopa Rinpoche accommodated an aesthetic that is more East Asian than Tibetan, in regard to the Maitreya Project statue. These were often whispered, backstage remarks to be sure, but I heard variations on the exact same comment too many times and from too many disparate sources to ignore: "The Maitreya Project's statue looks too Chinese." The aesthetic and pedigree of the statue were certainly unique and multicultural, but the comment may point to concerns about the hefty amount that Chinese/Taiwanese devotees contributed (or pledged) to the project. These complaints came from both heritage and nonheritage FPMTers, as well as heritage Tibetan Buddhists from outside the FPMT family,[6] and they reflect a general mistrust of the Chinese given simmering resentment at the long-term Chinese occupation of Tibet.

While I make no pretensions to expertise as an art historian, I have observed that there are multiple classical Tibetan representations of Maitreya, and the artistic renderings of the proposed Maitreya Project 2.0 statue seemed to move away from the type of Tibetan Maitreya style that is most prevalent in Tibetan Buddhist religious contexts today. For example, during a summer-long survey of Maitreya statues in Tibet in 2005, I was surprised to note that every single Maitreya statue that I found in *lha-khangs* in Tibet proper was outfitted with a crown (usually with a Shakyamuni Buddha represented in that headpiece). On the other hand, the representation of the MPI statue is iconographically different: here Maitreya sits without a crown (with no Shakyamuni Buddha image) and with a *stupa* instead. This—and other stylistic and iconographic differences between the standard Maitreya image in contemporary Tibetan monasteries and the image that has been produced for the Maitreya Project—has some Tibetan tongues wagging in disapproval.

The Maitreya Project's supporters acknowledged that the statue was not made in a conventional Tibetan aesthetic style. Peter Kedge stated in an interview that while the traditional proportionality would be maintained, the statue would not be representative of any specific national or regional aesthetic style (Bartholomew 2001). FPMT's effort to commission a Maitreya that did not conform precisely to traditional antecedents can be seen as a nod to their transnational nature. Perhaps like the Dhyana Buddha of Amaravati, India, studied by art historian Catherine Becker (2015), the Maitreya Project's statue was meant to be as all-inclusive as possible. Becker writes,

"Although the iconography of the Dhyana Buddha emphatically conveys the 'Buddha-ness' of this image, its style is far more ambiguous, thereby preventing this Buddha from being associated with a geographic region or historical moment. That would seem to be the point; by eschewing art historical specificity, the Dhyana Buddha is a Buddha for everyone" (2015, 271). MPI's Maitreya Buddha has evolved over time and space and been influenced by many people along the way, and as such, it is arguably a very transnational representation of the Maitreya Buddha. One might expect that this would be celebrated in the context of a transnational institution, but the fact remains that the perceived Sinicization of MPI's Maitreya remains a source of dispute among some Tibetan Buddhists. The face of transnationalism, it would seem, is not always a welcome one.

MPI as Archipelago

The Maitreya Project has long been one of the most important projects of FPMT. Although for much of the Maitreya Project 2.0 era, MPI listed on its website that its affiliation with FPMT was still "pending," the Maitreya Project was listed unambiguously as an FPMT project in FPMT literature and on its web pages. FPMT was also clearly listed as the community sponsoring the Maitreya Project in MPI literature and online materials.

MPI was itself legally decentralized: an institutional island chain of sorts. It had numerous legal components that operated independently of one another. According to MPI documents released in 2007, the main MPI corporate entity was based in Great Britain but was reincorporated in the Isle of Man (MPI 2007c, 2007d). There was also a corporate branch in India that was technically the domain of the main owner of the statue and Maitreya Project assets on the ground. Other MPI entities that existed at that time—located in Singapore, Hong Kong, the United States, France, and Australia—were primarily for fundraising and promotion.

Publicly, MPI sought to cast itself as a large operation for the benefit of potential donors, but even in its heyday there were only a few staff members and administrators managing the project. The MPI Coordination Team as reported in late 2007 on the Maitreya Project's website consisted of (1) the "director and CEO," Peter Kedge (a former businessman and longtime FPMT devotee who lived in Vancouver); (2) "executive director" of the Maitreya Project Trust and the Maitreya Project Society, as well as "Art Programme director," Tony Simmons (who was based in Australia but commuted periodically to India); (3) the "education director" (a position long held by David Thomas, a devotee who commuted between both Australia and India);

(4) the "liaison officer," the regional associate based in India, Babar Singh; (5) the public relations head, "media manager," Linda Gatter (based in Britain); and (6) the Relic Tour manager (at the time it was Stephanie Evans, a British national who worked primarily out of the United States).[7]

Other significant personages guiding the trajectory of MPI include the spiritual director, Lama Zopa Rinpoche, and his attendant Roger Kunsang.[8] Certainly the other members of the FPMT Inc. board of trustees also would have had influence on Maitreya Project policy in their own way. Also, there are two local boards in India that are also charged with responsibility for the project: (1) the Maitreya Project Trust (a "socio-spiritual trust"), which will eventually be entrusted with the Kushinagar site; (2) the Maitreya Project Society (registered as a "spiritual society") that is currently responsible for the Bodh Gaya site. Professional staff includes (1) the Relic Tour custodians, (2) the staff (kitchen, grounds, security) of the Maitreya Project headquarters in Bodh Gaya, India, and (3) the Maitreya Project schoolteachers and staff. The Maitreya Project has also periodically contracted engineers, architects, and other technical experts.

During my fieldwork period, the Maitreya Project ran two associated side projects: the Relic Tour, and the Maitreya Project School in Bodh Gaya. Since the Maitreya Project statue in Kushinagar was in limbo, these two side projects represented the only work that the Maitreya Project was doing that was concrete, active, and visible to the public eye.

The Maitreya Project School was started as a part of the local FPMT center, the Root Institute, but was subsequently handed over to the Maitreya Project at Lama Zopa Rinpoche's request, since the original Maitreya Project plans were expanded to include health and education components. The Maitreya Universal Education School, as MPI's school was called, closed its doors for lack of funding in 2010.

The Relic Tour was initiated to publicly display the relics (from past Buddhas, bodhisattvas, historical gurus, and teachers of India and Tibet) that Lama Zopa Rinpoche had collected to place inside a heart shrine of the giant Maitreya Project statue. This tour traveled the world, sometimes splitting into multiple simultaneously touring circuits.

The Maitreya Project website and literature listed several offices worldwide that one might have imagined were staffed with numerous, busy Maitreya Project employees. In practice, many of these Maitreya Project offices were not offices at all, but rather the mailing addresses of associates. For example, "the North American Maitreya Project office" has long been located inside other FPMT offices such as the former FPMT headquarters in Taos, New Mexico, or the Land of the Medicine Buddha in Soquel, California.

When I e-mailed to arrange a visit to the former in 2000, I received a phone call from an FPMT staffer telling me not to bother. The FPMT staffer told me that there was no one employed by the Maitreya Project based there; MPI literature and materials were housed there, and MPI donations were processed by FPMT staffers.

When I visited "the North American Maitreya Project headquarters" in Soquel in the summer of 2007, I was told that the Relic Tour and regional MPI were only technically based there; in practice, the FPMT center simply kept a shed with extra MPI publications and materials. An FPMT volunteer laughingly showed me the shed; it was full of Relic Tour souvenir booklets and also the foot-high Maitreya statues that were given to important sponsors. I was also shown the single desk that the Relic Tour coordinator used to use when she had temporarily been in residence there.

The Maitreya Project office in Uttar Pradesh, India, was located in Gorakhpur, which is about an hour and a half drive (or thirty-five miles of bad road) from Kushinagar. It was a private house on the upper floors and a private office on the lower floor; the building is owned by Babar Singh, who was the primary Indian broker managing the local politics and bureaucracy for the Maitreya Project. He had also been appointed to a government committee overseeing the land transfer. The home office is legitimately used for Maitreya Project work, but it is owned and operated by Singh, who is involved in many projects of his own. That is to say, it is not an office owned or operated by FPMT or MPI proper.

Babar Singh was the mover and shaker for the Maitreya Project on the Indian side, although unfortunately for the project he had a local reputation as a scoundrel of questionable character. Singh was neither an FPMT student nor devotee; he told me that he and his family were Hindus, but he noted that he believes in the Buddha too (as do most Hindus). In general, Kushinagari farmers reviled him and were quick to enumerate his many sins against the community. I have no evidence that Babar Singh is as villainous as locals believe, but it is an unassailable fact that MPI hired a regional representative that is widely despised and mistrusted by the large majority of local Kushinagaris. This type of decision—prioritizing the paperwork over the people—was one of the factors that mired Maitreya Project 2.0 in years of controversy.

The Maitreya Project office in Bodh Gaya, India, was the former home of the statue project Maitreya Project 1.0. In the midaughts, it was being used as a bureaucratic staging point for two ventures: (1) the Maitreya Project school, which was located just a short distance away; and (2) outreach and fundraising for the Maitreya Project, generally targeted at Buddhist pilgrims.

The fundraising was accomplished by positioning a large prototype of the MPI statue, which was housed in a large hangar in the middle of a large empty field, as a minor tourist attraction. During the pilgrimage season the Maitreya Project staff set up a fundraising video, put Buddhist relics in display cases, and hung giant *thangkas* in the hangar. The site was not a popular attraction, especially compared to the frenetic crowds of pilgrims at the Mahabodhi Temple in the town center, but the prototype statue did periodically receive busloads of pilgrims ready to pay their respects to the relics.

In India, in the midaughts, longtime FPMT devotees told me that the problem with the Maitreya Project was entirely financial—that is, donations were down; the controversy in Kushinagar was generally unknown to rank-and-file FPMTers at the time, but whispers about financial trouble ran rampant. The rumors of MPI's financial woes were confirmed when persistent questions from donors—following hard on the heels of some unflattering press—led the Maitreya Project leadership to release their finances on their website for the first time in 2007 (Kedge 2007c; MPI 2007c, 2007d).

The records for the project that were released in 2007 show earnings and expenditures from the early nineties to the end of the 2006 fiscal year. From 1990 to 2006, the Maitreya Project (in total from all its offices) brought in $12,667,000 and spent $19,033,000; during this period the Maitreya Project had allowed a deficit "financed by loans and creditors" of $6,366,000. According to the same document, the top expenditures during this period were the following: (1) for "Contractors, Consultants, Architects, and Engineers," a total of $8,289,000 was paid out; (2) for "Salaries & Allowances," a total of $3,112,000 was paid out; (3) for "Financial, interest, insurances, bank charges," there was $2,023,000 spent; (4) for "Marketing, Advertising, Fundraising," there was $1,468,000 paid out; (5) for "Travel, Accommodation, F & B," the total expenditure was $878,000. In the 2006 financial year, the Maitreya Project brought in $1,126,981 and paid out $1,590,893, leaving them with a deficit of $463,912 (MPI 2007c, 2007d).

In 2001, Peter Kedge noted that while the United States provided the larger number of contributions, Taiwan was the source of over one-third of the funding (Bartholomew 2001). Donations are made to the Maitreya Project in a number of ways. Donations are being collected as small, individual donations at centers, but these account for only a small percentage of the total. Merit boxes are placed at centers for people to deposit their small change toward many international FPMT projects, MPI included. Many large donors were tapped at the outset, most from Taiwan and other Asian countries where merit making by donating to the construction of a Buddhist statue or temple is a more traditional, mainstream practice. Donations were made online at the Maitreya Project's website (www.maitreyaproject.org), which functioned in several languages. As of spring 2010, on the MPI website, one could make a donation of $150 to receive a six-inch replica of the statue made in white resin. The website was careful to suggest to donors that the exchange is not consumerist in nature, but rather a merit-making one:

> Buddhism teaches that one should not sell sacred objects for personal profit. For that reason, we are not providing these statues simply as "for sale," thinking of them as goods to be bought and sold. Rather, we are making them available with the wish to benefit others by generating funds to enable us to carry out the charitable work of Maitreya Project.
>
> All of the proceeds from your donation will be used to build the Maitreya Project statue and support Maitreya Project's charitable activities in Kushinagar, in the state of Uttar Pradesh, and Bodhgaya, in the state of Bihar, both in northern India.
>
> From your side, please do not think that you are purchasing this statue. Rather, think that you are making a donation with the thought of creating benefit. By thinking in this way, you, and the millions of other beings who will receive the blessings of Maitreya Project, will receive only benefit.

Maitreya Project 1.0

According to David Thomas, a Maitreya Project administrator in Bodh Gaya in the aughts, the Maitreya Project Society of Bodh Gaya was established in 1994: "The formal presence here started then. The land was purchased, around forty acres, but small strips of land within that area were owned by the government and also a small family. The issues related to the land made it impossible to proceed." While it does seem that the land acquisition issues connected to an intractable state government regime in Bihar was the primary reason that Bodh Gaya's Maitreya Project 1.0 folded in favor of the advent of Maitreya Project 2.0, there were many other obstacles, and it is likely that it was the compounded issues presented by multiple problems that ultimately led to the cancellation of the original statue plan.[9]

From the outset, the plan met with controversy from several quarters at once. First of all, there were vocal opponents among the local Buddhist expatriate community. According to many of my informants, regardless of their feelings about the giant Maitreya statue itself, there were those among both nonheritage and heritage Buddhist communities who felt that Bodh Gaya itself or the spot they had chosen there was not the most appropriate place for the Maitreya project for various reasons. For example, a prominent Burmese monk who had been in Bodh Gaya for years felt that the idea of a giant statue was fine but that the Maitreya Project had picked the wrong place, since it was on desirable agricultural land. An American devotee of this monk described his guru's feelings this way:

> He thought it should be over by the Mahakala caves. The area by the caves, the land is not good, so no one would mind the statue over there. This is one of the more intelligent critiques of the statue plans. . . . He knows the complexity of land issues. He thinks they should have picked a site that no one wanted. He didn't say whether the statue was important or good. The Burmese have large statues in Burma too. They picked the wrong spot. He's the son of a farmer, so he thinks it's wasteful to take arable land. It wasn't going to work because people weren't going to give them the land they wanted.

In the end, the landowners surrounding the Maitreya Project headquarters did indicate resistance to selling off more land to MPI. The land problems with the government and its neighbors were a thorn in the side of the MPI statue organizers in Bodh Gaya. In tandem, there was also a popular, though unverifiable, rumor circulating among local Indians that the nearby air force base and the proposed reopening of the Gaya International Airport taken together would mean too many planes in the sky uncomfortably close to a five-hundred-foot statue with its head in the monsoon clouds.

Ralph, a Buddhist devotee and educator who had been coming to and living periodically in Bodh Gaya for decades, also noted that many people were upset that the Maitreya statue would be higher than the Mahabodhi Temple. Ralph felt that their concerns were quite right and that there would be something disrespectful about trumping the spot where Buddha became enlightened. "From an esoteric point of view it may really hurt the spiritual energy of the town," he said.

> I don't that you should build anything higher than the Mahabodhi temple. The Mahabodhi temple is about 180 feet, I think. . . . It used to bother me that the Maitreya Project statue would have been bigger than the temple. I thought that to dwarf the Mahabodhi Temple was wrong; as if the Maitreya would be looking down on a little model Mahabodhi. It wouldn't be far enough away. People would see the statue first and it would overshadow the temple. The Mahabodhi Temple shouldn't be overshadowed by any modern construction, even a statue. I think that a lot of people felt that.

Regarding this final observation, Ralph was quite right; his concerns were shared by many other people. I heard concern about the dwarfing of the *stupa* reiterated several times by Western Buddhists (mostly non-FPMTers), by Buddhists of Asian descent, and even by a few Indians working in foreign monasteries in Bodh Gaya; all indicated anxiety that the spiritual geography of Bodh Gaya would be shifted in a problematic way, or that the sacred energy of the place would be weakened, if the giant statue was built there.

Locally, there were many community members who worried about the socioeconomic effects of the giant statue project. Ralph and many others with special, lengthy connections to Bodh Gaya mentioned their concern about how the addition of a huge new project might change Bodh Gaya too quickly and that the corruption and graft might be excessive. He said, "Bracketing appropriateness questions, I was afraid that it would be terribly executed—that it would be a slow-rolling disaster that would transform Bodh Gaya. For the average Bodh Gaya resident the past thirty years, the changes have been good. They have more income than before. I was afraid it would destabilize the local economy. Those people out at the Maitreya Project don't know India well enough." If the recollections of local Indians and expatriates are to be believed, then the leadership of several dozen nonprofits, social service hubs, and schools in town felt that the Maitreya Project would hurt rather than help local Indians.

There is some evidence that even certain high-status Tibetans were against the idea of the MPI statue. The Dalai Lama, reportedly, was ambivalent about the idea initially, and only agreed to support it once the social service and education aspects were added to the plan. An informant from FPMT told me that an initial envoy from the project cried when the Dalai Lama failed to support the project after a first hearing. Also, there were rumblings, quiet ones, that certain Tibetan teachers, especially those outside the Gelugpa tradition, were less than enthusiastic. One Western student told me that his non-Gelugpa guru did not foresee an easy time for the project in India. He told me: "I have a Tibetan teacher, he said, it's a good project, but maybe in the wrong place. His concern was that it would destabilize everything here. There is too much corruption and greed for a project of that size to be done well here. It was the late nineties. . . . But it got the Dalai Lama's backing, so there was probably difficulty in speaking against it." The lay Tibetan refugee community in India was never of one mind about the project—not when it was initially scheduled to be in Bodh Gaya, nor later when it moved elsewhere—but in both iterations it was viewed as a nonheritage Buddhist project, and thus adjacent to their sphere of influence.

Though there is an outward appearance of intercommunal harmony in Bodh Gaya, there is a history of racial, ethnic, and class tensions between the various communities there. The colonial hangover haunts the dynamics between Westerners, especially whites, and Indians. Many past inequities have been maintained, in new forms, by the vagaries of neoliberal globalization. Some difficulties and misunderstandings between Tibetans and Indians go back to the period of mass resettlement of refugees into India. Indo-Tibetan relations are as interdependent as they are fraught (Falcone and Wangchuk 2008). Tibetans hold many unsavory stereotypes about Indians, as Indians do about Tibetans (Diehl 2002). In this complex ethnic landscape, MPI has been accused of institutionalized cultural insensitivity, and occasionally even outright racism, in some of their dealings with local people in India. There is a great deal of ambivalence about India and Indians within FPMT centers located on the subcontinent. There is a general sense that FPMT's pilgrimage-place centers function as refuges from India(ns) as opposed to refuges in India, and almost never as refuges for Indians.

In her article about the Maitreya Project, a nonheritage Tibetan Buddhist practitioner indicated that Western racism and ethnocentrism had led MPI to express condescension toward local Hindus (Cousens 2007). She wrote, "The project is being imposed by outsiders, and not ethnic Tibetans, but new Western Buddhists or newly converted Indian Buddhists, who appear to see the local Hindu culture as deficient." On the other hand, Ralph, my aforementioned FPMT informant, seemed to place the blame for any anti-Indian bias by FPMT at the feet of the ethnic Tibetans who serve as spiritual guides. Ralph phrased his concerns this way:

Lama Yeshe founded Root with the idea of giving back to local Indians. But amongst non-Tibetan Tibetan-practitioners there is a certain disdain for the locals. They don't value Indian culture. Lama Yeshe wasn't like that, but many Tibetans feel that. Westerners acculturate to Tibetan values in an exaggerated way. If Tibetans have tension with Indians, then it will be more so from the Westerners in the organization. The cultural bias, and the acculturation from Tibetans and then followers, is an important part of this. Some people come here in spite of India, but others, like [Helloise], love India. Tibetans and Western Tibetan Buddhists have this issue.

I have observed the gamut of interracial relations at Root: from devotees who make an extra effort to build respectful relationships with Indian staff to a quite obviously racist FPMT staffer who raged on and on about how all

Indians are liars and cheats. The latter attitude is not uncommon, and the fact that it is extant does serve to tarnish FPMT's overall reputation in the area.

I also met local Indians in Bodh Gaya who felt that the Root Institute was famously, excessively racist, even in a context where many Indians are critical of most outsiders for their treatment of local people. The Root Institute's optics are affected by their high walls, razor wire, armed patrols, and attached police station.[10] For example, they have a health clinic open to locals, but aside from staff, no local Indian is allowed beyond a certain point. Security is tight. The locals that I talked to said that they feel very unwelcome at Root, and often as if they are being assumed to be up to something. The non-profit leaders and social workers of Bodh Gaya cast aspersions on the Root Institute as a place that is "part of the problem." In sum, the Root Institute is known in Bodh Gaya for going overboard in their efforts to keep Indians out; the same bubble that makes Root feel snug and safe to those inside its walls can make it feel like an affront to those on the outside. I am not suggesting that FPMT, nor its center in Bodh Gaya, is a racist organization writ large, and yet it would be fair to say that as an organization it could be far more graceful and inclusive in its relations with local Indians than it has been thus far. I tend to agree with my informant, an FPMT student who lived with me at Root in 2006, when she said that she was embarrassed by the anti-Indian tendencies she had witnessed there. "They have a long way to go," she told me.

Persistent concerns about FPMT's anti-Indian bias has fed certain critiques of the Maitreya Project. One Bodh Gaya native, an Indian social worker, said that he protested against MPI because he thought that FPMT was anti-Indian, and therefore could not be trusted to carry out such an ambitious project in a responsible way. One local Indian civic group, Gram Ganrajya Manch, wrote an open letter to the Maitreya Project that voiced its concern and fear that the project would have unintentional and negative consequences for Bodh Gaya (Gaya Forum of Village Republics 1999b), and then followed-up with a dismayed community letter when they felt that they were being "ignored deliberately" (Gaya Forum of Village Republics 1999a). Gram Ganrajya Manch expressed two major concerns: 1) the image was disrespectful—"For the people here it is unfortunate that an image meant to represent such a great personality like the Buddha will be projected in such a monstrous form. We are distressed at this cultural insensitivity" (Gaya Forum of Village Republics 1999b); 2) the giant statue–led tourism would wreak havoc on the socioeconomics of the locality—"Our concern is also about the future effects of this Project on the villages of the area. We see clearly that our villages will no longer remain villages. They will degenerate into slums. We are afraid that the proclaimed values of the Maitreya statue—i.e. Maitri, loving kindness, compassion—will prove to be only wishful thinking. Instead we will have more greed and dependence on market forces, cut-throat competition and unemployment, disintegration of the community and cultural degeneration" (Gaya Forum of Village Republics 1999b); 3) the cost of the project in the face of poverty—"How can we justify the misuse of massive resources at the cost of the poor people?" (Gaya Forum of Village Republics 1999b). I myself did interviews with a number of locals who articulated versions of these arguments. Some of my local interviewees were as adamant as Gram Ganrajya Manch that the effects would be massively detrimental to the locality, explaining that an influx of tourists would not benefit the poorest of the poor who would just be pushed aside by the unkind forces of gentrification and capitalism. This is not to say that all local Indians in Bodh Gaya were opposed to Maitreya project 1.0, but it is a fact that MPI met substantial local resistance to their work.

Sister Theresa is a white, European woman who runs a Christian nonprofit in Bodh Gaya. She works very closely with underprivileged youth and women in some of the villages surrounding the tourist sector of Bodh Gaya. Her perception that FPMT has anti-Indian proclivities fueled Sister Theresa's antagonism to the MPI plan in Bodh Gaya. Although she sometimes collaborates with Buddhist nonprofits, she was critical of the Maitreya Project's "top-down activities" in Bodh Gaya. In 2006, she shared this recollection with me: "It's a corporation. The Maitreya Corporation is working with the government. I remember when it was supposed to be here. There were all sorts of petitions against it, and Christopher [Titmuss] wrote against it. There were women who went there and protested. . . . Such a huge waste of money. [MPI] were saying that it was the Christians who were against it, but that wasn't true, it was so many people." She told me when the Maitreya Project was based in Bodh Gaya there were several groups actively protesting the statue project. There were some rallies against the statue in Bodh Gaya that had been organized by locals afraid of rapid change, corruption, and an egregious waste of money in the face of enormous local poverty.

Sister Theresa explained to me that some of the local women she knew through her organization were so angry about the plan that they walked a picket line near the Maitreya Project land. She went on to say that when the Maitreya Project had an open house lunch, the dissenters were invited, but that the forum was not a discussion format: it was a one-sided, lectured advertisement for the statue. She and her social worker friends were frustrated that the Maitreya Project was dictating terms, rather than engaging in real dialogue with the local people about their needs and concerns.

During the early years of the project, the promoters of Maitreya Project 1.0 became enmeshed in a theological debate about whether statue building on such a grand scale is more of a vanity project rather than being truly Buddhist practice. Lama Zopa Rinpoche regularly emphasized the merit making that would come with statue building, but those in the other camp felt that building a mammoth holy object was actually the antithesis of true Buddha *dharma*. This controversy was sparked by expatriate Buddhists in Bodh Gaya and quickly spread into debate and discourse in the larger Western Buddhist communities.

My informant, Ralph, noted that an Insight Meditation community leader, Christopher Titmuss, was the first Westerner to raise a hue and cry about the statue and that he and his Buddhist community questioned its spiritual value: "He was asking, is it good to spend all of that money? In such a poor area why not spend it on something better? It's a waste of money. So do other things with that money—that was his view. In the late nineties, it was discussed a lot; from 1995 to 2000, it was discussed a lot over here over tea." It also became fodder for debate among those who were completely unconnected to the Bodh Gaya Buddhist community who debated its merits in Buddhist chat rooms online. The *Turning Wheel* magazine featured the Maitreya Project debate in 2001. Christopher Titmuss wrote a critical piece about its excesses: "is it skillful means (Sanskrit: Upaya) to build a $150,000,000 statue in the poorest and most economically deprived region in the whole of the sub-continent of India?" (Titmuss 2001, 32). A counterperspective lauding the MPI plans was provided by the Maitreya Project's public relations officer (Gatter 2001).

In addition to meeting resistance from some local Indians and expatriates, the Maitreya Project in Bodh Gaya encountered problems with the Bihar state government. Bihar, especially at the time, was considered one of the most corrupt state governments in all of India. The state government was run by Lalu Yadav Prashad and his family, though the man himself was in and out of prison for graft. Bihari politics being notoriously corrupt, one can well imagine that the Maitreya Project must have looked like a prime target for exploitation by the administration.

After a very long, thorough, and candid discussion with David Thomas, the administrator of the Maitreya Project headquarters (and the MPI school) in Bodh Gaya in 2007, about Kushinagari farmers' issues with Maitreya Project 2.0, I asked him why they had really left Bodh Gaya for Kushinagar. He told me that the Bihari state government had indeed tried to extract outrageous rent on a sliver of government land that ran through the organization's property. Furthermore, David told me that the reason the government has some of the land is that there are some old government-owned waterways (or "canals") that are on some strips of land that protrude into their property area. "They had wanted an astronomical sum of money for the land. The land prices have gone up all over Bodh Gaya quite a bit, but even while some of the land could be used, most of that contested land is pretty useless commercially," David reported. Other FPMT informants told the story by saying that the Bihari state government had tried to draw exorbitant *baksheesh* (Hindi for "tips" or "bribes"—here meaning extorted payments) from the Maitreya Project that they had been unwilling to pay.

The thirty-plus acres owned by the Maitreya Project in Bodh Gaya was initially supposed to be enough land for the statue and its constituent infrastructure. When I noted that there was a huge gap between the thirty to forty acres needed at the original site (for Maitreya Project 1.0)[11] and the 750 acres that was slated to be acquired at the Kushinagar site (for Maitreya Project 2.0), Mr. Thomas said, "Now we can see that forty acres wouldn't have been quite enough land. Now whether 750 acres is needed . . . that's another story."[12]

According to several FPMT informants with administrative experience in the organization, when the Bodh Gaya site became manifestly unfeasible due to both land acquisition and corruption issues, the Maitreya Project put out feelers for alternative locations, and the Uttar Pradeshi state government responded with interest. An informant in the Department of Culture in Uttar Pradesh told me that, on hearing about MPI's situation, a state official from the Sarnath area of Uttar Pradesh began courting the Maitreya Project to settle near Sarnath. The state government of Uttar Pradesh's Department of Culture, recognizing a potential boon to their tourism offerings, forwarded some proposals that gained traction quickly. Eventually, it became clear that the land in the Sarnath area was too expensive and there was not as much available as the project wanted. The Maitreya Project eventually, with the help of a divination by the Dalai Lama,[13] settled on the Kushinagar area, and the Uttar Pradeshi state government began its work to secure land there. Maitreya Project 1.0 was abandoned.[14]

The Maitreya Project Moves to Kushinagar

The Maitreya Project signed a Memorandum of Understanding (MoU) with the Uttar Pradeshi state government on May 9, 2003. From Uttar Pradesh state offices in Lucknow, I collected an internally circulated draft of the MoU, as well as a copy of the final, official, signed MoU.[15] The MoU leased the land from the state in perpetuity and for a pittance. Whether the Maitreya Project was given a deal too good to pass up, or whether their representatives twisted the arm of the state government into offering far, far more land than they initially wanted to do, is the subject of debate among my FPMT informants from Lucknow to Delhi to California. Lucknowi bureaucrats interviewed for my project indicated that they felt Maitreya Project representatives were "greedy" and "not good," but that their superiors had felt pressured to close the deal anyway. During an interview in 2006 with Mr. Chaturvedi, a bureaucrat at the state Department of Culture in Lucknow, he told the story this way:

> MR. CHATURVEDI: They are encroaching on seven hundred acres of land.
>
> JESSICA: Why so much land?
>
> MR. CHATURVEDI: They say that it is a big condition. We think that it is land grabbing. But they say that they will build a big auditorium where five thousand people can pray, and there will be a big environmental campus, and one big school free of cost from primary to an engineering college, and they will build a big hospital. Have you been to Bodh Gaya? There is a small Maitreya Project school there. Have you seen it? What is your impression?
>
> JESSICA: Yes, I've spent a lot of time there in the past. Actually, I think that the school is quite well run, but, well, it has consumed many of the resources of the Bodh Gaya Maitreya Project people, and that makes me nervous about the ability to carry out the Kushinagar plan responsibly. I mean they are doing one school well, but their resources to expand are limited, I think. The school is good though.
>
> MR. CHATURVEDI: Have you met [Babar Singh]?
>
> JESSICA: Yes.
>
> MR. CHATURVEDI: Honestly what do you think of him?
>
> JESSICA: Well, I don't know. . . . I didn't really spend much time [in Gorakhpur], it's hard to say. [I grimaced—my face likely revealing my opinion about his character.]
>
> MR. CHATURVEDI: Well, our feeling here at the department is that he is a poor choice to run this project. He is land-grabbing and trying to gain from this project. He is a bad man. We feel that he is really the problem. . . . Why have they contracted with that man? It is a shame because the project is now nowhere.

Mr. Chaturvedi went on saying that from his perspective the whole project was nothing but a glorified land grab masquerading as a Buddhist theme park. In addition, it had no substance aside from the paperwork in process designed to seize land from farmers: "The whole project is air. It is just on paper. The Maitreya Project has so much paper: red paper, green paper, blue paper!" Mr. Chaturvedi told me that he understood why farmers were unhappy with the project and said that he thought that they were very angry for good reason.

On another occasion, with disgust and sadness in her voice, a European-born FPMT nun, who had been based in India for several years, told me that the Maitreya Project was a blight on FPMT's good character. She told me about how a nonheritage FPMT monk, who had been a key staffer of MPI at the beginning of the project,[16] had himself gleefully told her and others the story of how he (and his staff) had kept demanding more and more land from the Uttar Pradeshi state government and how the latter had acquiesced, toppling under their demands, not unlike a house of cards. This nun and I bonded about our personal disappointment in MPI's endeavors, during the handful of times I visited her while in India.

Given the political issues faced in Bodh Gaya, some interlocutors hypothesized that the Maitreya Project's lesson number one from the Bodh Gaya era was this: get the state government on board. Another handful of project opponents said that they felt that the number one lesson learned was actually to keep the project from the prying eyes of meddling nonheritage Buddhist expatriates. In sharp contrast to Bodh Gaya, Kushinagar is not an area where there is a large community of expats who reside locally for extended periods of time. Aside from the Burmese and Thai *sanghas*, and one or two monks who may be stationed at various international monasteries (most of whom keep to themselves), Kushinagar is very light on outsiders. The fact that Kushinagar is practically devoid of Western Buddhists is one of the reasons that most FPMTers and donors had no idea that Maitreya Project 2.0 was facing substantive opposition there until the media blowup in 2007.

There was apparently a socioenvironmental impact study done for Bodh Gaya, but I was never permitted to access it. During my fieldwork period, it seemed that one had not yet been done for the Kushinagar locale, since FPMTers close to the project griped to me that it was odd that it had not been done. One source told me that the administrators were waiting for the land acquisition to go forward before taking such measures. As MPI contemplated a move to Kushinagar, there was no effort expended to reach out to the local community to see how such a large project might impact them. In fact, the interests and wishes of local Indian communities never seemed to be a motivating factor for MPI. No one, not even project supporters, argued that the reason for moving to Kushinagar from Bodh Gaya had anything to do with the desires of the local Kushinagari community. The anxieties of local Indians have consistently been treated as peripheral by MPI staffers.

The Maitreya Projects statue is viewed as a karmic boon for supporters of the project. The MPI operation spent much of its early period working to secure funds and design a memorable transnational Maitreya for a global Buddhist community. Despite the fact that the small FPMT affiliate has struggled with finances, they were able to envisage the art and engineering of a giant Maitreya statue, promote this vision to FPMT supporters, and sell their plan first to the state of Bihar and then later to the state of Uttar Pradesh. The challenges faced by MPI's first project iteration in Bodh Gaya, Maitreya Project 1.0, provided some insight into unexpected local ambivalences and resistance, a reality which, much to their chagrin, MPI would encounter again in Kushinagar in the future.

✖ CHAPTER 4

The Relics / *SARIRA*

Worship and Fundraising with the Relic Tour

In what one might consider the public relations coup of the millennia, the Maitreya Project's paramount ambassadors to the public were actual Buddhas themselves: specifically, a Buddha of the past (Kashyapa) and the Buddha of the present (the Shakyamuni Buddha). Lama Zopa Rinpoche's circulating collection of *ringsel* (Tibetan for "relics"), which purports to include relics of the Shakyamuni Buddha, his son Rahula, and the Buddha Kashyapa, as well as many, many other relics from Indian and Tibetan saints and teachers,[1] was put on tour to advertise the mission and plans of the Maitreya Project. By all accounts, the Relic Tour is the primary means of spreading the gospel of MPI, as it is a very popular traveling event that has made appearances all over the world.

The tour began in 2001 and has been so successful that the original collection was expanded, and the Relic Tour itself was split in two in order to facilitate more exposure and more fundraising. Occasionally, there are even three of these Maitreya Project relic collections traveling simultaneously in the Americas, Europe, and Asia. There is also a small relic collection in the Maitreya Project headquarters in Bodh Gaya that does not travel. Cristin, the primary guardian or custodian and coordinator of the Relic Tour, who cared for and traveled with the tour throughout the time of my fieldwork and beyond, told me in an interview in 2005 that the fact that Catholics put their relics on display inspired the Dalai Lama to suggest the need to put

Buddhist relics in public places. According to Cristin, it was this mandate that compelled Lama Zopa Rinpoche to circulate the collection of relics that were intended to eventually reside in the heart shrine of the giant Maitreya Project 2.0 statue.

Relics are very important in Tibetan Buddhism, as they are for most major forms of Buddhism (Trainor and Germano 2004). When relics were interred in the Mahabodhi Stupa in Bodh Gaya in February 2007, Tibetans thronged the processional, the Dalai Lama was on hand to participate in the ceremonies, and Tibetan Buddhists from across the heritage spectrum sought to gain admission to as many of the proceedings as possible. FPMT teachers are unequivocal in their assertion of the significance of relics as powerful holy objects. FPMTers know that Lama Zopa Rinpoche firmly believes in the efficacy, power, and significance of systematically authenticated relics, so most dedicated FPMT devotees regard the presence of relics as an unassailable sign, or proof positive, that a particular Buddhist teacher was indeed a realized master. Other FPMTers, especially those newer to the organization, struggled to believe in the power of relics, or in the authentication process, or both. While relics are present at various FPMT sites, many of FPMT's most significant relics are those circulating on behalf of the Maitreya Project.

Relics

Relics are the material remnants of famous Buddhist personages, which serve to embody, emanate, and echo the presence of the deceased (Collins 1998; Schopen 1991, 1997; Strong 2004; Trainor 1997). Devotees from a wide variety of Asian Buddhist traditions believe relics to be the bones and ash (or small pearl-like spherical deposits) that remain after the cremation of a holy teacher or Buddha. While relics of the Buddha and his disciples are thought to be most important, there are valuable relics from great lamas and Buddhist teachers throughout the ages. In practice, even the hair or nail clippings of a revered living teacher in the Tibetan tradition are considered relics. However popular relics are with many heritage Buddhists, they are a somewhat more challenging proposition for many nonheritage Tibetan Buddhists. Since the early days of Western Buddhism, recent converts have been known to express some ambivalence about the sacredness of relics.[2]

FPMT literature is unambiguously assertive about the power of lamas and considers the remains of lamas after death a gift to the living from the deceased. Lama Zopa Rinpoche writes that "relics are very precious. Relics are manifested and remains are left behind due to the kindness of holy beings for the sake of us sentient beings to collect merit and purify obscurations" (Courtin and Zopa 2003, 25). A video shown at every Relic Tour stop, the Maitreya Project DVD, shows a monk gathering small relics from a smoky cremation ground with a spoon, as a voice-over reports that relics are still being generated by important Buddhist lamas (MPI 2004a). Kopan Monastery, the central monastery of FPMT, located in Nepal, houses many relics, including those of Lama Konchog, a recently deceased teacher whose relics are on prominent display there (Courtin and Zopa 2003).

Trainor (1997) reports that relics are highly valued in Buddhist practice,[3] especially "relics of the Buddha," since they are thought to be efficacious in terms of removing obstacles from the path of Buddhist practice. Trainor (1997) and Strong (2004) both classify relics on the standard Theravadin threefold scale—corporeal relics, relics of use, and commemorative relics—but both foreground the first (and to some extent, the second) while disregarding the third type altogether.[4] Corporeal relics are physical remnants of the deceased, and usually represented by the dagaba, the *stupa*, that is, "relic chamber" in Sinhalese (Trainor 1997). Relics of use are objects/belongings of the deceased—robes, bowls, etc.—and are often represented in Theravadin traditions by the famous bodhi tree under which the Buddha attained enlightenment. Commemorative relics are images of the Buddha, that is, statues, paintings, etc.

Schopen argued that the relics themselves had historically served to make the Buddha "actually present and alive" to devotees (1997, 126). Calling the phenomenon, "the localization of presence," Trainor (1997, 97) argues that the relics serve to impart an air of sacredness to the sites they occupy. In effect, the sacralization of the relics is a means of affecting the presence of the Buddha. According to Trainor, while only Mahayana is known for its countless accessible Buddhas and bodhisattvas, even Theravadin Buddhist rituals evoke the presence of the historical Buddha through these sacred objects. Tambiah also notes that while an orthodox textual position would have Theravadins reject icons as anything other than mere reminders of the Buddha's great achievements, the tradition more or less came around to recognize "fiery energy" or "radiance" from Buddha images that are created in the true likeness of the Buddha (1984, 231).

Religious studies scholar John Strong (2004), like Trainor and Schopen, affirms the presence of the Buddha in Buddhist relic practices; Strong forwards an interpretation of the relics as an extension of the life of the Buddha. Strong argues that it is not enough to observe that the relics embody the Buddha, since the relics represent the extension of his biography into the present: "the relics continue to do things the Buddha did, to fill the roles the

Buddha filled; but they also do new things the Buddha never did. They write new chapters in the Buddha's life story" (2004, 8).

In Strong's (2004) interpretation, the Buddha's hagiography would not end at Mahaparinirvana, since the relics are pieces of the Buddha that propel his being indefinitely through time. In fact, there is a narrative that prophesies that in the future, when the decline of the *dharma* leads to a lapse in devotion to the relics, all the relics of the Buddha will magically reassemble, form an image of the Buddha, and then by bursting into flame, attain a final nirvana or final extinction of their own. Only after the relics are thus consumed in "the disappearance of relics," Strong explains, will the Buddha's biography be brought to its ultimate closure (2004, 224).[5] However compelling this view of the future Mahaparinirvana may be, there are also narratives in the Buddhist tradition that would preserve certain of Buddha's relics into Maitreya's era, making relics a material bridge between Buddhas (Strong 2004). Schopen's (1997) narration of a text in which the Buddha stood over the site of relics of the previous Buddha, Kashyapa, indicates that in some texts, Buddha relics are not thought to undergo their own ultimate Mahaparinirvana. In fact, some FPMT devotees, like many Tibetan Buddhists, believe that Kashyapa's relics are still in active circulation, and thus the Maitreya Project Relic Tour has relics reputed to come from both the Shakyamuni Buddha and the Kashyapa Buddha.

The presence of the Buddha accomplished by relics represents a slippage in both space and time. Strong's (2004) observation—regarding the continuing life of the Buddha through his relics—is proof positive that in some realms of the Buddhist tradition, at least, the presence of the Buddha in the present is not just affective, but quite literal indeed. The presence of the Buddha and others available through their relics makes these objects unique, for as Geary notes in reference to medieval relics, "like slaves, relics belong to that category, unusual in Western society, of objects that are both persons and things" (1986, 169). While relics are not viewed as unusual in the Asian societies where Buddhism has flourished for millennia, the personhood of relics poses something of a challenge to some nonheritage Buddhists in FPMT.

The Relic Tour

The relics are thought to embody the qualities of the masters from whom they came. A Relic Tour handout from 2008 reads: "These ringtsel are special because they hold the essence of the qualities of the spiritual masters. Their inner purity appears in the form of relics. The relics are physical evidence that the teacher attained qualities of compassion and wisdom before death." The relics then are thought to provide attendees with an opportunity to establish a direct connection with departed enlightened beings. The Relic Tour handout reports that "again and again, people have connected directly with the powerful loving energy emanating from the relics. Buddhists and non-Buddhists alike tell us that they feel inspired, healed and at peace simply by being in the presence of the relics. Each visitor touches the divine within them." The Relic Tour custodians have reported miracles. For example, one custodian reported to me that on a particularly rainy day at a stop in upstate New York in 2005 just as the opening ceremony began, the weather began to clear up and the sun came out. She downplayed this as just "a minor miracle," since she said that there were innumerable cases of miraculous events that she had both experienced and heard about.[6]

According to a custodian of the Relic Tour, suggested donations are one of the primary means toward soliciting funds for MPI, as well as the best way to get people from around the world invested in the fate of the Maitreya Project. At the Relic Tour sites, donations are not explicitly solicited as entry fees, but there are offering boxes in various places inside the room and outside as well. The motivations expressed by individuals who had donated at Relic Tour events were diverse. Of the people who made donations inside the Relic Tour shrine room, many gave donations to make merit and indicated that the offerings were an important and mandatory part of taking blessings. The offerings boxes were usually stuffed with cash and checks. I was told that it was most often Asian-American heritage Buddhists and longtime nonheritage practitioners who gave generously to MPI in tandem with their viewing of the relics. Of the people I interviewed who did not mention merit making, they most often gave donations because they saw others do it, had had a positive experience with the relics, or had an intention to donate specifically toward the Maitreya Project statue.

At the Relic Tour events, I found donors expressing desire for merit, desire to be blessed by the relics, and desire to make offerings to the Relic Tour or statue, but very often it was the desire for a specific souvenir that led a visitor to pay a preset suggested donation. Outside of every Relic Tour event there is a table where attendees can acquire souvenirs, such as Maitreya Project posters, postcards, DVDs, statues, and other Buddhist music CDs, charms, images, etc. Sometimes these exchanges were called "donations," sometimes "suggested donations," but they were guided by set prices in the strict sense of the word, since one could only receive an item in exchange for a set value, which was clearly listed next to items as a "suggested donation." While I served as a volunteer staffing the table at one Relic Tour event, I talked to other volunteers about this when a woman wanted to have a statue at half the price of the suggested donation. We were directed by the custodian not to allow the woman to proceed with the transaction unless she paid the full amount on the printed suggestion donation list. There were probably times that people paid less, since items were paid for by placing the money in a large offering box (although volunteers sometimes kept money in an envelope to help make change, when necessary), and thus it sometimes functioned essentially as an honor system.

The souvenir table was always set up next to a television that played the Maitreya Project DVD about the touted benefits of the statue plan on a continuous loop. According to the custodian, there was little difference in the merit accomplished by these various forms of donations at Relic Tour events: "Visitors have burned off one thousand years of negative *karma* in their visit to the relics, and by making donations they have created good *karma* that will lead to a connection between themselves and Maitreya. This is an enormously positive opportunity to make good merit." The donations pay for the traveling Relic Tour, but they also go a long way toward the running of MPI proper. In discussion with a custodian it was clear that if the Relic Tour stopped running, then MPI would be in ever more dire financial straits.[7]

The relics shift to a new region each weekend, where the custodians are invited by host institutions to display the relics for free to the public.[8]

FIGURE 6.   MPI Relic Tour at a Chinese temple in upstate New York in 2005.
Photo by the author.

Relic Tour stops are unique FPMT events in that they draw various types of devotees and onlookers depending on the locale; the audience represents the constituency of the host community, as opposed to the hosted community (FPMT). At an event in rural Pennsylvania in 2005, the Relic Tour was hosted by a Vietnamese temple–cum–community center, and the large majority of visitors that day were local Vietnamese Buddhists (with a handful of others, such as some local Korean Buddhists and a few white, nonheritage Buddhists). At the event hosted by the Namgyal Institute in Ithaca in 2006 there were a handful of heritage Buddhists (for example, there were several refugee Tibetan families who visited), but the large majority of visitors were not Tibetan; my field assistants noted strong showings from nonheritage Buddhists and curious local onlookers.[9]

The different venues also advertise to, and hence attract, very disparate constituencies. A Relic Tour event at the Soryarangsky Buddhist Temple in Philadelphia in November 2007 attracted an almost exclusively heritage Buddhist crowd, while the event at the FPMT center in San Francisco that year attracted a much more diverse crowd of both nonheritage and heritage Buddhists.

Although Relic Tour custodians told me in interviews that the relics sacralize every space—and so, from MPI's point of view the space itself is relatively unimportant—the character of various venues to some extent affected the sanctity or tone of the event. For example, the Relic Tour event at a major Chinese monastery in New York state hosted the relics in a grand altar room, so the mood was hushed and reverent, while at a Relic Tour event in a Vietnamese community center, there was a sense of familial ease, louder talking, and children running helter-skelter in and out of a much smaller altar room.

At the Namaste Yoga Center in Asheville, North Carolina, MPI's relics shared space with a small altar of Hindu deities and gurus. At the same site, the walls of the room were arranged with Tibetan *thangkas*, but sitting at the end of a long row of them was a large batik of the Hindu god Shiva. Despite Cristin's admonition that the relics completely transform the setting so that the space is the same everywhere, the environment actually did have quite a profound effect on the tone, ambiance, and aesthetic of a particular Relic Tour weekend. Therefore, I will describe one particular Relic Tour event in detail with the caveat that the tour is necessarily unique in each locale.

A Weekend in the Life of MPI's Relic Tour

On August 2, 2007, the Relic Tour altar was set up inside a day center for severely disabled persons located in Walnut Creek, a small city due east of Berkeley, California. Outside the venue, the souvenir table was set up with various Buddhist baubles, statues, and books that could be acquired with a suggested donation. Some of the souvenirs were directly produced by the Maitreya Project, such as posters of the statue-to-be, a Maitreya Project DVD, a brochure of the Relic Tour, Maitreya Project *tsatsas*, etc., while other souvenirs had been acquired specifically for resale. Next to the souvenir table, volunteers set up a TV playing the Maitreya Project DVD on a continuous loop.[10]

Volunteers helped set up the display, the Maitreya Project information panels, and the altars before the relics were put in their cases. Once the Relic Tour opening ceremony began in earnest, the volunteers and devotees all sat while visiting monks from a nearby temple performed an invocation blessing.

Then two long-term Relic Tour custodians, Cristin and Stephanie, prepared to lay out the relics. The two women, both nonordained white FPMTers, were dressed in Tibetan *chubas* (Tibetan dresses). They had tied white *khataks* (Tibetan offering scarves) around their mouths like masks to avoid any pollution or impropriety while handling the relics. One custodian hit "play" on a tape-deck, and suddenly New Agey Buddhist music filled the space.[11] In tandem, in a prayerful, slow, choreographed dance-like manner, the custodians did full prostrations, and then proceeded to reverently shuttle back and forth between the relic storage cases and the relic display cases with the relics themselves held up high on their crowns.

FIGURE 7.   MPI Relic Tour relic display, 2005.
Photo by the author.

Each relic (or set of relics) is encased in a container of its own and is labeled with the identifying tag of the name of the Buddhist master from whom it came; in each relic display case there are several of these smaller containers.[12] The relics were displayed in small glass cases that surround a centrally placed Maitreya Buddha statue (designed by the project as a model of the MPI statue slated for Kushinagar). The display was dotted with several other statues and images: fifteen small- to medium-sized Maitreya statues, one small Manjushri statue, one Vajrassatva statue, and one Manjushri image on a postcard.[13] At the front of the altar were saffron-infused water-bowl offerings, flowers, electric lights, and candles.

Custodians maintain a high level of vigilance and diligence regarding the relics in their care. When the relic display cases are still unlocked, the guardians are on high alert protecting the relics. At the Walnut Creek event in California, I observed Cristin anxiously tense and square herself to defend the relics as a visitor regrettably approached the inner circle—on his way to the restroom, it turned out—during one of the setup sequences that weekend.

Once the cases were carefully locked from the back, the music turned down, and the *khatak* scarves removed, the custodians and the monastics present led the entire audience in prayers and recitations. Custodians and volunteers handed out photocopied sheets of prayers in English to the congregation (that are collected at the end for later reuse).[14] The custodians then gave a talk about the authenticity and power of the relics and about the goals and significance of the Maitreya Project to FPMT. They discussed their hope that the giant statue would be built in Kushinagar. After the blessings, setup, chanting, and talks, the two women took up their stations and helped set up the visitors in lines. They would educate the public about the relics, suggest rituals that guests could do, help volunteers direct traffic, and protectively ensure that the relics were being monitored at all times.

The first thing seasoned devotees do as they approach the altar is generally prostrate three times, but since there are curiosity-seekers as well, sometimes people just approach the objects and begin (as directed by volunteers or staff) a clockwise circumambulation around the table. At the very front of the display, there was a large water bowl with a baby Buddha (pointing up at the sky) affixed to its center; devotees are invited to bathe the image by dipping a ladle into the bowl, while saying a blessing (which is helpfully written out on a piece of paper beside the bowl) to purify and be purified.[15] The relic caskets were dotted around the altar table, so that devotees slowly circumambulate the main MPI-replica statue at the center as they go from one small case to the other. In front of each case lay pieces of cloth on which some devotees placed their foreheads as they prayed or chanted mantras.

The "Golden Light Sutra" lay open at one place on the altar table, and devotees were invited to read about the benefits of the sutra.

Visitors generally prostrate, circumambulate, and then, when they can, they get in a queue to get direct blessings from one of the relics of the Shakyamuni Buddha. Still protected in its handheld case, the relic is placed onto a guest's forehead by a local Buddhist monk or nun. Some devotees sit and meditate, others do continuous rounds of circumambulations, some trace the Sanghatasutra in gold marker at one of three stations set up for that activity, while others read all about MPI's giant statue project on a large display that is set up adjacent to the altar. Devotees who spend several hours at a time at the Relic Tour often do all of the above more than once, but these activities are undertaken independently, and there is little formal instruction or direction.

The end of the day for the tour was marked with prayers and chanting.[16] Then, as taped music again played in the background, the two female custodians did ritual prostrations and performed the relic ensconcing. While they carefully placed each relic casket back into its protective traveling cases, they were joined in the closing ceremony by a Tibetan monk who had come to assist them with the weekend. Once all of the relics were safely stowed, the now-blessed saffron water offerings were distributed to members of the public interested in taking some for home altars. Leftover saffron water was placed in small, sealed containers for use the next day. At the very end of the weekend, event volunteers and some devotees helped the custodians to break down all of the display items.

This tour stop, like so many others, drew hundreds of visitors over the course of the three evenings and two full days. (Of course, sometimes a stop would draw thousands of visitors, and have long lines out the doors, so this was a medium-sized event by Relic Tour standards.) During the first opening chanting service, there were about seventy-five to eighty people in attendance. Throughout both full days there was a steady flow of people, so that most of the time there were at least about three dozen people with the relics.

The visitors at this stop were moderately diverse, mostly middle- to upper-class Americans, a reflection of the small city hosting the event. The crowd was mostly white, but there were many Asian-American families as well, and a few black and Latino visitors. There were several big Vietnamese and Chinese contingents that arrived in groups to visit the relics, and some Korean families. At any given time approximately one third of the attendees were of obvious Asian descent.

The venue organizers, Tom and Martie (and their preteenaged son), had already hosted four Relic Tour stops and attended some eight Relic Tour events all told. Tom, a white, nonheritage Buddhist, explained to me that the couple had been so deeply affected by the holy presence of the relics the first time they experienced it that they immediately booked a plane to attend the next weekend's Relic Tour event in Phoenix. Martie and Tom worked at the center for the disabled where the event was taking place (although Martie was training to become a paralegal), and it had been their shared dream to bring the relics here to their workplace. Tom was very enthusiastic about the fact that some of his disabled students had now been exposed to the power of the relics, both because some of them had come to the event in person with their family members and also because the space itself would bear a spiritual imprint from the relics that he knew would have a good impact on the center's beneficiaries in the future. Tom called himself a "serious" Buddhist practitioner, while Martie seemed more ambivalent about Buddhism as an institutional religion (although she seemed just as taken with the Relic Tour as Tom).

Tom told me that he was sometimes asked by visitors and journalists to defend the authenticity of the relics; when that happens he explains to them that the relics have gone through a process of validation by Lama Zopa Rinpoche. He tells visitors that the relics have not been carbon-dated and that he thinks such a process might have a problematic, unforeseen effect on the relics themselves, which is why he does not think it should be done in the future either. He told me that when confronted by naysayers he tells them narratives about how people leave the room glowing, about the miracles that have happened in the presence of the relics, and about how so many people feel moved by the relics. He told a person who had e-mailed him asking whether the relics had been scientifically tested that if the person would just come to the event then they would get their answer: "I said, you can just tell when you walk in that it's real. You can feel it." He articulated a very strong belief that certain objects have essential power, and he had recently become intrigued by crystals and other strong minerals that have powerful effects: "I can read the energies in crystals. I'm very sensitive to the energies in objects."

During the open hours of the Relic Tour weekend, Martie and Tom spent most of the time sitting outside with the souvenir table and also telling passersby to come inside to view the relics, but they also took occasional breaks inside doing circumambulations and "enjoying the relics." Martie and Tom helped to arrange for a relic to be brought outside each time someone came with their dogs, so that both the person and their pets could be blessed. At some point, a few dogs, including a cancer-stricken canine, were allowed into the relic room to circumambulate the relic display one at a time. Martie and

Tom had brought their dog with them to the event and kept him tied outside under the souvenir table for most of the weekend; Martie told me that she felt that relic blessings could have a very good impact on all creatures that came into contact with them.

Another set of devotees that I interviewed at the event was the multigenerational Yi family (Korean-American Buddhists). A young woman helped her elderly grandmother circle the relics, while the former's own mother held one of her daughter's children in her arms. Over the course of a few hours, the men and women of this large family circled the relics, prayed and took pictures in front of each case, made a donation, and then took a blessing from the Buddha relic given by the Tibetan Buddhist monk. They then sat in the chairs facing the relics to reflect on the sacred objects and the ambiance of the space. They were delighted to have had the opportunity to see relics in their town. The women of the family were especially talkative about how they felt "lucky," as the objects were "real" and "very strong." There were many couples and families like this, Asian and non-Asian, who came to pay their respects, receive a blessing from the relics, make a donation, and pick out a souvenir or two before leaving.

Angela, a volunteer at the 2007 Walnut Creek Relic Tour, a black woman from North Carolina who had self-identified as a serious FPMTer for years, had seen and volunteered for the Relic Tour before. Angela was an artist and said that she had a special connection with holy objects, including the relics. Indeed, her room at the FPMT center in San Francisco, which I had seen during an interview a few weeks before, was a veritable museum display of holy objects. She had several altars, each one immaculately kept, and each one arrayed with offerings of some kind.[17] Angela was confident in the "power of Buddhist objects" in and of themselves. She noted that holy objects must be treated with respect, and she knew that when she made Buddhist art it would have to be handled with care by her, by the gallery or museum owners, and by the buyer. (She was chagrined to remember once seeing someone use a Buddha head as a doorstop.) She observed that the difference between "sacred art" and "holy objects" was the consecration of the latter with relics or mantras. At the Relic Tour, Angela divided her time between doing practices and mantras inside the Relic Tour venue and helping out as a volunteer at the souvenir table.

As far as I could tell, the Relic Tour–going public at this event was comprised of some believers, like Tom and Martie, Angela, and the Yis—to the extent that they consider the relics to be immanently efficacious and powerful—but there was another set of attendees who seemed interested in the relics but still agnostic or openly doubtful about their efficacy and authenticity. These tour-goers (searchers, Buddhist students, and sightseers) made up a significant portion of the crowd. I met several nonheritage Buddhists at the Walnut Creek event who felt strongly that real Buddhism was about meditation and that while the relics were fascinating cultural artifacts, they were not particularly sacred objects. For example, this was the view of Bess, a white senior citizen who was affiliated with a Buddhist community in San Jose and emphasized that she was not currently connected to FPMT. (She had gone to meditations and teachings at their San Francisco center a number of times in the past, so I might call her a former FPMT student.) As I talked to Bess at a coffee shop after she had left the Relic Tour venue, she told me that she had come to view the relics out of curiosity. She said that when she arrived she had watched others interact with the altar to learn how she should do it; she then went through the motions of prostrations and walked around the relic display a few times. She said that she did not feel any special connection with the relics:

> I don't believe in it. It's culture. Mythology, or like that. I came here the way I would go to a museum. I respect the fact that Tibetans have preserved some of the Buddhist *dharma*, but they mixed it all up with their superstitions and traditions and stories. The relics are just that—objects mixed with stories. They don't have any special power in and of themselves. The Buddha wasn't present the way [my friend] told me that she felt him when she came to [another Relic Tour event elsewhere]. Even if one of these old Buddha relics was real, which I highly doubt, then I don't think it would have power . . . except what people give it. When I prostrated I thought about what if one of those ancient relics was actually real. I prostrated out of respect to that guru from long ago, but not with the thought that it was anything more than a single little old bone. I don't feel blissed out or blessed or anything. I am glad I came anyway, but just to see it, not the other stuff. Like a museum. Like going to the Met in New York City to see the old Buddha statues.

Bess was not alone in feeling that the narratives of miracles and bliss were constructed by the community.

Alex, a young white man who considered himself loosely FPMT-affiliated because of some courses he had taken in India years before, but generally "just Buddhist, if anything," also came out to the California event more out of curiosity than devotion. Alex told me he felt that the whole Relic Tour was just a nicely staged way to capture donations and interest for the statue project. He told me, "The Relic Tour is a performance by Buddhists instead of a Buddhist performance." He went on to say that he knew other Buddhists who would never speak openly about their ambiguous feelings about the relics and holy objects, as he had done, but that they would sometimes talk to him in private. "You see all those people in there, well, I'll bet half of them at least don't believe the relics are real, they are just going along with it. Like the emperor has no clothes. I'll tell you that straight up. The emperor has none. He's naked! They put on a good show though. It just makes me mad as a Buddhist a little. It's attachment! It's crazy." He told a story about how he felt that the devotees inside were watching each other, and each trying to outdo the other: "It's a holier-than-thou atmosphere. It's judgmental."

Alex and I had started talking because he had been watching the Maitreya Project video outside and said, "Five hundred feet? Is this a joke?" I had been minding the donations table diligently, but sensing his cynicism, I told him that I had just finished fieldwork in Kushinagar, and that it was all serious business. We talked for about ten minutes about the Maitreya Project. I briefly filled him in about the controversy there among the landowners, telling him how the statue project required taking land owned by small subsistence farmers. He was aghast and began a long tirade about how he thought that expensive statues were un-Buddhist, especially giant statues or gilded statues. He was reminded that he had heard about the Maitreya Project before, when it was slated to be built in Bodh Gaya, but he had since thought that the whole thing had been cancelled, and he had been glad to think so. Perhaps in earnest, or perhaps feeding off of my frustration with the statue effort, he said that he was sorry to have commuted in for the event, saying that he felt like he had been tricked into supporting the statue.

When I pressed Alex about why he came to the event since he considered himself "skeptical about all things holy," he said that he came expecting to see some *dharma* friends who had told him about the event. He also took this opportunity to confess that he had felt that he should give relics one more try; he was so unimpressed the first time he had seen relics (at a *stupa* consecration), but he wanted to come to this viewing to see if maybe the "lightning would strike" this time. We were talking after he had viewed the relics again, so he added, "No lightning. Maybe next time." He told me that he sometimes wanted to believe in the efficacy of relics and statues, but that his "natural skepticism" would not let him do so.

"I will say this," Alex said as he was about to walk away. "The statues—the small ones!—can be nice to look at." Another volunteer who had come out halfway through this exchange had caught the gist of his ambivalence, and after he was gone she told me, "Even the nonbelievers come around eventually. He'll realize that it was the relics themselves, the Buddhas and the gurus present in the room, that make the room feel that way. If it's his *karma* [he'll realize it]."

Some attendees treated the event like a museum exhibit: they came, they looked, and then they went. These visitors were novelty-seekers who had heard about the event and just wanted to come see relics for the pure spectacle of it. The fact that Martie actively solicited passersby made the number of these attendees higher than usual. When outside, Martie would approach everyone who passed through the open-air corridor, like a hawker outside a carnival tent. Martie approached two white, teenaged passersby, Samuel and his sister Andrea. Samuel went inside and looked around, while the sister of the young man peeked inside and then came right back out. Andrea paced back and forth and then yelled at her brother when he finally reappeared: "We're Christians! Mom is going to kill you. I'm going to tell. That is not Christian in there!"

A black family passing by decided to drop in, even though they said they were Christian and seemed unsure whether it would be suitable. "It was very pretty," the mom said to the volunteers as she exited. "I'll tell my friends about it." Another passing family took Martie's suggestion that they check out the tour; they went in and came right back out when their child started screaming. Martie leaned over to tell me, "Sometimes the kids get scared." Even a group of guys that looked like neighborhood toughs was coaxed inside, and while some of them hung back looking at the display from a distance, one of them walked around the table respectfully gazing down into the cases.

Two women, who seemed like a couple, arrived and immediately went inside. When they came back out to the souvenir desk, they excitedly told the volunteers that they had been at a café drinking coffee that morning and one of them had picked up an old edition of a local newspaper that had just so happened to advertise this very Relic Tour event. There was no address, so they called the reporter and left a message. The reporter called back with the address, and now here they were. "It was *karma!*," one of the women said. The other noted that she wasn't a Buddhist and didn't think it would affect her; she said, "But I felt it. I got goose-bumps. I didn't expect that." The volunteer sitting with me, Angela, was unfazed by their excitement and just nodded and smiled, as if it happened all the time.

Soon afterward, another volunteer pointed out an interracial couple and told us that they are Relic Tour regulars. She told me that they had actually first met at a Relic Tour event and were now married, despite resistance by his family from India: "I don't think either of them were Buddhist . . . but who cares? They were drawn to the relics and then to each other. It's a Relic Tour love story!"

Eladio, a Latino man who lived in an apartment in the building right above the Walnut Creek venue, was not a Buddhist, but he said he felt that he was "spiritually open" and had loved the "vibe" of the relics. He spontaneously decided to help out and spent half of the weekend opening the door for people going in and out of the Relic Tour venue. On the final morning of the event, Eladio came down and took up his station opening the door again and, addressing the volunteers sitting outside, said that the relics had been calling out to him in his sleep. He told us that he had had an anxiety dream in which he had been missing his clothes—they were lost or stolen—but he needed to come down to the event to help. In his dream, he had walked around naked, back and forth and back and forth, until finally he was clothed and could come downstairs and help out with the relic event. "What does that mean?" Eladio asked. After a moment he answered his own query, "It was some kind of *karma*. [The relics] were calling out to me."

During my visits across several Relic Tour events, it was made clear through literature, video, and speeches that these relics had been given Lama Zopa Rinpoche's personal seal of approval. Arguably, relics fall into Appadurai's category of "enclaved" commodities, or "objects whose commodity life is ideally brief, whose movement is restricted, and which are apparently not 'priced' the way other things might be" (1986, 24), since the social rules for their movement highlight their scarcity, authenticity, and sacredness. The question of the authentication of relics is less an issue regarding those objects encased in ancient *stupas*, but for those that have been on the move, there are methodologies in various Buddhist traditions for establishing the authenticity of a relic.

"Are the relics real?" This question hung in the air at Relic Tour events, especially among the nonheritage Buddhist community. While some informants articulated the question, others were content to either suspend disbelief or give FPMT the benefit of the doubt. The question of what is real and true often serves to underline the fluidity and ephemerality of realness and trueness along the way, for as Spooner writes, "Authenticity is a conceptualization of elusive, inadequately defined, other cultural, socially ordered genuineness" (1986, 225). Like the medieval relics that Geary (1986) explored in his work, Buddhist relics also undergo specific (e)valuations and are certified (and recertified over time as the object changes hands by gift, theft, or sale) according to certain socially constructed categories of value. A special expertise is necessary for this kind of evaluation, and so it falls to the guru to decide which relics are real and which are not. Spooner's (1986) essay on the question of authenticity in the realm of Oriental carpet consumption demonstrates that signs of real and authentic not only change over time but are manufactured just as surely as the objects themselves. The question of authenticity is also paramount within FPMT, but the heart of the negotiation of authenticity has less to do with taste (as it did with Spooner's informants), and more to do with faith.

In FPMT, to establish a relic as unquestionably authentic, Lama Zopa Rinpoche's personal certification is needed. If a venerated monastic proclaims a relic to be authentic, then it is for devotees to negotiate that realm of faith and guru devotion to determine whether to question or accept that proclamation. Most heritage Tibetan Buddhists would never think to question the validity of such a proclamation of authenticity, but as we have seen, FPMT's constituency runs the gamut of acculturation and faith. At MPI's Relic Tour events, there are those who wholly accept the authenticity of relics and holy objects, others who struggle to do so, and still others who remain (comfortably or uncomfortably) skeptical.

The Relic Tour is a fascinating space in which to observe the construction of authenticity and faith in FPMT, as well as to observe how the Maitreya Project 2.0 statue is being promoted and branded publicly. The Relic Tour custodians have long served as MPI's most assiduous public relations proponents, and the organization has reaped a steady, if modest, stream of funding through the traveling spectacle of Buddhist relic veneration.

✿ CHAPTER 5

Aspirations / *ASHA*

Hope, the Future Tense, and Making (Up) Progress on the Maitreya Project

At the FPMT center in Dharamsala, India, in the main *gompa*, off to the left side of the central altar, there is a modest Maitreya Project altar. The altar includes a small prototype of the MPI statue, an even smaller *tsatsa* of Maitreya, plus a colorful, postcard-sized early drawing of the Maitreya Project site. The statues are adorned with plastic flowers and flanked by Maitreya Project documents explaining the project goals and inviting people to make donations in the Tushita Center office. Indeed, there are monetary offerings, of various currencies from around the world, sitting at the feet of the statue. The *gompa* itself is full of statues, *thangkas*, and photos of lamas, but the only prominent sign in the room is MPI focused. The sign, which is taped up next the Maitreya Project altar, is printed on a single sheet of paper in large lettering; it reads, "Actualizing the Maitreya statue is the goal of my life," and then underneath, "Quote by Lama Zopa Rinpoche 2001."

FPMT has always had many projects in the pipeline, but the Maitreya Project dwarfed all others, both in the breadth of its ambitions and in the sizable frustration it heaped on FPMT devotees as it was deferred over and over again. If the Maitreya Project's statue existed in Kushinagar today as planned, the five-hundred-foot statue would now be one of the largest statues of a Buddha in the world, a veritable Buddhist skyscraper. Why would FPMT adherents desire to build such a gigantic statue? At least as

FIGURE 8.   A poster in the FPMT center in Dharamsala, India, that features a Lama Zopa Rinpoche quote and a very early MPI statue representation.
Photo by the author.

many FPMTers seemed to react as much in bemused surprise as with un-mitigated enthusiasm when first hearing of the plans to build a gargantuan Maitreya statue, and certainly there are also those who react with vocal cyni-cism about the project's motivations and means. I have heard many dozens of people, both inside and outside of FPMT, wonder why in the world Buddhists would seek to build a statue of Maitreya, as opposed to other popular Buddhas or bodhisattvas. Who is Maitreya, and why should we care about him? The answers to these questions provoke another flurry of questions: Are statue donors propitiating Maitreya now in Tushita heaven,[1] or hoping for some other more far-flung karmic rewards? Why pray to be born in the very distant, postapocalyptic era of Maitreya? Why would anyone desire this, as opposed to just desiring enlightenment right away?

This chapter will address the spectrum of aspirations, desires, and hopes that Buddhism, especially FPMT's brand of Tibetan Buddhism, itself stokes in its adherents. What do Buddhists want? Nirvana, of course, but how is it that the path to nirvana is sometimes paved with gold, wishing-trees, paradise on earth, or paradise in a pure land (Collins 1998)? I will investigate the specific prophecies surrounding the coming of the future Buddha and how they tie into FPMT's aspirations to build a statue for the future benefit of all sentient beings.

In general terms, hope is implicit in Buddhist belief and practice, since one would have to hope to attain a cure if one was to undertake the course of treatment: "Without some initial trust in the fact that there is a way out of suffering, without some seed of understanding of the nature of suffering and its cessation, we would never begin to look for the path and we would have no hope of finding it" (Gethin 1998, 166). However, hope is marked in its absence from the formula itself. Hope for the future manifests in Tibetan Buddhist theory and practices through various lenses, including fixation on nirvana and other Buddhist felicities (Collins 1998), oracles and prophecies, and eschatological literature regarding the future Buddha, Maitreya.

As we shall see, the Maitreya Buddha narrative is an "imaginative horizon" (Crapanzano 2004) in the Buddhist social landscape that has the potential to capture the imagination of practitioners like few other figures. Kitagawa (1981) and Holt (1993) have found that the future orientation of the Maitreya figure in the Buddhist tradition has allowed Buddhists to approach the figure with an open-ended quality that has lent itself to particularly creative practices. Kitagawa writes that "one of the most fascinating features of the Maitreya is wherever Buddhism was transplanted his figure evoked 'potential modes of creativeness' . . . in the peoples' religious apprehension and expression" (1981, 110).

In this chapter, Buddhist notions of hope for the future will be elucidated by paying close attention to the ethnographic data collected about the developing iterations of FPMT's future statue of the future Buddha. Through the lens of Buddhist aspirations for the future, I will explore the changing temporal orientations of the Maitreya Project and how the future statue of the Maitreya was planned, plotted, and reconceptualized again and again. I will trace the history of future thinking in FPMT's public discourses surrounding project progress and prophecies.

I will show that the Maitreya Buddha offers more than an opportunity to achieve nirvana in the distant future, but is also a temporal conduit to work on the problem of the present through a focus on the near future. Here I offer my contribution to Jane Guyer's (2007) invitation to anthropologists to attune ourselves to the near futures of our informants instead of just the present and distant future. If the problem of the present is in some way related to the gap, the unbearable distance and impossibility of ever achieving the horizon (for if we do, it is no longer the horizon), then one of our choices for engagement is that of imagination (Crapanzano 2004). Since the future is clouded by both hope and anxiety, imagination does its own magic on fact and fiction, in order to make the gap between now and then more bearable. I will trace the imaginative flights of the Maitreya Project with particular attention to their near futures, their shorter term goals, and their construction of hope. This chapter concerns what I call the future tense, that is, the anxious momentum provoked in the present by orientation toward future possibilities in opposition to one another.

The Future Buddha

The Maitreya Buddha, the Buddha of Loving-Kindness, will be reborn sometime in the future, in order to rediscover and resurrect the body of the Buddhist *dharma* long after it has been utterly lost to humanity. Practitioners in most, if not all, major Buddhist traditions propitiate Maitreya in order to make merit that will allow one to have direct personal access to Maitreya's teachings in another place or time.[2] Not only is Maitreya a ubiquitous figure found in most Buddhist traditions, he has a significant presence in many contemporary Buddhisms, including the Gelugpa Tibetan tradition.

The religious studies scholar Steven Collins (1998) showed how Buddhists have made space in their *dharma* practice for "felicities" other than nirvana, which itself is often approached indirectly; the Maitreya Buddha represents an alternative felicity that establishes a spatiotemporal transit point between now and nirvana. Chris Arthur impresses upon his readers that according to the letter of the text, even Maitreya's era will be impermanent: "he is a messiah who is not unique and who will not bring time to an end, but will act as a punctuation mark in the great cycles of time in which all beings are caught up and from which, according to Buddhist soteriology, they ought to seek release in the form of nirvana" (1997, 49).

Hope as an abstract concept is generally implicit in Buddhist traditions, emerging in forms such as the ontological promises of Maitreya (Kitagawa 1988; Sponberg 1988; Holt 1993). Sponberg argues that Maitreya is a manifestation of hope in Buddhism: "Though perhaps initially a minor figure in early Buddhist tradition, Maitreya thus came to represent a hope for the future, a time when all human beings could once again enjoy the spiritual and physical environment most favorable to enlightenment and the release from worldly suffering" (1988, 1). Sponberg also writes of the universality of this interpretation of the Maitreya: "In every Buddhist culture Maitreya is a symbol of hope, of the human aspiration for a better life in the future when the glories of the golden past will be regained" (1988, 2). This view is contiguous with Holt's view that in all Buddhist cosmologies Maitreya is a symbol of hope:

> Throughout the historical development of Buddhist traditions in Asian cultures and societies, veneration of the *bodhisattva* Maitreya (Pali: Metteya; Sinhala: *Maitri*; Tibetan: Byama-pa; Chinese: Mi-lo; and Japanese: Miroku) has consistently reflected eschatological visions of an ultimate spiritual salvation and, to a lesser extent, recurrent millennial dreams of collective redemption from the problematic conditions of this-worldly existence. Abiding in the splendid heavenly abode of Tusita in the upper strata of the Buddhist hierarchical cosmos, Maitreya is believed to be the future Buddha whose appearance in the human abode later in this world-cycle (*kalpa*) will re-establish *dharmic* norms of righteousness and provide the virtuous with an auspicious time and place to gain final fruition of the spiritual path: nirvana. . . . The figure of Maitreya, therefore, embodies the spiritual hope that righteous human beings may someday live in universal concord. (1993, 1)

Kitagawa recognizes that the Maitreya narrative holds an implicit promise that connects hope and faith in Buddhist theology: "Clearly, the notion that the future promises to be better than the present, leading to the triumph of the good at the end of the world, is based not on empirical observation, but on speculation and affirmation" (1988, 8). Kitagawa's claim is consistent with Crapanzano's idea that in contrast to the psychologically motivated notion of desire, "hope presupposes a metaphysics" (2004, 100); as a metaphysics, Buddhist ontology plants hopes in fertile ground. The eschatological quality of the Maitreya story does not preclude hope, for as we know, many eschatologies are utopian, apocalyptic, or both at once (Robbins and Palmer 1997);

in fact, for many Buddhists adherents, the era of Maitreya holds the promise of something beyond world ending. Buddhist devotees view Maitreya as the light at the end of the tunnel for themselves and others.

The coming of Maitreya Buddha is narrated in the *Anagatavamsa Desana* text in a Pali sutta that is attributed to the historical Buddha (Meddegama 1993), but scholars generally believe the text was composed later, as the cult of the Maitreya Buddha cannot be dated earlier than two centuries BCE (Holt 1993, 3).[3] In the *Anagatavamsa Desana*, the Shakyamuni Buddha tells an assembly of devotees the story of a previous Buddha, named Muhurta, who had long since foreordained that one of his particular devotees,[4] the Cakravartin Prabhavanta, would eventually be reborn as the future Buddha, Maitreya (Meddegama 1993). In some Buddhist texts there are other future Buddhas who are expected to come even after the Maitreya Buddha, but these texts are often marginalized, and the popular lay and monastic perspective is often that the Maitreya Buddha represents something akin to finality: "Accordingly, this figure's consummation of Buddhist heritage sometimes casts him in the role of an eschatological cosmic savior who, at the end of the empirical world order, will establish a utopian state of justice, peace, and truth" (Kitagawa 1988, 7).

In classical Buddhist theology, Maitreya is expected to be born on earth only when Buddhism has been lost from the world, but unlike some other messianic figures, he will not come at the pinnacle of darkness (Meddegama 1993). The old world must first be destroyed and then regenerate of its own accord, for he will come only once the minds of humanity have undergone enough of a resurgence to be able to receive the *dharma*. The *Anagatavamsa Desana* sutta prophesies that the state of the world will decline to the point that the maximum age of human life is ten years, children will marry but only love themselves, and humans will behave like animals (Meddegama 1993, 26). Then, deities will travel through all universes and warn of seven days of rain in which any person who gets wet will perceive other humans as game; yet only the "wise" will hide in caves while the others slaughter each other until the universes will all run red with blood (Meddegama 1993, 27). The wise who had survived the homicidal rain will naturally give up all killing, and with each subsequent generation humans will become wiser until their minds have ripened to the point that they are prepared to receive the Buddhist *dharma*; only then, many eons later, when humanity is again ready, will the Maitreya Buddha be reborn on earth. This act of deferred salvation makes the classical version of Maitreya an unusual messianic figure.

Jan Nattier made a significant contribution to Maitreya studies when she observed that various subcultural iterations of Maitreya have stoked various and sundry aspirations regarding Maitreya that can be expressed through four framings: "there/now," "there/later," "here/now," and "here/later" (1988, 25). Nattier's typology takes into account the outstanding questions of time and space, ascent and descent, near future or distant future. For example, for Mahayanists, the bodhisattva Maitreya is waiting in Tushita heaven for the right time to come to earth, which makes him a particularly accessible figure. The notion that Maitreya exists nirvana prior (or nirvana adjacent) means he is able to respond to the prayers of his devotees, which fosters a specific kind of hope: "Being compassionate, . . . he willingly grants help; and being a high god in his present birth, he has the power to do so. His cult thus offers its devotees the advantages of theism and Buddhism combined" (Robinson and Johnson 1977, 103). The devotee adhering to the "there/now" perspective hopes to ascend to Tushita heaven now to be taught by the bodhisattva Maitreya. On the other hand, if a believer hopes to ascend to Tushita heaven in the distant future to be taught by the Maitreya, then they are demonstrating a "there/later" perspective.

John Holt (1993, 1) considers the Maitreya story to be analogous to Judeo-Christian messianism, but Nattier (1988) offers a cautionary note that only one type of the four spatiotemporal types of Maitreya stories could be properly regarded as apocalyptic: the "here/now" possibility evokes the devotees' hopes that Maitreya will descend to earth now, during the present lifetime, to grant spiritual or material boons.[5] This apocalyptic form of the myth manifested when figures in history, especially in China, claimed to be Maitreya while engaging in revolution against empires (Nattier 1988, 31), but even today there are would-be gurus who claim to be Maitreya incarnate (Zablocki 2009).

The "here/later" Maitreya framework, which is the oldest and most popular of the four spatiotemporal interpretations, refers to a promise of messianic intervention and a utopia deferred (Nattier 1988). If a devotee believes in the "here/later" option, then (s)he anticipates that Maitreya will descend to earth to teach in the far distant future. This "here/later" eschatology of the Maitreya Buddha represents a contemporary distant millennialism that provides a receptacle of hope for a postapocalyptic future, not unlike the millennial hope of Tamils in Malaysia described by Andrew Willford (2006). In the *Anagatavamsa Desana* sutta, the Shakyamuni Buddha tells his disciples who will see the Maitreya and who will not; the historical Buddha is said to have noted that those "who engage in meritorious acts according to their individual capabilities will definitely see Maitreya" (Meddegama 1993, 52). Meritorious acts include such things as giving alms to temples, building temples, and making offerings. Hope is generated in the devotee that if they perform merit-making activities they will be reborn in the time of a living Buddha and thus have a great chance of reaching nirvana. Most of FPMT's discourse about the Maitreya Buddha takes a "here/later" view, but as we shall see there are multiple temporal futures that emerge through Tibetan versions of the tale.

Lama Yeshe and Lama Zopa Rinpoche's teachings on Maitreya emphasize the need to connect with Maitreya in the present in order to align our futures with his future. For example, Lama Yeshe once said:

> In the absolute sense, Maitreya is subject to neither death nor rebirth; he is forever benefiting all mother sentient beings. Furthermore, he once declared, "Anybody keeping just one vow of moral discipline purely during the time of Shakyamuni Buddha's teachings will become my personal disciple when I appear and I shall liberate all such disciples," and he faithfully keeps this promise, his sworn oath and pledge. Therefore, those of us fortunate enough to have met the teachings of Shakyamuni Buddha and maintained some level of pure discipline are guaranteed to make direct contact with Maitreya, become his disciple and quickly achieve enlightenment. (2008, 49)

FPMT discourses on Maitreya note that by helping to build the statue (through prayers and donations, especially) one explicitly connects one's *karma* stream to the era of the Maitreya Buddha; thus, by making an offering to MPI, one can aspire to be reborn when Maitreya once again returns to earth and makes the achievement of enlightenment a much easier matter for all contemporaneous humans.

When Lama Yeshe gave a talk to FPMTers about Maitreya in 1981, the classic version of the story narrated in the *Anagatavamsa Desana* was given a regional Tibetan twist: Maitreya manifests on earth as a learned spiritual teacher when human life expectancy declines to just ten years, that is, precisely at the pinnacle of darkness (Yeshe 2008, 46). In Lama Yeshe's telling, Guru Maitreya's teachings, especially those on loving-kindness, serve to turn the tide, and his message inspires spiritual changes that lead to an increase in human longevity. Then, much later, after many eons, when the time is right, Maitreya finally manifests again as a "universal teacher or founding buddha, like Shakyamuni" (Yeshe 2008, 46). Therefore, in an FPMT narrative such as this one, Maitreya does serve to play the role of a stereotypical messiah, in addition to his more traditional role of deferred savior. While Lama Yeshe's narrative is not ubiquitous among Tibetans or Nepalis, it is a familiar telling of the tale within heritage Tibetan Buddhist communities.

In an interview with a senior monk at the Namgyal Monastery in Ithaca, New York, in 2004, I asked about the tale of the future Buddha. Tenzin Lhun-drup explained to me that the Maitreya Buddha had been overtaken by the efforts of Shakyamuni, so had to wait in the wings, just like countless other Buddhas to come. Tenzin-la also told a narrative that represents Maitreya as a more direct savior figure:

> There will be one thousand Buddhas. Maitreya will be the fifth Bud-dha. They reside in Tushita heaven. Maitreya has three names: as a king, Gyelwar Champa; as a bodhisattva, Jetsun Champa; as a Buddha, Sanghye Champa. . . . He generates the *bodhi* mind, and altruism. . . . Forty-two eons before Shakyamuni he generated *bodhi* mind. Maitreya was skipped because of Shakyamuni Buddha's diligence. There is a prediction that Maitreya will come. Many Buddhas are there and they will choose their time to come. . . . When people's lifespan is only ten years, then that is when Maitreya comes. Lifespan will have degener-ated. Gyelwar Champa [will appear] as a king to help encourage people to improve. That body has radiance, and his words cool the angry little people. Humans will be the size of a thumb. Maitreya as a king will be the size of a forearm.

Tenzin-la's observation that the Maitreya would be very, very small com-pared to people today is an oft-repeated legend but not a universal one. A few critics of the Maitreya Project statue have seized on the idea of this wee Maitreya to argue that building a five-hundred-foot statue is wildly dis-proportionate and inappropriate in a very literal way. That is, from their perspective, it is especially incongruous for MPI to manufacture a giant Maitreya several hundred feet tall if one version of the traditional Tibetan Maitreya is just about a foot tall.

Within FPMT there is a wide variety of opinions about the Maitreya fig-ure; within a single FPMT retreat, he might be worshipped as a presence in Tushita heaven by some, hailed as a distant future promise by others, respected simply as a symbol of *maitri* by a handful of students, or even doubted as a cultural fiction by the more skeptical minds in the room. De-spite the range of reception Maitreya receives by various FPMTers, Mai-treya images and prayers are very prominent in FPMT circles, as they are in Gelugpa Tibetan Buddhism in general. Regardless, when Maitreya is invoked in Lama Zopa Rinpoche's Maitreya Project, and in all of FPMT's theologi-cal literature and practices for that matter, it is in the form of a "here/later" anticipation: either later at the pinnacle of darkness, or much later at the rebirth of Buddhism.

Envisioning the Maitreya Project

Lama Zopa Rinpoche is famous for articulating super-sized wishes to his community. Devotees and *sangha* laughed (and sometimes cringed) as they described to me how Rinpoche narrates his grand visions to them, and then places the responsibility fully in their hands just before getting chauffeured to the airport on the way to visit the next center. Angelica, a nun at an FPMT center in California, reminisced: "He looked at the land and thought for a little while, and said, 'A big *stupa* will go there, there will be a giant statue here, and a big nunnery over there.' Just like that." Angelica looked both awed and chagrined as she told me that story, since at the time, she and her peers were in the middle of an ambitious fundraising campaign to try bring those visions to fruition. Another informant, Maureen, an FPMT devotee and staffer at the Root Institute in Bodh Gaya, told me that Lama Zopa Rinpoche would rarely dwell on the outcomes of his plans; he was always dreaming up the next horizon. Maureen told me that she was working to make his most recent wish come true: a giant prayer wheel, even bigger than the last one. Lama Zopa Rinpoche is a visionary, Maureen explained.

The Maitreya Project statue is known to be Rinpoche's ultimate dream, his heart wish. The Maitreya Project statue was conceived not as an end in itself; it was a means to an end. Many ends are visualized, and many hopes are being expressed through its construction. The statue is desired because it will bring the future into the present, and the present into the future. It will accomplish this through the establishment of a direct karmic connection between donors and the Maitreya Buddha.

The Maitreya Project 2.0 statue was envisaged to last at least a millennium. According to Peter Kedge, "In the religious sense, like other great monuments, the Maitreya statue will surely be a source of spiritual inspiration to countless people during the 1000 years it is being built to endure" ("Peter Kedge International Director of Maitreya Project" 1997, 12). The optics of a thousand-year lifespan make the statue sound romantically long-lasting and durable. Many devotees saw this assertion of longevity as a promise that would allow them to make contributions toward posterity, but still others saw it as hubris. The ambition of structural longevity for one thousand years echoes Joseph Masco's (2005) observations on Yucca Mountain, the proposed site of nuclear waste storage meant to last for millennia. Although the narrative, the scheme, the vision is for "ten-thousand years," the engineers at Yucca Mountain found this statement to be the stuff of politics rather than attainable science.[6] Masco shows that the romance of the project's ambition can also be its soft, vulnerable underbelly. He writes, "What will happen a thousand years from now at Yucca Mountain, and who will be around to watch over the radioactive waste of the twentieth century? Can we imagine a nation-state that lasts one thousand years, let alone ten thousand?" (2005, 36).

The utopic image of Maitreya and the dystopic image of atomic waste seem at odds, but the open question for both projects is whether the projections of longevity are naive, ideological, or even disingenuous. Was the Maitreya Project statue's vaunted longevity meant to motivate feats of engineering or fundraising (or both)? The mammoth Maitreya statue and ghosts of future failure at Yucca Mountain seem to fuse in a dystopic, tongue-in-cheek, anti-MPI image made during the Maitreya Project 1.0 era, which was lightly circulated on some Buddhist listservs; in the homemade digital graphic, MPI's giant Maitreya statue is sitting alone, forsaken, in a postapocalyptic wasteland, being touched by a lizard monster looking for "a mate" ("The Metogpa Project" 2008). As a direct challenge to MPI's singularly rosy projection of the future, the graphic simultaneously haunts and mocks. In the image, the MPI's behemoth Maitreya comes face to face with "its own apocalyptic excess" (Masco 2005, 36).

FIGURE 9. The Metogpa Project. A graphic critique of Maitreya Project 1.0 circulated via Buddhist listservs.

Despite the fact that some nonheritage Buddhists were quite clearly antagonistic to the MPI's statue, the MPI statue was generally looked on favorably by FPMT devotees whom I interviewed in the aughts. For example, Tomas, a serious FPMT devotee from Europe—who was living and working in Delhi at the time of our interview—told me about his plans to eventually build a Maitreya statue in his own country:

> You know about the Maitreya Project? I would like to build a statue half the size in Belgium. In each continent Rinpoche wants giant statues. I will build a Maitreya statue. It will benefit so many people. Just by seeing these statues, it would purify. If you have a little bit of belief and circumambulate, it creates merit. The power of big statues, they draw people in and it can bring people to the *dharma*. You have to bring people to the *dharma*. What they do is up to them. . . . I dedicate to this regularly. Maybe it's too big to realize it on my own. I would have to start with a center. It would be so great. A seventy-five-meter statue would tower above so many other things.

Like many FPMTers, Tomas effusively supported MPI and its vision.

Other FPMTers accept MPI's mandate, but with muted enthusiasm. Stephen, an American nonheritage FPMT devotee (who was volunteering at the FPMT center in Bodh Gaya in 2006), told me that he gradually came to support the project, despite feeling ambivalence initially, because it was reputedly going to do so much good karmically and socioeconomically. Stephen said, "The Maitreya Project has grown on me." He went on to say that according to Lama Zopa Rinpoche even people who oppose and criticize the statue should be blessed by thinking about the image of Maitreya.

In public, Tibetan-in-exile religious leaders overwhelmingly supported the project. The Dalai Lama spoke about the potential benefits of the statue in 1998 when he blessed the land in Bodh Gaya that the Maitreya Statue was supposed to be built on:

> You should realize that this is a very holy and sacred project and I will therefore pray and wish that it will benefit the flourishing Buddhadharma and the well-being of sentient beings. From your own side it is very important to cultivate a correct motivation and try to pray and dedicate the success of the project to the well-being of sentient beings. . . . After the completion of this huge statue of Maitreya Buddha I'm sure many people out of devotion, and some visitors, will definitely visit this place. Even in the case of those who might visit this

statue just as a casual visitor though they do not have any special faith
I'm sure that merely seeing this holy statue and taking its picture will
leave a positive imprint in their minds. (Rose 1998, 36–37)

While I do not know the Dalai Lama's personal views on the Maitreya
Project, they are not thought to be uncomplicated; even among FPMT's
statue-cheerleaders there were frequently whispered stories about how the
Dalai Lama did not initially see the value of MPI's statue project, and that
his initial reticence is the reason that the school and health care project were
added to the planned complex.

Heritage Tibetan monastics are not of one mind about the statue, but
of the handful that I interviewed in exile, some are enthusiastic, especially
those in the Gelugpa tradition with the closest ties to FPMT institutions.
A Namgyal Monastery elder, Tenzin Lhundrup, told me in 2004 that he was
inordinately excited about the prospects of the project and had even made a
small donation to it himself. His feeling was that if it was not so enormous
then people would not come to see it and that lay people need these sorts of
things to make good *karma*. "FPMT tries to build the Maitreya statue, and we
try to achieve the *bodhi* mind, the seed of loving-kindness now that will be
nourished by Maitreya Buddha. FPMT tries to build the statue to encourage
people to go there and learn about Maitreya. If it's the biggest then people
will want to learn about Champa.[7] . . . Lay practitioners could only learn
from scholars. They do mantras, they say the name of Maitreya." When
I saw him again at a Losar celebration in 2008, Tenzin-la was disappointed
that the plan had run into "obstacles" but still enthusiastic about its potential.

If the Maitreya statue can itself be perceived as a form of "inalienable
wealth" (Weiner 1985) that offered the FPMT community the affective boon
of hope for better karmic futures (and ironically, a kind of affective permanence), it bolsters the notion that Buddhist gifting in this context is "strategic" (Bourdieu 1977), forward-thinking, and political. This is especially apparent when the heritage Tibetan monastics involved talk about how it could
potentially help ease the Tibetan political crisis through merit making. For
example, a lama who once served in the Tibetan-in-exile government (the
Central Tibetan Administration) seemed to highlight the Dalai Lama's apparent support of the project and connect it to the contemporary Tibetan
nationalism of the exile community: "There is some important connection
between Maitreya, the fifth Buddha, and our situation in exile. The Tibetan
political situation . . . Maitreya has a huge contribution to benefit for the
political situation. The future Buddha—by making a connection with the
Maitreya. By building this project it is cultivating love within the Tibetan

people, and even in the Chinese people who destroy our culture. Through the power of love it will reach and change the minds of people who harm us. Their minds may change." This lama was not alone in feeling that the statue would have positive future effects on the Tibetan cause, but he was the only ethnic Tibetan I interviewed who specifically prophesied that it would play a role in achieving a free (or autonomous) Tibet.

Highly visible Gelugpa monastics seemed to be publicly united behind the statue, but most lay heritage Tibetan Buddhists that I talked to in the midaughts remained ambivalent about the MPI's statue project. On the one hand, Tibetans in exile were confused about its status ("I thought it had been canceled"), very distant from the planning and fundraising ("they never asked us to make any contribution to it"), and resentful of the fact that it was a project being done entirely by "foreigners." Tibetan refugees in India often expressed to me their concerns about the design and aesthetic of the statue, as well as their perception that MPI relied too heavily on major East Asian (read: ethnically Chinese) funders. Still, many heritage Tibetan Buddhist informants were generally supportive of the statue idea in the abstract and quite keen to visit, should it ever be actualized.

Designs of the Future and Signs of the Future

Back in the days of Maitreya Project 1.0, there was a meeting of experts on the Maitreya Project land in Bodh Gaya in 1997 (Colony 1997). The configuration of experts invited included three Taiwanese architects, two Malaysian feng shui (geomancy) practitioners, and two Taiwanese specialists from a corporation peddling their assistance with the "computer-aided manufacturing" of statues. While the scientists looked on, the geomancers were busily "propitiating the guardian deities of the land to co-operate requesting that there be no mishaps and that all work be accomplished without obstacle" (Colony 1997, 12).[8] This example clearly demonstrates that FPMTers accepted and welcomed various types of expertise in their technologies of planning and envisioning of the future. MPI enabled various kinds of technologies of planning from the beginning, as evident in the description of how the Griffins used both traditional and modern techniques to make the MPI prototype. Architects' skill sets were judged to be as valuable as the advice of geomancers, and bureaucrats were asked to accommodate the divinations of lamas. In this section, I will focus on the technologies of forecasting used by MPI and its affiliates.

Predictions are a common form of expression for enlightened beings and teachers in Tibetan Buddhism. American Buddhists sometimes attribute a prophecy to the Shakyamuni Buddha that in effect would show that Buddhism was always supposed to end up in America: "2,500 years after I have passed away into Nirvana, the Highest doctrine will become spread in the country of the red-faced people" (Fields 1992, xi). According to Prebish, Padmasambhava, an Indian sage thought to have lived in the eighth or ninth century, was reputed to have said, "When the iron bird flies, and the horse runs on wheels, the Tibetan people will be scattered like ants across the World, and the dharma will come to the land of the red man" (1998, 6). These prophecies are oft-paraphrased in the halls of FPMT, sometimes by the teachers lecturing in courses, and sometimes just among fellow practitioners at the dinner table during a course. As one might expect given that FPMT is a relatively nonheritage Buddhist institution, prophecy talk is met with wonder and skepticism both.

Oracles (Tibetan: *kuten*, or *lapa*) are prevalent figures in Tibetan Buddhist history and culture. Some, such as those who advise the Dalai Lama while possessed by deities in order to assist in his decision making for the Tibetan state, are high state oracles; the current Dalai Lama has said that the oracles are just one set of advisors, and he himself is responsible for decision making (Ellington 1998). Most of these high state oracles are men, but there are significant exceptions to this rule, as some women in Tibetan history have attained the title of state oracle (Havnevik 2002). Aside from high state oracles and oracular monastic heads, in Tibet and in exile, there are multitudes of locally and regionally recognized minor oracles, both male and female (Diemberger 2005).

Casting divinations (Tibetan: *mos*) is a common facet of contemporary heritage Tibetan religious practices, likely a part of the indigenous tradition of Tibet that was adapted during the influx of Buddhism. Diviners often use dice, *malas*, or doughballs to tell the future for themselves and others. The diviner establishes a ritual connection with a particular deity who invests the divinations with supernatural insight. Lama Zopa Rinpoche is reputedly very fond of divinations.

According to Rosenberg and Harding, modern futures were supposedly predicated on a rejection of the prophet, but this became intractable when prophets failed to get the message: "as it turns out, what most characterizes the modern problem of the future is not its historical distance from the mode of prophecy but rather its hybrid and contradictory relationship to it" (2005, 6). Within FPMT there is simultaneously acceptance and mistrust of prophecy and divination. "I'm not surprised [the Maitreya Project's] a mess," offered one Western Tibetan Buddhist devotee, whose teacher is actually one of Lama Zopa Rinpoche's gurus. "It's always just a roll of the dice with FPMT. Rinpoche makes all of his decisions based on *mos*." There are others who feel that Lama Zopa Rinpoche's divinations are the best possible way to feel out the future and make choices accordingly. One devotee explained, "I believe in *mos* if they are being handled by a divine being. . . . Lama Zopa Rinpoche *is* a divine being." Guru devotion and faith play a significant part in whether divinations are accepted or rejected, but occasionally even the most devoted FPMTers may experience cultural dissonance regarding certain prophetic elements in the institution and have either to work through them or simply allow them to mentally flicker as temporary spaces of doubt.

There were also hushed discussions around common tables at FPMT centers in India about how Lama Zopa Rinpoche can look into the future and has made predictions about some of his devotees. One of the most common responses of devoted FPMTers wrestling with the discomfort of local protests about the Maitreya Project is to reason aloud that since Lama Zopa Rinpoche is omniscient and enlightened, he knows the future better than anyone else; therefore, whatever the MPI is up to, it must be for the best.

I have also been told by some FPMT devotees that Osel is able to divine the future. His former attendant noted that when Osel was a child he showed psychic qualities and the ability to tell the future. Another monk reported the following prophecy: "Again you are going to be a lama, and I will hold you in my arms" (Mackenzie 1995, 191). In her hagiography of Lama Osel, Mackenzie notes that other monks confirmed to her that he was able to see their past and future lives. Also, "at other times he would scare them witless by declaring they were going to the hell realms—whether these were true prophesies or false no one was in a position to judge" (Mackenzie 1995, 191). Osel, as an adult, in public at least, has not claimed these gifts, but that is irrelevant to those who still believe he possesses them.

The religious interpretation of incidental signs or omens is also a common phenomenon in Tibetan religious culture. Although Tibetan refugees often wonder about the prodigious bad luck encountered by the Maitreya Project, it is not common for FPMT devotees to consider the obstacles encountered by the project to be bad omens. The flexibility inherent in reading signs is that they can be interpreted to support a foregone conclusion. Perhaps not unlike the Christian charismatic healer and patient described at length by anthropologist Vincent Crapanzano in his work, my FPMT interlocutors could also easily read into the signs exactly what they wanted: "It is clear that these 'premonitions' are retrospective reevaluations of experiences that seem to have little on the surface to do with the revelation they purportedly foreshadow" (2004, 48).

In January 1998, when the Dalai Lama came to the Maitreya Project–owned land in Bodh Gaya, he gave a speech in support of the project, but soon afterwards a series of events took place that are often considered bad omens (fire, strange weather, postponement) according to Tibetan cultural norms, yet these were all interpreted publicly by FPMT devotees as auspicious happenings.[9]

> In a dramatic turn later, a fire broke out, destroying the large Shakyamuni tangka and part of the temporary tent structure on the Maitreya land. . . . Towards the end of His Holiness' teachings that day, following the Chenrezig initiation, there was an unexpected downpour of rain. His Holiness looked up in surprise, but continued teaching. While people were fully protected by the teaching tent, heavy rain meant that the Maitreya puja scheduled for the same evening to bless the Maitreya land had to be canceled. Mini-pujas were held on buses and by a few monks at the land. It was felt by most that all these conditions were auspicious signs. (Rose 1998, 37)

Peter Kedge narrated the event by noting that although the tent, Buddha *thangka*, offerings, and ritual implements had all burned, the throne that His Holiness had just occupied, plus the Maitreya *thangka*, had escaped damage in the fire (Kedge 1998). Still, he admitted that he found himself "wishing that auspiciousness could display itself in a slightly more friendly manner" (41). Publicly, FPMT would spin ostensibly bad news as good news, and what would seem bad omens in one light are interpreted as auspicious signs instead.[10]

When I visited the home office of the Maitreya Project's land broker Babar Singh, in 2006, he showed me that one of the small six-inch Maitreya Buddhas in his glass case kept slipping out of its box and falling forward so that its head hit the glass. Mr. Singh interpreted it as a good omen that the project would soon move ahead, and said, "See that one keeps coming out of its case on its own. It's ready!" Rather than see it as a retrograde state for a sacred art object, or a negative omen, he saw it as indisputably positive sign. As far as I can discern, in FPMT and MPI, challenging events are routinely publicly interpreted as good omens. I have yet to see any public reference to a bad omen as concerns any FPMT project, including Maitreya Project 2.0.

There is sometimes acknowledgement of temporary obstacles that can be removed through diligent practice. FPMTers usually talk about obstacles as if they were inevitable, and therefore nothing to be concerned about. In 2000, Lama Osel gave an interview in which he repeated a common refrain of FPMT devotees that obstacles are inevitable in a *dharma* project of this magnitude: "If you make something big, then always some obstacles come. Some people feel jealous, so many things" ("Lama Osel 'Eager for the Study of Buddhism'" 2000, 64). When the Maitreya Project faced obstructions in Bihar and considered whether to move, the Dalai Lama performed a dough-ball divination to decide if the project would relocate. Lama Zopa Rinpoche recounted, "His Holiness the Dalai Lama suggested that we check where to build the Maitreya statue, because in Bodhgaya there had been so many obstacles. In front of the main Guru Shakyamuni Buddha statue inside the Bodhgaya Mahabodhi Temple, His Holiness the Dalai Lama used the traditional method of mo [divination], using tsampa balls. The checking was done very carefully and His Holiness the Dalai Lama held my hand while he did the mo himself and the answer came. . . : Kushinagar" ("Letter from Lama Zopa Rinpoche" 2014).

Once the project moved to Kushinagar, supporters often argued that it had been a foregone conclusion and that the reason that the project had so many problems in Bodh Gaya was precisely because the project was always supposed to be done in Kushinagar. For example, Babar Singh, the Indian MPI staffer, said that he had done a careful study of the literature, which all pointed to his conclusion that the historical Buddha had foreseen the coming of the Maitreya Project to Kushinagar. He narrated to me how he had found a passage in a dusty text somewhere that described how the Buddha had berated a disciple who had complained that a "backward" hinterland such as the Malla kingdom was not a worthy site for the Mahaparinirvana; the Buddha reportedly said that in a previous era Kushinagar had been a very famous and large kingdom. Babar Singh told me, "[The Buddha] said that 'what was past will be again in the future. In time this city will rise again.' He visualized this and his prophecy is coming true. Kushinagar will again be a beautiful city. . . . I cannot prove this, but I believe that the Maitreya statue was meant to come to Kushinagar. The site of dying will be the site of rising. Kushinagar will rise up—the Buddha made this prophecy." Babar Singh used prophetic discourse to suggest that Maitreya Project 2.0 was foreordained within Buddhist literature. I do not think this narrative was invented for my benefit, as it seemed to me an oft-repeated story.

Tibetan refugees have not played a major part in the Maitreya Project effort, mostly given that few are FPMT students or serious devotees of Lama Zopa Rinpoche. However, Tibetan refugees in Dharamsala that I interviewed about the statue project were quick to point out that many of the delays, controversies, and problems experienced by the Maitreya Project were incontrovertibly bad omens in their view. Dozens of heritage Tibetan Buddhist informants indicated that the MPI statue was a Western project, both lamenting that the Maitreya Project was run and funded by non-Tibetans and wondering if perhaps the inauspicious signs of delay and rumors of corruption were not connected in some way to its very distance from the Tibetan exile community.

Making (Up) Progress

Rosenberg and Harding argue that the futures visualized in the past continue to live on in the present: "More and more, our sense of the future is conditioned by a knowledge of, and even a nostalgia for, futures that we have already lost" (2005, 3). Futures past haunt our present, but do they also affect our ability to have faith in futures future? By tracing the Maitreya Project 2.0 progress reports, one finds that it was consistently dogged by broken promises and failed progress, and yet the discourse was remarkably, cheerfully future-oriented.

Robin Weigman's piece "Feminism's Apocalyptic Futures" approaches the problem of the present without a tenable solution. As per Weigman's explication, the future of feminism is fraught because the present has failed to bring past promises to fruition in the now. It is the short-term nature of the promises of the past that makes the present seem uninhabitable to feminists lamenting "the failure of feminism's present tense" (Weigman 2000, 807). In the same way, the future imagery evoked in each of the updates forwarded by MPI is haunted by the short-term broken promises of the past. This haunting by futures past is especially apparent in the revising and re-revising of projected dates for goals to be accomplished. In 2000, the expected completion date for the Maitreya Project was 2005. In 2007, though ground had not yet been broken, those connected to the project still hoped that it would be complete by 2013. Going back, one is struck by the plethora of envisioned futures that have failed to come to fruition, as well as the repetition of promise after broken promise to both themselves and their donors.

There is clearly a wide gap between what is and what may be, but it is important to see the gap as itself fluid and constructed over time. The gap between reality and the ideal that is central to Paul Ricoeur's (1986) notion of utopian thought is cogently extended by Hiro Miyazaki (2003, 261) who observes that the gap gives the present its future directionality. By explicating the way that Japanese arbitragers handled and extended the temporal incongruities of a volatile market, Miyazaki argues that only by exposing the gap between "reality" and the "ideal" does one develop "prospective momentum" (2003, 261). I draw on Miyazaki's formulation here to show that each of these detailed narratives of progress from the Maitreya Project illuminated precisely that distance between what was and what will be in order to excite a feeling of optimism.

MPI has established a pattern of articulating their revision and redefinition of goals so as to forward a narrative of progress. The production of momentum by MPI was accomplished in the organization's public literature, in periodic e-mail updates to the organization's listserv, and also through articles in FPMT's *Mandala* magazine. One to four times a year between 2001 and 2007, MPI e-mailed updates to those registered as donors or interested parties on the Maitreya Project website. Almost every e-mailed "Latest Update" focused on what had been accomplished, as well as setting short-term goals for the next phase of work: for example, in the first half of the update from 2000, a small "success" was registered—"the Concept Design team's work was complete"—with language such as "milestone," "dynamic," "inspiring," "energizing," while the second half of the e-mail described the "ideal" in detail—the statue as it was conceived—"a quiet hallowed setting," surrounded by a "natural native woodland landscape," which is partially encircled by a "Living Wall" where most of the accommodations, management, and services will be located (MPI 2000).

While a mid-2001 update proclaimed "Construction phase begins," in fact the November 2001 update acknowledged a full stop on progress as new sites were being scouted for suitability (MPI 2001a, 2001b). The next set of updates over the course of a year built momentum hinting at a swift resolution, but on the ground things were taking much longer than expected. The project announced that an agreement with the Uttar Pradeshi state government had been reached as of May 2003, and that it would be "several months before Maitreya Project will take possession of a site" in Kushinagar (MPI 2003).

Over a year later, in August 2004, the Maitreya Project wrote that they hoped to take possession of the land later in that year itself, to open offices in Lucknow and Delhi, and to begin social programs in Kushinagar (MPI 2004b). The MPI update from December 2004 documents their hope that it will be "several months" before they can possess the land that would be acquired on their behalf (MPI 2004c).

In early 2005, the project staff wrote that they "expected" that the land would be under their control later in that calendar year and that the statue would be done five years from that time (Kedge 2005b). In a December 2005 update, Peter Kedge wrote that "there is intense and ongoing activity, particularly in India, where we make daily progress towards the taking over of our site of 750 acres of land in Kushinagar, Uttar Pradesh. . . . We are making good steady progress with our partners in shared vision, the Uttar Pradesh State Government" (Kedge 2005a).[11]

The August 2006 update reported that the government land acquisition was well underway: "Currently, 40% of the land is ready for handover and the government has completed most of the process for the remaining 60% of the land. Although we know all too well that timing cannot be guaranteed, we expect the land site process will be completed by the end of 2006 or early 2007" (Kedge 2006). This apparent progress was not evident on the ground, nor did locals agree with this rosy assessment.

The next of these progress updates was sent in June 2007 and simultaneously proclaimed with great fanfare that all obstacles to the land acquisition had been cleared, and yet it would take some time for the government to take the land: "We are delighted to announce that in compliance with the Indian Land Acquisition Act, the State Government of Uttar Pradesh has completed the necessary legal requirements for the acquisition of the 750 acre land site to be made available to Maitreya Project, in Kushinagar, UP in northern India. The State Government has not yet taken physical possession of the land site and it will still take further time before it is operationally under the control of the Project; nonetheless, this is a major milestone in the development of the Project and we are pleased to be able to share with you this news which has been eagerly awaited for so long" (MPI 2007a). The buildup during these updates generated a continuous effect of being on the cusp of a breakthrough, although during the summer of 2007 the Kushinagari farmers still occupied the coveted project land, steadfastly refused to budge, and moreover, reported to me over the phone that the government seemed less inclined to force them off their land.

In the fall of 2007, the Maitreya Project suffered some bad press,[12] and they felt compelled to issue some progress updates that were more defensive. The update issued in September 2007 was a sweeping repudiation of the charges leveled against the MPI regarding the challenges faced by the land acquisition: it said that no one would be forced off the land for the project (Kedge 2007b). The report picked a few difficult cases, such as the case of a leasee who also reputedly wanted compensation for eviction, and argued that the Maitreya Project had no legal standing in the land acquisition. This report was the first that eschewed the singsong sway between real and ideal in favor of a perfunctory question-and-answer style. It seemed that the performative momentum was dealt a blow here, as the progress reports changed in substance for a period after summer 2007.

The progress report issued in November 2007 was more specifically designed to refute accusations about a lack of transparency in decision making and finances. Peter Kedge wrote that all due diligence was being done to ensure a fair process of land acquisition and noted that cases of eminent domain are "always highly emotive, whether they take place in the US, the UK, India or elsewhere" (Kedge 2007a). For the first time, with the update, Kedge released the financial records of the organization. In addition, they also showed the bureaucratic structure of the Maitreya Project as a transnational institution. In that report, progress is not discussed in terms of short-term goals and specifics on what happens next; it was simply stated that the land acquisition will eventually go ahead: "keeping in mind the long-term, sustainable benefits Maitreya Project will bring to the local community, the Project remains dedicated in its attempt to locate at Kushinagar, and at present we have every faith that the land purchase will be achieved to the satisfaction of all parties" (Kedge 2007a).

A report issued in October 2008 was a nostalgia-laden look at the Maitreya Project's school in Bodh Gaya. The update was not a progress report on Maitreya Project 2.0 proper, but rather a celebration of the accomplishments of the school (MPI 2008a). The missive reprinted the school's newsletter, the *Good Heart*, instead of discussing the progress or lack thereof in Kushinagar. The deployment of nostalgia—the good old days when Bodh Gaya, and not Kushinagar, was the future site of the statue—was evident. The momentum of the updates here seemed to reverse and travel backwards in time, as there was no mention of Kushinagar at all. The accomplishments of the Bodh Gaya school, while substantial, were unique as a placeholder progress update from the Maitreya Project in contrast to their previous updates. The new hope in October 2008 was fueled by the children of Bodh Gaya and their brighter futures, as one student's poem included in the update shows: "We little children will make a new world" (MPI 2008a). The education reset was accomplished by mapping out the need for funds so that the Bodh Gaya school "can do so much more—with a little help from our sponsors" (MPI 2008a). This update was nostalgic, and I read it as a reset of the prospective momentum forward.

After the break, it took the Maitreya Project some time to get forward momentum rolling again. In 2008, the Maitreya Project revamped their website to focus on the proposed Maitreya Healthcare Project and the hoped-for education projects in Kushinagar. The Kushinagar health-care proposal, posted to the Maitreya Project website in early 2008, thus outlined a new real and a new ideal in detail. The new real glosses Kushinagar under an avalanche of statistics about poverty, illiteracy, and the lack of basic health care options for Indians in general, and Uttar Pradeshis more specifically. Only after eighteen pages of the national and regional information does one find a paragraph, a single paragraph, about the Kushinagar locale. The paragraph about Kushinagar constructed a convenient real by noting the dearth of health-care options (which is undeniable) but failed to mention that a Thai temple had a hospital under construction at the time.

Rather than focusing on the land acquisition (the old ideal), the health-care-brochure-as-project-update established a new target goal: the Maitreya Healthcare Project became the new ideal as opposed to the statue itself. The health-care plan was slated to roll out in phases; there were detailed costs attached, such as "Physiotherapy" capital expenses being 60,000 rupees, and liability insurance being 5,000 rupees (MPI 2008b). The health-care project had long been envisioned as a part of the project writ large, but the effect of rolling out the funding proposal seemed to be another strategy to reset the momentum.

The health-care-brochure-as-project-update detailed the hopes and expectations of the project without mentioning the people of Kushinagar, their resistance to the project, or the land acquisition. There was no sense of contingency; nothing to the effect of, "if the land is acquired, then we will proceed with phase one." The Maitreya Project hospital became the fantasy du jour. For nearly two years, the land acquisition controversy was all but erased—silenced, in MPI discourse.

In September 2009, the Maitreya Project update was another report addressing the questions they had received about the land acquisition controversy and promising that they would advocate for the local people in Kushinagar (MPI 2009). They discussed this in more specific language than ever before. Even as they made it clear that some land previously coveted would no longer be acquired, they anticipated further land acquisition issues in Kushinagar would be settled shortly. In addition, a smaller statue (150 feet) would be built in Bodh Gaya, and the report detailed progress toward that end.[13] The 2009 update was a jolt to the heart of FPMT's heart project—a dramatic return from nostalgia land and side projects to bring focus squarely back on the business of the statue through redefining the gap, eliciting hope, and keeping the tone cheery. The report ended thusly, "Thank you for your kind interest and attention. We hope that the above, which is current as of September 2009, conveys the highly positive spirit of cooperation within which the Project is moving forward in Kushinagar, Uttar Pradesh and Bodhgaya, Bihar" (MPI 2009).

The update issued in April 2010 was extraordinary in its breadth, style, and content: it reported on the successes and miracles of the Relic Tour and then explained that it would be closing the Maitreya Project school in Bodh Gaya indefinitely due to financial issues and asked for funding help in order to help transfer the students and staff of the school to another local program (MPI 2010). Yet it was the final section that gave new life to Maitreya

Project 2.0 hope again: it showed a photo of Richard Gere posed with Indian bureaucrats in Lucknow with an explanation that the Hollywood actor had successfully gone to advocate on behalf of MPI. This report again reset the gap and returned the progress updates to the genre of hope creation and optimism. It marked a vigorous return to the drama of early MPI updates. The April 2010 report reads, in part:

> In January 2010, members of Maitreya Project met with the Culture Secretary of Uttar Pradesh, Shri Awanish K. Awasthi. The meeting included the executive director of Maitreya Project Trust Tony Simmons, Maitreya Project advocate [Babar Singh], trustees from Maitreya Project Trust, and friend of Maitreya Project Richard Gere. Mr. Awasthi presented a plan and timetable for the state government to identify final land site boundaries that are agreeable to all stakeholders.
>
> In a series of meetings since then, which have been held daily in Lucknow, further progress has been made. Our understanding directly from state government is that the timetable for handover is now approximately June 2010. The fact that such an announcement has been made directly to representatives of Maitreya Project and also published widely in state government press releases indicates that Maitreya Project should soon be in a position to take possession of the landsite in Kushinagar.
>
> There have been many reasons why this process has been long and drawn out. Some of these reasons have been presented already and they include the difficult circumstances involved in dealing with the state government responsible for over 150 million people in an essentially rural and poor part of India. A system of "office rotation" that occurs within the Indian Administrative Service is frequently implemented and hinders continuity. Politics also plays a part. Nevertheless, this year, 2010, has seen strong determination from the side of the State Government of Uttar Pradesh as well as, of course, Maitreya Project to bringing this issue to full resolution. (MPI 2010)

The spring 2010 update, like all discourse coming out of MPI thus far, blamed any and all obstacles and delays solely on external causes. The update went on to note that once the land was seized, the education and health-care projects conceived for the area would finally begin. The fact that the health-care project was proposed to start long ago was glossed and forgotten. The land was once more at front and center, but this time would be different, it promised. The gap moves again, and after a slight pause, a new real and a new ideal are summarily unveiled.

The prospective momentum extant in the literature for Maitreya Project 2.0 had the effect of both creating and sustaining hope within FPMT for years, and yet it also perhaps frustrated hope for others, who pointed to the revisions upon revisions as evidence that the Maitreya Project's plans and promises cannot be trusted. Faith and hope, as compatriots, are intertwined in this process. I have shown how hope is manufactured even when it is frustrated or slowed; the Maitreya Project managed to reboot their momentum countless times by articulating a new ideal and a new real. Thus as each new gap was made manifest, the Maitreya Project busied itself with the work of fabricating and reframing it anew.

The Future Tense

What is the significance of these imaginary futures on the present? This section will revisit the work that both distant future thinking and near future thinking does in the present. Essentially, the work of projecting and imagining into the future is creative, comforting, but also profoundly anxiety provoking. Future horizons, frontiers, projects, progress, hopes—these are all ultimately unbridgeable. As soon as one reaches one's destination on the horizon, the future is later, the horizon is elsewhere. Of course, ultimately, the future is empty, and it always has been and always will be. Conventionally though, there are good reasons to examine the work that hope and aspiration for the future do in the present.

The Maitreya Project also portends its own excesses and places its horizon at a dizzying distance in the far-flung future of Maitreya, but simultaneously, like a time machine, the statue would forge a connection between now and then. The statue, and the planning, imaging, designing, fundraising, and bureaucratic work needed to be done to achieve it, these are the near futures that arise in one gap and create their own smaller gaps along the way. The gap is still gaps, and we simply have to look for them: between now and Maitreya's era; between now and the statue's construction phase; between now and the construction of a new school in Kushinagar; between now and the Maitreya Buddha statue's completion; between now and the next update.

The anticipation about the Maitreya's era is also somewhat deferred. The same creative energy and imaginations construct the statue, frame it, and delimit it. Planning, designing, and fundraising—they stoke enthusiasm and anxiety in turns. Rich engagements with hopeful futures in the now can expose the raw nerves of affective tension that can accompany the contingent, blank openness of what lies just beyond the horizon. The future tense evokes the crucial anxieties and ambivalences in the present with regard to divergent visions of what is to come.

The anthropologist Vincent Crapanzano wrote that narratives of world endings, hope, desire, waiting, prophecy are confrontations with the "imaginative horizons" that play at the distant edges of the known. He observes,

> What makes the inaccessibility of the hinterland terrifying is less its inaccessibility than its determining role in our perception of that which we take naively to be accessible: that which we actually perceive, experience, touch and feel. Imagined—or better still, imaginable—it remains elusive. . . . It is this elusiveness, this determining absence of the accessible, which is terrifying; for that which we perceive is always determined—up to a point, I'm compelled to say—by that absence, that imagined presence. It is more than contingency that frightens us. It is the artifice of factuality, of our empiricism, our realism, to which we blind ourselves—often through absurdist methodologies of truth and naively positivist philosophies. (Crapanzano 2004, 17)

Here Crapanzano notes the terror of the intangible that ought to be graspable, and anxiety of an absence where a presence should be. This is the tension that creeps up on someone who wants to have faith in progress, even as they are haunted by half-memories of broken promises. MPI has worked hard to erase contingency and to put the future in all too concrete terms through their projections, prophecies, and progress reports.

In his work on eschatological narratives, Crapanzano argues that death and world ending are inextricably linked: "According to Frank Kermode, Saint Augustine says that terror of world-ending is a substitute for the terror of dying. Kermode himself argues that the End, whether in life or story, is a figure for death. It is certainly true that death lurks in all apocalyptic thought. But might we not reverse Augustine's formula and say that the terror of death is a substitute for the terror of world-ending?" (2004, 201–202). The proposed Maitreya statue, and the Maitreya mythology, is rife with narrative strands of both world ending and death, and of course, world regeneration and future life. Arguably, there is a deep-seated anxiety evoked by the figure of Maitreya that is very essentially connected to the fear of death.

On the one hand, the fact that death is a topic of interest and opportunity in the religious discourse might make one pause at Ernest Becker's assertion that "the idea of death, the fear of it, haunts the human animal like nothing else; it is the mainspring of human activity—activity designed largely to avoid the fatality of death, to overcome it by denying in some way that it is the final destiny of man" (1973, ix). While I would suggest that fear of death may not be as universal as he insists,[14] I do recognize it as a general pattern in the human experience and a reality for many of my Buddhist informants, both heritage and nonheritage alike. Certainly, Tibetan Buddhism's preoccupation with death in text and practice does not mean that all Tibetan Buddhists the world over have somehow risen above anxiety about death. For example, the Buddha remains present to many Buddhist practitioners despite Mahaparinirvana, in terms of both the discourse of *kayas* (Sanskrit for "bodies," which refers to the Mahayana concept of a multiplicity of bodies of the Buddha), as well as the duplication of Buddhas past, present, and future through similar hagiographies. There are many ways in which death, endings, and absence are avoided or postponed in the tradition, and just as many ways in which affective permanence is established and maintained; I find that these philosophical and psychological moments expose a future tense that can manifest as anxiety about death. Ernest Becker may have overstated the case when he wrote that "religions like Hinduism and Buddhism performed the ingenious trick of pretending not to want to be reborn, which is a sort of negative magic: claiming not to want what you really want" (1973, 12), but I come back to his work and these words again and again, since there is something almost excruciatingly true embedded in this observation. Tibetan Buddhist discourse and practice often perform philosophical contortions to allow devotees to avoid what they fear the most: dissolution and real endings.

For Tibetan exiles, such as Lama Yeshe, anxiety about the end of Tibet (either its destruction, or its transformation into something unrecognizable), the end of the Dalai Lama (either death of the persona, or the abolition of the institution), and the end of the world (either as one meditates on one's own impermanence, or the impermanence of the world around you) can fold in on each other and the edges may blur, until they all signify the same fear. Maitreya could represent the inversion of fear, the hope for life, the sunrise that can only happen on the other side of a sunset, but it also acts to suppress and delay the inevitability of ending.

If the Buddha and the Buddhas meld together, then the future felicity of desiring to be born during the era of Maitreya is akin to a temporally sanctioned traveling backwards in time, for given that there is little practical difference between being in the presence of the historical Buddha and the anticipated Buddha, the love, respect, and reverence a Buddhist develops for the Buddha past can be transferred easily to the Buddha future. The religious power of the historical Buddha provides a touchstone or gold standard that the cult of Maitreya can draw from. The future Buddha is an affective, though not actual, resurrection of the historical Buddha.

The same temporal work is achieved and replicated through the reproduction of gurus in Tibetan Buddhism. The reincarnations of gurus have led to a suspension of impermanence, as the life of the lama simply continues in a child for our benefit. The reincarnation of regular laity is anonymous, but the practice of lama rebirth through *tulkus* is a form of affective immortality. This system has been embraced by FPMT, since their lamas have thus far all been reincarnated into identified *tulkus*. Once Lama Zopa Rinpoche shuffles off his moral coil, it will be interesting to see if Osel is charged with the responsibility to find Lama Zopa Rinpoche's *tulku*. In any case, as the creator/ initiator/director of the world's largest Buddha statue in the world—that is, the everlasting Maitreya Project statue—Lama Zopa Rinpoche perhaps hoped to attain yet another form of immortality.

Ultimately, the efficacy of the FPMT community's effort to seize on the anxiety of the present by gesturing to the future relies on faith in narratives of the past. Hope in the future is fed by the faith that Tibetan Buddhists evince in the stories of the future attributed to the historical Buddha. The Tibetan Buddhist hope that drives the Maitreya Project is dependent on prevailing faith in order to be grounded and internalized on a wide scale. Walter Benjamin's exploration of hope, as framed by Szondi (1986), attempts to recapture the present by looking for the future in the past.[15] The Maitreya myth is similar in that it relies heavily on mirroring the narrative of the historical Buddha's hagiography in order to create future hope out of faith in the past. The past is mined in order to create the forward momentum of hope for a utopian future in which the devotee will be able to meet an actual Buddha on the fast track to enlightenment.

In this chapter, by extending Miyazaki's (2003) formulation of prospective momentum, I illuminate how the MPI's deployment of the real (lack of actual progress) and the ideal (movement toward the completion of the statue) served to construct widespread hope for the Maitreya Project 2.0 statue among many FPMT devotees. By building a statue today that implicitly speaks to events they hope to transgress (the end of Buddhism, the end of the world, the end of FPMT, the end of a lineage, the end of themselves) and an event they hope will be achieved (the regeneration of world, the coming age of Maitreya, the rebirth of Buddhism), FPMT evokes the wide, anxiety-provoking gap between cosmic reals and ideals.

Each pregnant, hopeful aspiration—hope for enlightenment; hope for the Maitreya's era; hope for reincarnation of lamas; hope for continuation of the nation, lineage, organization, and self; hope for the biggest statue in the world; hope for progress—contains a seed of fear as well. The end of Lama

Yeshe's reign at FPMT, the end of a lineage, the end of the Dalai Lama, the end of Tibet, the end of the world as it once was, in institutional mythologies each potential ending recedes in favor of the forward motion toward hope for future utopias. There is tension implicit in the very articulation of a future possibility: between wanting something better and between wanting things to stay as they are; between wanting to know the future and wanting the future to remain unknowable; between desire for endings and fear of them. The future tense acknowledges the anxiety, the stress, of longing for something against the ultimately unknowable result, because it contains within it our deep human ambivalence about futures in contradistinction.

Crapanzano acknowledges the difficulty of this predicament in this way: "Of course, just as we desire fixity, we desire openness. We fear closure; we delight in possibility. Obviously each community has its own tolerance for openness and closure, fixity and looseness. But whether cultural—or individual—emphasis is given to one or the other, the fact remains that once the hinterland, once possibility is articulated, it is somehow fixed and constraining, determining further possibilities: the newly displaced hinterland" (2004, 23). Why build a Maitreya Buddha that should last one thousand years? *Karma* (check), faith (check), enlightenment (check), but one can also read this construction as a means of displacing the end and resetting the gap. Thus, we can also locate the Maitreya Project's futurity at the intersection between the simultaneous inevitability and unendurableness of impermanence: the impermanence of Buddhism within Buddhist cosmology, the impermanence of FPMT, and the impermanence of every single FPMTer from Lama Zopa Rinpoche to the newest student. The future tense is manifestly apparent in FPMT's struggle to articulate, construct, and manage its future possibilities and in the anxiety produced when a gap between real and ideal can be so fraught, so chaotic, and so contested that one may well tumble into the precipice between the two.

❧ PART 2

The Kushinagari Resistance

❧ CHAPTER 6

Holy Place / *TIRTHA*

Living in the Place of the Buddha's Death

Although reclaimed from obscurity by Indian and British archaeologists about a century and a half ago,[1] the town of Kushinagar today still feels so small and sleepy compared to other major Buddhist pilgrimage places in India that many pilgrims have remarked to me that the place seems utterly "dead." While it is tempting to dwell on the morbid in what is, after all, the place of the historical Buddha's death, in this chapter I push back against the stereotypical characterization of a "dead" Kushinagar by showing a panoramic view of vibrant "ethnoscapes" (Appadurai 1996) and "sacroscapes" (Tweed 2006) at play there today.

I will examine the current and potential future significance of sacred monuments that mark the location of Buddha's death and his cremation and how these spaces are currently envisioned and occupied by pilgrims, monastics, and locals; this chapter will also look outward from Kushinagar's sacred spaces and toward the secular ones that are intertwined with them. Here I am interested in what there is to be learned by panning out to look beyond the celebrated monuments and into the cultural lives of Kushinagar's many communities, including those that often remain invisible to passing pilgrims.

FPMT's plans to build the monolithic Maitreya Project 2.0 statue in Kushinagar would forever reshape the lives of the people who move through it. For more than a decade the Maitreya Project has been an object of fear (and sometimes hope) for various Kushinagari locals. As the chosen site for the

Maitreya Project 2.0 statue, Kushinagar as a place itself becomes a significant character in the story of the statue's prelife. The Kushinagari locals have borne the brunt of the Maitreya Project 2.0 plan's actual effects in the world, and their actions and fight have undermined the behemoth.

While the terrain of certain religious places has been well explored by anthropologists—for example, the relationship between the Australian landscape and the aboriginal Dreaming (Myers 1986) or the rich cultural worlds of Hindu pilgrimage places (Eck 1982; Grodzins Gold 1988; Parry 1994)—sacred Buddhist territoriality in India has not been so famously or exhaustively mapped. Where Buddhist pilgrimage spaces are discussed, most often they focus on the archaeological, historical, textual, or ritual significance of these places, rather than on the cultural life outside the sacred sites that is constrained and constructed by the very existence of the sites themselves.[2] By simultaneously looking at both the visible religiously significant landscapes and the oft-invisible social worlds just outside their walls, we can rebalance our perspectives on the living (and dead) aspects of Buddhist pilgrimage sites. Here I look at Kushinagar as a complex and layered cultural nexus where people of all Buddhist nations, and people of different walks of life—monk, sweeper, travel guide, merchant, archaeologist, *chaiwallah*—meet, interact, and affect one another in profound ways.[3] Through the exploration of various groups of people living in Kushinagar today, we can begin to perceive Kushinagar's many contested visions of the future.

This chapter will describe the cultural life extant in the place of the Buddha's death. With some special attention paid to Tibetan Buddhists (both heritage and nonheritage)—due to our continuing circumambulation of the Maitreya Project and its spheres of influence—I will examine the significance of the *stupas* that mark the location of Buddha's death and his cremation in the cultural landscapes of Kushinagar's pilgrims, monastics, and locals. For Tibetan Buddhists in exile, and also for Tibetan Buddhist converts, sacred landscapes themselves are a central aspect of religious ideologies, identities, and ritual practices, although these disparate constituencies may express their attachments to sacred spaces in divergent ways.

In continuing our circumambulation of the Maitreya Project, it is important to look at the full Kushinagari ethnoscape, not just as it applies to Buddhist monastics and pilgrims, but also as the home of the local Kushinagari farmers who are in the process of resisting some of the Buddhist plans that may displace them altogether. I look at locals' articulations of altogether different notions of sacred space that rely as heavily on ancestral claims as on particular religious connections to the land. I show some of the disparate effects that these sacred Buddhist spaces have had on the cultural and socio-economic worlds of contemporary Kushinagaris up to now.

Setting the Scene

The town of Kushinagar, which is located in the Kushinagar district of Uttar Pradesh, is home to several significant Buddhist sites, yet remains one of the least populated (and one of the least popular) of the main historically celebrated Buddhist locales in India. The Archaeological Survey of India (ASI) is currently responsible for the preservation and administration of several Buddhist holy sites in Kushinagar, as well as a museum of local Buddhist antiquities. The Mahaparinirvana Stupa—where the Shakyamuni Buddha uttered his final words, which are thought to be, "Vayadhamma sankhara appamadena sampadetha," and can be translated, "Everything is impermanent. Work toward your liberation with diligence"—lies at the geographic and spiritual heart of Kushinagar.

The actual *stupa* is dwarfed by a shrine set just in front of it, which houses a fifth-century CE red sandstone statue of the Shakyamuni Buddha reclining on his deathbed. This shrine is the center of the modest swirl of pilgrims who descend on the small Indian town every day, pray briefly, make offerings to the statue,[4] make offerings to the local Indian Buddhist "monks" who sit at the statue daily,[5] and then file back onto their air-conditioned tourist buses before either moving to the next pilgrimage site or spending a single evening in one of the four foreign-owned-and-operated upscale hotels in town.

As I have mentioned, Kushinagar is considered a dead pilgrimage site by some international Buddhists, especially in contrast to the bustling site of Buddha's enlightenment at Bodh Gaya or the similarly active Buddhist community in Sarnath, where the Buddha gave his first teaching. The 2,500th anniversary of the Buddha's death was officially celebrated by Indian state tourism departments during my doctoral research period in India, although, ironically perhaps, the anniversary was most conspicuously and grandly feted in more popular Buddhist pilgrimage sites than Kushinagar itself (such as Bodh Gaya and Sarnath). In an interview with the abbot of the main Thai monastery in Kushinagar in 2006, I asked him about how Kushinagar compares to other sacred sites, and he mentioned that when the princess of Thailand came to India for a pilgrimage she had loved Bodh Gaya most, especially the bodhi tree. He noted that Kushinagar was less safe for tourists, since there was little, if any, light on the roads after dark. He summed up the contrast this way: "Bodh Gaya is the place of enlightenment, it is hopeful,

FIGURE 10. The scene outside of the Mahaparinirvana Stupa park in Kushinagar, 2006. Photo by the author.

a light place. Kushinagar is a sorrowful, dark place, and people come for condolences. They come, but they don't stay for long." The abbot was absolutely right about Kushinagar's pilgrims—Buddhist tourists rarely remain in Kushinagar for long. Places like Bodh Gaya and Sarnath were chock-full of pilgrims who would stay for lengthier visits for study, prayer, meditation, or other *dharma* activities. Although the area is actually quite beautiful—vividly green, serene, and bucolic—foreign tourists do not linger in Kushinagar.

The government-run Buddha Museum in Kushinagar is often dark and empty. During my lengthy research visits in 2006 and 2007, I noticed that one newly constructed luxury hotel stood almost completely and consistently empty, waiting for someone to come and breathe some life into the premises. The other luxury hotels, all owned by Japanese business interests, were also quiet, although they would periodically attract a busload of pilgrims from a wealthier tour group. All of the luxury hotels boasted rooms that were nearly US$100 per night, which is quite expensive in Indian tourism circles. As far as anyone working at these hotels could recall at the time, very few people had ever stayed more than one night.

Ramabhar Stupa, the site of the Buddha's funeral pyre and the origin for all of the Buddha's relics, is also usually desolate. It is surrounded by the ruins of ancient monasteries, a reminder that the site was enthusiastically venerated once upon a time, before Buddhism receded in central India and the jungle reclaimed all of Kushinagar's former monuments. One can only imagine what it was like then, over a thousand years ago, when monks diligently made offerings and prayed daily in the shadows of the great *stupa*. Now there are just a few ASI-employed gardeners on the premises, who trim the hedges and offer candles and incense for profit to the handful of tour buses whose occupants step out quickly for often hurried devotional rituals and photographs.

Ramabhar is sometimes skipped by tourists altogether. Even in the busy season, it could be empty practically all day, with just one or two buses approaching for a short stop. When pilgrims of various ethnicities do stop at Ramabhar, it is often a very brief pause, as if the guide inside says to his charges, "Hurry up, everyone! Five minutes tops, we've got to get back on the road to Lumbini!" Also, I have seen whole buses of pilgrims take snaps of it from their air-conditioned coach, unwilling to take the time to even step outside for a single circumambulation. I watched buses of Tibetans acknowledge it with their prayers as their vehicles roll by for a quick *darshan* (Hindi: visual worship).

Along this quiet lane of sacred death sites, there is a row of monasteries and temples built by devotees from around the world—Sri Lanka, Japan, Burma, Thailand, China, Korea, and Tibet. Not unlike an embassy row in the capital city of some irrelevant state, most of the monasteries are shabby and practically deserted, symbolic gestures of devotion by long departed worshippers. Most of these house only a token monk or two (that too, often only during the tourist season), sometimes one who has lost a lottery or was otherwise sent against his will. Some of the foreign Buddhist shrines are maintained and operated solely by local Indian employees. There are two major exceptions to the observations above: (1) the Burmese vihara, which though arguably old and a bit run-down, is an actual, functioning monastery with a full contingent of monks living and worshipping there; (2) the main Thai temple, which is gorgeous and opulent, and occupied by a half (or full, depending on the time of year) clutch of rotating monks and volunteers from Thailand.

The soundscape in Kushinagar, like that of most Buddhist pilgrimage sites in India at the height of the season—in addition to the honks of bus horns, the shouts of vendors selling snacks and miniature souvenir Buddhas to tourists, the yaps of stray dogs in their packs, the thud of monkeys landing on tin roofs, the gush of hand-pumped water, the clinking chimes of bicycle riders asserting their space on the dirt road—is awash in the sounds of more than a dozen different languages. Significantly, many of these intercultural interactions are brief, but there are a handful of foreigners who remain in town. For the purposes of understanding the communities interacting with one another in Kushinagar, I have distinguished three main categories of people who are most often moving through the sacred and secular spaces of Kushinagar: pilgrims, temporary inhabitants and transplants, and locals.[6]

Buddhist Pilgrims in Kushinagar

It is a cool morning in January 2006. A bus pulls into the Burmese vihara parking lot, and a few dozen Burmese pilgrims, mostly middle-aged and elderly women, step gingerly out of their tourist coach. A few monks hurry out of the vihara to meet their guests. Later, when the pilgrims are ready, some of the monks take them through a side gate to the Mahaparinirvana Stupa, which stands just next door. The monks lead the pilgrims down a short path and past the red-robed Indian monks who sit at the *stupa* throughout the day. Inside the shrine, the Burmese pilgrims chant, make offerings, pay their respects, and offer money to the Indian monks sitting inside and outside the *stupa*. Some women take photos of the statue and their group outside the shrine. On their way back out to the bus (now waiting for them at the front gate), the pilgrims are hounded by local touts selling Kushinagar postcards, gold-painted reclining Buddhas made of plaster, and newspaper-wrapped Indian snacks. Beggars pull at the sleeves of the last women in line to embark, until another bus pulls up filled with pilgrims from Thailand, and the beggars wander off to try their luck with the new arrivals.

The visit that I have narrated above was unique in the particulars, and yet by virtue of the patterns that emerged after watching scores of such visits, I would argue that it was a typical pilgrimage stop in the essentials. This fact reminds me of a popular phrase in India, "same same, but different," since each busload was unlike the last (in dress, language, custom, personalities, dynamics, class, etc.), yet their interactions with the *stupas* followed the same general routine.

The first category of people that make up the ethnoscape of Kushinagar are the fleeting buses full of pilgrims that speed in and out of the town on a daily basis. Pilgrims, as Ann Grodzins Gold (1988) has noted, are those who make a round-trip from home to a sacred destination and then back again. I talked with many of these pilgrims over my many stays in Kushinagar, but as one might expect, it was hard to get to know the people that came and went so quickly. Instead I experienced the waves of pilgrims like tides at the beach: constant and omnipresent movement, yet every wave yielding up something new and different to the shore.

While most of the visitors to the *stupas* are foreign Buddhist pilgrims, there are some middle-class Indian visitors from the region who come to the park as a day trip to see the site and to picnic on the grounds. Hindu visitors do tend to see the *stupa* as part of their religious heritage, noting that Buddha is an avatar of Vishnu, a popular Hindu deity.[7] The Mahaparinirvana Park was also sometimes used as a cricket pitch for local and visiting Indians. At the end of a busy day, the ASI's Mahaparinirvana Park was littered with trash, which groundskeepers would often endeavor to clear by the next day.

Heritage Tibetan Buddhist pilgrims usually did the following at visits to the stupa: a set of three full prostrations; one circumambulation; light, incense, or cash offerings; then they headed back to the bus. Tibetan pilgrims either drove onward immediately or stayed the night in the Namgyal Monastery *dharamshala* (Hindi for "guest house"). In my time living there, only one Tibetan family stayed for longer than an overnight visit: a Tibetan *amchi* practicing Tibetan medicine stayed for five days to meet with pilgrims before deciding to move to more populous sites. Lay practitioners told me that by going to sacred sites, including Kushinagar, they are purifying negative *karmas*, which will help them move toward enlightenment. Both heritage Tibetan monastics and lay people feel that even being in close proximity to powerful sacred spaces such as the holy *stupas* of Indian Buddhist sites has immeasurable karmic value.

Nonheritage Tibetan Buddhist institutions have no permanent presence in Kushinagar. FPMT has no *dharma* center in Kushinagar, nor does it have an office, volunteers, or any other presence in the locale (nor does MPI, for that matter). Few of my FPMT informants spent any time in Kushinagar, and never more than a day of pilgrimage, if anything.[8] If they made it to Kushinagar, nonheritage Tibetan Buddhists tended to approach their pilgrimages there differently from heritage adherents. The few nonheritage Tibetan Buddhists I saw that did visit Kushinagar tended to take more time with the *stupas* than heritage Tibetan practitioners. They set up longer ceremonies and organized group meditation sessions at the sacred sites.

Temporary Residents and Transplants Living in Kushinagar

Under the heading of "temporary residents," I would include foreign-born and South Asian seasonal residents of Kushinagar, such as monastics who consider their home elsewhere or nongovernmental organization workers who consider their primary home elsewhere. "Transplants," on the other hand, are foreigners or South Asians who are heritage or nonheritage Buddhists who, though they were not born in Kushinagar, have, over time, made the town their primary home. These two communities are relatively small, but they are crucial insofar as they often play significant roles in mediating and facilitating many of the interactions between locals and pilgrims in Kushinagar.

Under the category of temporary residents, I could even subdivide again: short-term and recurrent temporary residents. The handful of Tibetan monks (two to four, in my experience) sent to mind the small Tibetan temple every year (usually assigned there for just a single season or two) would fall under the short-term group. A nonprofit worker who comes to Kushinagar religiously every year would be a recurrent temporary resident. The distinction is crucial, since the recurrent temporary residents have often established more personal and lasting relationships with local Indians. Short-term temporary residents, whether voluntarily or involuntarily in Kushinagar, rarely invest in the community or its other residents.

On the other hand, the Burmese abbot and some of his monks who have lived mainly or exclusively in Kushinagar for many years should be denoted transplants insofar as they feel that Kushinagar is a permanent adopted home. These community members live, work, and rest in Kushinagar and have chosen it because it is the place of the Buddha's death. Buddhist transplants tend to move to Kushinagar permanently because they believe that it is a particularly special and sacred space.

Recurrent temporary residents and transplants have invested time, money, blood, sweat, or tears in Kushinagar, and they generally have very strong opinions about its future prospects and potential. In terms of the Maitreya Project, as one would expect, short-term temporary residents were fairly ambivalent and unknowledgeable about the project altogether. Recurrent temporary residents and transplants, on the other hand, had much more complex ideas about the statue, most often supportive of the idea in the abstract, but critical of MPI's hands-off approach.

"*We* are Kushinagar"

Kushinagar proper is dominated by the tourist business, monasteries, *stupas*, supporting businesses, and a few schools, but most of the locals who work at those places actually live in adjacent villages. Truly, the nearby villages are often pulled into the orbit of the pilgrimage place proper whether they want to be or not. For the purposes of this study, I will speak of nearby villages as being part of the Kushinagar ethnoscape, since these are the locals that most often work and move within it. I speak of Kushinagar, then, as a "Greater Kushinagar," so that the neighboring villages' connections to the pilgrimage space can be illustrated properly and to resist the notion that the villages surrounding the pilgrimage sites are somehow separate from Kushinagar proper. In fact, the locals of these villages make up much of the social fabric of Kushinagari culture.

I admit to embracing the term "Greater Kushinagar" with some trepidation, since my informants in some of these villages, such as Dumari, Siswa Mahant, and Anirudhwa, very explicitly reinforced the fact that these villages have their own microcultures and small agricultural economies that do function almost entirely independently of the world of the Buddhist pilgrimage place.[9] Each *gaon* (Hindi for "village") has its own character and personality, and these villages remain always outside of the view of the pilgrims hurrying through town. However, when I asked one informant from nearby Siswa Mahant about whether the "people in Kushinagar" comprehended the frustration that local village farmers just outside of town felt about the Maitreya Project plans, he sharply dismissed my implicit differentiation, saying, "*We* are Kushinagar!"

Over the past few centuries, the nearby towns and villages extant in the prediscovery era have expanded and grown to surround the refurbished

FIGURE 11. Village women from the Kushinagar area discussing how they would be negatively impacted by Maitreya Project 2.0.
Photo by the author.

ruins, but their relationship with the infrastructures surrounding and supporting the sacred sites is actually quite ambivalent. In turns, locals are interdependent with and also increasingly frustrated with the incursions of outsiders (including archaeologists). For example, in my discussions with the villagers of the Greater Kushinagar area, they often express ambivalence about the value of the ASI's work and the latter's virtual stranglehold on building in the immediate vicinity of the *stupas*. Many of the villagers do not like the restrictions placed on them by the ASI, and they chafe at cooperating with officials, especially if it comes to ceding land to archaeological digs or other Buddhist endeavors, like the Maitreya Project.

The handful of archaeologists in the Kushinagar area (some of whom are longtime local residents, and others of whom are recurrent temporary residents) were not popular with local villagers due to occasionally combative relationships with one another. Some of these ASI employees believe that many of the old brick lanes found in area villages were made from bricks stolen from the ruins themselves. One of these men, as he walked through the Anirudhwa and Dumari villages, regularly yelled at local people, "Where did these bricks come from?!" Although he never believed their protestations of innocence, he barked his question incessantly, telling me that he hoped his badgering would at least make villagers think twice before plundering the nation's antiquities again. One of the ASI affiliates I interviewed also noted that if villagers accidentally uncover new archaeological spots, they usually cover them up promptly to avoid land seizure by the ASI. This suspicion was especially painful to some of the archaeologists I talked to, since they believe that there is still much in the area to be discovered, especially as regards any unearthed ruins from the Malla kingdom.

By all accounts, Greater Kushinagar is a relatively poor region in economic terms. The 2011 census reports 3,564,544 persons in the Kushinagar district, with an approximately 65 percent literacy rate overall (Census of India 2011). The Kushinagar district is considered exceptionally poor and underdeveloped, even in contrast to other districts in Uttar Pradesh, which itself is one of the poorer states in the nation.[10] The Human Development Index (HDI) is by no means a perfect means to measure poverty, but it does more accurately reflect the complexity of progress made than gross domestic product (GDP) alone, since it looks at three variables: life expectancy, educational attainment, and GDP per capita. In 2001, Uttar Pradesh was ranked fifteen out of seventeen states in terms of the HDI, but in 2005 it dropped to sixteenth of seventeen states in terms of the HDI ("Human Development Report 2006, Uttar Pradesh" 2006). The Kushinagar district was one of the lowest performers in terms of improving its HDI between 2001 and 2005;

its score indicated just a slight 0.0304 percent improvement. In the report cited above, the district ranked sixtieth out of seventy districts in terms of absolute human development indicators. Even more significantly, when the Uttar Pradesh report ranked its districts according to the deprivation index,[11] the Kushinagar district was ranked sixty-three of seventy.

The Gender Development Index (GDI) takes HDI data and adjusts for gender discrepancies ("Human Development Report 2006, Uttar Pradesh" 2006). In 2005, the Kushinagar district was ranked fifty-five out of seventy districts, with an underwhelming 0.4742 GDI. One reason for this is low GDI is that Kushinagar has a very low female literacy rate, ranking in the bottom handful of districts, with just 30 percent female literacy.

Much of the economy of Kushinagar proper is dependent on pilgrimage tourism, while most of the surrounding villages subsist on agriculture, both subsistence and cash-crop farming. The large majority of the district lives in rural areas, relying either on the cultivation of their own plots or agricultural labor wages (or a mix of the two) to feed mostly large extended families. The tourism and agricultural zones certainly have overlapping interests, as many farming families have one or more members who have found formal or informal work in the tourism industry.

There are a handful of Indians, some local Kushinagaris among them, who have donned Buddhist robes and go to the temple every day to beg for alms. While a few of these men may be duly pious toward the Buddha, it is common knowledge in Kushinagar that many of these men are not Buddhists in the way that most pilgrims think them to be. Many continue their worship of Hindu gods and goddesses, and some do not abstain from sexual relations. One foreign transplant I interviewed in 2006 said this about the local Indian monks: "Some of these Indian monks don't even know the teachings. Some are married. Some just want to get money." In Kushinagar, becoming a Buddhist monk is a career option, and a rather lucrative one at that. The monks themselves know that they are not exactly what foreign pilgrims think them to be, but none of my informants minded; one monk I interviewed said that he was being a devoted Vaishnavite by virtue of his worship of the Buddha's place of death. He considers himself a Buddhist, and a Hindu, and said that he "didn't mind" in the least that pilgrims may not like that he is a Hindu Buddhist: "I am my kind of Buddhist, and they are their kind of Buddhist."

Despite the fact that the largely Hindu local population is quite amiable toward the worship of the Buddha, there are very definite social boundaries between the international Buddhists and the local people of Kushinagar. Even where the physical walls are less imposing and concrete than those that hug the main Thai monastery, there is a very palpable ambivalence toward one another that sits between locals and foreigners. One might expect to find a strong symbiotic relationship between guests and hosts, but while there is certainly some flow from the pockets of Buddhist pilgrims into the local economy, the socioeconomic dynamic is fraught with inequality and tension.

Local–Outsider Entanglements in Kushinagar

So how has the influx of temporary residents, transplants, and pilgrims affected the lives of local Kushinagaris? Anil, a transplant from Calcutta who had moved to Kushinagar in 1993 with his family to start a business, gave a description of the way that Kushinagar had changed over the intervening decades:

> We started this [business] in 1996. At that time there were only two tea shops and one paan shop, and two other shops that were closed half the time. There was no light [i.e., electricity], so it was dark at night. [Before we started the business] during the day we would eat at the [Burmese] monastery, and at night we would eat at a dhaba. . . . In 1996, everything happened. Burmese tourists started coming more and more. Every week there were two buses. Before, there were few Western tourists. The only place to stay was the Burmese monastery. Back then there were hardly ten backpackers a year. After 1996, there were buses full of people coming. Developments started then.

His wife, Aishya, a Nepali-born Buddhist practitioner, added, "Gradually small shops started opening up. But the local people aren't getting much benefit from the tourists. Monasteries provide food and lodging for pilgrims. The monasteries are like hotels. Or else the benefits go to the major hotels themselves. . . . One percent of the benefits go to local people here. Now people are becoming poorer and not getting any spiritual work either. Monks are too busy running their monasteries and have no time to teach *dharma*. They are too busy running their business. . . . This place is very holy, but many unholy things happen here." I asked whether people are better or worse off than they were fifteen years before. Anil said, "It is developing. Buildings are coming. But, you see, people out there are fighting for money." I replied that it seems that there is still a long way to go in terms of developing for everyone. Anil said, "There is [still] the communications problem [referring to the lack of information technology infrastructure, and steady Internet and phone access]. And there is no airport."

Anil later extolled his hope that the Maitreya Project would come and improve the economic situation for businessmen like himself. "The Maitreya Project is good from an employment point of view. That's my perspective.

Fifty percent will lose their land at a cheap price, but five hundred thousand people will benefit." His wife, Aishya, who had previously talked at length about how the farmers stood to lose their land for a pittance, said, "The foreigners will bring money back to their own countries [like the monasteries do now]; how will this change with the statue?"

In another conversation several days later, Aishya told me that she was very much in favor of the Maitreya Project in theory but that she was angry about the way that it was being organized. She said, "The farmers here have so much difficulty. If you just talk to them. . . . I see these small, small dhabas, and I see them boiling milk for tea. The cream is going to the top. And the skim is left at the bottom. Here the temples are getting the cream, and the local people get the skim at the bottom. For example, if there are ten people in a jeep then the ten people will eat at the temple, but only the driver will eat at the dhaba." Although her husband agrees with her, he constantly sought to emphasize the positive developments over the many problems encountered along the way. Anil is keen for Kushinagar to develop further, and he admits that his compassion for the poorer locals aside, it is important to his business that the economy and the tourism industry continue to grow.

Some monasteries sponsor small health clinics or schools and encourage their devotees to give alms to the poor. The Thai monastery, the richest in the region, had a small health clinic outside their gates to benefit local people, and they were also planning to build a fully functioning Western-style hospital.[12] The Burmese pilgrims have funded an excellent school, in operation for decades, that has immense popular support from local people. However, many locals say that the charitable projects are mere gestures of compassion, not real work toward upending the systematic structures of poverty. One observation that I heard over and over was that the Buddhist charities were unintentionally creating a culture of beggars and entitlement. Yet, locals complain even more bitterly about monasteries such as the Tibetan monastery that do not even have social welfare and health charities for local Indians.

A Kushinagari couple removed their young daughter from a Buddhist school that was getting regular visits from wealthy pilgrimage groups who would shower the children with pencils, sweaters, and other goodies. The couple, businesspeople with a decent income from their business, claimed that their daughter was being trained to think like a beggar. They told me that one day their young daughter heard that another school was getting freebies, so she lied to her parents and snuck out to beg for her share of the bounty. Since my informants felt that the giveaways were costing their daughter her integrity—a price too heavy for them to pay—they took her out of the Buddhist school that was being overfrequented by Buddhist tourists. They found that at her new school their daughter is far enough away from

well-intentioned, but problematic, Buddhist charities that were
~~~eir distribution of loot and gifts.

~~~ people, both businessmen and farmers, also complain that most
of the donations (and tourist dollars for that matter) simply end up in the
hands of the monasteries, which all too eagerly, and sometimes forcibly, buy
large swathes of land, in the process driving up land prices and slowly displacing some of the poorest farmers. Many locals also complain that some of the
money is sent directly back to the home countries of the monasteries, and
money is not trickling down into their local economy effectively, at least not
to their satisfaction.[13]

When faced with such criticism from locals, monastics tend to articulate the counterpoint that they are beholden to a particular religious mission; they are not primarily social activists with the goal of revitalizing the
local economy. The monks at Namgyal in Kushinagar told me that since
their devotees were usually much poorer than the usual Thai or East Asian
devotees, it simply was not feasible for them to operate similar charitable
programs. Several locally based Buddhist monastics and lay people did argue
compellingly that the economic situation and educational opportunities of
the nearby villages had been revolutionized by the influx of pilgrims' rupees,
especially since the roads had been improved with the investment of Japanese interests in the early nineties. This progress has not gone unappreciated
by the local businesspeople, who admit as much, even while they note that
the effects are not as profound as they could, or should, have been. The Indian employees of foreign monasteries are especially likely to express their
appreciation of foreign Buddhists.

There are only a few modest nonprofits that are operating in the Kushinagar area. For example, the Maitri organization (no connection to FPMT
or the Maitreya Project) is a Japanese-based organization that has built and
funded several primary schools. The Japanese volunteers who come for
some time each year to administer their projects are the kind of short-term
temporary residents who work hard to make some personal connections to
locals, especially those attached to their educational projects. I found that my
local village informants were generally extremely positive in their evaluation
of groups like Maitri, which were doing collaborative social-development
work and building strong local relationships and networks.

Tibetan Buddhism in Kushinagar

The Namgyal Monastery is the only Tibetan monastery in town, and as such
the controversy regarding MPI's proposed statue instigated some particular

challenges for the monks. Most local villagers in Greater Kushinagar know that the project is Tibetan Buddhist, and therefore, for better or worse, Namgyal is sometimes dragged into the quagmire.

Kushinagar is a significant Buddhist pilgrimage site for Tibetans coming from Tibet, as well as those Tibetans on pilgrimage from inside the exile community. Tibetan pilgrims have long viewed sacred sites as being the abodes or repositories of sacred beings, such as Buddhas and deities. Huber writes, "Another vital aspect of Tibetan understanding of *né* that seems to closely parallel what can be discerned about early Indian Buddhist beliefs and practices is the idea that pilgrimage sites, as both sacred objects and their immediate physical surroundings, somehow physically embody both salvational power and superior morality" (2008, 61).

Pilgrimage as a religious phenomenon for Tibetans (geographically both internally in Tibet and externally to India) really only took shape as practice during the later period of the propagation of Buddhist teaching to Tibet, known to be from the late tenth century to the thirteenth century (Huber 2008). Tibetans' Kushinagar has not always been where it stands now. The terrain of Buddhist India shifts, as Toni Huber argued compellingly in *The Holy Land Reborn* (2008), so that the holy places of yesterday may go unrecognized, forgotten, and sometimes re-recognized in new ways. The Kushinagar of today was identified as the site marking the Buddha's death by archaeologists of the British Raj. Before that it was in ruins, forgotten, and buried, but that did not mean that Tibetan Buddhists shied away from finding a place designated "Kushinagar": their classical Kushinagar was several hundred miles away in Assam.[14]

While Kushinagar is clearly significant to Tibetan pilgrims, it is not as heavily trafficked by ethnic Tibetans as Bodh Gaya or Sarnath. The Tibetan monastery in Kushinagar, where I stayed for several of my research visits, was quite dilapidated. The Tibetan monastery had employed a local Indian caretaker during my preliminary visit in 2003; the caretaker was supervised by two monks during the high tourist season. Three years later, the Tibetan monastery had hired one elderly Tibetan, an ex-soldier, newly widowed, to be the primary caretaker. The caretaker was assisted by a local Indian worker and a Tibetan cook. These employees were all technically supervised by the elder of the two young adult monks who had been sent by their monastery in Dharamsala to look after the place during the high season, when busloads of Tibetan pilgrims might show up at the gate at any time of the night or day to sleep in the twenty or so simple rooms of the rundown guest house. The two or three seasonal monks, the crumbling monastery, and the decrepit guest facilities all stand in stark contrast to the well-kept, well-staffed, and fully functioning monastic facilities of the very same Tibetan monastic branch, Namgyal, in Bodh Gaya (not to mention the one in Ithaca, New York, in the United States!).

The aging Namgyal Monastery in Kushinagar also stands in sharp contrast to the opulence of the local Wat Thai Monastery, which enjoys the patronage of the Thai royal family. The Wat Thai is an enormous monastery with well-manicured gardens, a full *sangha*, and a host of male and female volunteers, all of whom are separated from the fields of sugarcane surrounding it by high walls topped with barbed wire, which are patrolled by armed guards. The Thai monastics do most of their prayers and rituals within their own compound, but accompany any Thai pilgrims to the Mahaparinirvana Stupa. A Thai abbot expressed his feeling that only the Thais really respected the place of Buddha's death as a truly significant pilgrimage site, and this is why so many of the other monasteries were in a state of disrepair. In his view, Tibetan Buddhism undervalues the importance of Kushinagar and death meditations. He said, "Tibetans don't like to come to Kushinagar. They have big monasteries in Sarnath and Bodh Gaya and Lumbini, but not here. Maybe because the Buddha died here. They think, he died here and that's the end, but we think he died here and so this is where we must continue the *dharma*. It is our work to carry it forward."

The Thai abbot was not the only Buddhist in town to consider Tibetans less invested in Kushinagar. The Burmese Temple is the oldest in the region, and it also houses an active *sangha*, which is quite a bit more active with the local community than other temples. The Burmese monks are a very visible presence at the Mahaparinirvana Temple. I did not spend much time at the Burmese monastery, but I did a handful of interviews with monks there, and their perspective, too, was that Tibetans and Kushinagaris did not have a healthy relationship. The monks said that Tibetan Buddhism undervalued Kushinagar as a pilgrimage site and that therefore it was strange that Tibetan Buddhists wanted to build a giant statue and complex there. The Burmese monks that I talked to felt that "the Tibetans" (meaning MPI) should work more closely with the local people. My Burmese informants felt that the relatively miniscule, fleeting presence of Tibetans in Kushinagar in the present made the ambitions of the Maitreya Project all the more jarring and inscrutable.

The "China Temple," which was renamed the Linh-Son Temple when it was taken over by Vietnamese devotees, was a small religious compound. Their plan was to continue hosting a few big events for monastics each year, but by and large while the grounds are impressively kept, there is only a devotee or two at a time living there with a few Indian employees. The female

Vietnamese Buddhist heading the Linh-Son Temple (where I also lived for some of my field visits, by the way) told me that she felt that Tibetans were estranged from Kushinagar by virtue of their quick visits. "It's not a good site to them. Tibet people pass quickly through Kushinagar just to say that they've been here, but if you go to Bodh Gaya, you see the difference. Tibet people—they love the bodhi tree. They stay there and do prostrations all day and night. They live there. Here they just come and go, like they are afraid." Speaking critically of the Maitreya Project (lumping together all Tibetan Buddhist institutions, whether Namgyal, MPI, or otherwise), she told me that if the locals were supposed to embrace Tibetan Buddhists, Tibetan Buddhists needed to embrace the locals first.

Significantly, there is very little socializing between monasteries. The Thai and Tibetan monks do not know each other well, the Burmese do not socialize with the Vietnamese laity running the Linh-Son Temple, and the local Indian monks mostly keep to themselves. Except for very occasional functions—on the Buddha's birthday, for example—when a devotee might sponsor a meal for all the monastics of the area, the monastics keep to their own compounds and their own communities. While the language barrier is no small matter, one Tibetan monk reminded me that "broken English" is a common language among most of Kushinagar's monastics and that, in fact, "We just don't want to talk to them."

My Tibetan monastic informants in Kushinagar tried to minimize the concerns of the other monastics by countering that Kushinagar is definitely an important pilgrimage site for Tibetans. One monk argued that if they were funded by a royal family they would have built a grander monastery. Another resident monk told me later that they wanted to upgrade their monastery, but they had been hampered by ASI restrictions on new construction work in such close proximity to the Mahaparinirvana Stupa. The monks at the Tibetan monastery did admit that Kushinagar was not as popular a pilgrimage station for them or lay people as other places, but for them personally it had a few perks. One monk laughingly told me, "I didn't want to come here because it was Kushinagar. I came because here I have more freedom. No discipline master here!" He went on to suggest that there was probably no need for a discipline master in such a placid town, saying, "I was glad to be here at first, but I am bored now."

Each time I arrived at the monastery in Kushinagar (I stayed in their guest house for some of my visits), I would have the company of Tibetan monks for the first few days that I did circumambulations around the *stupas*, but after that, they went back to their normal routine: tidying up the guest rooms after breakfast, playing cricket when there was no electricity, and watching videos when there was electricity. During the full moon, the elder of the monks in residence would sometimes do a short *puja* and light offering at the Ramabhar Stupa. While the caretaker was in residence, there were regular light offerings at the temple, but I observed that there were not regular *pujas* or even daily chanting and recitations; the monks themselves told me that they technically ought to be doing those rituals, but they were unmotivated to do anything much beyond tidying the guest rooms.

Without exception, during my fieldwork visits from 2003 to 2007, Tibetan monks in temporary residence in Kushinagar were loath to wear their robes. Although they wear robes while in residence at other Tibetan monasteries in India, in and out of the monastery compound in Kushinagar the monks wore lay clothes—usually jogging suits. My monastic informants felt better without them in Kushinagar. According to one monk, he believed that he would be harassed by the young Uttar Pradeshi men if he were to wear robes and that he was safer in "normal clothes." I asked whether the forthcoming Maitreya Project had affected the way that local people saw them, and my monastic informants said that while most local people did not connect the project with their monastery in particular, their Tibetanness had become more conspicuous and notorious. In point of fact, local Kushinagaris protesting against Maitreya Project 2.0 actually were not sure how much to blame Namgyal, and some did mistakenly think that the Tibetan monks in Kushinagar were directly complicit in the plan.

The majority of the land being acquired for Maitreya Project 2.0 was happening outside of Kushinagar proper, in the villages of Greater Kushinagar, so the Maitreya Project's slated land grab was far from the madding crowds hopping on and off buses at the Mahaparinirvana Temple. Strangely enough, very few pilgrims had any idea that there was a battle underway over the fate of Maitreya Project 2.0. Even heritage Tibetan Buddhists were generally ignorant of the situation. The heritage Tibetan monastics and laity whom I interviewed in Kushinagar, Bodh Gaya, and Dharamsala had all heard about the project, and while they tended to support it in theory, they had nothing to do with the planning or fundraising. Nor did they know much, if anything, about the local protests. It was clear to them that the Maitreya Project was an FPMT project, not a heritage Tibetan Buddhist project being forwarded by ethnic Tibetan refugees.

Even the Namgyal Monastery monks in Kushinagar did not understand the stakes, or the situation, from the perspective of anti–Maitreya Project activists. As I mentioned, the monks did not get out much, and as short-term temporary residents, they knew little about the politics and issues facing Greater Kushinagar. In a stunning understatement, a monk stationed at the

Namgyal Monastery in Kushinagar asked of the Maitreya Project, "It's not popular, right?" This query was posed just after I had returned from a day of raucous protests in front of the district magistrate's office (an hour away from Kushinagar). I told them the story, and they shrugged, saying that it had nothing to do with them.

The Tibetan monks were technically correct: Namgyal and FPMT are different institutions. Yet despite the fact that ethnic Tibetans have very little to do with FPMT's MPI project, I worried that if the land acquisition proposed for Maitreya Project 2.0 went forward, there would be additional trouble between ethnic Tibetans and dispossessed Indian farmers. The farmer-activists were not inclined to believe that Kushinagar was a place underfrequented and ignored by Tibetans, as the Thais and others seemed to believe. Some of my local Kushinagari informants mistakenly believed that Tibetan refugees had designs on their land and job opportunities. "[Tibetans] will swarm here, and take over Kushinagar," said one farmer-activist. "But we won't leave without a fight."

Kushinagar may seem like a modest collection of half-occupied monasteries in a sleepy Buddhist pilgrimage town to most visitors, but it is a rich translocal space of abundant "crossings" and "dwellings" (Tweed 2006). In this chapter I have examined the contours of Buddhist life at this space of Buddhism's most celebrated death and how this conglomeration of Buddhist visitors from disparate communities has become enmeshed with local Kushinagari communities in various ways. I traced the contours of Kushinagar in broad strokes in this chapter by asking, "What, and who, is Kushinagar?" In order to examine the interacting communities of Kushinagar, I categorize people roughly along a spectrum of those least to most tied (or committed) to the fate of the town: pilgrims, short-term and recurrent temporary visitors, transplants, and locals. I have introduced the locality here to set the stage for exploring the specific plight of local farmers fighting the Maitreya Project.

I have described how the pilgrimage industry is woven into the larger social fabric of the town and its environs, and perhaps how Buddhist tourism obfuscates the multireligious nature of Greater Kushinagar.[15] The refashioning of Kushinagar as a Buddhist place, especially in MPI's imaginary, echoes the hyperreal urban landscape of Kuala Lumpur, which has increasingly developing a modern Islamic aesthetic that falsifies and pretends to historical continuity (Willford 2006). This chapter introduced today's Kushinagaris as they face the new challenges of global tourism and the socioeconomic realities it brings, and as aspects of memory, mythology, and creativity negotiate for inclusion within the cultural milieu of old and new Buddhist and Hindu identities. Given its close kinship with FPMT's Gelugpa Tibetan Buddhism, I paid particular attention to the sole Tibetan Buddhist monastery in Kushinagar. The concern of local Indians about the Maitreya Project 2.0 plan lightly affected Buddhist monasteries in Kushinagar across the board, but the Tibetan *gompa* was especially scrutinized.

I mapped the social and cultural landscape of Greater Kushinagar atop its better-known sacred spaces. In sum, my research in Kushinagar, and the structure of this chapter, was akin to doing a series of wider and wider circumambulations around the sacred sites. I began by winding tight circles around Kushinagar's famed *stupas* and their sacroscapes, and then began making larger circles through the town seeking the outer edges of its socioeconomic milieu. By doing so, I discovered the ways in which the sacred spaces of Kushinagar proper extend outward to impact a Greater Kushinagar that largely remains outside the view of the average pilgrim.

✹ CHAPTER 7

Steadfastness / *ADITTHANA*

Indian Farmers Resist the Buddha of Love

Sandwiched between site visits to Kushinagar in 2006, during a visit to Delhi I arranged to meet Rina, a former university instructor of mine from several years before.[1] Rina was an Indian FPMTer, a nonheritage devotee of Lama Zopa Rinpoche, as well as an MPI trustee. We had tea and biscuits at her home and caught up with one another. We discussed her current classes and the department, and I started telling her about my research in Kushinagar. Since so few FPMTers at the time knew about the protests in Kushinagar, I figured that it was unlikely that Rina had heard about the controversy. I hoped that once I told her about the morass in Kushinagar she could help spread the word in FPMT and MPI circles. I was hoping she would be an ally. But when I told Rina about the anti–Maitreya Project protests, she reacted defensively.

Although I had spent the last several months watching the anxieties about the statue project haunt the local community there, Rina did not want to believe that FPMT had so thoroughly bungled its local relations in Kushinagar. The bureaucratic stasis, lack of construction, and absence of FPMTers in Kushinagar led her to insist over and over, like a broken record, that "nothing has happened in Kushinagar." I gave her facts and figures, and I shared stories about the farmer-activists and their resolute resistance in the face of the giant statue project.

"Nothing is happening there!" she insisted. I flatly disagreed. In fact, I told her that there was a great deal happening in Kushinagar as a direct result of the Maitreya Project. There was, I told her, a deep and frenetic current of mobilization and activism in Kushinagar, and some 95 percent of it was directed at derailing the Maitreya Project completely. Isn't a social movement directed against MPI something very significant and unfortunate? Surely outrage and fear aren't nothing, I pressed.

Rina tried to persuade me that there was no reason to be studying the Maitreya Project in Kushinagar at all. She said that Kushinagar was a nonissue for FPMT until the land acquisition. Despite her reticence, I asked her to tell other MPI trustees what I was telling her; I truly believed that MPI's relationships in Kushinagar could be fixed, but it would require a radical course correction. Rina shut down. I could tell she regretted inviting me to her home. When there was a natural break in the conversation, we quickly went through the motions of a polite farewell. Rina and I parted ways that day with a palpable sense that we had each disappointed one another in surprising ways. I never saw her again.

In this chapter, I share some of what I shared with Rina that day in Delhi. I detail the resistance movement that bubbled up in direct antagonism to MPI's statue plan. Also, I explain why Kushinagar's famers were cynical about MPI's claims that the statue project would bring them great benefits and what steps they took to keep the state government from acquiring their lands for the Maitreya Project.

In 2001, farmers from seven villages surrounding Kushinagar began hearing about the Maitreya Project and reading about it in local Hindi-medium periodicals. They learned that, according to the preliminary plans, the Maitreya Project land acquisition would likely divest many of them of their lands and livelihood. The initial proposed land acquisition for Maitreya Project 2.0 in Kushinagar would have ceded over 750 acres (a figure later decreased to 661 acres) to the Maitreya Project in perpetuity. The problem, from the local farming families' perspective, was not with the statue plan itself, but with the "land grab." Most farmers did not want to lose any of their land, but to add insult to injury, the proposed financial terms of land acquisition were extremely unsatisfactory to the large majority of the affected villagers. As a result of the state's effort to co-opt large tracts of land for the Buddhist project, the farmers of Greater Kushinagar engaged in more than a decade of agitations against the MPI statue.

This chapter will examine the Kushinagar controversy in detail, from the perspectives of various stakeholders. It will tell the story of the turmoil that the prelife of the statue caused in Kushinagar for over a decade, as well as the rifts it caused between the statue's supporters and detractors in the region. In this chapter, I will show that, indeed, something was very definitely happening in Kushinagar.

The Land Acquisition

When the Dalai Lama chose Kushinagar for the Maitreya Project over and above other statue relocation options,[2] MPI began finalizing their efforts to move their flagship statue project out of Bihar and over to Uttar Pradesh. The chief minister of Uttar Pradesh gave approval for Kushinagar to be the new location for the project in January 2002 ("Maitreya Project, Kushinagar" 2004). The state government then proceeded to hammer out plans and procedures with MPI, leading up to the signing of the MoU by representatives of the Maitreya Project Trust and the state government's Department of Culture in May 2003 ("Akhilesh Yadav to Lay Foundation" 2013; "Memorandum of Understanding" 2003).

The Maitreya Project statue plan was considered a future boon for Uttar Pradeshi tourism by the state government, so it planned to lease the land to the Maitreya Project for just one single Indian rupee in perpetuity ("Memorandum of Understanding" 2003). The MoU also details the fact that the Maitreya Project would be exempt from taxes, charges, duties, and fees ("Memorandum of Understanding" 2003, 13).

The land would be seized under the Land Acquisition Act (LAA) of 1894 that had been instituted by the British colonial government to forcibly acquire land for the purpose of railway construction.[3] Land acquisition in India is done in stages, but one hopes that the first stage will grant favorable provisional rates of compensation with the understanding that final rates may be slightly adjusted. But in Kushinagar, when the provisional rates of compensation were publicized, many of the farmers in the affected villages were utterly distraught. Although the published rates they found so outrageously low were still preliminary, the farmers had no reason to believe that they would be adequately adjusted upward in the future. The affected farmers in Greater Kushinagar were slated to lose some or all of their family plots to the Uttar Pradeshi state government, which planned to seize it on behalf of the Maitreya Project.

After discovering the Maitreya Project and Uttar Pradesh's plans for the Kushinagar area, the farmers who stood to lose their land were so incensed that they soon established an anti–Maitreya Project group called the Bhoomi Bachao Sangharsh Samiti (BBSS), which can be translated as the Council for the Struggle to Save the Land, or more simply, the Save the Land Association.

BBSS and its supporters immediately undertook several courses of action at once: they prevailed on the local district magistrate for help; they began consulting with social workers and lawyers in the community to see what their rights and options were on the matter; and they began holding local protests to make their views clear. Over the next few years, BBSS and its associates filed several lawsuits against aspects of the project, and while I was in the field, my informants hoped that ultimately the lawsuits would succeed in stopping the Maitreya Project from moving forward.[4] The farmers' perspectives on the matter were captured in this devastating headline from a local newspaper: "Government Wants to Erect Palace on the Fertile Land of the Poor" (2006).

The exact number of affected people from the seven targeted villages is itself a source of controversy: the public relations officer of MPI wrote that about fifty families would be displaced and that 1,100 plots were to be acquired (Gatter 2007b); a Maitreya Project representative told me during an interview that "1,100 families would be affected"; a local newspaper wrote that "1,400 families" would be directly affected ("Starvation Deaths of the Poor" 2006); another local newspaper wrote that the families and homes of

FIGURE 12. Protestors listen to speeches at a BBSS-organized anti-MPI rally in 2006. Photo by the author.

almost 1,400 farmers would be negatively impacted ("Fast Continues" 2007); in their speeches and interviews, the BBSS often estimated that two thousand families would be negatively impacted; during our interview, a bureaucrat directly in charge of the land acquisition told me that "three thousand families" would be affected (that is, he said, "three thousand households," and that "three thousand separate checks" would be cut). Freelance journalist Daniel Pepper did some independent research on the Maitreya Project in 2007 and published several articles that quoted the land acquisition officer in Deoria saying that "between 15,000 and 20,000 people will be displaced in the process" (Pepper 2007a, 2007b).[5]

According to my informants in Kushinagar, the affected farmers were worried and aggrieved about the plan from the very outset. The farmers generally focused on rallying against those who were most accessible: their local politicians and bureaucrats. Soon after the BBSS formed, they began leading protests against the bureaucrats responsible for developing the area with the Maitreya Project, especially targeting the district magistrates overseeing these efforts.

The essential issue for the farmers railing against the project is loss of land, livelihood, homes, and community. To most of my informants these losses

FIGURE 13.   A Kushinagar woman speaks against the Maitreya Project at BBSS rally.
Photo by the author.

were absolutely unacceptable financially, socially, culturally, and emotionally. Many farmers talked about how "land is mother," saying further that many of them have a deep connection to their particular plot of earth. They know their land, its temperament, its history, tricks for irrigation, its potential with various crops, and its shortcomings with others. In most cases, the land has been handed down for generations.[6] In these terms, the land owned by a particular family is not necessary an easily alienable object, even if it could have been replaced down to the precise acre, which it could not. In 2006, my BBSS informants noted that even if they were being offered reasonable compensation, land is not a renewable resource—land is finite in a particular locality. Even if farmers lost only their farmland, it would be nearly impossible to stay in their homes and buy replacement land. Since they would have to move to buy new land somewhere, they would effectively lose the investment of their homes, but go without compensation for the buildings.

One of the farmers asked despairingly, "Who would want to buy a home in such a place?" He referred to the fact that it was now perceived as a place devoid of prospects and under threat of future forcible acquisition. Another informant whose family's land was slated to be taken for Maitreya Project 2.0 explained that it was sinister that they were not taking all the houses—for most people, it was just the land. He said something to the effect of, "What good is a house with no more land nearby? It's useless. But they can say they did not displace us. They are cunning. They know that we will have to leave, but they won't even have to help us."

Finally, my BBSS informants all impressed on me over and over the fact that such a move would mean the deprivation of their tightly-knit communities, neighborhoods, and extended family networks. The plan to acquire land did not take into account the innumerable social costs of resettlement and starting over again in a distant locale amid strangers. These social considerations are among the strongest reasons that many of my local informants said that they would defend their property and livelihoods "to the death."

Even the relatively successful families that have stopped farming themselves because their primary income comes from the profits of a shop in town often keep their farmland and hire laborers to farm it; to these businessmen-landowners the land is considered an important investment and a supplemental source of income, and to the laborers it is their primary source of income. Land is clearly very significant in Kushinagar, even to those who no longer personally farm it.

Within the affected villages, 100 percent of the people I interviewed said that the provisional compensation was abominably low. The rates of compensation vary according to several factors, including the distance from the town of Kasia, its arability, and its accessibility to the main roads. The provisional values set by the government were between 10 percent and 50 percent of what the farmers themselves said their land was worth on the open market (if they were selling, which the large majority still resist for the reasons outlined above). The lion's share of my farming informants told me that they were being offered approximately 10 percent of their land's value. In addition to collecting the farmers' narratives about land rates, I independently confirmed BBSS's assertions about low compensation by interviewing other locals who had nothing to gain or lose personally; I checked into land rates by talking to Kushinagaris shopping for land in the area, and also by discussing the rates with the nonlandholding townspeople who wanted the Maitreya Project statue to come to the area. By triangulating data, I came to the conclusion that the farmers were indeed fighting against insufficient provisional compensation packages, and thus had every reason to protest for outcomes they could live with.

Usually in an interview, a person (or a family) would say that they were being offered a low rate of compensation, and then quickly acknowledge that they would not want to sell even if the rate was higher. For example, one woman, a teacher whose family would lose land to the MPI plan, said, "The value of the land is not correct. It [should be] more than one *lakh* [100,000 rupees] per *katha*,[7] but they are giving less than forty thousand [rupees] per *katha*. Or even six thousand [rupees] per *katha* sometimes! It is too low. We are not going to give the land. The government is giving unreasonable rates, but even if they give two *lakhs* per *katha*, then it would be a big problem and we wouldn't sell it." Her friend, another female teacher at a small private nonprofit school, told me, "I am ready to give you five acres of land, but first you give me five acres of land in the USA. Just give me five *katha* of land in your country. Foreigners don't understand. They think we are crazy, but if we take their land to build a statue of Hanuman in their country, then they will think we are crazy." The women both explained to me that the economic situation of their families would collapse if the land acquisition moved forward.

Furthermore, the BBSS and its members had no faith that the government was even capable of figuring out the proper market values, since the rates were being determined in part by the registered values reported by buyers and sellers to the local government in the past decade or so. Farmers freely acknowledged the open secret that everyone claims to pay far less than they actually do, in order to avoid high taxes (stamp duty) on their property transfers. This common practice, and its problematic effects on land compensation pricing, was never acknowledged publicly by the government; however, in an interview, the bureaucrats in the Land Acquisition Office (LAO) in Deoria conceded that it was normative practice among farmers to register at low rates and then pay the rest under the table. The LAO officers emphasized that the practice was illegal, so the unintended consequences being felt by the Kushinagari farmers now were not the problem of the state government; he said, that the effects were the fruits of their bad deeds come back to haunt them as *karma*.

National activists working against the LAA, such as members of a nonprofit called the National Alliance of People's Movements (NAPM), say that political use of the LAA has disenfranchised farmers by eminent domain in many Indian states. An economics professor in Delhi noted of land acquisitions in general:

> The record of state governments is dismal when it comes to fixing and updating the circle rates for land. . . . Since the demand for land is growing while the supply remains fixed, an average of the past prices will be less than the current market price. Also, in order to save on stamp duty, prices quoted in sale deeds are much lower than actual payments. This means that the very basis of determining compensation is faulty. What is just compensation has been debated for long. A just compensation should not leave the owners poorer than they would be in the absence of acquisition. (Singh 2007)

The scholarship on the troubling effects of displacing and disenfranchising the poor in order to pursue development options has been well argued elsewhere, especially in regards to the antagonism of scholars and activists regarding the paltry resettlement and rehabilitation packages offered to those affected by the Narmada River Dam project (D'Souza 2002; as well as the dozens of contributors in the two volumes edited by Dreze, Samson, and Singh in 1997 and Mohan Mathur and Marsden in 1998, respectively).

The fact that the government utilized misleading compensation rate figures on past property transfer registrations, in tandem with their concerns that a former district magistrate had reputedly twisted reports in order to make arable land seem barren, led the farmers to argue that the government had no idea what the real market value of land actually was in the area. The provisional values were to be followed by provisional payouts, and then, after the transfer was complete, the matter would be looked into once more by bureaucrats in Lucknow to see if there was a final extra payment needed in order to reach the appropriate government-determined final value. Farmers in Kushinagar, not unlike those fighting land acquisitions elsewhere, had zero confidence that they would be any more satisfied with future settlements than they were with the provisional settlements. Acknowledging the difficulties faced by other farmers protesting the Narmada Dam project and corporate projects in Bengal, BBSS farmers told me that they too would not concede without a fight, and indeed they aggressively resist the plan.

Value, of course, is notoriously controversial. Social scientists have long discussed the intractable nature of value, how it is a promiscuous notion, one that shifts according to cultural, economic, temporal, and other factors (e.g., Appadurai 1986; Maurer 2003; Myers 2001). For my informants, land is not just commodity, but also "mother." Land for some informants transcends livelihood as both kin and goddess. Market value is just one way of relating to their parcels of land, which is why many farmers insist that even if the compensation was fair, they would never consider selling. The slippery notion of value makes it easy for proponents of the Maitreya Project in FPMT to argue that Indian farmers are being greedy and hoping to get rich quick. Furthermore, they argue that the value is being set by the government, so the Maitreya Project has no reason to involve itself in the messy material matters of remuneration, since it is all a matter of Uttar Pradeshi policy and law.

When the land acquisition process technically progressed in earnest in 2005,[8] only a few dozen households of the more than a thousand affected would approve the initial rates of compensation; those who quickly capitulated were among the few for whom the rates for their portions of the land, which may have unarable (for example, waterlogged or flood-prone), may have been perceived as actually quite decent.[9] According to the BBSS, these few dozen households sold their land to the government quickly, despite the fact that most of their comrades tried to convince them to stand with the majority against the land acquisition.

The large majority did not accept forced LAA payments for the purchase of their land and homes. The actual physical, large-scale transfer of land to the government did not actually happen in 2005, as farmers simply refused en masse to sign over their land because the compensation rates were insufficient. They stayed put and defied the government to remove them. The local media clarified that compensation rates were the main cause of farmer distress, writing, "Clouds are again surrounding the efforts for bringing into effect the proposed Maitreya Project for Kushinagar due to the protests of the farmers. The farmers are maintaining that inappropriate value has been fixed for the land which was sustaining them. They are saying that now they will neither take the compensation nor give their land at any cost" ("Farmers Warn of Agitation" 2006).

Abhishek, a teacher at the Maitreya Project school in Bodh Gaya, originally hails from the Kushinagar area. As an Indian man with professional and social connections to MPI, he was diplomatic about the project but un-yielding in his criticism of how the land acquisition was unfolding. His main admonition regarding the value of land was that locals have no reason to trust that promised rates of compensation, whether low or not, whether pre-liminary or final, would be honored. I did not record this conversation with Abhishek, which took place in Bodh Gaya after an English-Hindi language exchange session, but I paraphrased it in my field notes (that I wrote down right afterward) this way:

> He told me, "Let's say I promise you one hundred rupees, but I say, just take ten now. Later I may get nothing. This has happened so many times, even here in Bodh Gaya. People know not to trust the govern-ment. To them land is everything. They may be illiterate, but they know that they live through the land and without it they have nothing. They are not stupid, just uneducated. A village was moved when they found some [old Buddhist] statue, and people were not given what they were promised. The people in Kushinagar are not being treated fairly."

I interviewed several dozen people in the Greater Kushinagar area, and while there were different opinions about MPI and the statue, I never talked to one local person (aside from regional and local bureaucrats) who believed that the farmers were being compensated appropriately.

If the compensation had been higher, would more farmers have agreed that the Maitreya Project would have helped the region's economic situation down the line? Perhaps some would have been more agreeable in that case, but even these farmers were not at all convinced that the Maitreya Project would improve their family's socioeconomic situation, even if they could somehow subsist and manage from the moment their land was seized to the grand opening of the statue complex many years later. Farmers also noted that under normal conditions it would be safe to assume that the market value of land will go up over time, so retaining their land would be a stable source of wealth ("like gold jewelry"); this fact made the prospect of relin-quishment that much harder to accept.

Despite the fact that my farming informants feared moving, some said that they feared the police and army more. If the compensation packages had been generous, some informants told me that they would still be frustrated and angry but would take the money anyway and try to do the best they could to resettle amicably. Most farmers would not have admitted to this in public. Still, in private some BBSSers acknowledged that many of their most stalwart comrades would probably assent to the acquisition if the price was

fair and there was no other option. One farmer, echoing many other interviewees, said, "What can I do? If the compensation was right, then I would
be a fool to fight the police." Then he told me, with equal parts bravado and
exhaustion, that since the proposed compensation was insulting, he would
be forced to fight for his land at any cost.

Upending Kushinagar's Future

In the Kushinagar area, the only visible signs of Maitreya Project 2.0 in 2006
were the anti–Maitreya Project slogans written as graffiti on building walls.
Otherwise, the farmers continued to farm, their children trudged back and
forth to school in their uniforms, and people celebrated holidays in much the
same ways they always had. Life did go on in the villages affected by the MPI
plan, but it was not all business as usual. It was not just that busy farmers had
to suddenly find the time in their schedules to organize and attend a series
of protests and agitations; the fear of forcible acquisition traumatized the
Kushinagar-area farmers in some ways for many years. The Maitreya Project
plan added another layer of precarity to lives already permeated with the
ever-present insecurity of potential rainfall, climate, and other production
issues, and of course, fluctuating crop prices.

Due to the cloud of uncertainty that seemed stalled over their heads, some
of my informants deferred repairs to their homes, put off building sheds, or
delayed purchasing needed equipment. Some farming families deferred their
children's weddings or cancelled plans for pilgrimage or family travels. Even
worse, I learned of several instances in which girl children were pulled out
of school and their marriages arranged sooner than their families would have
done otherwise, due in large part to the economic uncertainty gripping the
region. Although BBSS protests successfully paralyzed the efforts to co-opt
land for the statue, the plan lay in wait, in limbo, haunting the Kushinagari
people for nearly a decade.

Several farmers told me that if jobs had been promised to locals in relation to the statue, then they might have exchanged a bad deal on land for a
good work opportunity. This was a point that the BBSS had highlighted in
their dissent: they had asked the government officials to make a provision
that each family losing land would be given a job in the government or at the
Maitreya statue park, but this request was refused. According to two succes-
sive district magistrates and Lucknowi bureaucrats, the notion that affected
farmers would be guaranteed new jobs was never seriously entertained by
the government. A BBSS member told me that he had heard that any new

jobs would be given instead to ethnic Tibetans. This was a prevalent rumor in the trenches of the anti–Maitreya Project resistance:

> RAKESH: We heard that five thousand Tibetans will get Indian citizenship from this Maitreya Project.
> JESSICA: But what does that have to do with the statue?
> RAKESH: In 2001, the Maitreya Project came, and six years has been spent on discussion. The hidden aspect is that the Maitreya Project is asking for five thousand . . . citizenships. It is a secret discussion, a top secret matter. They will come to take care of the Maitreya Project.

Many of the BBSS activists believe that the MPI negotiated to have most of the jobs created by their giant statue complex in Kushinagar given to ethnic Tibetans instead of being granted to local Indians. I had not heard a word about Tibetan citizenship or Tibetan jobs from FPMTers, planners, or bureaucrats, so I told my informants that I highly doubted if there was any veracity to the hearsay.[10] The notion that Kushinagar would soon be overrun with Tibetan refugees hired to care for the giant statue was a common belief shared among many local Indian villagers.

The large majority of the Kushinagaris are Hindus, and from their perspective the Maitreya statue is not an idol of a foreign god. As I have mentioned before, the widespread belief in contemporary Hinduism is that the Buddha, or Buddha Bhagwan, is an avatar of Vishnu, a very significant, beloved Hindu deity. The fact that Buddhists do not concur on this theological point is irrelevant to local Hindus, as is the fact that this statue would not be a Shakyamuni Buddha statue, but rather a Maitreya Buddha one. That is, locally the giant statue was seen as a foreign project, but not as a project building a foreign deity.

The religiously motivated opposition by a Hindu priest against the Maitreya Project only came about because a large Hindu temple in the area would lose some of the land that it owned to the Maitreya Project plan:

> The Radha-Krishna Temple will be adversely affected by the Maitreya Project. This is the opinion of the BBSS, who is on the sixteenth day of their hunger strike. The Mahant Shiv Sharan of the Radha-Krishna Temple was speaking at the strike. He said that the Radha-Krishna Temple was losing a lot of arable land. God would not be looked after properly, and a lot of people would be left shelterless. With this plan, the agricultural land would be halted and many families will be

displaced. For this reason the plan should be moved somewhere else. ("Better Tourist Facilities" 2007).

While Buddha Bhagwan was not anyone's avowed enemy, my informants did say that they saw no need for another statue to be built when there were already so many holy sites in the area. The small Muslim community was working tirelessly with their Hindu neighbors against the Maitreya Project, which they also saw as a socioeconomic fight rather than a religious battle. It was not uncommon for a farmer to quip that the Buddha himself would certainly stand against the Maitreya Project for all of the suffering that it had already caused, and would yet cause.

Even some transplanted foreign Buddhists living in Kushinagar believed that Buddha would be antagonistic to MPI's plans. Many local Hindi-medium newspapers carried the story of how a Burmese abbot and several of his monks came to sit in support of the protestors in February 2007,[11] but only one local article noted that many of the Buddhist monks of the area were ambivalent about the costs and benefits of the project ("Maitreya Project: Chasm in the Buddhist Monk Ranks" 2007). My local informants felt that Buddha was in their corner, even if his transnational FPMT devotees were not.

Given the uptick in *Hindutva* (Hindu nationalist) sentiment in Uttar Pradesh (and India) in recent years, it is worth noting that there was little religious violence (communalism) in evidence in Greater Kushinagar during this period, although there have been flare ups in the Kushinagar district in recent years.[12] The lines between support and antagonism for the project did not fall neatly along religious lines: locals based their feelings about the statue on socioeconomic considerations, not religious ones. The BBSS resistance was made up of religious groups throughout the villages; I met Hindus, Muslims, and Sikhs staunchly allied against the project.

Notably, even the self-avowed Marxists, of which there are many in India, declined to demonize the religious aspects of the project. One Marxist gentleman noted the following at a rally: "We have been fighting. These leaders [politicians] are not good. . . . We will cancel this project. Until then we will fight, until we win. . . . This is nonviolent. We accept Buddha, but we will protest the Maitreya Project. They are robbing us. This is wrong." This speaker, railing against the Maitreya Project in 2006 in front of some two hundred farmers, eloquently argued that neither the Buddha nor Buddhists are the real problem; rather it was the economic robbery under the guise of development that they must fight against. In India, Marxism and religion can rest comfortably together, and indeed there were several very passionate Marxists involved in the BBSS protests for purely economic reasons.

Many Kushinagaris expressed anxiety about the socioeconomic effects on Kushinagar overall, as well as whether the region would gentrify as a result. This is to say that many Kushinagaris not only worried about their own financial situation but felt that the town would change in ways that would further improve conditions for some at the expense of others. For example, many farmers worried that new pollution restrictions—a wide circumference around the statue within which industry would be banned—would actually deter the kind of local development that they relied on. Some BBSS activists noted that small brick-making businesses, which spew smoke, would be pushed many kilometers away in order to keep the statue pristine. As potential workers and consumers of these factories, farmers were opposed to the strict pollution regulations that would accompany the Maitreya Project, because this would hurt the local economy, especially the smallest businesses and smallest farmers. They felt that Indians and Indian businesses would be pushed further and further away from their ancestral lands and that any benefits would accrue to others, to the wealthy, to the foreigners. Although farmers and social workers in the BBSS acknowledged the fact that some environmental regulations could benefit the air quality, they worried that it would come at the expense of the economic welfare of the very poor.

When I discussed the controversy with my FPMT informants, occasionally someone would suggest to me that the farmers were too traditional and provincial to see the larger economic benefits of MPI's plan. One of my FPMT informants said something to the effect of, "They are so ignorant that they are holding back the only thing that could save their kids from similar poverty." Other FPMTers I talked to also seemed to assume that farmers just myopically wanted their children to stay farmers. However, my farming informants were not romantic about their livelihoods, so it would be wrong to suggest that they saw their agricultural world as a bucolic paradise that they wished to preserve indefinitely. In antistatue speeches and interviews in 2007, farmers consistently indicated that they wanted better lives for themselves and their families. Almost every farmer I interviewed noted that they wanted their children to have options—in government, running a business, or working in large industrial sectors, or in agriculture. While Kushinagari farmers did not necessarily want their children to be farmers, they acknowledged both that maintaining the family farm was a fine, probable future for many of their children and that their family farms were certainly necessary in order to nurture and enable other possible futures. In other words, they felt that for the time being agriculture was the one stable, known economic entity, and if they were suddenly stripped of land with inadequate compensation, then their current livelihoods, and their dreams for the future, would be disastrously undermined. The planned land acquisition was viewed by locals as an endeavor that would foist destabilization, upheaval, and economic hardship on them and make better futures for their progeny increasingly untenable.

Kisan Ekta, Zindabad! Anger, Actions, and Threats

The farmers in Kushinagar were very angry, and they were fearful for what the future held for them, so they threw everything they had into stopping the Maitreya Project 2.0 statue plans. There were countless smaller protests in the affected villages, as well as organizational meetings, but there were dozens of major regional actions as well. In 2002, for example, the farmers blocked a major highway, the first of several times: "Scores of farmers blocked the national highway under a scorching sun in opposition to the acquisition of their lands by the state government for the Maitreya Project" ("Roads Blocked" 2002). I went to many protests, often chanting with them, "Kisan ekta, zindabad!," which is a punchy affirmation of farmers' solidarity.

BBSS arranged for the *tehsil* (Hindi: local government administrative unit) office and other municipal offices to be periodically encircled, an Indian protest tactic known as *gherao*-ing (Hindi: besiege). Farmers would surround the *tehsil* office to insist that local administrators hear their demands, which were relayed in writing and through the multiplicity of fiery speeches. For example, in 2004, a local Hindi newspaper reported: "Almost one thousand men and women surrounded the Kasia *Tehsil* office and chanted slogans on the 9th of September to stop the process of acquisition . . . of farming land, which was started by the administration in the name of development of this area by erecting a five-hundred-feet high idol of Lord Buddha" ("Demonstration and *Tehsil* Surrounded" 2004).

Another common resistance tactic was hunger strikes. Occasionally, this was one person, but more often it involved a group of people taking nothing but water. Hunger strikes sometimes took the form of fasting relays, in which multiple persons would take turns refusing food for shorter periods within a long stretch of days or weeks. This rotating tactic makes sense given that many of the strikers were active farmers (although some were members of farming families who themselves had other jobs) in an impoverished area who still needed to maintain enough strength to labor in their fields. The effect of the fasting relay is that the suffering (weakening, weight loss, and hunger) was shared by the community in a way that was a very strong statement of resistance but did not permit any one protestor to fully wither away for lack of sustenance.

The bulk of BBSS work and discourse was nonviolent agitation, but, while in the field, I did hear violence threatened time and time again from both the leadership and the rank and file of the anti–Maitreya Project movement. I cannot know for sure, but I do not believe that the threat of violence was an entirely empty one. There was a series of minor altercations and threats, and if the forcible land acquisition had proceeded as planned, then the environment of anxiety would have been primed to make more intense violence a likelihood.

Babar Singh once admitted to me that he would be attacked by villagers if he came to Kushinagar without his armed guards. (Even with his guards, in general, he stayed out of the Kushinagar vicinity.) Bureaucrats on business, and even the occasional tourists who strayed outside of the Buddhist tourist zone and onto the contested land, have been targeted as well. An informant narrated this story to me:

> One day Brahma Shankar Tripathi and some other gazetted officers, the farmers surrounded them for three hours. There were five thousand people and they said, "if you go anywhere we'll kill you." The district magistrate [one of the officers who was surrounded] wrote a letter to the governor and the Department of Tourism and Culture that concerned the matter. Ultimately, the district magistrate sent the letter and then the farmers released them. That district magistrate was then transferred—it was [Manav Khan]—he was the one who wrote the letter that supported the farmers, so then he was transferred. This place, Siswa Chowk, they kidnapped them here. The farmers were going to set fire to the car. They had already snatched the mobile phone from the officers. I controlled the people and told them to calm down. Otherwise, the ladies they had put the wood under the car to burn the car. They were so angry they would have done violence. There were five thousand people there. They would have killed people. I said to the district magistrate that the farmers don't know who you are; they think you are with the Maitreya Project, so they want to kill you.

"Were they bluffing?" various FPMTers have asked me, in various ways, when I retell this story. I still do not know—they certainly seemed deadly serious to me.

An altogether different altercation was covered in the local Hindi media under the heading, "Agitated Villagers Keep District Officer Captive for Two Hours": "Due to the negligence of an administrative officer of the district, agitated farmers kept the district officer captive for almost two hours. It was only coincidental that nothing untoward happened. Later the district officer and other officials were able to leave after appropriate assurance was given by them at the behest of some knowledgeable people" (2002). At their protests, it was not uncommon to see effigies of the politicians who supported MPI publicly burned. For example, in 2006 and 2007, farmers did full funeral processions, rites, and burning of the effigy of Chief Minister Mulayam Singh Yadav. In 2004, the farmers burned an effigy of their member of the legislative assembly (MLA), Tripathi ("Farmers Demonstrate against Maitreya" 2004).

The farmers also threatened Buddhists in the area in a direct and targeted way. For example, one of the local Buddhist abbots was threatened by a group of farmers, so in order to calm the situation he promised to join them in their hunger strike. He said, "It's a bad feeling. Some villagers came here to beat me." The abbot noted later in an interview that this was no ideological hardship, since a few dozen acres that belonged to his own monastery were being forcibly acquired at a very low price for the Maitreya Project. He did oppose the low rate of compensation, but he wished that he had not felt compelled to protest against the statue by threat of violence, since he noted that he was not explicitly antagonistic to the project itself. This abbot privately hoped the statue would be built, but in a downsized version that would not require forcible land acquisitions. He also predicted actual violence if the land was forcibly acquired: "If the project is passed then something terrible will happen. Something very bad." "You mean, something violent," I probed. "Yes, violence. The word *maitri* means friendship and love. If you work with love then you can achieve good things, but without it, what can you expect?" The local newspapers reported that some Buddhists were standing in solidarity with the hunger strike, but none of them noted that some participation had been in part due to antagonistic duress.

The draft MoU, especially, makes it clear that there was great concern about the possibility of local retaliation, as it asks specifically for government assistance in securing the lands and protection for Maitreya Project staff against any local violence in the wake of the acquisition ("Memorandum of Understanding Draft" 2002). The draft language states, "During the acquisition process when some disturbances may arise, the Government agrees to provide armed police personnel to accompany MPT [Maitreya Project Trust] Staff and Consultants during this sensitive phase." A bureaucrat in the Department of Culture explained to me that the phrase was pulled from the final language because the preceding phrase, which was retained, implicitly promised such protection for the site and the personnel at all phases from acquisition onward. "It did not look nice," he wryly noted of the deleted language. The final draft also retained language obligating the government to set up a police outpost at the site during preconstruction and construction phases. This aspect of the MoU exposes the fact that even at the earliest planning stages both the government and the Maitreya Project anticipated the possibility of resistance, decided to meet it with a police presence, and proceeded apace anyway.

Finally, even as a vocal supporter of the farmers' rights against the acquisition, I was personally threatened many times by farmers and villagers who did not initially (or in the case of some, ever) trust me, despite my assurances and the legitimatizing company of BBSS leaders. Especially at the beginning of my research in Kushinagar, it was not uncommon for some of the children in Anirudhwa village to throw stones or other things at me when I bicycled past them; usually, they would scream things in Hindi: "No Maitreya!" or "Go away!" It was not unreasonable of them to think that a young American woman interviewing people about the Maitreya Project could actually be doing so on behalf of the latter. Since there were many thousands of people affected, most of whom had to work all day, there were many people who did not see me at protests and did not know that my presence had been accepted by BBSS leadership. Even among those who did, some just did not believe my explanation about why I was in Kushinagar nor my assertions of support for their cause. I think some questioned why an American would come across the world to research their plight.[13] I do not blame some of the more cynical farmers for wondering if I was secretly an agent of their enemies.

While doing a survey about the land acquisition in 2006, in one hamlet, my translator and I sat down to do interviews, but we were chased away by an angry group of women who believed that I was a Maitreya Project staffer. Usually people who doubted my motivations would just refuse to cooperate. Sometimes I was on the receiving end of dirty looks, and very occasionally I was threatened as I moved through the MPI-affected *gaons*, with angry people telling me that I would be attacked or killed if I returned to their hamlet. I believe that by the end of my trips to Kushinagar most of the villagers felt that I was harmless at least, or an advocate at best, but even then there were still some people who did not trust me. For example, even during a stay in Kushinagar in 2007, late in my Indian fieldwork period, I met a woman who grabbed at my clothes, sank to the ground, and pleaded with me not to take her family's land.

In sum, I cannot say whether the discourse of violence was just a dramatic, rhetorical means of asserting their commitment to resistance or whether the threats were real, but it is only fair to report the extent to which violence was regularly threatened by the farmers. I heard these proclamations regularly in interviews and at (otherwise) nonviolent protests. The local media covered the "kill or be killed, I will not move" discourse as well. For example, in an article titled with a quote from a protestor, "Murder, Hanging . . . Whatever Happens, We Will Not Give Up Land," a local paper waxed anxious about the prospect of violence: "The government has issued notification for acquisition of 660.57 acres of land to give concrete shape to this project, but the villagers are not prepared to give up their land at any cost. They are not able to take the government's justification that the tourism industry will develop all round and employment opportunities will generate on a large scale with this project. In this situation if there is use of force at the administrative level, it will lead to an outburst of the people's anger ending in bloodshed" (2005). The next year a paper reported that farmers were willing to die for their cause: "The farmers under the aegis of *Council for the Struggle to Save the Land* announced on Sunday, the fourth day of the ongoing relay fast against the Maitreya Project, that they will fight to the finish. If needed they will give up their lives for the land" ("Announcement of Struggle" 2006). This is to say that in their public discourse, farmers agitating against MPI were vociferous in their assertions that they would fight to save their land.

Who Is Maitreya Project? It Is Difficult to Find Him!

Global institutions working in rural India often operate in the liminal spaces between the official and the patently unofficial; in postliberalization India, it is critical to underscore the intersectionality of transnational corporations with these bureaucratic entities (Sharma and Gupta 2006). As Gupta and Sharma have already articulated, the realms of the nonstate and the state (or the unofficial and the official) have always been intertwined, and any notion that they are pure and distinct is cultural wishful thinking rather than true to everyday practice. Globalization and technology have altered power dynamics to disenfranchise certain vulnerable populations in some unfamiliar ways, and indeed the local Indian protestors at odds with a transnational institution found themselves battling an unfamiliar opponent.

While admirable work has been done in bureaucratic state spaces in South Asia (Gupta 2013; Hull 2012), my work has consistently focused on the more conventional engagements with these phenomena, that is, how official spaces, agents, and materials are interpreted from the outside. I was never given access to the internal bureaucracies of the nonprofit I studied nor the local Indian bureaucracy working with them. Along with my Kushinagari villager informants I was on the outside of the Indian bureaucracy looking in, and my engagements with it in offices in Lucknow and in the Kushinagar district were intimidating and confusing. I saw the towering stacks of folders and portfolios leaning precariously in offices but rarely got a good look at what was inside them. While the study of the fuzziness and amorphousness—what Gupta calls "messiness" (2013)—of official business is worthy of serious scholarly attention, I was relegated to the periphery, much like my local farmer-activist informants.

There is a great deal of significant cultural practice happening between state and nonstate entities, and although these relationships may or may not always be recognized (by us or our informants) as semiofficial, there is much to gain in working to shed light on the dynamics between actors across the spectrum and the perceptions of these actors vis-à-vis one another as they exercise their disparate types of power. Suffice it to say, the semiofficial nooks and crannies of the Maitreya Project endeavor made for new challenges in local politics and activism in Kushinagar. One of the very clear ways that the semiofficial status of MPI manifested in the field was in its early invisibility to local villagers and the extent to which the existence of such a large, transnational organization met with incredulousness.

At first, some Kushinagari farmer-activists thought that the Maitreya Project was just a conspiracy between Babar Singh and a few investors overseas to create an empty shell corporation that would allow them to take valuable land at a pittance. The worldwide, globalized network of MPI was such an unfamiliar institutional form to the Kushinagari protestors that in the beginning of my research, I heard many false narratives about how the Maitreya Project was not a real organization. Some local interlocutors told me that MPI was just a scam concocted so that the state government and people like Babar Singh could profit at their expense.

Singh, a Hindu businessman who lived in a small city more than an hour away, was much maligned by people in Kushinagar. Not one single farmer that I interviewed in the Kushinagari area had a kind word to say about him. Singh's name was frequently, and vociferously, vilified by BBSS speakers at rallies. I never attended a rally or protest in which Babar Singh was not named first and foremost among the dastardly local politicians, bureaucrats, and businessmen who were trying to seize the farmers' land for their own profit. (A former district magistrate was also high on their list of enemies of the people, but he was transferred midway through my research period, leaving Babar Singh to bear the brunt of local antagonism.) At the first protest I witnessed in January 2006, a speaker railed against Singh for being in cahoots with the government and for taking and giving bribes. When I asked a BBSS organizer about this later, he said, "[Babar Singh] is the main person with the project. He is taking lots of commission. He is a dishonest man. He used to be with the Indo-Japan Association. He's been taking too much commission." Even the astutely diplomatic Abhishek—the Kushinagari native who was working for the Maitreya Project school in Bodh Gaya at the time—told me that the view of Babar Singh in the Kushinagar area was so universally negative that (whether Singh deserved his poor reputation or not) for the good of the statue project, MPI ought to sever all ties with him.

At a protest held in February 2007, over a year later, Babar Singh was still the central focal point for farmers' grievances: "The man behind all of this, [Babar Singh], is a land broker. He became very rich. He heads [Kompro] Agencies. He brought the Maitreya Project here. He met Brahma Shankar Tripathi and he said if you do work with us then you will get money. For the Indo-Japan society, he made thirty-five schools, and he would take commissions of billions of rupees. . . . Very corrupt person." When I enquired further about the notion of "billions of rupees" going astray, the informant and his compatriots said that it was an exaggeration, but the illegal "commissions" numbered "too many rupees to count." A Japanese woman running a nongovernmental organization in Kushinagar sadly confirmed to me that from her perspective, the widely circulated claim that Singh had defrauded her Indo-Japanese Association nonprofit several years before was all too true. Her staffers also discussed the alleged fraud with me and were notably appalled that MPI had hired him despite this well-known history.

It was not only farmers with land to lose that mistrusted and denigrated Babar Singh. Many Kushinagari businesspeople also openly discussed with me their views of Babar Singh by cataloguing alleged graft and corruption in his business dealings in the region. This impression of him as a rogue was shared even by those locals who had cordial personal relationships with him. Several state government bureaucrats in Lucknow also expressed their mistrust of Singh, who seems to strike many people, myself included, as extremely self-interested.

Babar Singh was so widely maligned that during the entirety of my fieldwork period, he had little to no direct contact with the Kushinagari farmers whose land he was working to acquire. Although Singh's home office building was a veritable armed fortress and he traveled with armed guards, the Kushinagari farmers who were threatened by the Maitreya Project's land acquisition plans often said with bluster that if Babar Singh were to drive up to their farmlands, they would kill him or die in the attempt.

The MoU signed by the Maitreya Project Trust and the Uttar Pradeshi state government stipulates a "zero tolerance" for corruption ("Memorandum of Understanding" 2003, 21). The Maitreya Project makes much of this declaration in their literature, although they did not have a single employee or volunteer living in Kushinagar, Deoria, or Padrauna to oversee (or collaborate with) the bureaucrats who were actually handling the day-to-day paperwork toward the pending land transfers. Therefore, in my view, MPI could not reasonably assert with confidence that corruption was not taking place, since they made no effort to supervise those who were actually doing the legwork on their land acquisition, nor did they work with local beneficiaries to ensure their satisfaction with the process. Among both Kushinagari farmers and businesspeople, there are very outspoken critics of the land-acquisition process in Kushinagar who have publicly accused both the Maitreya Project representative, Babar Singh, and local government bureaucrats of significant corruption already. Petty corruption was acknowledged as a fact of life during several of my interviews with local Kushinagari statue supporters (mostly small business owners, but also some of the nonlandholding villagers) as well. I cannot say whether Babar Singh deserves his unsavory reputation, but it is an indisputable fact that MPI's sole regional representative is widely reviled and mistrusted by local Kushinagaris.

Given the conventional wisdom about Singh, it is understandable perhaps that some BBSS supporters mistakenly thought that MPI was just a front for Singh's own financial interests. A BBSS leader initially believed that the MPI "headquarters" was actually Babar Singh's own house in Gorakhpur, so that view fed his suspicions that the whole project was nothing more than a well-orchestrated regional swindle. The global, transnational nature of FPMT and the Maitreya Project was completely unfamiliar and confusing to the protestors, who were initially skeptical that the statue was ever really a true plan.

The notion that there was a transnational organization trying to acquire their land that basically operated through e-mail and overseas phone calls was an untenable, alien notion to many of my farming informants. There were very few Internet-savvy farmers in the affected villages in the aughts; even now, very few of my Kushinagari informants have e-mail accounts. However, some of the families had college-educated children with some technical knowledge, and at some point the son of an MPI-affected farmer printed out sections from the Maitreya Project website. These pages were passed around at meetings in 2006, but even that was not convincing proof to many of the farmers that MPI was real. Some of the BBSS leadership believed, or at least thought it possible, that the MPI website was all design, a vacant shell with no real organization, funders, or devotees behind it.

Some seasoned, urban, veteran activists who passed through Kushinagar (most from the NAPM) assured BBSS that global corporations behave as

such and that the plan may well be real. This did not change any[...]
ment of their plight but simply shifted their sense of who was res[...]
their suffering. Candidly, a few BBSS leaders said that they wer[...]
the Maitreya Project statue plan was indeed real, since they then would be
fighting an organization that was perhaps out of their league. One informant
said, "If we are fighting the Buddhist Coca-Cola, then how can we hope to
win?" Since the Kushinagari locals had little to no contact with FPMT or
MPI, they puzzled about how an organization like the Maitreya Project could
operate without real local headquarters. One informant called MPI "a head
without a body."

During one conversation, I watched as some of my informants in BBSS
argued about where they should go to protest if the decision makers were really all so far away. When I told them that the leader of the Maitreya Project,
Peter Kedge, lived in Canada, and that he was Babar Singh's boss in regard
to the statue project, they were crestfallen. Aneesh said, "How can we fight
an enemy who is so far away? Our stones cannot hit them there. Our micro-
phones are not loud enough." Among Aneesh's circle of friends, there was
some sense that if the fight could not be won locally, then they had no chance
of success. The Maitreya Project, at that point, was perceived as a kind of
phantom—a spectral presence with the power to haunt and hurt—not a real
antagonist with form and substance.

Others felt more hope, since they recognized that perhaps if the Maitreya
Project was a real Buddhist organization, then they could potentially be rea-
soned with. A few of these farmers traveled to Bodh Gaya to find the Maitreya Project office there, and to make appeals to this office. BBSS supporters told me their first visit to Bodh Gaya only made them more convinced
that the organization was a sham, since the offices were on undeveloped
land and they did not see any school there.[14] However, I was informed that
on a second, later visit, they finally made their way to the Maitreya Project
School, which at least gave them the sense that their antagonists were really
from a Buddhist organization with some actual projects underway. As far as
I can tell, this recognition did not change BBSS's strategy in practice, but it
did help some of the Kushinagari activists to get a better sense of the nature
of their adversary.

Playing Politics with the Maitreya Project

The state, regional, and local government officials in Uttar Pradesh have
brought political considerations to bear regarding both the statue and the
farmers' resistance to it. Local politicians are thoroughly enmeshed in

Maitreya Project debates. At the state level, the elected chief ministers, representatives, and party heads in Lucknow, Uttar Pradesh, have all weighed in on the statue project one way or the other.

Uttar Pradesh's chief minister from 2000 to 2002, Rajnath Singh of the Bharatiya Janata Party (the BJP), heralded the Maitreya Project as his initiative, and he had claimed credit for it for his party. He has repeatedly emphasized that it would be bigger than the Bamiyan statues that the Taliban had destroyed in Afghanistan ("Rajnath Promises Buddha Statue" 2016). Since the BJP is a Hindu fundamentalist party with an implicit (and sometimes explicit) anti-Muslim agenda, the emphasis on building a statue grander than the one that the Taliban tore down can be read as a political maneuver, or dog whistle, tapping into anti-Muslim sentiments. This rhetoric was repeated in later election cycles, such as at an event in 2016 when Rajnath Singh retold the story of how upset he was when he saw the Bamiyan Buddhas destroyed on television: "He added, 'As the then CM [chief minister], I announced that a larger statue of Lord Buddha would be set up in Kushinagar. . . . Later, I laid the foundation of the same. . . . Since then, the work is pending. I reiterate the announcement and the promise that I would get the construction of the Buddha statue done in Kushinagar, if God gives me a chance'" ("Rajnath Promises Buddha Statue" 2016). During the midaughts, when the BJP was out of power at the state level, the party participated in some anti–Maitreya Project protests as a way to try to get dismayed farmers to vote for Rajnath Singh in the next election.

Madame Mayawati, out of power during the bulk of my fieldwork period in India (though subsequently reelected in spring 2007 around the time that I left India), is the head of the Bahujan Samaj Party (BSP). The BSP was founded as a political party for *dalits*, also known as untouchables. Several of my Kushinagari informants, both pro and con regarding the statue, told me that Mayawati had said to her core *dalit* community during her 2002–3 tenure in state office something to the effect of, "I'm building this statue for you—it is a gift." This quote was paraphrased by my Indian informants in Lucknow and Kushinagar several times, so even if it was never uttered as such, it is widely attributed to her. The Maitreya Project was widely seen as a pet project for Mayawati ("What Will Happen?" 2012).[15]

The Chief Minister from 2003 to 2007 was Mulayam Singh Yadav, head of the Samajwadi Party (SP). Mulayam Singh Yadav was reputedly opposed to the statue project while out of office, but supported the project while in power. He even went so far as to tell the farmers that the plan would be postponed for a reevaluation all the while allowing the plan to move forward unopposed.

The state-level politics summarized above trickled down to intense political debates at the regional and local levels. Membership of the BBSS and other farmers' advocacy groups have little respect for the integrity of political promises made about the Maitreya statue. A veritable parade of regional ministers dependent on farming constituencies in the Kushinagar district would pass through the area declaring their opposition to the Maitreya Project in public. The shared sentiment among most farmers in the greater Kushinagar area is that regional and local politicians were reliably pro-Maitreya (in action, if not in speech) while they were in positions of power, but whenever they were out of power they would promise vehemently to oppose the plan if returned to power.

Since it had become politically dangerous to crow too loudly about pro-Maitreya activities in the midaughts, the MLAs had long since stopped vocally supporting the project in public, but the farmers widely believed that their elected representatives were indeed helping to advance the Maitreya Project's interests in secret. In general, the sense from the anti-MPI contingent can be summed up by the musings of a local Kushinagari schoolteacher: "One thing is clear: there is no political party for the poor."

The farmers' mistrust of politicians and bureaucrats stems in part from all of the doublespeak they experienced as regards the project plans. For example, one government official first promised that the farmers would be consulted about the compensation and then reneged on that promise.

> Opposing statements of state Culture Secretary and Secretary of Maitreya Project, Shailesh Krishna, on the form of acquisition of seven hundred acres of land for the construction of a five-hundred-foot-high statue of Buddha . . . has led to much anger among the affected farmers. Whereas they were earlier assured that their land will be bought only after personal dialogue and on the basis of the price agreed upon by them, Shailesh Krishna issued a statement last week that land will be acquired for the purpose within three to four months and farmers will be paid compensation on the basis of the government circle rate and seven hundred acres of land will be acquired. ("Unrest among Farmers" 2002)

Although the land was obviously not acquired in 2002, due to BBSS agitations, these kinds of reversals and betrayals led the farmers to constantly worry that their representatives were working against their best interests.

The Great Betrayal

In 2006, Brahma Shankar Tripathi, the MLA for the region, was caught by the locals having a meeting with Babar Singh in Kushinagar, and "one thousand" local farmers reputedly surrounded the hotel to protest. When I came back to Kushinagar a few weeks after the drama, I got a detailed eyewitness report from Raj and Aneesh that I corroborated with other farmers and businessmen later.

> RAJ: The hunger strike was from 10th August to 26th August. It was kept by some men, and also women and children. They were senseless because they would lose everything. One day the MLA of this area was here in Kushinagar with the Maitreya Project broker, [Babar Singh]. They were staying in Pathak Niwas [hotel] and we came to know. The farmers all came, the women came, and they really showed that they were angry. The MLA had said to us that, "I have no idea about this person, I have no relation to [Babar Singh]," but now he was caught. Women were the most angry and they showed it with so much yelling and commotion.
>
> ANEESH: The women were holding their shoes and shouting. They wanted to beat those men with their shoes. They were so angry. It was something.
>
> RAJ: People were saying, "We respect the Lord Buddha, but if he will take our land, our lives, then we will kill him." So the MLA assured the farmers that he would help them. On 14th August evening this happened. There were five hundred women and over five hundred men. So the MLA said, "I will take you to CM [chief minister] Mulayam Yadav Singh." On the 15th of August India got freedom, and on that day we were freed also!

Raj and Aneesh continued their story: they told me that a bus was soon chartered by the MLA that took some of the BBSS-affiliated farmers to Lucknow.

In Lucknow, they were feted at a breakfast by the chief minister, Mulayam Singh Yadav, who told them that their struggle had been successful and their prayers were answered. According to Raj and Aneesh, the chief minister said that he would immediately fax the district magistrate to put a hold on the project until a commission was constituted to look into the whole project again, including recollecting and reanalyzing contentious statistics and data. His assurances were apparently unambiguous, and everyone who attended felt that he had clearly said that the whole project would not happen without a great deal of further research, work, and the farmers' consent. The fact that the land would be resurveyed as part of the commission was key to my informants, since they felt that the district magistrate who had orchestrated the setting of the provisional rates was corrupt and had been paid to misrepresent the vitality and quality of the land; a resurvey, Raj and Aneesh assured me, meant that the large majority of nearly seven hundred acres at stake would be apprised as fully arable, and the whole Maitreya Project would be cancelled as a result.

"They can't take such arable land," Raj said.

And Aneesh noted that even if they did, they would have to pay more appropriately generous compensation per acre. So the farmers returned home triumphant from Lucknow. When I asked others about the story, BBSS members and agitators all reported to me that the MPI plan had been officially "cancelled" or "postponed" by the chief minister, so everything could finally go back to normal.

But just the day before I spoke to Raj and Aneesh, MPI had issued an update report to their listserv (and posted it on their website) saying that the news from Kushinagar was good and that they were many steps closer to acquiring the land. I was concerned: both the farmers and the Maitreya Project were simultaneously trumpeting their success and touting incommensurable facts in the process.

In order to discern the truth about the alleged pause on Maitreya Project 2.0, with some members of the BBSS I then traveled to Padrauna, the seat of the district government, to interview the new district magistrate, Mr. A. N. Chatterji. My BBSS friends and I waited for hours before we were eventually shown into a large office. The district magistrate was polite. When pressed, much to the dismay of the farmers, the district magistrate said that the plan was absolutely going forward and that there had been no official order from the chief minister to halt or alter course in any way.

The conversation I had with this district magistrate was very different than my interaction with his predecessor; the former district magistrate had been curt and suspicious, while this new district magistrate was happy to talk, although he said he knew very little about the details of the Maitreya Project and its proposed effects. Mr. Chatterji supported the Maitreya Project, he told me, but had a great deal of compassion for the farmers. He acknowledged that plans had not been worked out yet to mitigate the trials of displaced persons and those who would be unable to make a living after the acquisition, but he promised that he would look into the progress being made on this score. About this, he said, "We will try to strike a balance between the needs of the project and the farmers. Perhaps though, this goes to show that whatever level of civilization, the rule of the jungle still prevails. Might is right." We proceeded to have a provocative and candid talk about power, diplomacy, and politics, including American exceptionalism. Although the conversation was amiable enough, the discussion was difficult.

When we departed, Mr. Chatterji smiled and shook our hands. My comrades and I were wholly spent by a day of travel, waiting, and emotional, challenging interviews and terrible news. The BBSS representatives with me were nothing short of distraught. On the bus back to the village, we talked.

SHASHI: It's very bad news, but I think he is telling us the truth.

RAJ: We had a very unlucky day. We waited and waited, and in the end it was very bad news.

JESSICA: So the CM [chief minister] was dishonest.

SHASHI: The CM [chief minister] is very liar.

RAJ: This DM [district magistrate] is very sincere and honest, but what he said is very bad for us to hear.

SHASHI: The numbers he gave are very wrong. Definitely. There are 1,400 families affected.

RAJ: He didn't know very much about the [Maitreya] project. I think he was a little embarrassed that he couldn't answer your questions. He will learn more about it now, so that he can talk about it.

SHASHI: What kind of DM [district magistrate] knows so little about such a big thing? If I were DM [district magistrate] I would know everything. The CM [chief minister] is a liar. He lied to my face. He had sent for his personal assistant, and they sent a fax to the DM [district magistrate] of Kushinagar ordering a resurvey of the land. He said, "I am a son of a farmer too, and your land is safe." He is a liar. The DM [district magistrate] seems honest, so I think he told the truth.

JESSICA: Well, he definitely seemed honest to me. I think he felt bad to tell us the bad news. He looked like he felt guilty.

SHASHI: The leaders in India . . . this is our problem in India. Our leaders are liars. They say that the farmers are the backbone of the nation. That farmers are everything, but they are treated like nothing and told lies. This is truly an unlucky day.

We traveled the rest of the thirty minutes back to Kushinagar in near silence. I had rarely felt so tired, even after longer days canvassing the affected villages in the heat of the full sun; the news had felt like a punch in the gut. We all felt bruised. Shashi said that the BBSS would be meeting soon to strategize their next steps.

The farmers, having been alerted to the fact that they had been misled deliberately by the chief minister, began their protests again. They quickly returned to their peaceful actions: calling another series of rotating fasts and sit-ins. The local Hindi-medium newspapers covered the protests and fasts regularly. Weary, angry volunteers took turns fasting at a central location. Fasters were inevitably joined by whoever from the community was free to sit in solidarity with them, as well as a parade of politicians and others offering support.

Many months later, in February 2007, yet another hunger strike was in full force, and the broken promises of the CM [chief minister] were still being discussed at rallies and covered in the local papers.

> The hunger strike and fast of the farmers are continuing on the twenty-sixth consecutive day for the removal of the Maitreya Project from Kushinagar under the banner of the *Bhoomi Bachao Sangharsh Samiti* [BBSS]. The enraged farmers on *dharna* are arguing that even the order of the chief minister is proving to be ineffective, as at this point no secretary-level investigating team has arrived as promised. At the same time, in the region, a public debate has ensued on the Maitreya Project as to where the farmers should go. . . . Because of effective measures not being taken until now, it appears difficult to answer the piercing questions of the enraged, dissatisfied farmers. All eyes are focused on whether the fear of losing their lands will transform the hunger strike of the farmers into a movement or the government will again examine its facts. Only time will tell. ("Fast Continues" 2007)

Although politicians from various parties were coming to sit with the fasting protestors, the farmers were loath to believe their promises of support. Even when Tripathi later came to say that the chief minister, if reelected, would indeed finally convene his committee or investigating team to put the brakes on the land acquisition, the farmers kept up their *dharna*. And even when the chief minister announced that he would order a probe into the Maitreya Project land acquisition, the farmers refused to stop fasting until they actually saw results. The activists told me that they were tired of political promises, and they wanted to actually see that the government's actions would match their rhetoric.

In an interview with me, one of the leaders of the BBSS expressed outrage, cynicism, and desperation:

> On 17th of February, a cabinet minister from this locality, Brahma Shankar Tripathi, he said, "I have talked with the CM [chief minister], and now everything should be stopped. They will make a committee and survey and then give to the CM [chief minister]." . . . The local villagers do not trust these assurances. Let them promise, but we will continue. They all say the same thing. They make the same promises. They all promise to cancel the project, and then they forget. The politicians are all talking with the farmers and saying, "support me"

[in the election]. The farmers know very well. Farmers aren't making any promises to politicians. They are having no confidence. They will not stop their protest. The media is highlighting this. In the *Rashtriya Sahara* newspaper they said the farmers are angry. They said that if our request is not accepted then we will abduct the foreigners, and we will just give them Indian food to eat.

I started laughing when he said this, but he said that they were quite serious. Discomfited, I shifted in my seat, took a few moments to collect myself, and then resumed asking questions.

Welcome, Maitreya!

While there was widespread local resistance to Maitreya Project 2.0, there were also many locals who viewed the project as a potential boon to the region; it is reasonably expected to attract more tourist and infrastructure dollars that would expand and develop the local economy. At first glance, it seemed that businesspeople were keen on the project while farmers opposed it, but this is an oversimplification. There are many businesspeople who desire the project, but not all of them. Most local farmers are antagonistic to the Maitreya Project, but not all of them.

I interviewed several dozen businesspeople in Kushinagar proper and in the nearby town of Kasia: from chai stall vendors to photography studio owners and hospitality industry employees and owners, everyone did believe that Maitreya Project 2.0 would boost tourism. Still, businesspeople who owned land that was slated to be acquired, or who had family members who would lose land to the project, were all very much against the land acquisition; some of these people talked wistfully about alternative sites for the project, some railed against the project as a whole, and still others felt that the government and Maitreya Project brokers were perpetrating fraud. However, businesspeople who had no land being acquired were almost all enthusiastic about the forthcoming Maitreya Project, although some felt that the controversy had put the plans in danger, so their critiques of MPI were not with the statue plan but rather on the mismanagement of the project.

Some pro–Maitreya Project vendors felt strongly that the Maitreya Project would bring much-needed benefits to their region and to their own business opportunities; therefore, they said, the farmers should stop their fight for the benefit of the region as a whole. Other pro–Maitreya Project elements noted that despite their own optimism at the prospect of the Maitreya Project in Kushinagar, the farmers were getting a very raw deal, and it would be a shame that their future boom would come at the expense of poor villagers.

Anil Thakur, a Buddhist businessman in Kushinagar, had been patiently waiting for the Maitreya Project for years, since he felt strongly that it would help revitalize the economy as a whole, as well as his own business interests. He was quick to note that he was not only hoping for the Maitreya Project because of the rosy prospects for his wallet; he desires that the statue be built because he thinks will be good for Buddhism. Mr. Thakur told me that he and his wife have actually foreseen the Maitreya Project:

> I know that even if the Maitreya statue doesn't come here now, it will in the future. I have seen it, it will be over there on that side. [Here he gestures toward Anirudhwa.] And it will be facing north. Once my wife and I were out sleeping on the roof. . . . We used to do that. Suddenly the sky was white, and then against the southern horizon it turned a fierce red color. And then it was like a fire burning, and we thought that maybe the Thai temple was on fire; we both saw it and were talking about it like that. This was on the 1st of August in 1998. But it wasn't a fire, and then we saw two columns of light that were coming out of the Mahaparinirvana Stupa. We were amazed. We put our hands together and did like this. [He closes his eyes in prayer.] We questioned people carefully the next day, like the chowkidar who stayed there, but no one had seen anything. Only we saw it. We still don't know what it was. We told our guru, and he wrote it all down. He writes books sometimes. He thinks that it may have had something to do with one of the ancient relics. We're not sure.

Mr. Thakur was amiable and talkative, especially since he seemed to have a somewhat complex relationship with the Maitreya Project. I supported his business by coming by at least a few times a week, and we would talk at length.

Mr. Thakur and his wife were transplanted Buddhist businesspeople who owned land on the far side of Kushinagar, that is, far from the MPI's future land. Therefore, they had everything to gain by the coming of the Maitreya statue and nothing to lose. However, in the course of most conversations Mr. Thakur would tie himself in knots by both supporting the statue plan and railing against it. He would talk about how much economic and spiritual good the statue could bring to Kushinagar, and then he would angrily vent about how the Maitreya Project was stupidly relying on "thugs" to do their dirty work for them. He and his wife would discuss at length how the farmers were being fleeced by the government and how sad it was that a *dharma* project was hurting so many people. Then he might say how he still hoped that despite all the obstacles, the plan might be brought to fruition soon.

For example, one of our conversations began on the topic of how the whole region would benefit from the statue project. He talked about his own plans to expand his business, a plan that would not stand a chance of success under the current economic conditions in Kushinagar. Then when I started talking about the farmers' problems with the plan, Mr. Thakur passionately said that they are being done a terrible injustice.

> MR. THAKUR: The checks have been cut and sent out. Some people have already deposited those checks. I have seen one of them myself at the bank. Many people have not withdrawn the money, however. The people who have sold are from this side—they are not as strong as the people on the other side who have formed an organization against the acquisition. There are rumors that the documents are being given to poor people where everything is in pen, but the amount to be received is in pencil. They would change the numbers afterwards. I have not seen this, but this is being said. I think that the authorities should investigate this claim. The farmers are not educated so they just put down their thumbprint. . . .
>
> JESSICA: You said last time that the government rates were very low. . . .
>
> MR. THAKUR: There is one man who had a parcel of land he was going to sell several years back—before the Maitreya Project. Someone was going to put a plant there. He was offered sixty-four *lakhs* [for his lot]. He demanded one *crore*, but the buyer wouldn't go up so high. The government acquisition rate [per *katha*] for that land: fifty-five thousand rupees only! Of course, he is really regretting that decision! This shows the difference between government rates and market prices. Of course, every farmer is getting different, different rates per *katha*. . . .
>
> JESSICA: Yeah—depending on where it is in relation to the road, right . . .?
>
> MR. THAKUR: We have lost interest in it. We used to be interested in helping bring it to Kushinagar, but now it is such a mess. We thought it could be done with consideration to the *dharma*, but that isn't what's happening. Anyway, we'll see.

Mr. Thakur told me a few days after this that he still was very hopeful that the Maitreya Project would come. He reiterated both his sadness for the farmers and his desire to see economic boons that will trickle down to help the whole community. He looked almost guilty as he ended the conversation by saying that he was praying for it.

Mr. Thakur was not the only person whose feelings about the statue were fraught and complex. I conducted several interviews with local farmers slated to lose land to MPI who actually supported the statue in theory but were simply antagonistic to the way that the plan had been carried out. These interviews were few and far between, but the sentiment was reiterated enough times to catch my attention. These were most often farmers who talk about the prospects for their children, specifically hoping that the statue could bring an economic boom that would mean better jobs for their progeny in the future. Each of these farmers said the same thing: the statue is most welcome, provided that it does not destroy my family's economic well-being in the short term. A few of these men even spoke with regret at the lost opportunity to the region, saying that it is a shame that the Maitreya Project must be opposed tooth and nail, since it could have been a good thing. These farmers usually blamed Babar Singh and corrupt government officials for the problems that beset the project planning and development.

I interviewed some businessmen and white-collar workers who had good jobs in the nearby town of Kasia, but whose family land was staked for land acquisition, and their opinions about the statue were generally ambivalent: they liked the idea of the statue, but agreed with the landowners that the rates of compensation were intractably low. For example, I interviewed Mr. Reddy, a Kasia lawyer with a good job, whose finances were not at all dependent on his father's plot of land that was slated to be acquired. He was outraged that the family land was being forcibly acquired at a low rate of compensation, but still he acknowledged that the region as a whole would be better off should the MPI build its statue. Mr. Reddy said: "We want the Maitreya Project to come. We know it will be good for us. But the government is giving us too little money for our land. The broker, [Babar Singh], he doesn't have a good reputation here. They are only giving us thirteen thousand or fourteen thousand per *katha*, but the land is worth one hundred thousand per *katha*. We won't sell at this low price. . . . Still, the Maitreya Project would be good for the people here. We want the development that it will bring." Mr. Reddy told me that if the land acquisition went forward his father (and other semidependent family members in that household) could survive economically due to Mr. Reddy's financial support, but he told me that he had other extended family members who would face dire financial straits. Mr. Reddy was not involved in the protests but said that he could understand why so many farmers were protesting. He said that he supported the fight for higher compensation, but not the fight against the project.

Young adults, such as college students, living in the affected villages were generally more likely to support the MPI statue as a potential economic windfall. I met Kapil Guha only once, during a canvassing of Anirudhwa village. He reported to me that his extended family of fourteen people was being supported tolerably on five acres of land, since the family income was being supplemented by a few wage earners engaged in the informal sector. He told me, "Both the farm and the businesses are important to feed the whole family. We grow wheat, paddy, sugarcane, pulses (*daal*), vegetables, and maize. Most of the harvest we eat and only some, a little bit, we sell. The sugarcane we sell." He reported that he was in his third year of college nearby, studying economics and history.

"It is my hope to be a teacher or a civil servant with a government job. I don't want to do business," he said.

Kapil's family had been spared the threat of losing land to the Maitreya Project plan, but the MPI plan had thrown many of his friends and neighbors into an anxious downward spiral, so he felt very ambivalent about the plan. Kapil was at once critical of the plan and its implementation and simultaneously hopeful about the potential for further economic development of his region. Kapil said:

Kushinagar should develop as a tourist place. There have been a lot of changes. The fertility of the land is increasing and infrastructure is better. This is improving. Electricity has come. Before, in previous time, all the homes were mud. At present time, all are burnt bricks and cement. Education is better now, there is more. The facilities have also increased. I want more development in every field. The [Maitreya Project] would be good for Kushinagar, but there are problems. The Maitreya Project would bring big problems too. I don't want the village to be removed. It would destroy some villagers, and it wants to take fertile land.

He went on to say that if the plan could happen without displacing people or wasting good farmland, then he would support it wholeheartedly. Kapil's perspective was not an uncommon refrain among local young people: the statue would bring economic development, but the government should not be permitted to forcibly acquire land from villages and farmers in order to bring that boon to fruition.

The grassroots anti–Maitreya Project movement was at a low to medium boil throughout my fieldwork period. A person coming to Kushinagar to study something else, say kinship or rural Hindu festivals, would have heard about the resistance movement immediately, because it was an unavoidable, ubiquitous, hot topic of conversation in the region. Although it was a local and regional obsession, it was not heavily covered in the national or international press. I once told an Indian journalist at a national level English-medium newspaper about the MPI controversy in Kushinagar, and he replied, "Get in touch with me again once the blood starts flowing."

In March 2007, a BBSS-organized hunger strike was in full swing. Some of my informants had already "lost kilos" due to their participation in the fasting relay. While some farmers were hopeful that after the upcoming state elections there would be a more favorable climate for the chief minister to finally cancel the project once and for all, most were worried that after the elections any and all promises would be quickly forgotten.

As I sat with the protestors, an elderly gentleman who was one of the hunger strikers offered me a collection of Hindi newspaper clippings about the project, which he had been saving from the beginning of the agitations against the statue.[16] He asked me to share the news with the world: "Tell them that we are fighting, and that we have been from the beginning. Please go, tell them all."

Rakesh was another of the hunger strikers. When I asked him about the political situation and upcoming election, he spread the blame equally to all the parties, reiterating the mantra that the farmers could trust no one but themselves. Rakesh said, "All the political parties are responsible. The BJP, the BSP, the SP. They are all dishonest. We don't trust any of these political parties." But, he told me, the hunger strikes would continue until the politicians actually hear them and cancel the statue project.

At some point, Tripathi, the local representative I mentioned before, reported to the BBSS that the chief minister wanted to appoint a commission to look into the matter, but it was too late to really do anything, since state-level elections were about to take place. The farmers were livid at these excuses and continued their protests.

CHAPTER 8

Loving-Kindness / *MAITRI*

Contested Notions of Ethics, Values, and Progress

As the Maitreya Project 2.0 plan hung over them like a dark, threatening cloud, the farmers of Kushinagar desperately fought to get the project cancelled. Plan-affected villagers felt insecure and anxious—the police could come at any day to force them off their land against their will. How many sleepless nights have been foisted on the farmers of small plots in Greater Kushinagar? How did a spiritually inspired Buddhist development project end up inspiring such fear and chaos in an area FPMT ostensibly wanted to help? In this chapter, I will frame the Maitreya Project land controversy by discussing it in terms of values. Here I put two very disparate types of values side by side: the values of Engaged Buddhism and the values of economic development.

Was FPMT's five-hundred-foot statue of the Maitreya Buddha being made with loving-kindness? In Tibetan Buddhism, as in other traditions, loving-kindness, or *maitri* in Sanskrit,[1] is considered a significant idea in theory and practice. Developing loving-kindness for all beings is one way of developing *bodhicitta* and hence a way toward enlightenment for the benefit of all. The Maitreya Buddha is the embodiment of loving-kindness, the Buddha of desiring happiness for all sentient beings. My BBSS informants were cognizant of the disconnect between their current suffering as potential victims of the statue plan and the moral values espoused by Buddhist communities. In these terms, I will take a closer look at the values of FPMT and the Maitreya Project as they are demonstrated through the work of statue building and Engaged Buddhism.

Given the fact that FPMT teaches its adherents to value *maitri*, I ask: How could the Maitreya Project allow so much suffering, uncertainty, and fear to prevail in Kushinagar—just in the planning, pre-acquisition stage alone? How could FPMT's spiritual leaders simultaneously rescue goats from slaughter, pray for world peace and happiness, and dedicate clouds of offerings toward the hope that all sentient beings will be spared suffering, all the while championing MPI plans that alarmed, outraged, and incited a whole region of hard-working small-farming families for more than a decade? This chapter exposes the "friction" that Anna Tsing discusses in her work on global connections and crisis; Tsing writes, "Friction refuses the lie that global power operates as a well-oiled machine. Furthermore, difference sometimes inspires insurrection. Friction can be the fly in the elephant's nose" (2005, 6).

Akhil Gupta explicates how it is the responsibility of the anthropologist to show the ways that local identity and a local sense of place are increasingly affected by the momentum produced by globalization:

> The changing global configuration of postcoloniality and late capitalism have resulted in the repartitioning and reinscription of space. . . .
> To grasp the nature of these changes, we need to be bifocal in our analytic vision. On the one side, we need to investigate processes of place making, of how feelings of belonging to an imagined community bind identity to spatial location such that differences between communities and places are created. At the same time, we also need to situate these processes within systematic developments that reinscribe and reterritorialize space in the global political economy." (Gupta 1997, 179–180)

In this chapter, I discuss some of the political and economic forces at national and global levels that affect how Kushinagaris see themselves and how they have processed the coming of the Maitreya Project into their lives.

The intractable, uncompromising, top-down nature of the MPI plan met with extreme anger and frustration from those it diligently sought to displace and disenfranchise. This ethnographic narrative could be added to the many stories of local resistance to globalizing forces of development (e.g., Fortun 2001; Ong 1987; Scott 1985; Taussig 1980; Tsing 2005; Turner 1993). As in Terence Turner's (1993) reports of the Kayapo in Brazil who succeeded in getting a World Bank dam project canceled, the resistance in Kushinagar has not been futile in the least. BBSS and the Kushinagari farmers put up a show of force that thwarted the speedy acquisition of land that the Maitreya Project had once anticipated. Kushinagaris do desire progress, but most are wary of the way that development was unfolding in this case study: transnational Buddhists and the capitalists of the tourism industry would win at the expense of the poor and lower-middle class of rural Kushinagar.

This chapter is about loving-kindness in theory and in practice—in action and in absence. The loving-kindness of MPI has manifested in a way that is iconographically recognizable to FPMTers, but in practice there was little *maitri* in their dealings with the Kushinagari farmers who were threatened with the loss of their land. This chapter is about values, ethics, and disparate cultural perspectives on what is right and what is wrong.

Buddhist Values

There is good and evil aplenty in Tibetan Buddhism; the hierarchy of heavens over hells demonstrates clearly that good motivations beget better rebirths, and bad motivations lead to lesser rebirths. One's actions and their consequences matter, but one's motivations are also of concern in terms of karmic accumulation.

Buddhist ethics,[2] in part, hinge on adherence to the eightfold path, which is thought to direct the way toward enlightenment and out of *samsara*. The eightfold path consists of (1) right view, (2) right intention, (3) right speech, (4) right action, (5) right livelihood, (6) right effort, (7) right mindfulness, and (8) right concentration (Williams and Tribe 2000). The three Buddhist jewels—wisdom, morality, and meditation/mindfulness—classify right speech, right action, and right livelihood as the three elements of the eightfold path that fall under the jewel of morality.[3] Another popular categorization of the above concepts is known as the "six perfections": giving, ethics, patience, effort, concentration, and wisdom.

The realization of *anatman* (Sanskrit: doctrine of "non-self") is also an important value that elucidates ethical thought and action. The minimization of the ego, to whatever extent, allows for more compassion, giving, and kindness, in general. The Dalai Lama writes, "Concerning ethics, the root practice of a bodhisattva is to restrain self-centeredness. Since the practice of charity cannot involve any harm to others if it is to succeed, it is necessary to overcome the very root of any tendency to harm others. This must be done through eliminating self-centeredness, since a solely altruistic attitude leaves no room for harming others. Thus, the ethic of restraining self-centeredness is crucial" (Gyatso 2000, 101).

Thich Nhat Hanh coined the term "Engaged Buddhism" in the 1960s in the context of Buddhist monastics protesting against the Vietnam War on moral terms (Queen 2000). Engaged Buddhism most commonly refers to the ways that Buddhist practices can be deployed in a political, social-justice-oriented manner. The Maitreya Project staff consider their colossus to be a fundamentally Engaged Buddhist endeavor, even though it is primarily a holy-object construction project, because the giant statue would be flanked by medical facilities and educational projects.

While Engaged Buddhism is considered a contemporary movement encompassing a wide variety of practices, there are those who might argue that to some extent all Buddhism is inherently engaged, and always has been so (Kraft 2000, 493; Queen 2000, 24). Engaged Buddhism, for some, means general mindfulness and kindness in everyday life. For others it means ethical living in general, while for still others it means collective political action or volunteering for social justice projects. While this range of perspectives shows that engagement is a fluid and flexible notion used by various people in various ways, it most generally refers to social action, such as work in prisons, antiwar activism, volunteering, and charitable work. The notion that this sort of work is the same as Buddhist collective actions past is not accepted by most Engaged Buddhists. Thich Nhat Hanh's devotees point to Buddhist collective antiwar action in Vietnam in the 1960s, such as strikes, boycotts, and noncooperation with the government, as a break with even past efforts at Buddhist politicking in the region (Hunt-Perry and Fine 2000). Although it is acknowledged that there have always been Buddhists who act with the Buddha's moral lessons in mind, Engaged Buddhist proponents seek to amplify the general lessons of right action and direct them, full tilt, toward helping others in a hands-on manner. The ethics of engagement is a paradigm shift in Queen's view simply because the level of vocal activism and policy-change work that has been championed in Engaged Buddhism is not characteristic of normative social practices in Theravada or Mahayana traditions (2000).[4]

Engaged Buddhism is now a veritable movement with advocates, activists, and practitioners that sing its praises as religious ethics in action. The Engaged Buddhist literature, however, is almost completely written from the perspective of Engaged Buddhists and its proponents, whether academics or practitioners, and in these narratives Engaged Buddhism is often portrayed as a panacea (Chappell 2003; Eppsteiner 1985; King 2005; Kotler 1996; Kraft 1999; Queen and King 1996; Queen 2000; Puri 2006). In my unpublished master's thesis, I argued that Engaged Buddhism was a promising movement toward responsible Buddhist socioeconomic development (Falcone 2001), but I acknowledged that it was important to look to results and not just intentions. In reference to the Maitreya Project, which was one of my case studies, I wrote that by tapping into Buddhist values, FPMT had activated the social capital of Buddhist morality for the benefit of social justice projects in India (Falcone 2001). I argued that the early work being done on Maitreya

Project 1.0 in Bodh Gaya evinced far too little participation and input from the desired beneficiaries of the project, but I was hopeful that the moral underpinning of the project would mean positive outcomes. In the early aughts I still naively thought that the Buddhist ethics and beliefs of institutional actors would ensure commitment to ethical and careful engagement with local beneficiaries. In other words, I too was once a believer in the Engaged Buddhist brand.

David Loy (1997) has argued that as consumerism and free market capitalism have increasingly become our new contemporary religion, traditional religions must reassert the values of generosity and renunciation for the betterment of the general populace. But while Loy carefully critiques the market, he ignores the fact that Buddhist society, law, and politics have also been prone to inequality, hierarchy, and, yes, even greed. While it is clear that Engaged Buddhism has inspired some very beneficial projects and practices,[5] it has also become increasingly apparent to me in the intervening years since completing my master's thesis that Engaged Buddhism is no cure-all, not even in the Buddhist world.[6]

Nor is everything that is done in the name of Engaged Buddhism actually beneficial for everyone affected. In Bodh Gaya, for example, there are vocal complaints that many Buddhist charitable-works nonprofits are corrupt, and the money often is diverted away from the projects that Buddhists have donated to support (Rodriguez 2012). This concern is also a pressing one in Kushinagar, where there was palpable concern that charitable Engaged Buddhist projects support a sense of entitlement and dependence among regular beneficiaries. Not unlike the appropriation of grassroots terminology like "participatory development" and "action research" by the World Bank in the nineties, the term "Engaged Buddhism" can be co-opted by Buddhist groups to make their routine work seem more en vogue and appealing to donors. At times, Buddhist projects with a charitable component may in fact be more complex, more self-gratifying, and more self-serving than the institutions would care to admit.

There is no doubt that FPMT has made charitable giving an important platform of their Buddhist practice. FPMT has many humanitarian projects in the works. And to be completely fair, several of my FPMT informants made the case to me that although Engaged Buddhism is popular in some circles, charitable social projects are not an easy sell to everyone, especially in contrast to pure dharma projects.

ROBBIE: The health program is a gift to the Indian people from the Tibetans, who they have been kind to.

JESSICA: You mentioned some tension. Is there any tension between Root [religious] resources and the health program resources?

ROBBIE: From my perspective there have not been tensions between resources. We are experiencing extreme generosity directed toward the health program at present. We need to generate more money and we are meeting with success. Some recent donations were unparalleled in our history here. Well, maybe not since the group of Singaporeans gave the money to build this place. . . . Some years ago the health program had to be curtailed because of lack of funds. Some programs and staff were curtailed, so there was an attempt to raise more money, and it was sufficient to keep the program functioning. We've tried to turn it from a clinic to a health program. That's when I was invited to come. I communicate a lot with donors. . . . We've made proposals to donors for child health programs. It takes immense energy to generate more funds. . . . There was a Theravadin monk who came with a group. When they left they gave a lot of money to our program. The teacher said, I wish I could convince Chinese people to give to health clinics instead of to gilding statues. They think nothing of spending enormous amounts for such things. But there are enough of both kinds of people to go around.

The charitable project—the health program at the Root Institute—is financed independently; the religious work and the health care work coexist in the same compound at Root, but both are essentially self-sufficient. Robbie diplomatically noted that there is enough money for both projects, but other health project volunteers at Root felt strongly that the health projects were underfunded in contrast to money for *dharma* objects like new statues and prayer wheels. Donors must specifically give to charitable works versus more explicitly religious works, showing that the distinction between the two remains intact in FPMT centers. It is admirable that FPMT advocates for engaged, charitable practices as a part of their religious milieu.

Is MPI's statue an Engaged Buddhist project or a *dharma* project, or both? Certainly the Maitreya Project advocates in FPMT consider it an Engaged Buddhist project, although as a holy object it comes with enormous *dharma* benefits. The proposed development and economic stimulus entailed in the Maitreya Project 2.0 project literature make it clear that the number one benefit that will accrue to Kushinagar is the enhanced opportunities afforded by increased regional prosperity. A hospital project plan is supposed to be built on the Maitreya Project grounds. In addition, the Maitreya Project 2.0 plan promises to build a school, perhaps one even going up to the university level. The health-care and education projects are integrated into the MPI plan, and a glance at the project website in 2010 showed that, at that point, those elements were highlighted almost above and beyond the more strictly religious aspects of the project.

The Maitreya Project supporters always supposed that Maitreya Project 2.0 would change the socioeconomic and karmic landscape of Kushinagar for the better. In my interviews with project staff and supporters in 2006 and 2007, they almost always talked of the "revitalization" of Kushinagar through the trickle-down benefits of increased tourism to the region. "It will benefit everyone," said one ardent supporter, an FPMT student named Arlen, whom I interviewed in Delhi; he asserted, "Even the cows and bugs of Kushinagar will benefit." As I've mentioned previously, MPI staffer Babar Singh even articulated a belief (or PR sound-bite) that the Maitreya Buddha would someday rise in the very place the Maitreya Buddha statue would be built, in Kushinagar itself, to the benefit of all beings.

My argument that a top-down develop-mentality—that is, the unexamined faith in the promises of neoliberal economic development and global capitalism— is partly to blame for the Maitreya Project–induced crisis in Kushinagar was established in my earlier publications about MPI (Falcone 2007a, 2007b, 2011). MPI has never conceded that there have been consequences to their unwillingness to engage in grassroots or participatory strategies of local engagement. Their public relations discourse championed a top-down growth model of economic development throughout the duration of the Maitreya Project 2.0 era.

My local informants in Kushinagar would likely take issue with any wholly optimistic appraisal of the karmic and socioeconomic benefits of the project, and not just due to concerns about the outcome of a forcible land acquisition. The proposed project sparked a protracted land battle in Greater Kushinagar that has dragged on for over a decade with its own negative effects, and thus the fight in Kushinagar has already caused emotional and economic wounds, if nothing else.

Special Land Acquisitions

The forcible land acquisition of the parcel for the statue project must be understood in terms of its place in a globalizing world, in which India's relatively new neoliberal agenda has allowed the British colonial legislation, the LAA, to be leveraged by states to acquire tracts of land for international corporate interests. Economic liberalization in India, which arguably began under the watch of Rajiv Gandhi in the 1990s, has continued apace under various political parties since then. This shift has met with resistance, as people's movements have grown organically against various projects, such as the Narmada Dam, the Nandigram special economic zone (SEZ), and other SEZs (Banerjee 2007). The anti–Maitreya Project agitation in Kushinagar must be framed within the larger discourses of globalization and development in India today, especially in relation to discontent about the trajectory of neoliberal policies and their untoward consequences.

In India, forcible land acquisition of farmland under cultivation is very serious business. As Hari Mohan Mathur (2011) observes in his edited volume on forcible land acquisition in India, the private sector has demanded more and more land in an effort to build more factories, office buildings, and malls. While he notes that it is often politically unpopular to do so, the Indian government has not shied away from working with private interests to force farmers off their land through laws of eminent domain. Mohan Mathur also argues that backlash against more large-scale land acquisitions led the government to hastily revise their national resettlement policies in 2007, and yet even this was widely seen by farmers, activists, and many scholars as merely an effort to mitigate the earlier political damage, as opposed to a genuine effort to significantly improve the legislation on forcible land acquisition, compensation, and resettlement. In contemporary India, there have been several high-profile and sometimes violent farmers' resistance movements to forcible land acquisition to private interests, such as the highly publicized cases of Nandigram and Singhur in West Bengal, and the anti–POSCO Corporation case in Orissa.

According to local Kushinagari bureaucrats, roughly 4.6 miles around the project site would be turned into the Kushinagar Special Development Area (KSDA), an SEZ that would have harsh restrictions on polluting industry, but lesser restrictions on tourist and business development. While the Maitreya Project's Linda Gatter (2007b) painted the KSDA as a special regulatory area with municipal bylaws and centralized management that would curtail any opportunism, the Kushinagari farmers felt that it would just allow the bureaucrats to extend favors to their friends while ignoring those with lesser means and connections. In the same article, Gatter wrote, "The Special Development Area status was enacted specifically because it would be irresponsible to build the Project without a carefully considered planning context to complement it." While the KSDA was envisioned as a religious SEZ, and therefore somewhat different than the industrial SEZs being set up and protested against around the country throughout the aughts, it should be viewed through the lens of national discourses about SEZs.

SEZs were often set up with reliance on land acquisition powers of the LAA, but the viability of this strategy has been called into question, especially by advocates for the poor. In one legal petition filed with the Supreme Court against the use of the LAA to seize land for industry and corporate interests, the petitioners wrote that the system was rigged against the poor: "A strategy under which the State allies with corporations who dispossess people of their livelihood is nothing but developmental terrorism" (Prakash 2007). The Supreme Court replied to the petition by ordering the national and state governments to issue a justification for their overly expansive use of the term "public purpose" in seizing farmland for corporate and development projects (Prakash 2007). The Kushinagari farmers' position may have been strengthened by the national-level legal challenges to the use of the LAA by state governments. There was agitation against SEZs all over India during my fieldwork period. One journalist even noted that nationwide, in areas where there are plans for SEZs, those regions are plagued by a dearth of marriages; the fear of possible future land acquisition has led to a grinding halt in marriage proposals and weddings (Pattnaik 2007). For locals in areas of government-sponsored economic anxiety, normal social mores are upended; life goes on, but not as before, and not for the better.

Anti-SEZ protests were given even more attention by the national press after the West Bengal violence over SEZs culminated in 2007. The state government of West Bengal had arranged for several SEZs, including a few in areas that saw widespread dissent about land acquisition plans, most notably Nandigram and Singhur. The SEZs were proposed and pursued under the administration of Buddhadeb Bhattacharjee, of the Communist Party of India-Marxist, also known as the CPI-M. The state government had seized hundreds of acres of agricultural land for a Tata car manufacturing scheme in the town of Singhur. Even after the land acquisition the farmers tangled with police to regain their land ("Singhur Flares Up Again" 2007), and eventually the corporation pulled out of the state completely ("Tata Pulls Out of Singhur" 2008).

Approximately ten thousand to fourteen thousand acres of mostly agricultural land in Nandigram were set to be acquired by the state of West Bengal via the LAA on behalf of an Indonesian-owned chemical corporation. The affected farmers set up the Committee to Resist Eviction from the Land (Bhumi Ucched Pratirodh Committee, hereafter BUPC). In 2007, fearing the land acquisition was imminent, the BUPC endeavored to defend their land by setting up blockades along the roads, cutting off communication with outsiders, and refusing to let any police or military into the area. On March 14, 2007, the CPI-M determined that the state government must restore the rule of law to Nandigram and sent a few thousand armed policemen and CPI-M party cadre members to break the BUPC's resistance movement. When the government stormed the area, the BUPC members, including men, women, and children, stood in opposition to the police, and in the intervening chaos between fourteen and fifty Nandigram locals were shot and killed by the invading forces ("Red-hand Buddha" 2007; "Nandigram Turns Blood Red" 2007; "Red Terror Continues in Nandigram's Bylanes" 2007). Human Rights Watch asserted that there had been at least thirty deaths in the violence, hundreds of injuries, and thousands displaced in a political vendetta that had largely gone unpunished in the intervening year ("India" 2008). The BUPC, which maintained control of Nandigram immediately following the attempted recapture, responded by driving CPI-M supporters in Nandigram out of their homes. The immediate effect of the violence was that technically the SEZ plan was put on hold, although not cancelled. Opposition parties in West Bengal condemned the CPI-M's actions in Nandigram, as did many of CPI-M's national allies. In both November 2007 and May 2008, fresh tensions between the BUPC and the CPI-M cadres led to renewed violence and aggression against BUPC members ("Red Terror Continues in Nandigram's Bylanes" 2007; "Fresh Violence in Nandigram" 2008).

While the state government has been ordered by their High Court to pay restitution to some BUPC victims, there have been no criminal charges levied successfully against perpetrators of the violence in Nandigram. The CPI-M has paid a political price, as they experienced some backlash in the May 2008 elections. Amnesty International's India Office produced a report that asserted that CPI-M especially had been guilty of perpetrating human rights violations including murder, rape, and kidnapping of Nandigram dissidents ("Urgent Need to Address Large Scale Human Rights Abuses" 2008). Both of the aforementioned reports by Human Rights Watch and Amnesty International highlight the need for politically independent tribunals to prosecute the perpetrators of the violence in Nandigram.

I find the CPI-M's assault on a people's movement in Nandigram on behalf of corporate interests to be an interesting parallel with Kushinagar's predicament at the hands of a Tibetan Buddhist religious project. I am not the only person to draw this parallel, as both my Kushinagari informants and the NAPM leaders advocating on their behalf were also cognizant that the lessons of Nandigram may serve as a cautionary tale should the Uttar Pradesh state government follow MPI down the globalization rabbit hole. For example, when I talked with staunch BBSS activist Shashi in March 2007, he reported to me, "I went to talk to the ADM [assistant district magistrate] in Kasia and I said, 'Do you want a Nandigram or Singhur? Is that what you want?' He said 'no,' but he has done nothing to help us. The Buddhist people don't want violence for the Buddha, but it will happen this way." In addition to the obvious similarities between the Nandigram and Kushinagar impasses—institutions working to displace farmers for their own ends—one simply could not have two more surprising antagonists. According to their own stated missions, their own ideologies, one might expect both Communists and Buddhists to be far more attuned to the suffering of poor, rural farmers. In the aftermath of the violence in West Bengal, the national government of India, the Centre, generally took the stance that SEZ development should be pursued only in cases where there was no forcible land acquisition (F. Ahmad 2007). However, where states were restricted from seizing land for SEZs, there were loopholes available, such as the fact that land could be acquired if the project was not technically called an SEZ (Singh 2007).

Another media topic that received constant coverage during my fieldwork period was the rise in starvation deaths and farmer suicides in many agricultural regions of India. There is a link to be made between the SEZ issue and the rash of farmer suicides; in general, the Indian government had turned toward industry and increasingly left small agriculturalists to their own devices. A BBC article about rural Indian starvation deaths noted that nongovernmental organizations in the area estimated that between 2003 and 2006 there were fifty-two such deaths in the Kushinagar district (Pandey 2008). Drought and poor crop yields in various states had led to financial ruin for thousands of farmers. Some farmers committed suicide when crops failed and bankruptcy ensued, since they felt that only the subsequent government payouts to their widows would sustain their families. I did not hear about any starvation deaths in the areas slated to be acquired by the MPI, but there were some rumblings about starvation deaths in the district. My Kushinagari informants all knew about the national trend of farmers' starvation and suicide; the literate farmers read about the rise of cases in various states in their Hindi newspapers and talked about it with their nonliterate friends. In interviews it was not uncommon for a farmer to bring up these deaths and say that starvation will happen to them also if their arable lands are forcibly acquired for the MPI statue. One man indicated that he would commit suicide if the land was taken, since that would be his only option. Some farmers talked about how disingenuous it was that on the one hand the state government was talking about helping farmers in dire straits, but on the other hand they were all set to doom the Kushinagari farmers to the ranks of those already in financial ruin.

"The Maitreya Project Is Wrong"

In stark contrast to the stated goals of my Buddhist informants in FPMT, and the very morals and notion of justice they espouse, the anti-MPI Kushinagaris believed that the Maitreya Project was an unjust monstrosity. My BBSS informants often articulated a general sense of injustice, in which the poor stayed poor, and in which they were almost doomed to be disenfranchised at every turn. Some people attributed this structural stratification to globalization, but much more often during my research my informants would call the land acquisition a form of "colonization"; as they saw it, MPI, a foreign power, was moving in to colonize their land and their livelihoods. One very memorable Kushinagari informant, one of many who were not really sure where I stood, even linked me to the forerunners of the colonial presence, in the context of scathingly criticizing the mission of MPI:

> SANJAY: I am a teacher in primary school . . . eight kilometers away—at a government junior high school. My school is safe. There are eleven schools which will be taken by the Maitreya Project. Primary, intermediate, and up to twelfth class.
>
> JESSICA: How big is your family?
>
> SANJAY: I have three children; one girl and two boys. My eldest is in the ninth class, and one girl in fourth class. I want them to be doctors and engineers.
>
> JESSICA: Will the Maitreya Project land acquisition hurt you? If it happens . . .
>
> SANJAY: I will lose two *bigha* and forty *katha*. I live in a joint family of twenty-two people. Four brothers and two sisters. . . . My house will also be taken. The cost of the house was eight *lakhs* [that is, eight hundred thousand rupees], but the government [compensation] rate is just twenty thousand rupees.
>
> JESSICA: Do you think your protests will halt the project?
>
> SANJAY: We will win against the Maitreya Project. I am 100 percent sure that we will be successful. [Around 1600 CE] the East India Company came from London. The East India Company was also a "project." The Maitreya Project is like the East India Company. And you are like Thomas Roe. Thomas Roe met Jahangir, and he made a promise [to him]. He said the British are simply salesmen.

He went on to say that obviously Roe had perpetrated a great scam and gave the British a political foothold to gain ever more influence in India. I admit that this speech, especially the fact that I was implicitly being mistaken for a stalwart MPI ally, took me by surprise. I quickly reiterated that I supported their protest: "But I'm not trying to convince you that the Maitreya Project will be good for you. I'm not paving the way [for them]. I hope you all win in your struggle," I said.

But Sanjay just smiled thinly, lifted his eyebrows, and bobbled his head, as if to say, "We'll see." Sanjay, like many others, was not working his land himself, but rather was contributing to the joint family income while some of his brothers worked the family land. Later that afternoon, after I interviewed others from his village, he approached me and said, "We are stronger now. You tell them that we can't be colonized again."

At other times, an elderly family member or two recounted that they could remember the British leaving when they were children and that if Gandhi were still alive, he would be fighting against the Maitreya Project. "We will not be colonized again," said an old woman, after spending fifteen minutes tugging at her clothes ("How will we afford clothes?") and rubbing her belly ("What will we eat? Where will we get our *chapatis*?") to show her anger at MPI's plans. This particular old woman told me that she remembered seeing Gandhi when she was a child; her father took her to see him during the salt tax protests. Irate, and yelling to whomever was in earshot, she said that even as an old woman she would fight to the death for her family's land if the Maitreya Project ever came for it.

Some of the BBSS leadership, however, began to attribute their plight to globalization and the policies of an increasingly neoliberal India. From the beginning, Marxist groups in the area (e.g., student groups and local political affiliates) took an eager interest in the anti–Maitreya Project protests, and their representatives often took the microphone to give speeches at protests. The MPI controversy in Kushinagar is a textbook case of the unintended local and regional consequences of global capital, and naturally fueled some spirited local Marxist rhetoric.

In 2006, a local connection to an Asha for Education social worker led the BBSS to invite two famous activists, Sandeep Pandey and his wife, Arundhati Dhuru,[7] to a local anti-MPI rally. Sandeep and his wife are also very prominent members of the NAPM, which boasts other celebrated Indian activists, such as Medha Patekar, who has battled tirelessly against the Narmada Dam project's propensity to displace countless villagers. The entrance of the NAPM into the anti–Maitreya Project battle raised the profile of the struggle from a local one to a more national one. Some BBSS members were invited to NAPM activist trainings and subsequently began talking more about how their struggle was people's resistance to global capitalism.

FIGURE 14. Local family from Greater Kushinagar poses in 2006. In interviews with the author, various members of this family emphasized that the Maitreya Project would hurt their family's socioeconomic situation.
Photo by the author.

After working with BBSS for a few years, Sandeep Pandey was somewhat frustrated, because he felt that too few Kushinagaris realized the extent to which their particular fight was a symptom of neoliberal globalization. When I interviewed him in Lucknow in 2007, Pandey told me: "The problem with the anti–Maitreya Project struggle is that they are not putting up a holistic struggle. They are only fighting for better compensation, so it is not giving the people strength. It is not an ideological struggle there. They are dealing with the same-same politicians, but only fighting against the Maitreya Project, not for their rights holistically." By this measure, Sandeep Pandey was correct: farmers by and large had little interest in revolution, and they just wanted the Maitreya Project to relocate.[8]

The Maitreya Project seems to be yet another development plan with good intentions and poor follow-through. There have been so many projects studied in the anthropology of development literature that teach us that development projects often go awry (Escobar 1995; Ferguson 1994; Sachs 1992). Ferguson goes so far as to remind his readers that in the world of development, failures are the rule, rather than the exception. Ferguson also observes that the most successful work of development industries is its self-maintenance, as well as its role as a purveyor of excessive governmentality. The Maitreya Project and its partner, the Uttar Pradeshi state government, have proceeded by laboring under the assumption that the top-down economic development of Kushinagar would be beneficial to everyone. As Escobar notes, in the 1970s development discourse became widely naturalized: "Development had achieved the status of a certainty in the social imaginary" (1995, 5). Vandana Shiva (1988) has called the naturalization of development discourse a form of violence against the poor and considers development to be "maldevelopment."

While I am critical of the develop-mentality that projects linear progress with neoliberal economic development,[9] Kushinagaris, in general, seem less interested in the problems with development and globalization, and more interested in how their villages may have more and more access to the luxuries that the Indian middle class already enjoys. Kushinagaris have bought into the idea posed by Latouche: "economic development as the trickle-down effect of industrial growth" (1997, 137). For Kushinagaris, development and progress were indeed good futures to work toward; the farmers' resistance was never in opposition to development itself; their resistance was in opposition to the fact that, as far as they could tell, the plan would preclude progress and development for them. In other words, my Kushinagari informants generally saw MPI's plan as maldevelopment, but they would not have viewed all economic development in those terms. They simply wanted progress that would not come at their expense.

The Kushinagari farmers who protested against the statue plan almost all noted that if they themselves were confident that their families would benefit along the way, then they would indeed be converts to the statue plan. Some of my interlocutors did not even dispute the contested development notion that a local economic boom would eventually trickle down to benefit them; instead they explained that they would not be able to survive the loss of so many pounds of flesh in the interim. Many hoped that it would be moved nearby, close enough that the region would benefit, but far enough away that they would not be the victims of poorly executed eminent domain.

While the revolution may not yet have come to Kushinagar with the totality that would please the leadership of Asha for Education and NAPM, the speeches at protests and the discussions with farmers in interviews in their homes demonstrated that some farmers have gradually recognized that their enemies were no longer just local and regional despots, but instead transnational outsiders: the global economy, the free market fetish, and the threat of outsiders coming back in to take more land, seize more control, and make more money.

Some of the farmers in the Kushinagar area who are protesting against the Maitreya Project do recognize themselves that their plight is a result of the global forces adversely affecting their local community. While many farmers do want higher standards of living and more opportunity for their children, some also recognize globalization as a symptom of neoliberal free market economics, in which the rich get richer and the poor bear the brunt of progress. Marxism is not a dirty word in the *gaons* of Kushinagar, and it is not surprising, therefore, that many villagers seem to take seriously the notion that the government ought to spread the wealth of the rich around to allow the most vulnerable economic groups to improve their lots in life. My informants, especially those connected with NAPM or in the BBSS leadership, spoke Marxist theory with fluency and passion and convinced many listeners of the truth of their view.

While the anticolonization rhetoric outstripped the Marxist discourse, in many speeches these two strands of thoughts are becoming intertwined with postcolonial awareness of "never again." Never again, they say, will we be dispossessed and abused by white people from far away. The postcolonial experience has affected my informants: they have personally thrived, or failed to thrive, under certain conditions that cannot be uncoupled from the history of the nation and its political economy. Not entirely unlike Gupta's (1998) explication of the postcolonial condition according to his informants (who were also peasant farmers in Uttar Pradesh), the postcolonial condition as an ethnographic frame is useful insofar as it helps to illuminate the experiences and views of our informants. Some anti-MPI protesters have come to believe that their current fight against a global organization echoes past resistance against colonial domination. The villagers of Greater Kushinagar have skillfully weighed the good, bad, and ugly of the type of international development proposed by MPI and their local advocates. Those with the most to lose put up an extraordinary show of resistance against the threat of dispossession by state and global forces that sometimes seemed indomitable. The anti–Maitreya Project activism has spawned moments of very acute local social solidarity, as well as more awareness of the larger economic forces affecting the locality today. Therefore, while the statue plan has brought constant fear and uncertainty about the future to Greater Kushinagar, there is a tiny glint and gleam of a silver lining: the MPI resistance has arguably left the villagers better informed and better organized than ever before.

There is certainly no clear-cut delineation between the modern and the traditional in Kushinagar. Farmers would oppose the idea that they are against progress or development. In fact, they want the trappings of modernity so much that they are unwilling to slip backward, which is what they fear they will face should their land be forcibly acquired. The villagers insist that, despite the work yet to be done, they are now more modern, more educated, more progressive, more successful and more stable than their parents' generation had been. They would oppose any suggestion that they are the "traditional" side of an imaginary binary on which the Maitreya Project was a putative "modern."

The Maitreya Project, of course, in building a five-hundred-foot statue of a future Buddha, could just as easily be deemed on the traditional, religious, end of things in contrast to farmers eager to modernize. To some extent, both the idea of "hybrid cultures" deployed by Arturo Escobar (1995) or even Gupta's notion of "hybridity" (1998, 6) captures the complexity and tangle of the modern and traditional, especially if terms like "modern" and "traditional" are understood as always already in flux. Although we can envision a hypothetical situation in which the values of MPI and BBSS aligned harmoniously—Indic religious values see potential spiritual value in Buddhist statue-building enterprises, and both communities could envision better socioeconomic ends—in the end, the particular type of state-led, top-down economic development championed by MPI led statue supporters and opponents to collide passionately and spectacularly.

In *The Making of Buddhist Modernism*, David McMahan writes, "one recurring theme in the interaction of Buddhism and the West is the hope that Buddhism might have solutions to the formidable problems of modernity—solutions that the West has missed in its drive to technological development and material well-being" (2008, 259). He goes on to say that barring the most Orientalist of these hopeful articulations, it would be folly to suggest that Buddhism is necessarily devoid of such alternative visions; that said, he argues, Buddhism could itself be converted to neoliberal globalization in the process. This latter possibility, "that [Buddhism] could accommodate itself so completely to mainstream western values and assumptions that it no longer is alternative to them and thus accedes the resources it has for critiquing them" (McMahan 2008, 260), is precisely, and tragically, how the Maitreya Project's grand experiment in Engaged Buddhism has played out in the Greater Kushinagar area.

The development strategy of the Maitreya Project and its partners advocates a top-down strategy that is, according to many development studies scholars (e.g., Chambers 1983; Chaudhari 1985; Holland and Blackburn 1998; Nelson and Wright 1997; Setty 1991), demonstrably less effective than grassroots development or participatory development. If development is even to be considered a viable ethical possibility, then this story, like so many others before it (e.g., Barnett 1977; Chambers 1983; Gardner and Lewis 1996), demonstrates the need for development strategies that are less beholden to global capitalism and more committed to equality, direct engagement, and real collaboration.

More cooperation, communication, and mutual respect could have led to compromises that may have gotten locals on board with Maitreya Project 2.0 many years ago. The stalemate in Kushinagar is largely a result of the structural violence of the situation: a global organization with access to first-world wealth has worked with a state government to get more arable land than it needed from thousands of people who depend on it for subsistence. As such, the Maitreya Project controversy is another narrative detailing the unintended, high local costs of neoliberal globalization.

In this chapter, the politics of the controversy is set against its poetics. Who determines value? The value of land, the value of kindness, or the value of an economic theory? Who is to say what is right and what is wrong? In facing these intractable questions, I have juxtaposed the moral aspirations of FPMT for a type of socially Engaged Buddhism with the details of the land controversy that lay bare the fraught dynamics at play in Kushinagar's socioeconomic world. Although espousing the mantle of Engaged Buddhism, MPI embraced a model of progress that relies on tired, trickle down approaches to neoliberal economic development. In sum, I have demonstrated that according to their own, self-articulated values of Engaged Buddhism, charity, and *maitri*, not only has MPI failed the people of Kushinagar, they have failed themselves.

❧ CHAPTER 9

Compassion / *KARUNA*

Reflections on Engaged Anthropology

In January 2006, I met Christopher Titmuss, a Buddhist teacher in the Insight Meditation community, told him about my research project, and subsequently asked him for an interview.

"The Maitreya Project," he said slowly. "That bloody Maitreya Project."

For many years prior to that moment, he had argued against what he considered the unethical excesses of the project (see Titmuss 2001). What struck me most at the time was how unbelievably tired he sounded. I did not understand it then, but now I feel it deep in my bones; it is tightness across the chest and a weight to carry: Maitreya Project fatigue. In part, it is the heaviness of the judgments of some of our nonheritage Buddhist peers who think, "Why would anyone push back against such a sunny dream?"

I began discussing my burgeoning concerns with any and all accessible FPMTers and Maitreya Project staff several months after my arrival in India for full-time research in late 2005. It had only taken a few months for me to realize that the communication gap between the farmers and the Buddhists was increasingly perilous, and growing more so as the days before the proposed land acquisition ticked away. These first inquiries of MPI staffers were fairly routine: Why wasn't there an FPMT presence in the area? Why wasn't there an MPI office in Kushinagar? Why was Babar Singh the only regional staffer, since he was wildly unpopular in Kushinagar? Should not someone, anyone, from MPI go talk to the farmers and discuss their future with them? As time passed my questions became increasingly despondent and impassioned. Don't you think that the compensation is too low? Why isn't it your problem?—isn't the land being taken for your statue? How can you build a statue of loving-kindness in a manner that is causing so much collateral suffering?

During the second half of my research period, having checked and re-checked my facts in Kushinagar, I began talking more openly about the controversy in Kushinagar with FPMTers of various stripes in Bodh Gaya, Delhi, and California. I met with a whole range of responses: surprise, incredulity, anger, fear, anxiety. Mostly there was a great deal of doubt. Finally, nearly eighteen months after the incident on the bridge narrated in the introduction, I began publicly writing about the Maitreya Project (Falcone 2007a).

In this chapter, I will reflect on my methods, my positionality, my advocacy, and my writing, since readers are entitled to read this book with an understanding of its authorial framing. It is best to say this clearly and firmly right here at the outset: I didn't swoop in to save the Kushinagaris; they worked to save themselves. Yet it would be problematic to write myself out of the book altogether, especially since I did become an advocate for the BBSS farmer-activists in the process of doing my research. Here I explore the ways that my scholarship evolved into an ethical, engaged anthropology. Furthermore, I consider how my identity as a white, female, nonheritage Buddhist anthropologist came with particular challenges (and privileges) in the field, which shaped my authorial vantage point.

Advocacy Anthropology

Anthropologists derive what authority they have from "being there" (Geertz 1988, 1); they travel to the field, listen, learn, soak it all in—the good, bad, and ugly. They write it all down, and they write it up. And, sometimes, they take sides. Some anthropologists choose to serve as activists or advocates on behalf of certain individual informants or groups of interlocutors (for example, see Fortun 2001, Scheper-Hughes 1995, or Turner 1993). Indeed, there is a long, respectable history of activist anthropology that I ardently celebrate as an important subgenre of anthropological work. This research project was not initially meant to be a contribution to that genre; I came to it entirely by accident. I choose to study the Maitreya Project because it fascinated me. I did not come to the project hoping to capture a car wreck in slow motion.

While my master's research on FPMT had disabused me of the notion that their centers were utopian spaces occupied by the perfection of wisdom incarnate (Falcone 2001), I did still hope, with a great deal of naiveté perhaps, that the Maitreya Project would be a Buddhist project done with the mindfulness and excessive attention to the details necessary to mitigate the kind of collateral damage that so often accompanies development projects. Another ethnographer of a Tibetan Buddhist community, Daniel Capper, admitted that when he began his research he certainly expected "a worldly utopia" (2002, 35), but he eventually reset his expectations on observing the sometimes "unenlightened" actions of his informants. He noted that his expectations were naive, and I can do no less.

Anthropologists seek to understand the beliefs, values, and practices of various subcultures, and then we do our best to represent our interlocutors fairly, in all their spectacular complexity. While we have a professional obligation to seek and receive informed consent from those we interview, anthropologists do not have an obligation to see eye-to-eye with their informants. Indeed, it is difficult for me to imagine a scenario in which an anthropologist is completely simpatico with each and every interlocutor. There are many anthropologists who are studying communities that they know from the outset will test their personal moral compass, and yet they go into the field and get down to work, really trying to get to the bottom of the internal cultural logic that drives behaviors that they themselves may never personally condone. I have done this work myself. I studied with Hindu extremist groups to do my best to understand their beliefs and practices, despite knowing full well that I would never give credence to political views predicated on divisive ethno-nationalist hate (Falcone 2010a, 2012b and 2016). An anthropologist studying child marriage practices in India, or female genital mutilation in Somalia, seeks to understand the power dynamics, belief systems, and cultural logics that motivate such practices, but neither anthropologist nor reader need necessarily conclude that such practices are moral.

In the fall of 2005, at the outset of my doctoral research, I requested permission to volunteer in the Maitreya Project office in Gorakhpur. My request was understandably refused, but I was taken aback at how MPI officials proceeded to dissuade my work in Kushinagar. Although I came with a certified Indian research visa granted for the topic, one MPI staffer enthusiastically pitched alternative projects for me to pursue. I persisted with my research on the Maitreya Project plan, albeit with a new commitment to look at the project from the point of view of FPMT supporters and Kushinagari antagonists. I had to study the project from the outside. Thus, I proceeded to "circumambulate" the planned statue.

The anger directed at the project by most Kushinagaris was so pointed and vehement that in the summer of 2006, I began writing e-mails and letters to the Maitreya Project to try to "call in" and ask them to consider a course correction.[1] At first, I tried to work within the organization, because I believed for some time that MPI officials simply did not know about the resistance of the farmers in Kushinagar. Their repeated insistence that I was wrong to believe the farmers led me to redouble my efforts to verify and check my data. When I met with lower-level MPI and FPMT staff, I was completely open with them about my research and my advocacy. For example, in late 2006 and early 2007, I allowed several Maitreya Project affiliates (a few Relic Tour custodians, Maitreya Project administrators, FPMT *sangha*, and Maitreya Project board members) to interview me at length about my experiences in Kushinagar before I interviewed them about their views on the Maitreya Project. I did not conduct "gotcha" interviews.

MPI did not have a presence in Kushinagar, so if MPI as an institution was truly ignorant of the situation there, then they should have made an effort to discern the facts; if they did not care to trust my assessment, then they could have sent a team in. However, if MPI was feigning ignorance, then they should not be allowed to continue that charade. If nothing else, my interventions denied them the option of claiming ignorance; by carrying the stories of BBSS's resistance to MPI staffers and advocates, I insisted on their responsibility. FPMT interlocutors responded to my news in a variety of ways: I was sometimes welcomed, sometimes ignored, and sometimes treated as a pariah. I was not taken seriously by those who had the power to do anything about the project.

I sometimes wonder if I my research trajectory would have been different had I been a male researcher, rather than a female one. Surely, a male researcher would not have (1) been consistently dismissed as "naive," (2) been accused of "becoming increasing shrill," as I was portrayed in an internal MPI communication (as related to me by multiple MPI insiders in personal communication), or (3) been told in an e-mail from a highly ranked MPI administrator that my ethnographic research in India (eleven months of work at that point) was merely "research." Two female Relic Tour staffers complained to me of patronizing and patriarchal attitudes in the MPI ranks that had negatively affected them and then told me that these issues were also at play in the way that my engagements were being so neatly dismissed out of hand. During my fieldwork, an MPI administrator telephoned my male advisor at Cornell University to ask that my project be curtailed, and to insist that I be put on a tighter leash. In fact, several male mentors and peers—such as my PhD advisor, my college religious studies professor, and other Buddhist friends and informants—have been occasionally called on to bring me to heel. I find myself wondering if a male scholar would have been treated thus.

When I finally acknowledged that the Maitreya Project leadership had taken a firm position of antagonism to the Kushinagari resistance and to me, I decided to alter my course of action. My somewhat underwhelming activist aim: whistle-blowing. I went public with my dissent in 2007. I wrote about my concern with MPI's plans and practices in the *Wild River Review* (Falcone 2007a), a well-regarded literary journal. In my contribution, I essentially discussed the controversy on the ground, the failure of MPI to mitigate the anxiety of local farmers, and the gap between MPI's predicted outcomes and the futures that seemed more probable given the institution's policy of studied negligence. The Maitreya Project issued a rebuttal urging readers to dare to dream, calling me "cynical," and saying that MPI was confident that all would be well in the end, and that they would engage with local stakeholders at the appropriate time, which would be after the land acquisition (Gatter 2007b). In my view, their response was an unnerving, tone-deaf public relations fluff piece. In my detailed response, I implored MPI to go work with the local community post haste; I maintained that a policy of "willful naiveté" to the fraught situation on the ground was not an effective strategy for developing a long-term partnership with the community (Falcone 2007b). I was not happy to be debating MPI in the press, but the alternative—to slink back to Ithaca to write my dissertation in silence—smacked of complicity, a selfishness that I found insupportable.

Lest I be the only voice (in an English medium) expressing concern about the situation in Kushinagar, I actively alerted dozens of journalists and press outlets about the story several times. I suggested that it was a story worth covering and invited them to do so. Most journalists I contacted politely declined, but some told me to e-mail them again if violence actually ensued (in other words, if it bleeds, it reads). In the fall of 2007, a freelance journalist, Daniel Pepper, did pick up the story tip and independently went to Kushinagar to cover the story himself. Pepper wrote an article that was circulated widely from the *Christian Science Monitor* (Pepper 2007a) to the *Washington Times* (Pepper 2007b) and in many other news outlets. I see the Daniel Pepper articles (and to some small extent, the *Wild River Review* debate) as a particular turning point for the project, and I call this moment "the media blowup."

By late 2007, FPMTers had heard from multiple voices that cast doubt on the integrity of the process in Kushinagar, as well as many counterreassurances from Maitreya Project staffers that any such criticism was malicious or sensationalist. At this point, many FPMTers were aware of the controversy and trying to sort through the opposing narratives: some took recourse in their faith in their guru's decisions, some discussed the problems with one another, and some expressed concern to the Maitreya Project staffers about whether everything in the process was truly as it should be.

After the media blowup, my other acts of advocacy involved the following: (1) continuing to speak with Maitreya Project affiliates (such as the custodians of the Relic Tour in 2008), as well as FPMTers who crossed my path, about my critique of the process; and (2) circulating an e-petition with supporters connected to Asha for Education (and also the NAPM). I sent the petition with a few hundred signatures from all over the world to the Maitreya Project in 2009. These were admittedly small gestures of advocacy. I had to do something; I wish I had done more.

After my *Wild River Review* articles were published, I was met with icy silence from MPI leadership, and I have received no written missives since then. In North Carolina in 2008, I tiptoed into a public Relic Tour event terrified that the custodians would ask me to leave; I was not expelled from the premises, but my short discussion with the head custodian at the time, who I had met with several times before, was especially tense and uncomfortable.

A very prominent MPI and FPMT leader, one of Lama Zopa Rinpoche's main attendants, called me in early October 2009 in response to a note that I written to him. My letter to him stated that despite a recent public statement by the Maitreya Project arguing that everything had been finally worked out with the farmers, the farmers' advocacy group had issued a statement in July 2009 to refute MPI's rosy public relations picture. I asked him to please mind the farmers. In our October 2009 phone call, this MPI leader was entirely uncritical about MPI's work in India; he told me they had no intention of shifting gears in their dealings with Indian locals. His only admission of a Maitreya Project misstep was to agree with me that they had underestimated the obstacles and difficulties of their plan. He said that they had lost some of their major donors and were now searching for new ones. I asked, Because of the economic downturn? Or because of resistance on the ground? Or lack of integrity of Indian partners or staff? No, he said, because of "our obstacles." He told me that I was making things difficult for them at a "critical" and "sensitive" juncture in the project. He indicated that he was ready to stop talking, so we agreed to disagree, and the call ended abruptly. I wonder if the call was as profoundly discomfiting to him as it was to me. I had finally and totally burned my admittedly tenuous bridge to MPI to an ashy, blackened crisp.

Readers of this book should know that my personal religious ties to FPMT made my struggles with the Maitreya Project a particularly painful fieldwork experience. While in the field doing this work, I was myself a nonheritage

Tibetan Buddhist, and thus I struggled intensely and earnestly with issues of Buddhist morality and Buddhist practice. In fact, I was an FPMTer myself. I had first taken refuge with Lama Zopa Rinpoche at an FPMT retreat while still a college student in the late nineties. I had done numerous retreats and courses with FPMT as a student since then. I am not sure if I ever truly crossed the line from being an FPMT student to FPMT devotee, but if I am being honest with myself I did go through a period of intense devotion when I lived and volunteered at the Root Institute for a few months in 2000. My practice down-shifted on my return to the United States in the summer of 2001, but I continued to meditate, to make offerings at a home altar, to chant the Green Tara mantra regularly, and to see the FPMT community as my *sangha*. When I began my doctoral work for this project, I still considered myself a part of the FPMT family.

My study of the prelife of a statue, Maitreya Project 2.0, has been intellectually stimulating but spiritually challenging. For example, my work on this research project has made me wary of devotional practices that are dependent on unwavering loyalty to spiritual teachers. As this project unfolded, my disappointment in FPMT leaders grew to the point that I went through a personal crisis of faith. As time went on it became clear to me that FPMT and I were hopelessly out of sync; I did not trust them as moral arbiters anymore. I still consider myself a nonheritage Buddhist, but I am no longer an FPMT student. My first *sangha* is now lost to me.

There is something else, reader, another factor in those countless sleepless nights: I am not a confrontational person. It is a personal weakness, but there it is. I assiduously avoid conflict, because I am deeply shaken when the antagonism and anger of others falls on me. As I endeavored to be heard by FPMT leaders, I was usually ignored and occasionally undermined, but the enmity I sometimes encountered has been profoundly personally taxing. Even now, years since I last tangled with them, I wonder and worry if the FPMT public relations machine will respond to this book with public personal attacks or perhaps an internal whisper campaign. When this book is published, I wonder what my FPMT friends will think and whether they will turn their backs on me. I am not cut out for this kind of thing—it is not in my character to be a rabble-rouser. And so, for years, I fantasized about just dropping this whole book altogether.

So, to publish or not to publish? As an academic, I earned tenure on the strength of my other publications, so I do not need this book to keep my university job. Nor do scholarly monographs like this one tend to make much money.[2] Given the emotional turmoil that has accompanied my work on this research, perhaps it would have been best for me to file my dissertation and then just walk away from this project altogether. However, I could not and I cannot. It pains me to think it, but my farmer-activist informants, the friends I left behind in Kushinagar, probably think I took their stories and ran. I publish this book because I feel I must, because to fail to do so would be a breach of the trust expressed by those whose voices I promised to carry further than their chants could reach. And so I will reach down deep, steady my breath, and send this book out into the world.

MPI Works to Control the Message

After the media blowup, the Maitreya Project administrators continued to work to acquire the land in Kushinagar, but much of their focus was wrapped up in public relations and fundraising. The public image of the Maitreya Project was a matter of the utmost concern to its administrators, and they were aggressive in their public deflections. For example, when the unsavory media attention came to light in 2007, almost every time the story was reposted to a Buddhist website or blog, MPI's media manager Linda Gatter would post the same crafted rebuttal, or variations thereupon, much of which had been taken verbatim from Kedge's contemporaneous Maitreya Project Update (Kedge 2007b). When *Vassa: A Blog for SCUBA* posted links to the Pepper article and discussed the story, the first comment, posted by Linda Gatter, was a form letter repudiating the news report. When someone replied to Pepper's article with an editorial piece titled "Proponents of the Maitreya Project Heartless, Arrogant" (McLeod 2007), Linda Gatter posted a version of the same reply (Gatter 2007a). MPI was in frantic damage-control mode. The Maitreya Project has consistently refused to acknowledge one single misstep in their Kushinagar relations along the way. Controlling the message means not having to say you're sorry.

When the *Wikipedia* page about the Maitreya Project was anonymously retooled by Tony Simmons, just after the media blowup, to mirror exactly what was posted to the MPI website, Wikipedia editors contested the objectivity of the edits and started a prolonged web battle or "edit war" over the right to control the content of the "Maitreya Project" *Wikipedia* web page. For a period of time, every single time someone would contest the veracity of the claims and take down Simmons's edits, he would challenge them, and vice versa. Several times editors tagged the page with a dispute of the neutrality of the point of view, and Simmons would delete the neutrality addendum.

The dispute raged on, as more senior editors were called on to resolve the dispute. In the context of official *Wikipedia* mediation, Simmons accused one of the editors of religious bias after she called his version of the page an "advertisement" and noted that his account was "a single-purpose account" working only on the Maitreya Project page; he deleted the "point of view" tags again and responded with the following: "Your inability to state a case clearly makes one wonder if there is a hidden religious agenda afoot. As I consider myself a neutral editor, thus I feel that I am entitled to remove this tag again as the article has been further edited." His account was then tagged for "conflict of interest," and the *Wikipedia* editors demanded that he identify his affiliations. At this point, Tony Simmons was unmasked as an MPI administrator.

Only after being thus exposed did Tony Simmons concede and allow many of the edits to stand, including reports of the controversy and links to opposing views that he had tried to erase from the page. Before this concession, he wrote that the Pepper article contained "deliberately fabricated" material and was a "witch hunt"; he suggested that it should be removed, but this suggestion was refused by the other active editors on the page who suggested that Simmons's opinion (and a letter he brandished from a bureaucrat in India) were not enough evidence to refute articles published in reputable international news outlets.

The debate continued for weeks before Tony Simmons bowed out, acknowledging that the conflict-of-interest concerns had made it difficult for him to function as an editor on the "Maitreya Project" page. However, he noted that he would periodically revisit the page, since he said that there were enemies of the project who would like to skew the public record. Simmons was not the only FPMTer to be accused of lack of evidence and neutrality in their *Wikipedia* edits. Later, another FPMTer popped up to try to insert a sentence about how thousands of FPMTers had made offerings of candles in support of the project, but editors asked him to back up the assertion with a citation, which he failed to produce. He tried to say that he had himself witnessed the offerings, but this was unconvincing to the editors involved, so the sentence was removed.

The *Wikipedia* edits were archived, and the internal dialogues about the edits were completely public, so I observed the *Wikipedia* morass from the e-sidelines and did not contribute to the discussion. The *Wikipedia* debates were a public stage on which the Maitreya Project and FPMT leadership tried to take control of the way that the statue project was being publicly represented. The *Wikipedia* guidelines frustrated the ability of MPIers to control the message. Notably, all of their public work on this front involved trying to deny the land acquisition controversy, as opposed to actually acknowledging it or saying that they would take steps to improve the situation. *Wikipedia's* editors, mostly volunteers who had risen in the ranks of editorial leadership, worked to make a page that referenced both MPI's assertions about the project and its future, as well as the viewpoint of its critics.

Reflections on Fieldwork

I have argued elsewhere (Falcone 2010b, 2013) that the reflexive turn ushered in by Jay Ruby (1982), Clifford and Marcus (1986), and others was a step in the right direction, but I believe that social scientists would do well to push reflexivity further toward more unflinching examinations of both the self and other. For example, in one article, drawing on two disparate bodies of scholars—Tibetan Gelugpa monastics and American anthropologists—I observed that for all of their analytical tools for the study of power, hierarchy, and ideologies, both communities seem to have trouble using their theoretical tools on their own institutions (Falcone 2010b).[3] Extending that thinking to the research at hand, I draw on Boyer's *Spirit and System* (2005), as he wrestles with the same phenomenon in terms of the gaps and synergies between the theory and practice enacted by his German media informants. Thus, echoing the Buddhist notions of my FPMT informants, I posit a meditative thinking that would allow an anthropologist to go beyond traditional reflexivity, that is, concern about representation, bias, and co-constitutionality, and begin to publicly and unabashedly explore academic culture and knowledge-production practices in a more personal, probing, and mindful manner. In *A Vulnerable Observer* (1996), Ruth Behar notes that in contrast to much of normative past and present anthropological thinking, the personal does have an important place in the public documents of anthropology. She argues that returning the self to the text does not mean "exposure for its own sake," or vulnerability for its own sake, since it ought to add to the integrity of the argument along the way (Behar 1996, 14).

Throughout my fieldwork and writing I relentlessly questioned my own authority, authorship, ethos, sociality, and subjectivity to achieve the end of punctuating my work on "them" with vulnerable gestures to an "I" that is no more or less fluid, under construction, and in process. Despite the ethical tightrope I walked, or maybe because of it, I view my book research itself as a moral, even Buddhist-influenced, practice. Every single day in the field, I wrestled with my conscience, and while I found no easy answers,[4] I allowed my desire for ethical action to guide my decisions in the field and afterward. I view my work on this project as modeled on the very Buddhist concepts—*karuna*, *maitri*, *dhyana*, mindfulness, interdependence, and emptiness—that I learned in both academic and FPMT contexts.

Crapanzano (1980) tells his readers that both informant and ethnographer are re-created through the process of fieldwork, and Rabinow (1977) tells his audience that understanding of the self comes through the detour of understanding the other. My informants on both sides deeply affected me, and I would venture to say that I affected them to some extent as well; through engagement, we changed each other. There are obvious moments of interrelationality and less obvious ones. I remember a teacher at a school in Siswa Mahant saying that the students did not understand why an unmarried woman was permitted to travel alone to another country; the students were asking a lot of questions about gender expectations—I was stretching their worldview just by being there. I recall moments in which my interconnection with my subjects was muddled, such as when I sat with FPMTers doing sincere prayers to defeat the obstacles to the Maitreya Project while simultaneously wondering if I had unwittingly become one of those obstacles.

Fieldwork is hard; it is the very worst and very best thing about anthropology. When I think about this fieldwork, I feel equal parts exhausted and grateful. It was hard to be doing research on such a controversial topic; so many of my informants were angry. I had to push myself out the door some mornings. I was the object of gossip in various field contexts in ways that still bother me. I was sexually harassed more than once. I fetishized my fieldnotes and archival material and had recurring nightmares that I had lost them all. I was engaged in months of warfare with disease-bearing mosquitos. And yet, still, I feel incredibly lucky to have had the opportunity to do this work. Even as my faith in FPMT disintegrated, my presence in the sacred places of Buddhism was fortifying in surprising ways. I was often conflicted about the best ways to serve as an advocate for the BBSS and what the unintended consequences of own my actions might be, but unlike MPI, my steps were guided by the local knowledge and local relationships gleaned from being on the ground in India. I know that I have become a better person for it. The people of Kushinagar were angry, but many of my interlocutors were also incredibly generous, hospitable, and kind. I miss it.

While I have worked to be as objective as possible while collecting narratives from all of the stakeholders involved with the Maitreya Project as proponents or protestors, I primarily honor the well-established conventions of my discipline: the politics of ethnography refuse any real objectivity or any claim to a perfect truth. I echo what Tweed has written about fieldworkers:

> Culturally mediated objects enter and leave my sensorial and conceptual horizon. The horizon shifts as I do. And my position (including my gender, class, and race) obscures some things as it illuminates others.

But let me be clear: I am not apologizing. Theorists have been more or less self-conscious and their interpretations have been more or less subtle, but there have been no supra-locative accounts of religion. No theorist has hovered; no interpretation has been ungrounded. All theorists stand in a particular place. Every one of them. The difference? Some interpreters have said so." (2006, 18)

Tweed is correct when he writes that it is best to acknowledge where one stands and the inherently partial nature of one's truth, even as one offers up as responsible and well-crafted an interpretation as one can muster. He writes, "To say that a cloud of sand blows up as we traverse the path is not to say we are not on the move and cannot offer representations along the way. To say we cannot have a God's-eye view, and to acknowledge blind spots, is not to say we can see nothing at all" (Tweed 2006, 28). I have shared my positionality, my crisis of faith, my advocacy, my anxieties, and my own intentionality so that readers might understand the hands that have crafted the face of this narrative.

I continue to feel deeply frustrated with the Maitreya Project, and my book must be read in this light. As a former FPMT student, a past donor to the statue project, and a current friend to many FPMTers, I am simultaneously disappointed by the gaps that I perceived between institutional rhetoric and their subsequent (in)actions and cognizant that FPMT still does a lot of good work in the world. Despite my antipathy for some of MPI's policies and practices, I have a great deal of empathy for many of their goals and motivations. As much as I am compelled to root for the farmer-activists of Kushinagar, I know that they are not perfect—their threats of violence disturbed me greatly. I have endeavored to be as even-handed and fair as possible to both the statue-makers and the Kushinagari resistance, but it is conceivable that in doing so, I have written a book that will ultimately be dissatisfying to nearly all of my informants.

Debating with Love

Although I saw my research as itself an exercise in compassionate practice, I sometimes wondered if the fact that I was engaged in a sharp debate with MPI had compromised my experiment in doing Buddhist-inspired fieldwork. Yet, by debating with, and for, *maitri*, I found myself well within the bounds of Buddhist practice. Tibetan Buddhist monastic debate is frenetic and competitive, but it is seen as an important heritage Tibetan Buddhist practice in monastic and scholarly contexts. As I reflect on my advocacy anthropology, I look to the Tibetan Buddhist tradition of debate to show that such engagement can itself be an ethical practice. I share an excerpt from an interview I conducted with a famous, learned Tibetan Buddhist monk and let him have the last word on the matter.

Fieldnotes, May 27, 2006

Kirti Tenshab Rinpoche was a highly respected lama, the abbot of Kirti Monastery in Dharamsala, and one of Lama Zopa Rinpoche's own teachers. Sadly, he passed away a few short months after this interview.

> JESSICA: In Tibetan debate, there is often a great deal of enthusiasm and also disagreement. Can there be loving-kindness in the midst of scholastic competition?
>
> KIRTI RINPOCHE: When you criticize or debate with them you should think of helping others. When you bring up questions it will inspire them to think more. You are helping the knowledge and intelligence to grow. Your motivation must be sincere to help them, and it will help them to increase their wisdom. It is good to have altruistic motivation before you criticize people. So the sincere and positive motivation is always the thing. In the monasteries there is the study of philosophy. Monks gather in groups for debate. The rest will challenge the person—the person who is sitting is being challenged by many people. This means that he learns so many more ways to answer questions. When you criticize and debate it helps to receive this intelligence. It raises doubts and helps them to raise more questions. In the West, there are conferences and seminars; scholars gather and everyone has ideas. More questions raised, and more doubts raised. It is very good to have this environment to debate—it helps everyone.
>
> JESSICA: I am just wondering about the antagonistic side of debate . . . often we feel that we have to take a side—and if I say that I am right, and he is wrong . . . it feels inconsistent with *maitri* somehow.
>
> KIRTI RINPOCHE: Sometimes when there is a conference, a person who is being attacked, that person may feel embarrassed. They may take it negatively, but this is unfortunate for him. There's nothing that can be done. But you should be trying to help them. They may take it negatively, but you should still see that debate is generally a good thing.

❦ CONCLUSION

Faith / *SHRADDHA*

*Guru Devotion, Authority, and Belief
in the Shadow of the Maitreya Project*

There is a saying very popular with nonheritage Buddhist practitioners, like my FPMT informants: "When you are ready, the guru will find you." Some FPMT students are still waiting for that bolt of lightning, but others, FPMT devotees and *sangha*, have come to believe that Lama Zopa Rinpoche is a true and trusted guru. On the FPMT path, a serious practitioner must have faith in and through the gurus; guru devotion is a part of the spiritual path forward. Tomas, a devotee from Belgium, had taken a few FPMT courses and then worked in a center for a few years before meeting the FPMT head lama. Here he tells the story of how he finally met Lama Zopa Rinpoche: "I was supposed to go to Ladakh. I thought that maybe it wasn't enough time. I unpacked everything and went to Tushita Dharamsala instead. He was there. He must have called me. He was so busy. When he came out and blessed everyone, it was like the feeling I got from the Dalai Lama. It was so powerful. The behavior of a holy being."

Tomas, like almost all of the devotees that I interviewed, was utterly taken with his guru, and Lama Zopa Rinpoche was very beloved among the devotees. They kept photographs of their main teachers on their altars and made offerings to them. Many attended regular guru *pujas* at centers, or chanted long life prayers for their gurus at home. What Daniel Capper calls "enchantment"—the love of guru that his nonheritage informants felt for their Tibetan teachers at an American Buddhist center (2002, 10)—was clearly in evidence in every FPMT context in which I have studied. Tibetan Buddhist gurus are often believed to be omniscient, and their devotees are supposed to cultivate a deep dependence and trust in their spiritual authority.

In the Tibetan Buddhist tradition, once one recognizes a guru, one is expected to demonstrate unswerving faith in that teacher; dissent against one's guru is thought to be extremely karmically disadvantageous. So what does one do if one is an FPMT devotee but against the Maitreya Project? Can one speak out against the heart project of one's guru?

MPI staffers and FPMTers displaced their responsibility for Maitreya Project 2.0 by placing their trust in the strength of two ideological pillars: globalization and guru devotion. Arguably, when it comes to the land acquisition controversy in Kushinagar, FPMTers failed to take notice of what was happening in their name and with their donation money. Instead, FPMTers evinced strong faith: (1) faith in the guru to the extent that some devotees felt that an FPMT project should be unswervingly supported without question—"Lama Zopa Rinpoche is in charge, so I trust that it is all being handled appropriately"; (2) faith in the top-down, international development strategies chosen by MPI—"more money will go to that impoverished place, so it will all come out right in the end." In previous chapters, I have discussed the myriad issues with the latter kind of trust—develop-mentality—and how MPI has compromised the lives of Indian farmers by seizing on the power of the state through the promise of economic growth. In this chapter, I will look at the role that faith in religious teachers and leaders played in how news about the MPI controversy in Kushinagar was received by FPMTers.

The notion of guru devotion partially explains why MPI's questionable behavior in Kushinagar was tolerated for so long.[1] The Maitreya Project is an FPMT project and therefore under the spiritual purview of Lama Zopa Rinpoche. If a guru is supposedly omniscient, then how would a devotee register a critique of a policy or practice under the guru's institutional purview? For devotees, this line of questioning may lead to even more discomfiting thoughts: If my trust in Lama Zopa Rinpoche to properly steward the Maitreya Project was misplaced, then how can I trust him completely, as I am supposed to do? This chapter hinges on the theme of authority and faith, because this is one of the keys to understanding how and why the Maitreya Project 2.0 story unfolded as it did.

Guru Devotion and Agency

Guru devotion in the classical Tibetan Buddhist sense manifests in a number of ways. The guru has attained such a special level of prominence in Tibetan

Buddhism that their refuge prayers usually involve practitioners taking refuge in the Buddha, the *dharma*, the *sangha*, and the guru. Guru devotion plays a role in the ways Tibetan Buddhist monastic institutions organize authority; monastic institutions are quite hierarchical as a rule and generally continue in that vein in Tibet and in exile (Dreyfus 2003).

Guru devotion is a means to an end, but not the end itself (Berzin 2000; Butterfield 1994; Capper 2002; Dorje 1998; Rabten 1974). In Vajrayana Buddhism, faith in a guru is a necessary step along the path—and here the guru is seen as a Buddha—so after practitioners carefully choose a guru, a devotional relationship is imperative (Kongtrul 1999). In the context of discussing guru devotional practices, Lama Yeshe wrote that it is useful and proper to envision one's root guru as the central guru of an important ritual visualization: "Seeing the essence of Vajradhara as your own root guru brings a feeling of closeness, of personal kindness; and visualizing the guru in the aspect of Vajradhara brings inspiration and realizations quickly" (Yeshe 1998, 60). In Vajrayana practice, the guru is a guide, but the guru is also an object of worship (Wayman 1987).

In Tibetan Buddhist contexts, guru devotion often manifests ritually through regular guru *pujas* (in Tibetan, *lama chopa* rituals, for example) and sociologically through the circulation of miracles attributed to the guru. FPMT centers hold regular guru pujas—in my experience, usually one or two a month. In FPMT, there were two means of circulating miracle attributions to gurus: through print and web media, and through personal storytelling. In the FPMT centers I stayed at in India during my fieldwork, there were lists of miracles collated and posted to bulletin boards; these were specific moments, captured and circulated through a listserv. I remember reading one about how, one evening, Lama Zopa Rinpoche became alarmed at all of the bugs getting pummeled by the car he was in, so he prayed, and the bugs seemed to part to avoid the windshield from that point on.

Word of miraculous activities is often spread through the FPMT grapevine in person. One morning in Bodh Gaya, I sat at a table with a number of FPMTers, and the most senior of us told stories about the guru miracles they have witnessed with their own eyes. During an interview about holy objects a few days later, a longtime FPMT nonheritage monk (with white Christian and Hindu Indian roots) told me a story that emphasized two lessons at once: (1) the power of Buddha images, and (2) the omniscient wisdom and compassion of the gurus.

Once, His Holiness the Dalai Lama was being escorted back to the Gaya railway station. Lama Zopa Rinpoche and I and others were waiting for him at the railway station. There was a big drawing of a Buddha at the station that had been put there for him. Rinpoche stopped His Holiness to look at the image. It was incredible: one holy image in the background and then two holy beings. . . . Rinpoche did this for my benefit. He didn't need to show the Dalai Lama, [since the Dalai Lama already] knew! So this is a very powerful image that I will never forget. Rinpoche has taught us that these holy objects are very powerful. If I can remember this image at the time of my death, then that will be very beneficial.

Stories like this one emphasize the omniscience and the kindness of the guru and show how reverential narratives spread within a relatively nonheritage Buddhist institution to reinforce a subculture of guru devotion.

One's recognition of the guru, and one's ability to clearly see their perfection, is perceived as the result of one's karma. In a foreword to a book cobbled together from some of Lama Yeshe's discourses, Lama Zopa Rinpoche takes the opportunity to expound at great length on the qualities of his guru's, that is Lama Yeshe's, own "holy mind" (Z. Rinpoche 1998, x), "holy speech" (Z. Rinpoche 1998, viii), and "holy body" (Z. Rinpoche 1998, vii). Lama Zopa Rinpoche writes that the more highly developed one's mind the more one will be able to recognize the perfections of true lamas like Lama Yeshe: "The unimaginable secret qualities and actions of a Buddha are the objects of knowledge only of the omniscient minds of other Buddhas. Therefore, there is no way that ordinary beings could understand Lama Yeshe's secret qualities; they could only see his qualities in accordance with the level of their mind" (1998, vii). On the other hand, to fail to see the perfections of one's guru is seen as a reflection of one's karmic limitations.

Fear of disobeying or questioning the guru is prevalent in FPMT text and practice. In certain Tibetan sutras and commentaries, there are specific narrations about the fact that those who are guilty of a "breach of guru devotion" that could come from "antagonistic" or "distorted" thinking about one's gurus will have to submit to the suffering of hell in response. While Alexander Berzin (2000) notes that the texts only impugn certain actions as deserving of rebirth in hell realms, many Western devotees have deep fears about "breach of guru devotion" that lead to deep guilt about doubts in the teacher's qualifications, enlightenment status, teachings, or actions. Berzin defends the Tibetan tradition, saying that there is little to fear if one engages in close readings of the sutras themselves. My primary interest is not in what the actual texts say, but in how they are understood by FPMTers, especially core devotees and *sangha*, since they have the most power in the organization. Within FPMT there is a great deal of flexibility for newcomers who question doctrine and dogma, but for devotees and monastic *sangha* the culture of guru devotion lends itself to anxieties about avoiding anything, whether internal or external, that could be interpreted as wavering or waning guru devotion.

In general, the institutional FPMT narrative is that any doubts and dissension are a sign of one's own karmic weaknesses and obstacles, and never weaknesses or mistakes of FPMT as an institution, nor of Lama Zopa Rinpoche as spiritual leader. There is precedence for this view in Tibetan Buddhism more widely; Gyatrul Rinpoche wrote, "Generally, whenever students see faults in the teacher and when teachers see faults in the students, it is a sign of the individual's own shortcomings" (1999, 16). Furthermore, it is seen as very karmically negative to criticize one's guru. Gyatrul Rinpoche says, "Expressing the faults of the root teacher is the same as finding fault with the Buddha. . . . To express fault in the sublime objects of refuge only serves to blatantly demonstrate your own shortcomings" (1999, 17).

In FPMT, the lamas are seen as faultless ethical guides. Ethical questions within FPMT are often sent straight to the top, but when they are dealt with in a more localized way, people often refer to the guru's blessing of the bureaucratic chain of command in order to diffuse disagreement. For example, I watched with great interest an intense battle of wills over the use of mosquito plug-ins at the Root Institute during my research period: the director of the Institute allowed them, and bought them for rooms with the center's funds, but an FPMT nun-in-residence at the center felt that the plug-ins were killing mosquitoes and therefore should be disallowed. The plug-ins were supposed to paralyze or neutralize the mosquitoes, not actually kill them, which is why the center director thought she could permit them. The nun perceived inert mosquitoes everywhere and felt that despite the chemical explanation offered, the mosquitoes were still being killed. Even if they were just immobilized, she told me, they cannot fly away, and we step on them by accident. The nun went so far as to remove the plug-ins from the *gompas* and some other rooms and throw them away.

I was present in the Root Institute library one day when the director confronted the nun and told her that she was stealing from Lama Zopa Rinpoche by throwing away his things; the director said that since she was the center director, Lama Zopa Rinpoche's will was being done through her. The center director asserted that this policy was accepted up the hierarchical chain; it had been vetted already. The nun protested, but she was told again that if she waged a guerilla war against the plug-ins, then she would be asked to leave. The nun told me later that she would write a letter to Lama Zopa Rinpoche to resolve the issue. She felt that while he had appointed the center director, he still needed to be alerted to such ethical and moral issues. I do not know what happened in the end, but when I left just a month or so later the plug-ins were still in widespread use at Root. Both women appealed to their belief in Lama Zopa Rinpoche's wisdom and authority to settle their ethical conundrum.

Similarly, sometimes skepticism about the Maitreya Project by FPMTers is attenuated by deference to the guru. If a devotee is ambivalent about an FPMT project, they often place their trust in the fact that it is their guru's wish, and that is that. Natalie, a Brazilian woman who had taken monastic robes with FPMT, told me, "Guru devotion is the most important thing. I can train my mind—everything is the manifestation of the guru." She noted in our interview that she felt very strongly about her love for her primary guru, Lama Zopa Rinpoche, but that she was not above doubts about certain things that he believed in. For example, she struggled with relics and also the ability to see holy objects as more than just objects. She told me:

> I have respect for relics. . . . I try to get it. In Bodh Gaya, I saw some of the relics on display. Sometimes they just put them out. A piece of robe of Lama Tsongkhapa, and other things. I don't know the profundity, I mean I see that it's holy. I know I may be purified. . . . Now I see just frames and pictures, I have to train my mind to see that they are not what they appear to be, and with that there are blessings. If you see that thing—they say there is power in the object. That's difficult. The power of statues and mantras and prayer wheels. It is very difficult to see the power of the blessing. I have to try to see the emptiness—it is not as it is.

Significantly, she saw her doubts as signs of her own weaknesses and poor *karma*. Her strong guru devotion was the antidote she trusted to eventually allay her doubts. For example, her initial doubts about the Maitreya Project were subjugated to her faith in the guru; she told me that since he was so kind, the project could only have the best possible effects.

Natalie was also one of many who linked her faith in the morality of the Maitreya Project directly to her faith in the goodness of Lama Zopa Rinpoche. She said:

> At first I thought the Maitreya Project was a bit strange. Why should the project be so big? It's not just a statue, it's such a big project. Everything is about my faith in my guru. I know that will benefit people. I saw that everything Rinpoche does is so beneficial. For me that's true,

so then when I think of how beneficial it will be for the world . . . I think about the statue, not the other stuff. When I pray I think about how the statue itself can benefit others. The power of the object can purify and give blessings. [Garbled, missing sentence.] Whoever sees it will get blessed. It's harder for the public, who are more beginners, it's harder for them to get it. We *sangha* do *puja* every night—we dedicate for everything, but there are special *pujas* we do especially for the Maitreya statue. Now we are reading the sanghata sutra. The renovation of the *gompa* here and also the Maitreya Project are the two main things we dedicate merit to here. Sometimes Lama Zopa Rinpoche says, "Please all centers should do such a prayers or mantras for the statue." Lama Zopa Rinpoche was here in March. We were five monastics in Delhi, and we went to say goodbye. We called Roger. He said that Rinpoche is asking us to read seven sanghata sutras to remove obstacles to Maitreya. In fact, most of the *sangha* is involved in prayers for the project. Even centers read the sutras and mantras for it.

Natalie observed here that most of her colleagues also participated in offering dedications to the Maitreya Project, and that they were a high priority for Lama Zopa Rinpoche and his entourage. Any doubts that she may have had about the viability or desirability of the Maitreya Project were completely subsumed by her faith in her guru. During my research period, I met a lot of FPMT devotees like Natalie: guru devotion was a factor that strongly affected how they processed MPI, the statue, and any news of the controversy in Kushinagar.

A Buddhist from America who has spent a great deal of time with various communities in Bodh Gaya felt that guru devotion has impeded internal debates in FPMT:

You know, even most Tibetans and Western Tibetan Buddhists looked at the Maitreya Project with skepticism and asked, "Why?" Of course at the Root Institute they toe the party line. They are devoted to Lama Zopa Rinpoche. What he says goes. Other Tibetan groups are a little more skeptical. Everyone respects the Dalai Lama but some people are willing to diverge from his view more than others. Some Tibetan Buddhists might say, if people are hungry, then maybe don't build a big statue now; if you have a surplus okay, but if not, then you are extracting it from people.

This informant, and several other like-minded interlocutors, expressed a strong view that guru devotion to Lama Zopa Rinpoche has limited the quality and quantity of dissent among committed FPMT devotees. Capper (2002, 181) argued that although his nonheritage informants at a relatively nonheritage Tibetan Buddhist center were intensely devoted to their gurus, they were generally able to maintain their ability to think independently. While FPMTers, even dedicated devotees and monastic *sangha*, are obviously able to think independently, I would argue that the culture of guru devotion at FPMT does sometimes limit the ability of devotees to vocally question their teachers' decisions. My research on guru devotion in FPMT tracks more closely with what Victor Sogen Hori (1998) noted about guru devotion in Zen contexts: nonheritage practitioners may be translating the idea into practice without the institutionalized social constraints that temper the practice in heritage communities.

Guru devotion in FPMT is seen as a necessity for devotees and monastics. For serious FPMT devotees, doubts must be worked through and can be interpreted as tests of one's devotion. This is not to say that everyone capitulates to this expectation, however. A few of my informants, from across the faith continuum—searchers to *sangha*—after discovering the controversy, expressed some very deep misgivings about the project's effects on Kushinagar; some have turned their backs on the project, either cancelling Relic Tour visits, refusing to make more donations, or finding another *sangha* with which to practice. Others stayed true to FPMT, but nursed their uncertainties uncomfortably. FPMTers can find it difficult to stay within the organization if they harbor intense doubts, since skepticism is not respected after one has reached a certain stage in the teachings.

In addition to the notion that a devotee's own negative *karmas* are responsible for any doubts about one's guru or their plans, *karma* also came up in the set of explanations regarding how the guru's plans were so grand that there were inevitably karmic issues to work through. I found this perspective articulated many times. This interpretation of obstacles is often directly linked to one's faith in the guru, as was very clearly demonstrated in an interview quoted below with an American devotee and staff member of the Root Institute who had been living and working at the Indian center for several months at this point.

> MAUREEN: With the Maitreya statue project there is such inspiration with what they want to do in this world. This is a gift they are giving. They have helped the *dharma* to spread. That he wants to do this crazy thing, and I would call it crazy to spend so much money on something so beautiful. He always wants to do something bigger and better. The Maitreya Project is like the centerpiece of the FPMT family. This is what Lama Zopa Rinpoche sends out requests

about most often: to do special *pujas* for its benefit. Lama Zopa Rinpoche says that the FPMT hasn't even started yet, like a baby that hasn't even stood up yet. Through the obstacles we are clearing through the Maitreya Project we will be able to really blossom. We haven't even started yet. We are trying to do something beneficial for the world. . . . There have been so many disappointments, so many starts and stops. A meeting was coming up, and they thought that everything would go ahead. It was just so close. But Rinpoche has undying enthusiasm. Whatever disappointments there are, they don't last very long. He is so unfazed. Because this was Lama Yeshe's wish, he will not stop. That was what Lama wanted, and he will do whatever it takes. There were some disappointments just to get the land. They worked so hard. They tried to get the land [in Bodh Gaya]. They will do good things with it still. They needed far more land, this was just the initial plot, but then there were big government problems. The government is so supportive in UP [Uttar Pradesh]. The land situation is okay in Kushinagar, but now the lack of money is holding us back. The main obstacle now is finances.

JESSICA: Um, well, actually I have been to Kushinagar, and there's a lot more going on. Protest . . . a lot of anger.

MAUREEN: This is life. You keep doing more *pujas* and more practices. Rinpoche has said that when we are trying to do something, sometimes there are *maras*.

JESSICA: What are *maras*?

MAUREEN: *Maras* are negative *karmas*. The wish to do something this big for other beings is highly beneficial. *Karma* that would have ripened as going to hell realms can become smaller obstacles. Of course there will be problems. This is a good sign. This is *lo jong*—so rejoice! If there were no problems, if it was easy, what would we learn? With *bodhicitta* we must bear hardships for others. Sometimes a strong sense of fear comes in my heart that when [the Maitreya Project statue] is finished maybe it would be a target for terrorism. When I have this fear I try to think of impermanence; it would just be part of the process. The process is just as important as the statue itself. From the emptiness of the project now. . . . Where is it now, when will it start, where will it end? I find it a constant source of lessons, so I am grateful to Rinpoche.

I found Maureen's interview fascinating—I had never heard anyone discuss their fears about the statue becoming a potential terrorist target before—but in its laser focus on faith in the guru and trust that any inevitable karmic issues would be worked through, her views fit squarely within normative FPMT discourse.

Intuiting Skillful Means

Another explanation given about the methods and choices of Lama Zopa Rinpoche, and his handpicked staffers, with regards to the Maitreya Project was that they were using skillful means to accomplish the highest possible goals. An informant deeply enmeshed in FPMT, and a regular donor to the Maitreya Project, said of the controversy, "Well, it may look bad to you, but lama is using skillful means. Even the people protesting, even you, you are all planting seeds that will bring you closer to Maitreya."

Upaya (Sanskrit for "skillful means") is a concept that emerged in early Mahayana to assert that advanced Buddhist practitioners have access to a spectrum of truths that they can engage with in various ways and means, depending on the context (Pye 1978); for example, gurus, bodhisattvas, and Buddhas might need to oversimplify the truest truths in order to produce the best possible effects in a particular person, audience, or setting. Pye explains:

> In Mahayana Buddhism the various forms of Buddhist teaching and practice are declared to be provisional means, all skilfully set up by the Buddha for the benefit of the unenlightened. A Buddhist who makes progress himself comes to recognise this provisional quality in the forms of his religion, and though using the means provided for him he has to learn not to be wrongly attached to them. He leaves them behind, like a raft left lying on the bank by a man who has crossed a stream and needs it no more. An advanced follower of Buddhism, usually named by Mahayana Buddhists a *Bodhisattva*, continues to use such provisional means in order to lead other living things towards nirvana. (1978, 1)

The concept of skillful means is often used to indicate that true Buddhist wisdom requires one to act and speak according to Buddhist morality in spirit, if not in letter. When it comes to skillful means, sometimes complex discourses must be truncated or simplified in order to achieve the best possible benefit for a particular audience, and sometimes violence must be done in the spirit of nonviolence. And as we shall see, some Buddhists may claim that some suffering must be caused in the discharge of a plan that will ultimately have a positive karmic balance.

One author claimed that *upaya* was a "social and cultural relativism" that reverberated positively with postmodern values (Hubbard 2006, 161). The

Tibetan Buddhist lama Chögyam Trungpa Rinpoche was reported to have advocated skillful means in the form of "ruthless compassion" in situations in which advanced practitioners queried about whether it was ethical to use violence in order to do a greater good (Feuerstein 1990, 249). Feuerstein reports that Chögyam Trungpa's recommendation assumes the maturity and goodness of the practitioners; thus the author is ill at ease with what is purportedly a slippery ethical slope: "Trungpa's unqualified answer that violence is a valid means in the spiritual process is alarming. However, this belief reflects an attitude that is common in spiritual circles and is closely associated with the paternalism so prevalent in the spiritual traditions, which treats the seeker or disciple as a child. This has repeatedly led to situations of abuse" (1990, 249).

Skillful means also refers to knowing when to give and when not to give. Lama Yeshe himself gave a lecture in 1975, in which he noted that not all giving is created equal. There are right and wrong ways to give. Lama Yeshe stated:

> Westerners over emphasize physical action. For example, many people believe that they're being religious when they give money to the poor or to worthy causes but often what they're doing is just an ego trip. Instead of their giving becoming an antidote to dissatisfaction and attachment it simply causes increased dissatisfaction and egocentricity and therefore has nothing to do with religion. Such people are taking the religious idea that it's good to give and believe that they're giving, but from the Buddhist point of view charity is not what you give but why and how. . . . Therefore we have to carefully check our supposedly religious actions to make sure that they do in fact bring benefit and don't cause more confusion for themselves and others. (2008, 18)

From my perspective, this is one of the few critiques of uncritical charitable giving that I have read from inside the world of Tibetan Buddhism. Ironically, also from my perspective, the Maitreya Project itself was being accused by affected Kushinagari farmers of giving in a way that would not benefit the donors and causing "confusion for themselves and others." Even more ironic, again from my perspective, is that the 1975 lectures were printed in a volume called *Universal Love*, which was commissioned and sponsored by the Maitreya Project itself.

From that same volume, additional qualifications on Buddhist gifting reveal an ethical parsing unfamiliar to me in the actual contemporary practices of FPMT: during a question-and-answer session that followed the lecture quoted above, Lama Yeshe discussed how sometimes it is better, more moral, to withhold gifts.

> Q: Do you also have to check to see whether what you're giving is appropriate?
>
> LAMA: Yes, that's a good point too. For example, if you give money to somebody who then goes and gets drunk, instead of helping that person, you've given harm. That's just a simple example; there are many more.
>
> Q: Would it then be charitable *not* to give that person money?
>
> LAMA: Yes, that's right. (Yeshe 2008, 24)

If the farmer-activists of Kushinagar had known that Lama Yeshe had said this, they doubtlessly would have wished that the founder's words could be harnessed to help them convince FPMTers that MPI's complicity in a controversial large-scale rural land acquisition meant that ultimately the Maitreya Project was doing more harm than good.

Skillful means is often used to lend nuance to arguments and action about ethics and morality. What is good and what is bad, what is true and what is false, what is right and what is wrong—none of these are black and white in Buddhism, especially where *upaya* is concerned. The logic of skillful means is commonly deployed within FPMT to explain how an enlightened being like Lama Zopa Rinpoche might do something that appears unjust, when really he knows that the benefits will trickle down to everyone (even the Indian villagers angry at him now). Faithful devotees found comfort in the fact that if their lama was using skillful means, then it was not for them to judge one way or the other, since he knew better than they did. Thus, *upaya* is often evoked as an explanation, or excuse, that effectively limits devotees' means to question inconsistencies, injustices, or unethical activities.[2]

Another tack offered by devotees: in order to do real good, sometimes a little injustice was acceptable collateral damage. These interviewees felt that even if there was a land acquisition issue, only a fraction of people would be hurt in contrast to the immense benefits that would be accrued to all sentient beings. The perspective that perhaps "a few eggs must be broken to make an omelet" was not uncommon in discussion about the controversy with FPMTers.

A German FPMT devotee that I interviewed in Bodh Gaya said, "Maybe it's just the only way that it can happen. Maybe there's no way that it can happen without someone getting hurt. Maybe it's impossible for everyone to benefit." Ultimately, she acknowledged that there was a problem with the way locals were being treated in Kushinagar, but in the end, she seemed to indicate that if the guru had led them down this path, then perhaps it was all justifiable toward the greater good. A dedicated FPMTer, she felt that it was Lama Zopa Rinpoche's place to consider these weighty issues, not hers.

The perspective that, as a realized being, Lama Zopa Rinpoche must know the facts of the case, as well as how best to proceed to ensure the best possible outcome, was also articulated by Pamela, a nonheritage Buddhist FPMTer who attended FPMT center programs in Delhi. Pamela told me, "How could Rinpoche not know? He must have known for a long time. . . . You don't know how seriously to take these things. The student is stuck between the truth of reality and the desire of the master. Even when it was in Bodh Gaya there was controversy. Christopher Titmuss used to criticize it. I have to wonder if maybe Lama Zopa Rinpoche has perceived the greater long-term benefits of the statue, and we just can't perceive it." Without specifically naming "skillful means" or "guru devotion," Pamela points directly to these two phenomena. During the whole of our conversation, I watched her vacillate about her own opinion regarding the Maitreya Project controversy: I listened to her despair; I watched her struggle internally to sort through competing ethical and moral compulsions; and in the end, in front of me at least, she placed her trust in her gurus to know and to do the right thing.

In another conversation, a nonheritage FPMT monk shrugged and said that realistically there was always a cost-benefit analysis at play even in matters of *dharma* practice. "I would definitely sacrifice a few farm families' happiness for the religious good of the rest of the world," he said. Skillful means in this context was used by FPMTers to suggest that the appearance of bad behavior on FPMT's part (for example, causing suffering, displacing persons from their farmland, breaking a few eggs) was actually just a crooked path toward the best of all possible outcomes.

Who Is Responsible?

Another perspective that made the rounds among FPMTers is that the Tibetan Buddhist notions of *karma* allow for karmic intermediaries that block one from acquiring negative *karmas* oneself. For example, one student brought up the fact of how Tibetan monks, even the Dalai Lama, can eat meat, provided that meat was not specifically killed on their behalf. In Lhasa, for example, Muslims, who settled in Tibet centuries ago, do the karmically impure work of slaughtering animals. I observed this practice myself in Lhasa in 2005, and it is an ongoing arrangement: some Buddhists pay Muslim butchers to incur the negative *karma* of killing so that they can remain meat-eaters with a lesser karmic cost. Moreover, Tibetan Buddhists in Lhasa who make ritual panoramas or boxes in order to draw the ill fortune out of their households will still often set those boxes near the Muslim neighborhood of the Barkhor, so that they can be destroyed by those who disbelieve in karmic consequences. These karmic intermediaries run defense for Buddhists who are not keen to take the impurity on themselves. There does not seem to be karmic backlash to these practices; that is, according to the cosmic calculus of *karma* as understood by these practitioners, Buddhists do not achieve a doubly negative *karma* for thus putting the karmic balances of others at risk. This relates to the Maitreya Project only insofar as FPMTers confronted with the controversy have occasionally connected the tendency to allow others to kill animals for Buddhist consumption with the sense that the Maitreya Project seemed comfortable allowing the Uttar Pradeshi state government to cause suffering in order to acquire land on their behalf. I heard variations of this argument many times from FPMT practitioners, sometimes as an excuse and sometimes as an explanation.

For example, Jennifer, a white American FPMT student, brought up this interpretation of skillful means when we talked about the controversy in Kushinagar. Jennifer was one of my roommates at FPMT's center in Bodh Gaya (while volunteering at a local nonprofit, just after she had taken a few FPMT courses), and while she liked the organization, she did not feel committed to it. Jennifer was deeply saddened about the controversy in Kushinagar that I had narrated to her. As it became clear to her that FPMT had no presence in Kushinagar proper, and seemed to be saying that they would not communicate with farmers until after the acquisition, her disappointment turned to anger.

Jennifer said, "I hate that Tibetans will eat meat just because someone else killed the cow. I think that's what's happening here. They [the Maitreya Project staffers] don't care that the Uttar Pradesh police will beat people out of their houses. They don't care that the farmers will fight back against the police. They don't care that people are cursing the Buddha."

At this point I explained to Jennifer that the Buddha himself was not being blamed by farmers, since they respect Buddha as an avatar of Vishnu; I told her that since none of the farmers knew who Lama Zopa Rinpoche was, they tended to blame the Dalai Lama (as the public face of Tibetan Buddhism) and Babar Singh (as MPI's widely maligned local operative).

She then continued, "Oh, then they are making so much bad *karma*! But the Maitreya Project doesn't care about the collateral bad *karma* that is being created. They just care that they will get the good *karma* from building the damn statue."

Jennifer was an FPMT student; she had taken refuge in FPMT and been to several courses over as many years, but had not really committed to FPMT or its teachers. She was volunteering at a local educational charity and going to the Mahabodhi Stupa on a regular basis. She told me that she did not feel that Lama Zopa Rinpoche was necessarily to blame, but that she would not be surprised if he had consented to all of the poor decisions made in the Maitreya Project planning. She felt that he did not really understand Engaged Buddhism. Her perspective was not singular, but neither was it normative or institutionally sanctioned FPMT thinking. Jennifer's view that FPMT was behaving badly, and that the guru was culpable, was a perspective that I heard only from the outskirts of the community, most often from uncommitted students or searchers.

Aside from the popular argument that the guru knows best, there was another common response to the Maitreya Project controversy by FPMTers: the guru must not know anything about it. After a candid discussion with Gertie, a German FPMT devotee in residence at the Root Institute, about my opinions of the injustices being perpetrated in Kushinagar, she seemed genuinely upset. At the very end of our discussion she felt unwilling to believe that her guru could have any knowledge of the situation.

> GERTIE: There are many of us who don't know anything about that. I thought the land was secure, but that there were money troubles—an inability to fundraise enough money. Many of us really want the statue. It will be good for those poor people.
>
> JESSICA: But the people who are suffering the most probably won't get the benefits of the statue.
>
> GERTIE: You should e-mail Lama Zopa Rinpoche. He must not know about it. You should tell him.

Gertie's reaction was not at all unusual among FPMT practitioners; I was often told that Lama Zopa Rinpoche's advisors and the Maitreya Project staff could be hiding information from him out of ignorance, as they were just fellow seekers on the path and not omniscient. I was advised over and over again to try to tell him—which, of course, I did try to do several times.[3] This view, which is represented here by Gertie, blurs the notion that the guru is enlightened and omniscient. Can an omniscient guru be misled by underlings? Thus, it is thus worth noting that not all committed FPMTers hold the belief that Lama Zopa Rinpoche is perfect and all-knowing, although most know that it is deemed proper to hold that view and thus they strive to do so.

The FPMT devotees and monastics that I met who believed that the Maitreya Project was indeed acting in bad faith were sometimes willing to believe that the lama was uninformed (or testing them as a community), but none of them, not one, ever said that they thought Lama Zopa Rinpoche himself bore any responsibility for the controversy or had himself made any mistakes along the way. Although Berzin (2000) argues that guru devotion should not be taken as absolute acceptance of everything the guru says or does, he also explains that many Westerners are so anxious about transgressing their commitments of devotion that they are far too judgmental of themselves when they feel doubt. It is this excess of guru devotion that helps explicate why even FPMTers who may have wanted to question the Maitreya Project may have refrained from doing so, and why some who did question the implementation of Maitreya Project 2.0 often saw it as a failure of everything and everyone, except Lama Zopa Rinpoche himself.

(Still) Waiting for Maitreya

> VLADIMIR: (*musingly*). The last moment . . . (*He meditates*). Hope deferred maketh something sick, who said that? (Beckett 1954, 8)

During my fieldwork period, MPI staff remained active in light fundraising and cheerleading for the statue project. They said that they were simply waiting for the land to be acquired before they could move ahead in earnest. The Maitreya Project staffers waited for the Uttar Pradeshi state government to take the land. "Until we get Kushinagar, I'm twiddling my thumbs," said one staffer in 2006. FPMTers and others who supported the project waited impatiently. Lama Zopa Rinpoche, by all accounts, was also waiting.

Waiting is one of the faces of hope. In Crapanzano's (1985) ethnography of South African whites before apartheid fell, he finds his informants waiting for something, anything, to happen. Depressed, anxious, and wondering what would happen in the future, the South African white community did nothing to work toward preparation for the major changes headed their way. The point is that hope can be paralyzing. Crapanzano writes that hope "is the field of desire in waiting" (1985, 45). Crapanzano's white South African informants were afraid of the coming political changes and took refuge in leaving their futures to their faith. In 2006, there was something similarly passive and paralyzed about FPMT's relationship to the Maitreya Project. Devotees and monastics were hopeful and anxious, but they generally did nothing, said nothing, and just trusted in their leaders to sort out whatever issues the project faced. The response to conflict or controversy was icy silence, defensiveness, or rationalizations. These devotees, too, waited for their giant statue.

Figure 15. The author sits in solidarity with the anti-MPI hunger strike in a village in Greater Kushinagar in 2007.
From the author's photo collection.

At the same time, in Kushinagar, the air was thick, melancholy even, with waiting. The farmers of Kushinagar were waiting to slough off their panic mode. They were waiting for notification that the end of their world was not nigh, but until then they resolved to sit in a show of determined resistance. The BBSS waited for the cessation of hostilities, fasts, protests, and strikes. They waited day by day for the official, and true, word that the project would be cancelled or moved far away, so that their lives could return to normal after many years of struggle.

The waiting that my informants on both sides endured represents one of those all-important gaps (Crapanzano 2004): this is a gap between what is anticipated and what may yet happen, and it is one plane on which the future unfurls in the present. This gap is no strategic delay (Bourdieu 1977)—waiting is something else entirely. This story of the Maitreya Project 2.0 and its many interlocutors is not one of passivity, but it is one in which all eyes were locked—straining and aching—on the horizon.

And yet, for a story about a five-hundred-foot statue that had not been built, we must acknowledge both the frenetic activity and the stillnesses.

There were decisions and donations made. There were protests and meetings organized. There were two communities that stood at an unbridgeable impasse in opposition to one another's dreams. There was so much great hope, and such crippling anxiety. It should not be written out of the history of the Maitreya Project in India that its plans and process created a future tense that caused clear and present effects across the world. Donors from Taipei to Asheville, devotees from Mexico City to Delhi, and *sangha* from Berlin to Lhasa, FPMTers from various backgrounds and nations worked hard to create the greatest statue that never was. And farmer-activists from the green hamlets of Kushinagar worked just as hard to see that if the colossus did manage to come to fruition it would not come at their expense.

 Epilogue

Rebirth/ *SAMSARA*

The Future of the Maitreya Project

In the fall of 2012, the Kushinagar statue that I had been studying, Maitreya Project 2.0, was canceled (MPI 2012). The MPI website announced the cancellation and the reshuffling of leadership. First, the project would leave Kushinagar altogether and shift back to Bodh Gaya, where MPI would make do with a smaller statue. Second, the CEO, Peter Kedge, would be replaced with a new leader, Nita Ing. A door was summarily closed. I could almost hear the cheers of my Kushinagari farming informants. It had been a few years since I had seen Raj, Shashi, and Aneesh, but I could imagine Raj's excited smiles and Aneesh's emotional relief. Knowing Shashi's penchant for breaking into song and poetry, I had a feeling he regaled his friends and family with songs of celebration. The BBSS had prevailed.[1]

FPMT and MPI, as institutions, have thus far declined to publicly reflect on the weaknesses of the policies and decisions that led to the spate of local Kushinagari protests against them. Even as the 2012 update outlined the end of the five-hundred-foot Maitreya Project 2.0 statue, MPI administrators refused to even acknowledge the suffering they had caused in Kushinagar (MPI 2012). In a letter update, Lama Zopa Rinpoche shows compassion only for the difficulties experienced by the CEO, Peter Kedge. He wrote, "Peter also worked for many years in India, bearing many hardships and experiencing problems and difficulties there. The key difficulty, however, has been acquiring sufficient land together in one parcel. . . . There have also been other significant setbacks, such as major donors being unable to fulfill their commitments through difficult economic conditions and untimely death" (MPI 2012). Although the difficulty of land acquisition is mentioned as a direct cause of the cancellation, the fact that the Maitreya Project was embroiled in a conflict with local people was entirely unremarked on. Lama Zopa Rinpoche acknowledged MPI's fault in only one way—being irresponsible with funds and fundraising: "Regarding the Maitreya statue, it's true that we made some mistakes. This was due to karma. We discovered much later that we made some wrong decisions with respect to expecting more money for Maitreya after we spent some or hoping to get a big amount and so forth. That didn't work out. So we did make some mistakes along the way" (MPI 2012). To the very bitter end of the Maitreya Project 2.0 plan, FPMT and MPI ignored the local Kushinagaris, as well as the tumult their own statue project endeavors had caused.

I remember feeling a mix of emotions, but primarily I was thrilled for the farmer activists of the BBSS. So that's the end, I thought. The statue in Bodh Gaya would be built on land already owned by MPI, so there was little danger of inciting the degree of resistance they had faced in Kushinagar with Maitreya Project 2.0. Furthermore, they had announced a more modest version of the statue, so perhaps it would even meet with less anxiety from Bodh Gaya residents than they had articulated about the Maitreya Project 1.0 version originally planned there. I was cautiously optimistic for a happy ending for the Indian farmers of both localities. And maybe FPMTers would still be happy with a medium-sized statue in Bodh Gaya. Perhaps it would be a win-win-win.

But then, in December 2013, after a flurry of backstage work and activity, and with little anticipatory fanfare, the Maitreya Project broke ground and laid a foundation stone for a Maitreya statue . . . in Kushinagar. I learned about the grand groundbreaking ceremony, which was attended by Lama Zopa Rinpoche and the chief minister of Uttar Pradesh, through the articles posted on the FPMT website. In FPMT's *Mandala* magazine, they announced the following a few months later: "On December 13, 2013, the Maitreya Buddha Kushinagar Project took an enormous step forward: the state government of Uttar Pradesh handed over an initial tranche of 275 acres (111 hectares) of land for the statue, which will be at least 200 feet (61 meters) tall" ("An Update from Kushinagar" 2014, 18). The actual signing over of a parcel seems to have taken place much later, in August 2016 ("Govt Grants Land" 2016).

In my article "Maitreya, or the Love of Buddhism" (Falcone 2012a), I focused on the nonevent of Maitreya Project 1.0, which was the Bodh Gaya version of the statue that was officially cancelled in 2003. In that article, I made the argument that there is not one Maitreya Project statue plan, but rather, there are many iterations. I argued then that even a potential return to the Bodh Gaya region would not be a revisitation of Maitreya Project 1.0, but rather a new version: a reincarnation into a new body, rather than a revitalization of an old one. I stand by that argument now, as I look toward new reincarnations of the Maitreya Project statue: Maitreya Project 3.0 (to be built in Kushinagar), and its twin that was visualized as Maitreya Project 3.1 (to be located in Bodh Gaya).

What will this new Kushinagar statue look like? From 2013 onwards, I noted with interest that in the MPI literature the height of the Maitreya Project 3.0 statue was not fixed; "at least 200 feet" was the new height language from MPI ("An Update from Kushinagar" 2014, 18). Would MPI's new Kushinagar statue (3.0) be a scaled-down version, as they had planned for the new Bodh Gaya statue (3.1)? On its new website, in 2016, an earlier letter from Lama Zopa Rinpoche announcing plans to pursue statues in both Bodh Gaya and Kushinagar was reprinted in part, and there he made a slightly more definitive statement about the Kushinagar project statue: "The Maitreya Statue would be about 13 stories in height. The total land area will be about 270 acres" ("Maitreya Project History" 2016). Thirteen stories is about 140 feet, less than a third of the height envisioned for Maitreya Project 2.0.

There is still little known about the new plans. The details for Maitreya Project 3.0 and 3.1 remain somewhat mysterious to those outside the inner circles of FPMT. The old Maitreya Project website for Maitreya Project 2.0 (www.maitreyaproject.org) remained frozen in time for several years; the only thing on the page was the 2012 cancellation announcement, and it remained there like a sullied relic from 2012 until 2016.[2] The *Mandala* article touting the ground-breaking in Kushinagar also promised a new webpage ("An Update from Kushinagar" 2014), which was not operational until over a year later (www.mbpkushinagar.org), and when it did go up it discussed most of its plans in general terms sans specifics. On the new Maitreya Project 3.0 website, the land acquisition issues, which figured so centrally to the story of MPI and Kushinagar, are utterly and improbably absent in the Maitreya Project's own telling of their history ("Maitreya Project History" 2016).

When the Kushinagari land for Maitreya Project 3.0 was signed over, it was covered in the national Indian news, although it did not receive much attention outside of the region. The actual amount signed over to MPI was less than two hundred acres, much of which was acquired from farmers. A *Times of India* article reports:

> "Altogether 195.81 acres of land has been given to Maitreya Project Trust (MPT) on a lease of Re 1. The government has also waived off Rs 35 crore stamp duty. The land is spread over Kasia, Sabia, Bindwalia and Anirudhwa villages. While 179.12 acres have been acquired from farmers, 16.69 acres belong to the government," Kasia sub-registrar Anupama Pandey said. The MoU was signed way back in 2003 but a lengthy land acquisition process put the plan on hold. Notices were also issued for acquiring of land but 69 farmers got a stay from Allahabad high court. ("Govt Grants Land" 2016)

The land signed over in 2016 was a little more than a quarter of the 750 acres once coveted by MPI. Will they simply use the portion already given to them, or is there another phase of land acquisition being planned for Maitreya Project 3.0? The language from 2014 implies more land is promised; "initial tranche" implies later parcels will be acquired ("An Update from Kushinagar" 2014, 18). Today, my cautious optimism is mitigated by a pronounced anxiety that MPI will slip back into old patterns of indifference about the effects of its project on locals and again embrace a top-down develop-mentality that pits the project against the poor. I have been out of the field for many years, so I cannot speak to what is actually happening in Kushinagar today, but I know that my hopes and my fears are shared by others, especially by local Kushinagari farmers, but also by some FPMTers who want the statue to be built with loving-kindness or not at all.

Aramis—a new French technology in the transportation realm—did not come into being because its makers never negotiated and coaxed it into being; according to Bruno Latour (1996), they did not love it enough to compromise with either the technology or the sociocultural realities of the moment. Arguably, Maitreya Project 1.0 and 2.0 were similarly denied the grounded compromises, understanding, and support needed to come into existence.[3] One interpretation of the inability of the Maitreya Project to manifest a statue thus far, despite several decades of trying, is that it is essentially a failure of love, that is, a failure of precisely the loving-kindness that the statue is meant to glorify. It remains to be seen whether the Maitreya Project makers—engineers, artists, bureaucrats, Buddhist devotees, donors—will "love" any future Maitreya Project iteration enough to merge "body and soul" (Latour 1996, 288) and finally bring a giant statue to fruition.

And so it begins, again.

🍎 Appendix

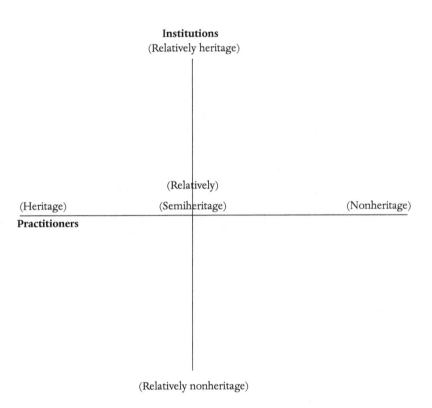

Institutions
(Relatively heritage)

(Relatively)
(Heritage)   (Semiheritage)   (Nonheritage)
Practitioners

(Relatively nonheritage)

Figure 16. The heritage spectrum

✿ Notes

Introduction

1. The task of building the biggest statue was not uncontested at that point, however, as there were other projects in the works trying to outdo MPI's statue plan. For example, Chinese Buddhists fundraised for a Vairocana Buddha statue that would be slightly taller than MPI's statue ("China Enters Biggest Buddhist Statue Race" 2001); they delivered on that promise in 2008, as the finished Spring Temple Buddha reached a stunning 502 feet tall (inclusive of throne and building/pedestal). The global Buddhist moment has created the conditions for several other colossal Buddhist statues in the past twenty-five years, for example, (1) the giant Amitabha Buddha in Japan, the Ushiku Daibutsu, which is 390 feet (inclusive of pedestal), finished in 1993; (2) the Kuanyin of Sanya, China, enshrined in 2005, which is 345 feet tall (Feng 2005); and (3) a giant 380-foot Buddha statue in Myanmar completed in 2008 (Baker 2016). Gigantic Buddha statues seem to be a symptom of neoliberal globalization, a point that Kajri Jain effectively makes in her work on the emergence of colossal statues in post-liberalization India. In reference to colossal statues in India, Jain writes: "Tracing how this form of spectacle and its exhibition value are enmeshed in the imaginaries, spatial politics, material processes and heterogeneous temporalities of uneven development, I highlight its territorial aspects and its capacities as an assemblage that brings together religion, aesthetics, politics and business" (2016, 329). Although Jain focuses on local/regional Indian creations as opposed to internationally funded statues, her work speaks to how Maitreya Project 2.0 can be read as a cultural symptom of neoliberal globalization.

2. I initially assumed, as had some of my local informants—wrongly as it turned out—that the Maitreya Project 2.0 statue was to be built "right there," since that was the spot shown in the MPI web photos. I learned later that the land in the picture was supposed to be acquired for the grand statue park, but the exact spot actually envisioned for the main statue site was in an even more heavily populated area nearby.

3. I first took refuge at an FPMT function led by Lama Zopa Rinpoche in Florida in the late nineties. "Taking refuge" is a manner of ritually self-identifying as a Buddhist.

4. While I utilize the conventional delineation of "Western" and "Eastern" with respect to the terminology used by so many of my informants, I must note here that the binary is, of course, exceedingly oversimplistic, erasing some of the historical contingencies of these imaginaries.

5. There are four primary Tibetan Buddhist sects recognized today: Nyingma, Sakya, Kagyu, and Gelugpa. Jonang practitioners sometimes argue that it should be considered the fifth important Tibetan Buddhist sect. There are sectarian differences

in lineage, Tantric ritual practices, and other aspects of practice; however, all of the schools follow Nagarjuna's Mahayana Buddhism and emphasize the efficacy of Vajrayana (Tantric) ritual and practice (Powers 1995).

6. The Maitreya Project 2.0 initial land acquisition figure of 750 acres was soon reduced to 661 acres. Since media reports often touted the number as 700 acres, note that the Maitreya Project 2.0 land acquisition acreage varies from 660 to 750 at various times in various sources.

7. Circumambulations of holy objects hold the connotation of both giving respect to the object and taking merit from one's proximity. Proper circumambulations are done clockwise and are called *nang khor* in Tibetan. Counterclockwise circumambulations, also called *chi khor* in Tibetan, are considered improper in normative Tibetan Buddhist practice. My friends and I sometimes joked that contrary to plan, I sometimes seemed to be circumambulating the Maitreya Project counterclockwise. There are culturally appropriate times and places for *chi khor*, however, in certain Tantric practices (Snellgrove 1987). *Chi khor* is also often associated with Bonpos, another set of religious practitioners in Tibet, although there are times and places that Bonpos circulate clockwise, and other times and places when Buddhists circumambulate counterclockwise (Huber 1999). Huber also notes that on certain popular mountain cult circumambulations, women are forbidden from making the full clockwise circumambulations and must proceed counterclockwise on specific paths (1999, 121). Huber wonders along with a colleague if the left-circling of women is a relic of the left-handed practices associated with the feminine path of the highest yoga Tantra (1999, 253). Like the women excluded from the full men's path around Pure Crystal Mountain in Tibet who had to proceed by going *nang khor* halfway and then *chi khor* halfway, perhaps one could say that I did both. From my point of view, as an anthropologist and a Buddhist, with due attention to my professional ethics, I very diligently endeavored to research *maitri* (Sanskrit: loving-kindness) with *maitri*.

8. I was not permitted to do research in MPI's Gorakhpur office, and it was perfectly appropriate for MPI to bar me. However, I was taken aback at some of the ways MPI tried to deter my research in Kushinagar. One MPI staffer aggressively tried to talk me into abandoning the project. In an episode almost comedic in retrospect, he pulled out an encyclopedia and looked up "anthropology," and then proceeded to try to think of other cultural questions I could research for my dissertation. Later, another MPI official called my doctoral advisor at Cornell University and tried to get him to curb my research. While MPI could restrict me from researching within MPI offices, they could not ban me from the Uttar Pradeshi villages or from FPMT centers that permitted me to do research therein. Hugh Gusterson (1996) did fieldwork on the Livermore National Laboratory without ever getting full clearance to work inside of it; he learned instead by encircling it, working at its periphery, and doing interviews with willing individuals who worked in the lab (and in the neighborhood). I took Gusterson's work as a successful model for sociologically seeing a large institution, despite the fact that it endeavored not to be seen.

9. The relevant center directors gave me permission to conduct my research in those specific FPMT centers. Throughout my research period I secured permissions from regional institutional heads and directors, as well, of course, as getting consent from the individuals with whom I conducted interviews.

10. To be more specific about the timing of particular inquiries: I was based in India from December 2005 to April 2007. I primarily divided my time in India between (1) the statue's prospective home in Kushinagar, (2) the statue's current bureaucratic home on the drawing boards in Lucknow and elsewhere, and (3) the statue's spiritual home in the thoughts and prayers of devotees from the three FPMT centers in Bodh Gaya, Dharamsala, and Delhi. In India, I completed two lengthy stints in Dharamsala, two in Bodh Gaya, several in Kushinagar, several in Delhi, and one in Lucknow. During the fall of 2005 and the summer of 2007, bookending my fourteen-plus months of fieldwork in India, I followed the Relic Tour to several different sites and also conducted short-term research at three FPMT institutions in California.

11. I conducted interviews in Kushinagar in Hindi and English. Since many villagers spoke the local Hindi vernacular, Bhojpuri (the Northern Bhojpuri dialect, also known as Gorakhpuri), I supplemented my Hindi proficiency with Bhojpuri language training while in the field. Still, my nascent Bhojpuri was not sufficient for solo one-on-one interviewing, so while working in the villages of Greater Kushinagar, I relied heavily on a handful of short-term translators and research assistants.

12. The bridge as a structure also reverberated with me on a personal level as a person stuck between two unyielding groups that never really met. Stretched between FPMT statue advocates and Kushinagari anti-statue activists, I often wrestled with the unexpected responsibilities of advocacy anthropology. In this manuscript, I have endeavored to background myself, but it would be disingenuous to try to write myself out of the drama altogether, as I was an active participant observer, and my advocacy work did affect the unfolding of the narrative to some small degree. I took no pleasure in this fact, and thus I have tried to consolidate the bulk of my self-reflexivity and activism into chapter 9, so readers can take it or leave it as they like.

13. The Relic Tour ceased operations in 2015, after fifteen years of regular traveling (sometimes with multiple relic caches traveling on separate routes).

14. For more on the Natra Mangala, or eye ceremony, see Coomaraswamy 1956. In his novel, Ondaatje beautifully writes about ceremony: "The other man, facing him, holds up the mirror, and the artificer puts the brush over his shoulder, and paints the eyes without looking directly at the face. He uses just the reflection to guide him—so only the mirror receives the direct image of the glance being created. No human eye can meet the Buddha's during the process of creation. Around him the mantras continue" (2000, 99). Donald Swearer's (2004) work on the ritual of consecration, or "opening the eyes," of a new Buddha statue in Thailand stresses that Buddha images of the past, present, and future become a corporeal presence as the object is thus anthropomorphized.

15. Acknowledging the Maussian roots of the notion that an object can extend and retain the personhood of those who meaningfully handle it, Gell (1998) forwards a theory of agency for objects: while the "primary" agency lies with a person, he asserts that the "secondary" agency of objects is significant in and of itself. For example, Gell explains, "The little girl's doll is not a self-sufficient agent like an (idealized) human being, even the girl herself does not think so. But the doll is an emanation or manifestation of agency (actually, primarily the child's own), a mirror, vehicle, or channel of agency, and hence, a source of such potent experiences of the co-presence of an agent as to make no difference" (1998, 20).

1. Community/*SANGHA*

1. In this book, I will follow Paul Williams's definition of *sangha* as "the community of practitioners who are in their different ways and at different levels following and realizing the dharma" (Williams and Tribe 2000, 2). In classical terms, it is also sometimes used to mean the Buddhist community of those who are ordained, including those lay devotees who keep lay precepts. In FPMT, the *sangha* often refers to the FPMT Buddhist community writ large (monastics, devotees, and students), but it is also used to refer just to the FPMT Gelugpa Tibetan monastic community in particular. Since I have seen this word used in both contexts in FPMT and elsewhere, I will qualify the latter use by noting that it is the "monastic *sangha*."

2. In Tibetan Buddhism, the case of a reincarnation born previous to the death of the reincarnated is called *madeh tulku* and is still considered a rare occurrence.

3. *Tulkus* are identified, usually at a very young age, as the reincarnation of a significant Buddhist personality (usually male lamas or learned monastic teachers, but also sometimes very accomplished women or laity). Through a ritualized series of tests, elders generally search for, formally recognize, and eventually enthrone the *tulku*. There is occasionally institutional disagreement; for example, there are currently two Karmapa throne-holders, as the sect has divided over a *tulku* recognition controversy. Moreover, the People's Republic of China has taken an increasingly controlling hand in the recognition of *tulkus* who now stand in direct competition with the status of those recognized by the Dalai Lama and his Tibetan government in exile.

4. For a longer exposition on the practices and tempos of Gelugpa meditation practices in and outside of heritage monastic institutions, see Falcone 2010b.

5. Many years after her death, Zina's reincarnation was identified as the newborn son of one of her relatives in Paris (Mackenzie 1995, 119).

6. Another teacher attaining global prominence at this time was the Dalai Lama himself, who began attracting devotees to public lectures and private audiences, but unlike FPMT's lamas, the Dalai Lama did not invest in the building of centers far and wide or develop an education program for Western converts. Yet another important Tibetan Buddhist monastic, Geshe Sopa, was appointed to the faculty of the University of Wisconsin in the late sixties and taught a generation of Tibetan Buddhist studies faculty and practitioners (many of whom were studying both experientially and academically). Geshe Sopa did not crave a monastic and educational empire like the FPMT lamas and instead established a single center, the Deer Park Buddhist Center, where he lived and periodically taught until his death in 2014.

7. Monastic travel for purposes of pilgrimage, teaching, institutionalized meditation retreats, and intermonastery debate was not uncommon in preexile Tibet (Sopa 1983; Huber 2008), nor was it uncommon for a main monastic center to have several branch monastic centers in the same tradition scattered elsewhere. Huber's (2008) work on international religious pilgrimage also demonstrates that there was concerted effort at various historical points to establish connections with sites and communities in India especially. While global travel is therefore not new to Tibetan Buddhism, the jet-set nature of FPMT's monastic travel certainly adds a unique dynamic to globalized teachings today.

8. There are a handful of other Tibetan Buddhist nonheritage groups whose institutional reach and scope are fairly expansive—Shambhala International and Karma Triyana Dharmachakra, for example (Seager 1999).

9. In FPMT, the notion that it is the defilements of the followers that cause the death of a lama is still in wide circulation among devotees; although there is not universal belief in this principle, I heard the belief that Lama Yeshe's death was due to the karmic shortcomings of his followers stated as fact in several contexts, including during a guru *puja* being done for the health of a senior Tibetan lama, during lunch conversations, and during discussions about the Maitreya Project controversy. Lama Zopa Rinpoche has blamed the "problems regarding our center in England, Manjushri Institute" for the rapid decline of Lama Yeshe's health (Wangmo 2005, 281). Once Lama Zopa Rinpoche caused commotion and upset among FPMT devotees when he told them that Lama Yeshe could have lived another ten years, but that his lifespan had been dependent on the integrity of the prayers and *karma* of his followers, who had essentially failed to muster the conviction to keep him healthy (Mackenzie 1988).

10. Foreign *tulkus* (reincarnations) are a rare phenomenon. There are just a handful of Western *tulkus* who have been identified by Tibetan lineage holders from all the major Tibetan sects. Most of these *tulkus* were the male progeny of nonheritage Tibetan Buddhist devotees, but there have also been a few adult Western men (e.g., Steven Seagal) and women (such as Catherine Burroughs, aka Jetsunma Akhon Lhama) who were recognized as *tulkus* over the past few decades as well.

11. For more on Osel and his trajectory, see his FPMT biography (2009b). Also, I have published a scholarly article that details his early journey in FPMT, his self-proclaimed doubts about his time in the monastery, and his eventual return to the FPMT organization (Falcone 2017).

12. Buddhism is Buddhisms. Faure writes: "Buddhism is itself double, hybrid, bastardized. On the one hand, it is a powerful intellectual system with tendencies both rationalist and abstract, almost structuralist and universalist. On the other, it is a form of local, pagan, quasi-shamanistic thought. By the same token, it is irreducibly plural. As the eminent Indianist Paul Mus has remarked, there are not just two, but at least half a dozen Buddhisms" (2004, x). The religious studies scholar Thomas Tweed writes that "every tradition, including Buddhism, is a flowing together of currents. . . . There is no pure substratum, no static and independent core called 'Buddhism'—in the founder's day or in later generations. What we have come to call 'Buddhism' was always becoming, being made and remade over and over again in contact and exchange, as it was carried along in the flow of things" (2011, 23).

13. Buddhism's many journeys over as many centuries with its subsequent movement of ideas, objects, and people, has been traced admirably by other scholars (Batchelor 1994; Baumann 2001; Collins 1998).

14. Perhaps David Harvey's (1989) notion of increasingly fast "time-space compressions" is useful in showing that while change is ubiquitous in human history, the speed of certain temporal transformations (such as the temporal moment at the end of the twentieth century) has set the stage for a historically particular moment. It is the frequency of time-space compressions given new technologies that have made global Buddhism especially unique in its own right.

15. To me, "TransBuddhism," as a term, reads as overly nebulous. Also, TransBuddhist could perhaps accidentally evoke the word "trans" (transgender) and be taken to refer to a transgender Buddhist subject.

16. So when did Buddhism go global? One thousand years ago, even as Buddhism dominated many parts of Asia, was not the notion of the world different? Even before globalization, Buddhism should not be taken as a purely Asian phenomenon, since Buddhist notions have influenced Western thinkers for many centuries as well (Batchelor 1994; Faure 2004; Inada and Jacobson 1984). Although one can argue that Buddhism has always already been globalized, there is a new valence to the contemporary movements that have leaped new oceans and been invited into new homes, all the while taking on different forms and meanings than before. I refer to this new movement as global Buddhism with full understanding that it is simply the newest stanza of a very old song.

17. I follow current anthropological conventions here in noting that ethnicity refers to a group with common cultural traits, language, descent, and so on. Ethno-racial distinctions hinging on racial identity are one type of ethnic classification. Ethnicity is historically, politically, and culturally constructed, often in manifestly hierarchical ways (Ong 2003; Williams 1989). The ethnic categories used in this book are fluid ones; for example, "The grouping 'Asian American' is not a natural or static category; it is a socially constructed unity, a situationally specific position, assumed for political reasons" (Lowe 1996, 82).

18. I am not the only scholar to find Nattier's categories problematic (see Cheah 2011 and Rocha 2006), but no critique, including mine, suggests that Nattier was explicitly, intentionally setting one of her types of Buddhists above another.

19. In order to make the analytic more useful to scholars studying various Buddhist subcultures—for example, Chinese Buddhists who are practicing Tibetan Buddhism in a monastic complex in occupied Tibet, or white Americans in Manhattan, Kansas, practicing a form of Korean Buddhism—I think heritage spectrum definitions could take more precise, case-study-specific forms. Frankly, the heuristic could be useful in different contexts and with different religions or subcultures at play. In my anthropology classes, I have used the "heritage spectrum of practitioners" terminology to discuss the diversity of Muslim practitioners in the United States. I have used the terms in my ethnomusicology course to discuss topics like old-time music and dance (differentiating Appalachian heritage practitioners from the nonheritage practitioners of middle-class contra dances).

20. I take enculturation, not genetics, to be grounds for religious heritage. The child of Korean American Protestant Christians who finds Buddhism later in life (thus, a nonheritage Buddhist practitioner) hardly belongs in the same category as a Korean American who was raised by parents and surrounded by family who are Buddhists (a heritage Buddhist practitioner). The fact that there are Asians in the West who have converted to Buddhism (or adopted a particular Buddhist tradition) is the reason that Janet McLellan's two Buddhisms binary—"Asian" and "non-Asian," in reference to Buddhists in Canada (1999, 20)—felt insufficient for my use.

21. If we were comparing Osel to Stefanie on the semiheritage spectrum, Osel would be placed further toward the heritage end in contrast to Stefanie, who would be further toward the nonheritage end.

22. While I do sometimes use the term "convert," I do so with caution and some trepidation, since it fits some nonheritage Buddhist experiences and not others. In my experience and that of other researchers of nonheritage practitioners, many so-called converts reject or "dislike" (McAra 2007, 165) the appellation. It is the unsatisfactory nature of the term "convert" that made Tweed's "cradle versus convert" distinction untenable to me (Tweed 2002, 19), even as a binary.

23. In a survey of American converts to Buddhism, Coleman (2001) found that over 20 percent of his respondents also identified as followers of another religion.

24. If the traditions being evaluated are quite close, a scholar might decide that "semiheritage" is a more appropriate qualifier. For example, depending on the framing of a study, I could see converts from Jodo Shinsu Japanese Buddhism to Zen Japanese Buddhism labeled either nonheritage practitioners or semiheritage practitioners.

25. For example, Wilt, a black American, who is now a nonheritage Buddhist (albeit actively maintaining connections to other religious traditions), told me that he first heard about Buddhism while reading a book about a famous Hindu guru titled *Autobiography of a Yogi*. It made him curious enough to seek out texts about Buddhism, which had spurred his new religious practices. Another new FPMTer, a Dutch woman volunteering at the Root Institute, had initially come to India looking for a spiritual path specifically because she had read some of Osho's books. (Osho, also known as Rajneesh, was an Indian spiritual teacher who drew from many traditions, including Hinduism and Buddhism).

26. Up until late 2008, FPMT membership levels could buy certain privileges; the extent of those privileges depended on the level ($30–$5,000/year) one had subscribed to. Membership at the $30/year (or "Golden Fish") level bought a subscription to *Mandala* magazine (FPMT's quarterly periodical), its e-zine, and a discount at the FPMT e-store. Membership at the "Victory Banner" level ($5,000/year) included the above, plus free videos, access to online learning, special mention in *Mandala* magazine, the merit of being honored at the "yearly Patron Puja," as well the additional "great merit" of helping FPMT with its publishing efforts (FPMT 2008a; FPMT 2008b). In 2009, the FPMT membership concept delineated above was scrapped in favor of encouraging donations through a "Friends of FPMT" formulation. The Friends of FPMT has four ranks, which correspond to the Buddhist story of the Four Harmonious Friends: FPMT Membership is available for free, and entails listserv access and limited access to the Online Learning Center; FPMT Basic Friendship is available for a $5–$25/month donation and includes the above, plus a subscription to *Mandala* magazine; FPMT Dharma Supporters give between $30 and $99 per month and have access to all of the above, plus unlimited access to the Online Learning Center; FPMT Patron status is given to all those donors who give more than $100 per month to FPMT for all of the above, as well as getting the benefit of a yearly *puja* for patrons (FPMT 2010).

27. These ideal types, like Weber's (1968), leave much to be desired but are necessary to avoid lengthy explanations throughout the body of the book. When I refer to "searchers," "students," "devotees" and "monastics" throughout, I am using this parlance. When I refer to "FPMTers" or "FPMT practitioners," I am referring FPMT-connected people across the faith continuum from student to monastic.

28. Thomas Tweed has coined the term "Buddhist sympathizer" to refer to those who evince interest in Buddhism without self-identifying as Buddhist, in contrast to the "Buddhist adherent" who self-identifies as a Buddhist practitioner (1999, 2002). I might place my term "searcher" under Tweed's rubric of "sympathizer," while the disparate commitments of "devotees" and the "monastic *sangha*" would be better understood as fitting under Tweed's category of "adherents." Since students are active, engaged learners in a *sangha* (or multiple *sanghas*) but may or may not self-identify as Buddhist, there is no clear way to map this category onto Tweed's typology.

29. Devotees are not necessarily singular in their commitments to gurus or organizations, so this measure has to do with whether someone has committed to FPMT, and not to whether they have only committed to FPMT. Based on her experience, an FPMT devotee could consider Lama Yeshe, the Karmapa, and Sakhyong Mipham Rinpoche to be her root gurus, despite the fact that those lamas represent different Tibetan orders.

30. Monastics are ordained at various levels. The ethnic Tibetan and Mongolian youth and children who have entered into FPMT monasteries and nunneries take a more formal ordination when they grow older.

31. There are sociocultural differences between FPMTers around the world, of course, but I have not visited the majority of FPMT's 150 plus centers, nor studied these regional differences in earnest. The following is a compilation of triangulated reflections from longtime FPMTers about the nature of those regional differences in very broad strokes. In general, my informants tell me that FPMT's European and North American practitioners are thought to be keener on meditation, and less inclined toward merit-making donations for holy objects, than Asian devotees, and even Latin American devotees. One American devotee who had spent time in European and American centers observed that "Europeans are a bit more cynical. Americans are a little more wide-eyed and willing to go along with things." I have observed this pattern to a certain degree, but I have met wholly faithful Europeans and many cynical, detached Americans. European centers are reputedly somewhat more formal and reserved than American centers, according to informants who have visited a handful in both regions. Latin American centers are thought to be even more ritualistic than North American centers. Devotees from Mexico and Brazil, for example, are more accepting of holy objects than Americans, Canadians, and the French, but they are less tolerant than East Asian FPMTers. East Asian devotees are reputedly major donors who make the bulk of FPMT's holy objects projects possible; according to all of my FPMT interviews on the subject, East Asian FPMTers are thought to be less focused on meditation and keener on merit-making activities than Western FPMTers. Indian practitioners, mostly elderly, educated Hindus, are often engaged in spiritual development activities at FPMT centers that, to some extent, run in tandem with their continuing Hindu beliefs and practices. Many Asian devotees grew up with the notion of merit making and therefore make larger donations for the karmic benefit of themselves and their ancestors.

32. Some of these individuals may be considered white, or "of Spanish descent," according to the particular ethnic delineations of their native countries (Fish 2012).

33. In 2017, all five of the FPMT international board of trustees were men (FPMT 2017b). At the same time, of the resident teachers listed on the FPMT website, forty-nine were male and eight were female (FPMT 2017c).

34. Alexander Berzin (2000) constructed a model of how different generations—the Baby Boomers, the "Me" generation, and Generation X—met Tibetan Buddhism in different ways, but I have found the model to be so oversimplified as to be less than useful for my purposes. Suffice it to say that I have met FPMT staff, volunteers, *sangha*, devotees, students, and dropouts from each of those generations.

35. Whiteness as a category is always sociohistorically constructed, of course, and is defined and delimited variably in all communities with notable changes over time. Latin American categories of race, in particular, are difficult to distinguish as an outside observer, which is why I have already noted the complexity of that categorization.

2. The Teachings/ *DHARMA*

1. Previously, the international headquarters of FPMT were located in Taos, New Mexico, Soquel, California, and Kathmandu, Nepal (listed from most to least recent).

2. In Tibetan Buddhism, in the case of circumambulation with nonhuman, sentient beings, the latter are slated to receive merit, but the human circumambulator is also expected to receive good merit.

3. The Jang winter debate sessions were a longtime tradition preexile between the three most celebrated monastic colleges—Sera Je, Ganden, and Drepung. Although the FPMT website claims to have single-handedly revived the Jang tradition in exile (FPMT 2008d), according to another history, the exile branches of these monasteries kept the practice individually until 1980 and then revived the tradition of a joint meeting together themselves in 1981 (Zopa 2003). This narrative notes that the debate sessions are seven plus hours per day. Since only two hundred monks from Sera Je could travel to these debates initially, one of Lama Zopa Rinpoche's FPMT funds subsequently sponsored more attendance to these debates.

4. In brief, the construction of holy objects, such as statues, *stupas*, and prayer wheels, in Tibetan Buddhism, as in other Buddhisms, generates karmic merit.

5. The appellation of "heart" indicates a special devotion in Tibetan Buddhism; e.g., one's primary disciple is one's "heart disciple." This term is probably derived from the Tibetan *thuk*, which bestows the sense of something close to one's heart.

6. Why preservation? Was Mahayana endangered? One could argue that at the outset of the organization, in the seventies, in exile from Tibet, Lama Yeshe and his peers may have legitimately feared for the future of the Tibetan Buddha *dharma*. The relocation (or duplication) of once mighty Tibetan monastic institutions in exile was in a nascent period, and perhaps the lamas recognized that support from Westerners would be a significant factor in the success or failure of these endeavors.

7. In *The Sound of Two Hands Clapping* (2003), Georges Dreyfus describes the three acumens or *"prajnas"* as the "acumen arising from listening" (165), the "acumen arising from thinking" (165), and the "acumen arising from meditation" (166). Dreyfus demonstrates that meditation is just one level of reflection, which must be preceded by other important steps in learning and comprehension. For more on traditional pedagogies and the acumens, see Dreyfus (2003) and Sopa (1983).

8. Tibetan monastic pedagogy hinges on memorization and traditional debate (Cozort 2003; Dreyfus 2003), while FPMT has abandoned attempts to include debate

methods in its pedagogical practices (Cozort 2003). Daniel Cozort wrote that in FPMT centers practitioners found the traditional debate style too academic; they were themselves more interested in practice. The jettisoning of debate, as well as intensive memorization, has been supplanted by more Western academic pedagogies like discussion-oriented classes, review sessions, and quizzes and exams (Cozort 2003). There are also innovations in some of the FPMT educational programs that were not necessarily common in either Western universities or Tibetan monasteries, such as weekly meditation sessions, retreats, journals for self-evaluation of behaviors, and community service.

9. Interestingly, Osel's public persona on his return to the FPMT fold after a long absence tends toward the eclectic. In an article about Osel, I wrote: "Despite noting in 2012 that he did not self-identify as Buddhist (Jenkins 2012), Osel's Facebook activity seems to indicate a gradual gravitation back towards an acceptance of Buddhist philosophy and practice, albeit within an eclectic, big tent spiritual framework that is staunchly inclusive of other traditions as well" (Falcone 2017, 231). In the future, if Osel is to be a star in FPMT's leadership constellation, FPMT may either have to adjust its institutional perspective on multidemoninational spirituality, or Osel may be pressured to fall in line with the institution's current policies on the matter.

10. At the Manjushri Institute, there was a power struggle between Lama Yeshe (and his supporters) and the resident lama, Geshe Kelsang Gyatso (and his supporters), in the eighties, as the latter began to split off from FPMT centralization. At the time, the Manjushri Institute was considered a central FPMT monastery, one of the "early jewels in the FPMT crown . . . the model on which FPMT centres would pattern themselves" (Kay 2004, 56). Lama Yeshe asked Geshe Kelsang to resign so that a "more suitable *geshe*, one committed totally to FPMT objectives" could take over, but since many local practitioners petitioned for him to stay, Geshe Kelsang decided to remain, effectively going against the express wishes of the centralized authority of FPMT (Kay 2004, 61). The Manjushri Institute informally broke off contentious talks with FPMT in 1984, legally won possession of Institute assets in 1991, and eventually became the founding "mother centre" of a new relatively nonheritage Buddhist institution, the New Kadampa Tradition (Kay 2004, 111). In 2003, the group became the New Kadampa Tradition—International Kadampa Buddhist Union, which has a Buddhist pedigree in the Phabhongkha Rinpoche lineage, and which incidentally diverges from the FPMT teachings on numerous religious positions. Most notably, the New Kadampas are a group aligned against the Dalai Lama's restriction on the propitiation of the Shugden deity, and therefore extremely controversial in the realm of Tibetan Buddhism in general, and Western Tibetan Buddhism in particular. For more on the Shugden controversy, see Dreyfus 1998, and for more on the role of the FPMT and the Manjushri Institute, see Kay 2004 and Cozort 2003.

11. That said, Abby, a popular and well-regarded FPMT nun from Pennsylvania, took Buddhist ordination yet acknowledges that she is also still ethnically and culturally Jewish. Similarly, Natalie, who grew up Catholic in a small town in Brazil, became an FPMT nun only after being able to mediate her Catholicism.

12. Other semi- and nonheritage Buddhist groups tend to make their own claim to superior practice. For example, the Insight Meditation community headed by Christopher Titmuss forwards a competing claim to better Buddhist practice. He noted in his lectures in Sarnath in February 2006 and in Bodh Gaya in January 2007 that

statues and centers were unnecessary for *dharma* practice; often his teaching spaces reflected this tenet—the one Buddha statue in any given space was rarely the center of attention. Those who gravitate toward Insight Meditation Buddhism(s) tend to say that they were turned off by the guru devotion and holy object worship in Tibetan Buddhisms. Serious FPMT devotees have often already explored their options and necessarily bypassed these and other, alternative, nonheritage Buddhist *sanghas*.

13. Merit multiplication is a common practice in karmic religions, like Buddhism and Hinduism, and in practice it takes many forms. For example, Copeman (2005/6) argues that merit multiplication is foregrounded in religious blood-bank advertising very consciously, so that Hindu donors will feel that through the technological process of "centrifuge technology" their one donation becomes several donations: the result is that the generosity of blood banking becomes more generous and the productivity of the bank increases. The appeal of this karmic arithmetic was very significant to Copeman's heritage Hindu informants, but it was a complex, and sometimes divisive, issue for my nonheritage Tibetan Buddhist FPMT informants.

14. In the unabbreviated "Dedication Prayers for Special Occasions" from the same volume (Z. Rinpoche 2004), the Maitreya Project is given one third of the total space for dedications. In the abbreviated version that we chanted at the event narrated in the chapter, about one half the space is dedicated to the success of the Maitreya Project.

15. Mahasiddhas are great accomplished masters. Je Tsongkhapa (1357–1419) was an important monastic, who is usually credited with the founding of the Gelugpa sect of Tibetan Buddhism.

16. It may seem counterintuitive to suggest that any tradition with antecedents could be deemed completely nonheritage, which is why I found it potentially mollifying to use the qualifier "relatively." Of course, the qualifier "relatively" is necessarily implied across a spectrum already, but I find that it has the added benefit of signaling to readers whether one is referring to the heritage spectrum for practitioners (which does not make use of the qualifier) or the heritage spectrum for institutions (which uses the qualifier).

17. The spectrum is a useful, although imperfect, heuristic for seeing differences in practice in various Buddhist institutions today. I do not see all institutions under a single category as identical, however. One could compare similar institutions to one another according to the extent to which they comport with the mainstream norms of their antecedent institutions. For example, Triratna Buddhist Community (formerly, the Friends of the Western Buddhist Order) was founded by a nonheritage Buddhist and based on ethnographic material about their institutional practices (McAra 2007). I would, preliminarily, plot them further toward the nonheritage pole than FPMT; that is, arguably, although both are relatively nonheritage institutions, Triratna is a relatively more nonheritage Tibetan Buddhist institution than FPMT. Also, I would say that, in contrast with FPMT, the type of "detraditionizers" discussed by scholar David McMahan (2008, 245)—such as today's Rochester Zen Center and the Princeton Area Zen group—would be on the more extreme end of this nonheritage segment of the institutional heritage spectrum.

18. This is not to say that the heritage and nonheritage practitioners never came together for practice; parallel congregations are not necessarily strictly isolated (Numrich 1996).

19. As an Ithaca resident during my graduate studies in anthropology, I spent a lot of time at Namgyal, including a few years of Tibetan language instruction with one of the monks living there. As a short-term resident in Dharamsala in 2000 and multiple times in 2006–7, I gleaned a general sense of the character, spaces, and tempo of the Namgyal Monastery in India.

20. This categorization of a particular institution along the heritage spectrum of institutions is based on the available data regarding the sum of practices and beliefs within the community; that is, on balance, FPMT is a relatively nonheritage Tibetan Buddhist organization. This is not to ignore the handful of projects under the FPMT, Inc., umbrella that might be seen as practicing heritage Buddhisms (Mu Monastery in Nepal, for example). If one were to look at FPMT at a micro level, one would find that its affiliated groups practice across the spectrum. However, in sum, the nonheritage projects and practices far outweigh the outlying heritage ones, and thus it is most sociologically expedient to call FPMT a relatively nonheritage institution.

21. Again, "Tibetophilia" among Westerners has been well documented in Keila Diehl's work (2002). In addition, my own coauthored work has examined some of the costs and benefits of the Western romanticization of Tibetans (Falcone and Wangchuk 2008).

22. For more about the Mu Monastery's affiliation with FPMT, see the Kopan website ("Tsum Monastic Communities" 2017).

3. The Statue/*MURTI*

1. Just to reiterate my terms, I define my retronyms as follows: the initial period in Bodh Gaya is Maitreya Project 1.0; the following period in Kushinagar from 2003 to 2012 represents the biography of Maitreya Project 2.0.

2. There is a long tradition of building large statues in Asia, but it is notable that the statues are getting more prodigious than ever in the age of neoliberal globalization. Philip Lutgendorf (1994), for example, has written about the giant Hanuman statues emerging in ever larger forms as various sponsors sought to build the biggest one. Catherine Becker has explored other Buddhist giants in India, such as Andhra Pradesh's Hussain Sagar Buddha and the Dhyana Buddha, in the context of looking at a regional spate of construction, during what she calls "a Golden Age for colossal images in India" (2015, 164). Kajri Jain (2016) has written about how the booming automotive and cement industries in postliberalization India have enabled a commensurate investment in giant religious statues.

3. Sadly, the director passed away in 2014, and the studio has been defunct ever since.

4. There is no ethnographic evidence that heritage Buddhist practitioners see karmic benefits as accruing to another person or to no-person. Ohnuma wrote, "The gift given for the sake of merit clearly involves time lag between the gift and its recompense—in this case, one that frequently extends into a future lifetime (and, in fact, to a 'different' person altogether)—again allowing the subjective experience of pure generosity to coexist with the objective truth of exchange" (2005, 119). Similarly, while discussing Buddhist gifting practices at Thai funeral casinos, Alan Klima wrote that generosity is pure because the object and the self are transitory and impermanent: "What if there is no 'thing' given, no 'one' and no 'other one' in the first

and last place?" (2002, 269). As he articulates his hypothesis that the merits of a gift settle on a future self, Klima writes, "Generosity brings a return to someone else, a stranger, some other person in the future (even in the next moment) to whom you might habitually refer as 'yourself.' One is being generous in giving a good inheritance over to that person, and inconsiderate by leaving a bad inheritance, whether we are referring to 'this life' or 'between lives' (there is no essential difference)" (272). Given my interviews with Buddhists in the field, I view these aforementioned notions of disinterested Buddhist giving as academic, and outside the pale of lived Buddhist understanding and experience. Even neophyte Buddhists with ambivalence about karmic cosmology, if they make offerings, usually do so with the knowledge that they are making a gesture that reaps social benefits: it supports a cause one believes in, reifies an identity one aspires to, shows that one is cognizant of community expectations in a particular social context, or demonstrates to onlookers that one is acting as part of a community. Givers in karmic traditions that believe in karma expect a form of karmic return for their offerings (and indeed reap social benefits as well). Givers in karmic traditions that do not believe in karma are generally aware that there are sociocultural benefits that accrue with adherence to the social conventions of generosity. This is not to say that these offerings are not heartfelt or sincere, but from an anthropological perspective they should not be viewed as disinterested.

5. Baudrillard might also see the loss of perceived authenticity as an opportunity to see things outside the pastiche of narcissism he describes thusly: "The fascination of handicraft derives from an object's having passed through the hands of someone the marks of whose labour are still inscribed thereupon: we are fascinated by what has been created, and is therefore unique, because the moment of creation cannot be reproduced. . . . Authenticity always stems from the Father: the Father is the source of value here" (2008, 81).

6. Ethnic Tibetans who do not recognize the image as their own told me that they worried that the aesthetic represents too much accommodation to ethnic Chinese (or Taiwanese) devotees whose political ideas about Tibet so often run counter to their own. Overall, my Tibetan-in-exile informants felt that the East Asian influence on the MPI statue design was heavy-handed and represented the source of the donations, rather than the source of the tradition. My basis for concluding that this was a general concern for Tibetan interlocutors is that it was brought up repeatedly in the dozens of formal and semi-formal interviews that I did with Tibetan refugees in Dharamsala, Delhi, Saranath, Bodh Gaya, and in a small hamlet in Himachal Pradesh.

7. Note, once more, that I have used pseudonyms for many of the MPI people listed above, since during my interviews with them I offered to do so. I have not changed the names of the three prominent members of the team who published about, and spoke quite publicly for, the Maitreya Project—and whom I have never officially interviewed—since their views are a matter of public record: Peter Kedge, Tony Simmons, and Linda Gatter.

8. A reminder that I have also not changed the names of the lamas of FPMT and Roger Kunsang, since they are public personalities whom I have never formally interviewed. Everything cited by name in regards to these personages are, therefore, public proclamations or publications.

9. I explored the story of Maitreya Project 1.0 in greater length in Falcone 2012a.

10. While these policing accoutrements and precautions may have been honestly acquired—they were the direct result of a raid on the compound by local gangsters—they look to all the world like a compound under siege.

11. A report by Peter Kedge observed that the Bihar state government's land ceiling prohibited MPI from purchasing more than fifty acres of land in Bihar, a fact which limited their possibilities there from the outset (Kedge 2007b).

12. The MPI staffers and administrators I spoke to never could explain why 750 acres was initially coveted in Kushinagar nor why 600-plus acres was needed; none of them even tried to justify the vast acreage.

13. The oft-repeated claim that the Dalai Lama chose Kushinagar with a divination ritual was confirmed by Lama Zopa Rinpoche ("Letter from Lama Zopa Rinpoche" 2014).

14. While the main statue plan shifted to Uttar Pradesh, the notion of a more modest statue in Bihar was eventually reintroduced after the Lalu Yadav Prashad–led Rashtriya Janata Dal faction lost elections in 2005; there was a transfer of power in Bihar, and the subsequent administration was more obliging to the Maitreya Project and its staff. During my main research period in India from 2005 to 2007 there were media reports and discussions in FPMT circles about reinvesting in the Bodh Gaya land and building another Maitreya statue there, though perhaps at a lesser scale than the giant one planned in Kushinagar. The secondary plans for the Maitreya statue in Bodh Gaya were only about 170 feet, as opposed to the 500 feet of the primary statue. During my fieldwork period, the Bodh Gaya office was quietly pursuing the development of the land, including a statue project, school, and clinic. If one wanted to name that iteration, one could call the rumors about an attenuated vision of a Bodh Gaya statue in the aughts Maitreya Project 2.1.

15. While much of the two documents, draft and final language, remained similar in spirit and in detail, there are some interesting divergences; the draft, I believe, should not be overlooked, as I follow Ann Stoler's (2002) assertion that drafts too have a special place in the unraveling of cultural logics and social histories.

16. This man had disrobed and was no longer a part of FPMT at the time of the nun's narration.

4. The Relics/*SARIRA*

1. There are relics from thirty plus Indian and Tibetan masters on display at the Relic Tour, but not all of them are popular with everyone, and this had led to certain communities boycotting the Relic Tour at times. For example, Nyingmapas are not entirely fond of Pabongkha, a historical personage whose relics are found in the Relic Tour collection, since he was so vehemently pro-Gelugpa that he arguably worked to undermine the interests of other sects, such as the Nyingma tradition. The current, fourteenth Dalai Lama has donated relics to the tour, but he is vastly unpopular with a very small sect called the New Kadampas, given that he has called for the cessation of the propitiation of one of their central deities, Shugden. Lama Zopa Rinpoche is himself not very popular with the New Kadampas, so as far as I could discern they tend to steer clear of the tour. For more on the Shugden controversy, in general terms, see Dreyfus 1998. The tour is fairly Gelugpa-leaning, although monks and nuns of various communities are invited not only to see the relics but to help the tour by sitting in chairs and giving blessings to attendees. However, MPI has balked

at non-Buddhist ritual specialists. According to a Relic Tour custodian, a non-FPMT, non-Buddhist, indigenous American was traveling with the tour for a while, until the decision was made at a higher administrative level that his presence was less than appropriate, and thus he was not allowed to continue on.

2. For example, the Buddhists Theosophy Society wrestled with relics. Colonel Olcott disagreed on this point with his Sri Lankan protégé, Angarika Dharmapala, and their parting of ways is thought to have been occasioned by Dharmapala's sense that Olcott had failed to pay proper respect to a relic (Strong 2008).

3. Trainor (1997) is immediately concerned with the prevalence of an ambivalent attitude toward scholarly work on relics and their place in Buddhist ritual. Trainor critiques the notion that the earliest texts represent the truest and most authentic Buddhism possible and that ritual was simply a degeneration of the tradition. Rhys Davids and other Orientalist scholars as well as missionaries began the textual reification of Buddhism as if it the tradition were buried in the pages of text, unintentionally effecting change in Buddhist practice in Sri Lanka and elsewhere.

4. Otherwise unqualified reference to "relics" will refer to the first of these categories as per standard contemporary meaning.

5. While Strong is perceptive to identify a new nuance regarding relics in some aspects of literature and practice, he perhaps overemphasizes the notion that relics can "best be understood as *expressions and extensions of his biography*" (2004, 229), by insinuating that it is always so.

6. A temporary Relic Tour custodian, a man who toured with the relics for a summer in Mexico, seemed less than convinced of the relics' power. While giving a talk to a group of Buddhist practitioners about the relics, he mentioned that he had heard about relic miracles, but had never experienced any, so he characterized himself as personally "doubtful." He told his audience that he was not sure if the relics were even authentic, though he said he supposed at least a few probably were. He was not the only FPMTer to wonder about the relics' efficacy.

7. Between 1990 and 2006, MPI had taken in about $12.5 million in donations, but had spent approximately $19 million, leaving them a $6.5 million deficit (MPI 2007c). The Relic Tour monies, thus, were a useful source of guaranteed, regular income for MPI.

8. This section is based on ethnographic observations of eight disparate Relic Tour weekends, of which I attended four of these American Relic Tour weekends myself and volunteered two additional times. I have also sent research assistants in my stead to take notes and do interviews at additional events; the Relic Tour came to Ithaca while I was in the field in India, so I won funding to train a small team of undergraduates to attend the event and take field notes. In addition, I asked a few friends and family to go and take photographs at distant venues, and to take notes regarding audience size, etc. (I have also visited MPI's nontraveling relics in Bodh Gaya several times, but I view that set as separate from the Relic Tour, so I do not include it here.)

9. Incidentally, this was also, roughly, the make-up of the crowd in attendance when the Namaste Yoga Center hosted the Relic Tour in Asheville, North Carolina, in mid-October 2008.

10. Many of my informants in FPMT, whether interviewed in India or the United States, reported that it was this very film that provided their first exposure to the MPI statue plan in India.

11. During this opening ceremony it was a piece called "Just Tara" that had been given to one of the custodians, but the custodians told me that there are many other musical albums that have been used.

12. In a later Relic Tour stop, nearly every relic was flanked by a card that added illustrations to the former labels. There was a *thangka*-like picture illustration of each ancient master and actual photo representations of more recent Buddhist teachers and masters.

13. Manjushri is a bodhisattva associated with wisdom; Vajrassatva is a bodhisattva associated with power. The exact make-up of the altar varies from year to year, and sometimes site to site, but in general it is fairly similar over time and space. The kind of flowers sitting in the vases on either side of the central Maitreya Project statue, and how the arrangements are done, likewise varies. In Asheville, North Carolina, in 2008 it was roses; in Walnut Creek, California, in 2007 it was a varied arrangement. Also in Asheville there were several large crystals arrayed around the whole altar.

14. The "Suggested Prayers While in the Presence of the Relics" handout included a "Prayer of Refuge and Developing Bodhicitta" (repeated three times), "The Four Immeasurables," the "Seven Limb Prayer," and several mantras, such as the "Wisdom Mantra," the "Buddha Shakyamuni Mantra," the "Chenrezig Mantra" (often repeated seven times), the "Tara Mantra" (sometimes repeated seven times), the "Maitreya Mantra" (sometimes repeated seven times), followed by the dedication: "By the merit I have gathered from all these acts of virtue done in this way, may all the sufferings of every being disappear."

15. For more on the bathing the Buddha ritual, see Bentor 1996 and Boucher 2002.

16. At the end of the weekend, at this point in the day, gifts, such as small Maitreya Project replica statues, gold bodhi tree leaves, and Maitreya Project thank-you cards were distributed to the main organizers and volunteers.

17. She had a small altar for Lama Zopa Rinpoche and Lama Yeshe (with a few deity representations) and one set of water bowls. Another larger altar for photos of teachers and gurus also included *stupas*, a vase collected with blessed strings that had come off, and other collected blessed things from teachers, such as a tissue from Lama Zopa Rinpoche and a piece of Ani Robina Courtin's robe. This larger guru altar had two sets of water-bowl offerings. She had one altar for *dharma* books with one water-bowl offering. The final altar, the central one, was arrayed with dozens of statues and images of Tibetan deities, *stupas*, and beautiful stones with a set of water bowls at the fore. There was an individual water-bowl offering for Tara. Angela was quite enamored with the mandala set and *mala* that Lama Zopa Rinpoche had given her. She also had received another *mala* as a gift, and made one herself. She would get many of her *malas* and other holy objects, such as wealth vases, blessed by gurus.

5. Aspirations/*ASHA*

1. Tushita heaven is a pure land, in which Maitreya is believed to reside.

2. In the Mahayana tradition, there are many texts that are attributed to Maitreya, who is said to have dictated them to Asanga, so therefore many practitioners do technically believe that they have the teachings of the Maitreya bodhisattva to draw on in the here and now.

3. Some scholars believe that the origins of the Maitreya Buddha in the tradition can probably be attributed to the contact between Buddhism and other world religions such as Zoroastrianism, Jainism, and Hinduism (Kitagawa 1988; Holt 1993). Kitagawa has argued that ancient Persian Zoroastrianism's myth of Saosyant, the future messiah, preordained to save humanity from evil by defeating the devil and establishing a paradise on earth, deeply influenced both Judeo-Christian and Buddhist traditions (1988, 9). However, Kitagawa does not conclude that Maitreya is simply a Buddhist version of Zoroastrianism's Saosyant, because he notes that Indic traditions may have had compelling influence as well; Kitagawa points to the possibly pre-Vedic Indic ideal of the divinely empowered super monarch, the cakravartin, who, "has a special place in the cosmic scheme as the final unifier of the earthly realm" (1988, 9). On the other hand, Holt notes that while Zoroastrianism may have had significant influence in the advent of the Maitreya narratives, the Indic religion of Jainism may have actually been the tradition to inspire tales of a future Buddha: "it may be that the emergent belief in a future buddha owes its origins to antecedent Jain traditions regarding the continuing lineage of tirthankaras ('ford-makers': spiritual 'victors' exemplifying the way leading to the ultimate spiritual realization)" (1993, 2). Conversely, Steven Collins (1998) remains unconvinced that Metteyya is a development from a Persian savior deity but admits that the name might have been borrowed, since he feels that the idea of future and past Buddhas is intrinsic to the fact of Buddhism's plurality of Buddhas. While Kitagawa (1988) and Holt (1993) are convinced that the Maitreya is a product of contact with other religious traditions, both Nattier (1988) and Jaini (1988) note that the controversy is far from resolved and that the origins of the Maitreya Buddha remain ambiguous.

4. The prophesy itself is important, since many of the previous-life, prelife, and life stories of the Maitreya Buddha precisely mirror those of the Shakyamuni Buddha's hagiography; since the Buddhist sacred texts tell that the Shakyamuni's coming had been prophesied, it is not surprising that Maitreya's coming would also be foreordained. The coming Maitreya Buddha will be born into the imperfect world of *samsara* as a human, a royal heir—precisely mirroring the narrative of the historical Buddha. Before attaining enlightenment, he will be a prince who renounces his material wealth and comfort in favor of the pursuit of enlightenment. He is said to attain enlightenment in much the same way as narrated in Shakyamuni Buddha's hagiography: besting Mara, Lord of the Dead, while sitting under a bodhi tree in deep contemplation. He will then deliver sermons that "save the world" (Meddegama 1993, 45), by delivering the listeners to nirvana and ending their cyclical rebirths. In this way, Maitreya's story can be seen as a cyclical reiteration of Shakyamuni's hagiography.

5. Nattier (1988, 34) is quick to point out that the messiah in classical Buddhism is quite different from Judeo-Christian messiahs: Maitreya does not bring about the world ending and the world rebirth—the reborn world is only reinvigorated, spiritually enlightened, and completed by the appearance of the Maitreya Buddha.

6. Masco asked a Yucca Mountain engineer if the proposed ten-thousand-year plan had affected the complexity of the engineering project, and the latter said it had not (2005). Surprised, Masco followed up, "Do you ever feel like you are building something for the ages here, like the pyramids of Egypt, because it will last for thousands of years?" (35–36) The engineer replied, "I don't like to think about those

kinds of things. . . . I'll guarantee this tunnel for one hundred years." In sum, according to Masco, the Yucca Mountain site's deep dark secret is thus revealed; it was a false promise, and something of a national hoax.

7. Champa is the name of the Maitreya Buddha in Tibet and its environs.

8. The geomancers reported that the "three resident deities had all agreed." (Colony 1997, 12).

9. It is not uncommon for Tibetans to have very flexible ways of interpreting signs. For example, a Tibetan Buddhist religious scholar once told me that when there are competing institutions or individuals, the same events are often deemed both auspicious and inauspicious, depending entirely on whose side a particular interpreter is on.

10. This example of the fire at the Maitreya Project site was reprised when an Italian FPMT center burned to the ground in December 2008. The FPMT international headquarters sent the CPMT e-list a copy of a letter Lama Zopa Rinpoche wrote to the gutted center about how something burning can be interpreted as an auspicious sign. After retelling the story of the fire at the Maitreya Project site, and specifically mentioning that both Ribur Rinpoche and one of the Dalai Lama's ritual attendants said that it was an auspicious sign, Lama Zopa Rinpoche wrote about how the fire at the center was a good omen: "I think that what has happened at Lama Tsong Khapa Institute with the blazing fire destroying the Gompa is an auspicious sign—that you have overcome all the problems by this blazing fire. . . . Even though there was much work and effort done for this Gompa, its burning gives us the opportunity to build an Enlightened Gompa, and for the encouraging Gompa not [to be used as] a place to eat pizza and mozzarella" ("Recent Fire" 2008).

11. Given this update, I found myself quite shocked when I visited the land in January 2006 at the beginning of my fieldwork and discovered that several thousand people still occupied the land in question and that they had no intention of ever moving. The residents of the project area had been protesting against the plans at a local level, and in August 2006 met with the chief minister of Uttar Pradesh, who agreed to cancel the project. Just a few weeks later, when I returned to Kushinagar, the farmers told me of their triumph; it was the same day that the "Maitreya Project Update, August 2006" was publicly released and posted.

12. To be perfectly candid, I was actively participating in the media coverage, both as an occasional author and a quoted source in articles by Daniel Pepper, a professional journalist. For more, see Falcone (2007a, 2007b), Gatter (2007a, 2007b), Pepper (2007a, 2007b). Furthermore, I was busily contacting media outlets and encouraging them to cover the story on the ground in Kushinagar.

13. Since it is Maitreya Project 2.0's close kin, I call this proposed medium-sized Bodh Gaya statue Maitreya Project 2.1.

14. The Tibetan Buddhist stance on human life is that it is a precious opportunity to work toward enlightenment in order to defeat the samsaric cycle of rebirth. The Tibetan Buddhist thinking about death in large part revolves around the fact that one should try to transcend it; one popular meditation on death in the tradition emphasizes three points: the inescapable fact of death, the uncertainty of the time and place of death, and the notion that only one's meditative acumen can help one at the time of death (the Thirteenth Dalai Lama; cf. Mullin 1998; McDonald 1984). There are many different kinds of death meditations from both sutric and Tantric traditions,

some of which help the meditator to visualize his/her path through the *bardos*, the stages of the afterlife, in order to be prepared to face death with the best state of mind to accomplish a good rebirth or enlightenment, but it is widely acknowledged that most Tibetan Buddhists, whether lay or monastic, do not do regular death meditations (Geshe Ngawang Dargye; cf. Mullin 1998).

15. Szondi argues that Benjamin reflects on his childhood by concentrating heartily on the moments of the past that portend the future: "he is sent back into the past, a past, however, which is open, not completed, and which promises the future Benjamin's tense is not the perfect, but the future perfect in the fullness of the paradox: being future and past at the same time" (1986, 153). Benjamin works to gain a sense of mastery over temporality by casting historians in the role of archaeologists of historical artifacts of the future. Benjamin's solution to the problem of the present is to take ownership of the past in order to reinfuse the present moment with hope.

6. Holy Place/*TIRTHA*

1. Kushinagar was among many sites that were rediscovered at this time.

2. A collected volume on Bodh Gaya has begun to redress this imbalance by focusing on contemporary sociocultural realities at that sacred site (Doyle 2012; Geary 2012; Rodriguez 2012) in addition to looking as relevant historical and archaeological questions.

3. Here I am, in part, doing what Ann Grodzins Gold describes as one type of anthropological study of pilgrimage sites (albeit not the goal undertaken in her own book, which focused instead on pilgrims and their return journeys): "Research may focus on the specialists in pilgrim centers who serve these transient journeyers—the bewildering hierarchies and networks of priests and other ritual experts, of guides, barbers, rest-house keepers, sweet-makers, vendors of flowers and incense" (1988, 1). In my work, I am indeed interested in those who make a living from the sites in various ways, but I am also attuned to the ways in which the world of the pilgrimage center invades other, apparently unrelated local spheres. For example, even the lives of small subsistence farmers in the region are deeply affected by their vicinity to the famous Buddhist sites of Kushinagar.

4. Some of the offering money goes to the ASI for upkeep of the site.

5. Many of these local "Indian monks" are not what tourists think they are. As I got to know some of them, I learned that many of these men have robed for the economic largesse only, they are widely known to be noncelibate (some have families of their own), and they tend to view their commitment to Buddhism only within the bounds of an inclusive Hindu identity.

6. These categories are mainly useful for a macro view of the cultural landscape of Kushinagar, as individually people may fall between two categories, shift from one category to the other over time, or frustrate the definitions altogether. With that caveat in mind, the next few sections will explore the Kushinagaris through this lens.

7. Buddhists in Kushinagar tended to disagree that Buddha should be considered an avatar of Vishnu, saying that this perspective was a symptom of Hinduism's ancient attempt to co-opt the Buddha. However, in practice, Buddhists and Hindus shared the site without ever getting into intense theological discussions about the matter with one another.

8. Most of my nonheritage Tibetan Buddhist interviewees in Bodh Gaya and Dharamsala had never been to Kushinagar but noted that they would like to visit someday when given the opportunity. One of my FPMT interviewees in Bodh Gaya, who had done a tour of nearly a dozen other Buddhist sites, told me that she had skipped the place of the Buddha's death: "We did a Buddhist pilgrimage, but Kushinagar was kind of off the beaten track. Also my friend who had gone there a few years before said that it was like a ghost town, so there wasn't much point anyway."

9. Attention to Greater Kushinagar is meant to provide an inclusive manner of speaking about the people who affect, and are affected by, the larger Kushinagari socioeconomic milieu, but a focus on a Greater Kushinagar area does not erase or devalue the distinct cultures of the villages themselves that have rich identities from their own side.

10. India is itself in the "Medium Human Development" range of HDI as compared to other countries (Human Development Index 2006, 285); it ranked 126 out of 177 countries.

11. The Deprivation Index, related to the HDI, expresses the lack of access to basic amenities in terms of the quality of habitat.

12. I asked the abbot whether this would be done in addition to, or in cooperation with, the Maitreya Project, which also said that it would build and operate a hospital in Kushinagar. The abbot replied that it would be separate from the MPI's proposed hospital, but not irrelevant to MPI's plans: "if the hospital happens it could benefit the Maitreya Project. If an accident happens [during statue construction] then the hospital will be there to help. It will be a good benefit to the project."

13. This ambivalence is not particular to Kushinagar. I heard the same complaints from locals in Sarnath, Bodh Gaya, and Dharamsala, who are just as dependent on, and also often just as resentful of, foreign Buddhists.

14. Huber traced a long period from at least the late sixteenth or early seventeenth century to the late nineteenth to mid-twentieth century, in which Tibetan conventional wisdom indicated that Kushinagar was in present-day Assam, in the town of Hajo (2008, 129). In surveying Tibetan lay informants on the matter in the mid-2000s, I found none who remember that it was the case that Tibetans once identified Kushinagar as being anywhere other than in Uttar Pradesh, but Huber's well-documented evidence shows plainly that the Tibetan community, in collusion and cooperation with locals, had replicated a whole host of holy sites around an Assamese "Kushinagar," including another famous bodhi tree. Huber shows that only in the twentieth century did compelling archaeological evidence and Buddhist modernism motivate pilgrims to shift their Kushinagar from Assam to Uttar Pradesh; at that time, Amdo Gendun Chopel published his ubiquitous *Guide to India*, which not only dismisses the Assamese Kushinagar in favor of the Uttar Pradeshi Kushinagar, but for the first time, according to Huber (2008), the former instructs Tibetan pilgrims in how to authenticate their pilgrimage sites in accordance with modern methodologies.

15. The tunnel vision of some promoters of religious tourism has been known to have overwhelmed and obfuscated the multireligious realities of localities before (Guha-Thakurta 2004; Ray 2012), such as in other Buddhist spaces in India that are

not primarily peopled by Buddhists but are being self-consciously remade (for example, Andhra Pradesh as discussed in C. Becker 2015; Bodh Gaya, Bihar, as discussed by Doyle 2012 and Guha-Thakurta 2004).

7. Steadfastness/*ADITTHANA*

1. In 2001, I took graduate courses in anthropology and sociology at Jawaharlal Nehru University in Delhi, and Rina had been one of my instructors. We had stayed in touch after I returned to the United States, as we had had some fruitful personal conversations about Tibetan Buddhist practice.

2. See "Letter from Lama Zopa Rinpoche" (2014).

3. The LAA was the law of the land in India as regards land acquisition until 2013 when the Right to Fair Compensation and Transparency in Land Acquisition, Rehabilitation, and Resettlement Act was passed.

4. For example, as it was described to me by a group of BBSS supporters, one lawsuit argued that the district magistrate who had signed off on a previous survey of the land had been corrupt and been bribed by an MPI official to say that the quality of the land was poor, unarable, and cheap. The lawsuit was working toward an official resurvey of the land to show that indeed much of the land was rich, arable, and valuable. At least some of this work through the legal system was effective, as the Allahabad High Court ruled in favor of plaintiffs working against MPI's land acquisition: "Notices were also issued for acquiring of land but 69 farmers got a stay from Allahabad high court" (Bano 2016).

5. Frankly, the figure of fifteen to twenty thousand displaced persons seems inconsistent with the general information I collected about estimated project consequences, as I report above. I have some theories about where that number may come from: (1) perhaps Pepper asked the government official how many people would ultimately be "affected" and these figures actually do include estimates from multiple phases of the process (whereas most of the estimates I collected just discuss the effects of the first acquisition); (2) perhaps Pepper asked how many people would ultimately be "displaced" and these figures include multiple phases of the process, not just the first acquisition. Although I had interviewed bureaucrats in that same office before Pepper, I may have been given answers about the effects of the first phase only. I failed to specifically ask about the effects of all combined phases future, so I cannot rule out either of the above possibilities.

6. If the archaeological documents are to be believed, then some 150 years ago much of the immediate Kushinagar surroundings were natural forest or jungle, and so not under cultivation. According to an interview with a source in the ASI, the discovery of the site led to new infrastructure, new communities, and expansion of farmlands throughout the region. Hence, while much of the land to be acquired is ancestral land handed down through many generations, it is probably historically inaccurate to suggest that it has been in the family from ancient times.

7. Land is measured in *katha*, but throughout South Asia the size of a *katha* is not fixed, so this should be read as a fraction of an acre.

8. A "Section 6" notification was published in June 2005, which technically made the land acquisition a point of fact; however, most farmers resisted any attempts to

force checks or compensation on them and refused to sign anything giving up their land. Therefore, while these steps were taken legally, in actuality the process had ground to a halt for years after this.

9. I never met any of the land-owners who took government payouts for their parcels, but this handful of apparently satisfied customers was acknowledged by both MPI and BBSS.

10. I investigated the "Tibetan citizenship and jobs" rumor quite aggressively, but I was never able to find the source, and I believe that it was entirely baseless gossip.

11. None of the local media coverage mentioned that the Buddhist monks sitting in solidarity had been compelled to participate in the demonstration by threats of violence. While the primary monk, Bhante Gyaneshwar, was fundamentally opposed to the project given what he perceived as an excessive land-grab (one that took some forty acres of his temple's lands as well), he only began showing up at the strikes because of violent threats against him by local farmers.

12. Although there were periodic Hindu-Muslim disputes in the district (and even some communal riots in the region during my fieldwork period), the Kushinagaris in the *gaons* who were to be impacted by the land acquisition said that communalism had never been a problem in their area. I have researched aspects of *Hindutva* communalism in the past (Falcone 2010a, 2012b, 2016), so I was actually a little surprised that there was so little evidence of it in Kushinagar during my fieldwork period. It seemed to me that the Muslims and Hindus in the locality got along well, and even when communal riots raged just an hour's drive away, the camaraderie in the Kushinagari area seemed undiminished. I acknowledge that there may be more to this part of the story, and perhaps underneath a facade of brotherly love there were tensions and prejudices that I was unaware of. I can only report that despite my repeated inquiries into the question of communal friction, the Hindus and Muslims of the area seemed to have neighborly concern for one another and were certainly fighting against the Maitreya Project as a unified front.

13. Most farmers had never heard of anthropology. I would often say, "I am a student of culture, and I want to learn about you and tell others about your story." In response, many of my informants often told me that their "culture" (what they would define as temples, rituals, and beliefs) had nothing to do with my questions about the Maitreya Project. I was also asked dozens of times, "Who are you writing a report for?" In this context, it is quite difficult to explain a PhD dissertation, or a book that might take a decade to publish. I explained that my work would hopefully be published someday. They knew I was not a journalist, nor a "professor," and at the time I was still a "student." My work and my presence remained mysterious to many Kushinagari locals. Even those whom I had interviewed, who necessarily had given me informed consent to share their stories publicly, did not always seem to understand why I had come so far (and spent so much perfectly good money!) to talk with them. This is to say, my explanation of my research project was not entirely comprehensible to all of my local Kushinagari informants.

14. This makes a certain amount of sense, since the school was located rather far from the MPI grounds, over near the Root Institute.

15. There is public uncertainty about whether Mayawati is a Buddhist practitioner or not. MPI has said that Mayawati is a "devout Buddhist" (Gatter 2008, 33), but in the media it has been reported that she is not a Buddhist (Shah 2016), and she

has publicly proclaimed that she will convert to Buddhism only if her party wins at the national level (which, incidentally, does not seem a very likely proposition). The *dalit*–Buddhist connection goes back to the mass Buddhist conversion ceremonies organized by famed *dalit* lawyer and reformer B. R. Ambedkar.

16. I photocopied his collection. I translated some of these articles, but there were dozens and it was slow going, so I had a translator work through some as well. Therefore, for this project, I had access to all of the Hindi-medium clippings in the local media about the project from the first announcements through the spring of 2007.

8. Loving-Kindness/*MAITRI*

1. Loving-kindness is one of four immeasurables, along with compassion (Sanskrit: *karuna*), joy (Sanskrit: *mudita*), and equanimity (Sanskrit: *upeksha*). Most often loving-kindness is considered the corollary of compassion. Loving-kindness is known to be the desire for others to be happy; compassion, on the other hand, refers to the desire for others to be free of suffering. Compassion and loving-kindness in the Tibetan Buddhist traditions, then, are often thought to be two sides of the same coin (Lief 1998, 12). Lief tells her audience that her root teacher, Chögyam Trungpa Rinpoche, used to say that *maitri* involved friendliness to others, but also friendliness and love toward oneself.

2. Perhaps "Buddhist morality" is more useful terminology than "Buddhist ethics," but I use them interchangeably in this book. Damien Keown makes the argument that Buddhism as a general tradition writ large has no formal branch of "ethics," noting that while rife with morality, the tradition simply has no branch of philosophical inquiry devoted to the study of morality. In contrasting the ethical debates in Plato's writing with that in Buddhist discourse, he writes, "A Buddhist version of this problem might ask whether certain acts are bad because they are punished by karma, or whether they are punished by karma because they are bad. Although this is clearly an important question, I have never seen the problem posed in these terms by Buddhist authors" (Keown 2006, 49). Keown goes so far as to suggest that the absence of ethics as a genre of thinking may have been due to the authoritarian, nondemocratic nature of Buddhist kingdoms, and the assumption within the monastic communities that the *vinaya* (Sanskrit: monastic disciplinary order) is absolute. Keown suggests that the development of Buddhist ethics really begins with the advent of Engaged Buddhism. In doing so, he explicitly connects the philosophical questions relating to Buddhist morality with the social justice questions of Engaged Buddhism.

3. Right speech is communication that does not promote divisions, gossip, or lies. Right action includes avoiding acts that harm any living being, refraining from taking what is not given, and not engaging in sexual misconduct (the details of which depend on one's particular commitments or vows) (Williams and Tribe 2000). Finally, acceding to the mandate to right livelihood involves ensuring that one's career path never betrays right speech or right action.

4. Christopher Queen (2000) identifies four types of Buddhist ethics that are overlapping and sometimes fluid: (1) discipline, (2) virtue, (3) altruism, and (4) engagement. Discipline refers to right action, while virtue refers to right mental intentions (such as compassion and loving-kindness). Queen goes on to explain that generosity is the

aspect of ethics, especially in Mahayana literature, that focuses on benefiting all other beings; on the path to bodhisattvahood generosity is a means to an end.

5. For example, in my view, FPMT's health projects in Bodh Gaya and its environs are good examples of how Buddhist groups can sponsor sustainable, well-planned programs that are beneficial to those in need. Also, just to throw out one more example among many, dozens of Buddhist groups have begun offering meditation courses, anger management training, and educational materials to inmates in prisons in the West (Parkum and Stulz 2000).

6. For an example of how Buddhist engagement can have unintended negative outcomes, some scholars have hypothesized that an increase in civic engagement in the world of Sinhalese Buddhism made it more palatable for Sri Lankan monastics to undertake active political careers, which in turn contributed to increased religious nationalism (Tambiah 1992; Trawick 2007); the subsequent increase in monastic militancy in Sri Lanka was one element feeding the brutal quarter-century-long civil war that finally ended in 2009.

7. At their insistence, I have not changed their names, especially since their names have been reported in the local and regional press. Sandeep Pandey is one of the founders of Asha for Education, an international nonprofit with branches in colleges and universities throughout the United States. In the interest of full disclosure, I was a member and occasional fund-raiser with the Asha for Education chapter at Cornell University from 2003 to 2008. On his return to India, Sandeep Pandey settled in Lucknow and has been a celebrated social worker and activist ever since (even winning the prestigious Magasaysay Award). He and his wife work to ensure the smooth running of Asha for Education schools and projects working tirelessly on behalf of the poorest of the poor. During my tenure there, they were training social workers to help them survey villages in Uttar Pradesh to audit a government program to help the economically disenfranchised.

8. Because of the anti–Maitreya Project protests, the NAPM had their annual conference in Kushinagar in the summer of 2008. The NAPM leaders were invested in trying to convince villagers that they should be less focused on just anti-MPI statue agitations and more focused on the revolution against neoliberal capitalism writ large.

9. While neoliberal economic development as a global system and as an ideology is anathema to me as a scholar, it is only fair to note that I make that judgment from a position of privilege; as a white, middle-class American I have already personally benefited from the fruits of a globalized economy that feeds off the poor. Even as a struggling graduate student, living on between $10,000 and $20,000 for many years, I had access to luxuries (like a computer, iPod, and digital voice recorder, and the resources for global travel) that some of my rural Indian informants could only dream of.

9. Compassion/*KARUNA*

1. "Call-out" culture is the tendency for like-minded people to publicly shame one another for perceived imperfections or insensitivities in words, policy, or practice. According to the queer body-positivity activist Asam Ahmad (2015), call-out culture often makes a public spectacle of constructive criticism. Ahmad argues that although call-out culture may sometimes play an important role in activism, it can be counterproductive and alienate potential allies. Although I did not think about it

in those terms at the time, during the period that I was trying to advocate for change by privately e-mailing and meeting with MPI staffers, I was endeavoring to "call in," instead of "call out," MPI with regards to the unintended consequences of their well-intentioned plan.

2. Lest I be painted as an opportunist by any of my informants, it is a known fact that first academic monographs make their authors little to nothing. I will be pleasantly surprised if my royalties even come close to the expense accrued by my preliminary visit to Kushinagar in 2003. This is not to say that I gain nothing; I am showing productivity in my academic milieu. I may get cited, and the *hau* of my work may circulate as part of conventional scholarly exchange practices (Falcone 2013).

3. There are, of course, some important exceptions, such as Bourdieu's (1988, 1990) excellent work turning the sociological lens onto academic subjects, Dominic Boyer's (2003) work on the fashion of academic theory, and Tony Crook's (2007) clever refractions of his positionality through the framing of his subject matter. I have endeavored to be introspective about the cultural conditions of my research and scholarship as these esteemed thinkers, as demonstrated in my own articles on the anthropology of anthropology, "the *Hau* of Theory" (Falcone 2013), and "A Meditation on Meditation" (Falcone 2010b). In my dissertation, I put reflexive intervals in between each chapter about the Maitreya Project; I used my field data, and the theory I had used to analyze it, as a mirror to look into and reflect on the knowledge-production practices at hand.

4. Indeed, our professional codes of conduct offer little guidance in the vagaries of complex fieldwork realities. I have written at length elsewhere about how the AAA Code of Ethics, as quasi-legal bureaucratic document, seems unequal to the task of effectively acknowledging the true messiness of doing ethical ethnographic research (Falcone 2010a).

Conclusion

1. It was my impression that even after the media blowup, there was still considerable skepticism in FPMT circles about the validity of the farmers' protests in Kushinagar. I was considered naive by many who found it far easier to believe in my failings than to question FPMT's leadership. After all, what could a thirty-something, white American woman know about culture, land prices, or local politics in agrarian India? It was far easier for FPMTers to doubt me, my conclusions, or my motivations than to doubt their guru's heart project, the persons entrusted to see their guru's wishes through, or their guru himself. While I argue that the thoughtless, top-down imposition of the statue project onto the small farmers of Kushinagar is ideologically hypocritical, I understand that the cultural logics of Buddhist guru devotion do not make a straightforward dismissal of MPI's motivations and actions an easy proposition for devotees.

2. Such is the power of skillful means that it can be used to justify almost anything. *Upaya*, thus, can give gurus a free hand to engage in questionable behavior—whether for good or ill.

3. I was not granted an audience with Lama Zopa Rinpoche in the years that I worked on this project, although I requested one each time I was in his immediate vicinity for teachings and talks (in India and the United States). I asked Rinpoche's

handlers for an opportunity to tell him what was happening on the ground in Kushinagar, as I had done with other FPMT and MPI *sangha*. It goes without saying that one cannot just e-mail Lama Zopa Rinpoche. I was never offered a direct e-mail address or a direct phone number. I believe the only direct exchange I have ever had with Lama Zopa Rinpoche was when it was my turn to approach his throne during my refuge ceremony in 1998; he scribbled a *dharma* name into an FPMT refuge booklet and handed it to me, and I thanked him profusely.

Epilogue

1. To be fair, the cancellation in 2012 was probably due to equal measures of Kushinagari activism, regional Indian politics, and internal MPI funding issues.

2. In the fall of 2016, the old webpage (www.maitreyaproject.org) began redirecting web traffic to an FPMT page on the Maitreya Projects (http://fpmt.org/projects/other/maitreya/).

3. See my article about Maitreya Project 1.0 for more on love as a method of co-constitution for objects and interlocutors (Falcone 2012a).

❧ GLOSSARY

aditthana (Sanskrit) steadfast, resolute, determined

amchi (Tibetan) doctor

anatman (Sanskrit) doctrine of nonself

asha (Sanskrit) hope

baksheesh (Hindi) tips or bribe

bhadrasana (Sanskrit) particular seated pose

bigha (Hindi) domestic land measurement (large); disparate acreage according to regional differences. *Bigha* are divided into smaller parcels, *katha*.

bodhi (Sanskrit) mind of enlightenment, perfect knowledge

bodhicitta (Sanskrit) desire to achieve enlightenment for all sentient beings

chapati (Hindi) (or, *chapati-roti*) unleavened bread, a staple Indian food

chi khor (Tibetan) counterclockwise circumambulation

chuba (Tibetan) Tibetan-style wrap dress

crore (Hindi) ten million

dalit (Hindi) refers those known as "untouchables" in terms of the Indian caste system

darshan (Sanskrit) view; referring to an auspicious viewing of a holy person, object, or site

dharamshala (Hindi) guest house

dharma (Sanskrit) multiple definitions in various traditions. For the purposes of this book, read as religious order; religious practice; the Buddhist teachings.

dharna (Hindi) nonviolent, sit-in protest

dhyana (Sanskrit) meditation

gaali (Hindi) abusive language; profanity

gaon (Hindi) village

geshe (Tibetan) high Tibetan monastic degree

gherao (Hindi) besiege, surround; refers to a protest tactic

gompa (Tibetan) monastery

Hindutva (Hindi) Hindu nationalism

kalpa (Sanskrit) era

karma (Sanskrit) cosmological causal system in Buddhism, Hinduism, Jainism, etc.

karuna (Sanskrit) compassion

katha (Hindi) domestic land measurement (small); disparate acreage according to regional differences; a fraction of a *bigha*

kayas (Sanskrit) refers to the Mahayana concept of the multiple "bodies" of the Buddha

khatak (Tibetan) offering scarf

kora (Tibetan) circling, usually a clockwise circumambulation

kuten (Tibetan) oracle

lakh (Hindi) one hundred thousand

lama chopa (Tibetan) guru devotional practice; guru yoga

lapa (Tibetan) oracle

lha-khang (Tibetan) chapel or altar room

lo jong (Tibetan) mental training

madeh tulku (Tibetan) the phenomenon of reincarnation before death

maitri (Sanskrit) loving-kindness

mala (Sanskrit) necklace, rosary

maras (Sanskrit) obstacles, negative karmas

mos (Tibetan) divinations

muboli (Hindi) declared-to-be (e.g. adoptive)

mudita (Sanskrit) joy

murti (Sanskrit) statue

nang khor (Tibetan) clockwise circumambulation

puja (Sanskrit) prayer

ringsel (Tibetan) relics

samsara (Sanskrit) cyclical rebirth

sangha (Sanskrit) community

sarira (Sanskrit) body; holy relics

shraddha (Sanskrit) placing faith

stupa (Sanskrit) particular holy object or relic receptacle, usually a dome-like structure

tehsil (Hindi) local, municipal administrative unit

thangka (Tibetan) particular style of Tibetan Buddhist painting

tirtha (Sanskrit) "crossing place"; holy place

tsatsa (Tibetan) Buddhist statues made as part of a particular ritual/meditation practice

tulku (Tibetan) reincarnate lama

upaya (Sanskrit) skillful means

upeksha (Sanskrit) equanimity

vikas (Hindi) economic development

vinaya (Sanskrit) monastic discipline

wallah (Hindi) doer/maker, as in *chaiwallah*

wang (Tibetan) empowerment

✿ BIBLIOGRAPHY

Newspaper Articles and Reports with No Author Indicated (in Chronological Order)

(1996). "Maitreya Project Moves Ahead." *Mandala*. November/December: 11.

(1996). "News India/Nepal." *Mandala*. August: 26.

(1997). "Peter Kedge International Director of Maitreya Project." *Mandala*. September/October: 12.

(2000). "Lama Osel 'Eager for the Study of Buddhism.'" *Mandala*. March/April: 62–64.

(2001). "China Enters Biggest Buddhist Statue Race." *BBC News*. May 6. www.bbc.co.uk. Accessed: October 2015.

(2002). "Agitated Villagers Keep District Officer Captive for Two Hours." *Rashtriya Sahara*. October 4. [Hindi]

(2002). "Memorandum of Understanding Draft." Lucknow, Department of Culture—Uttar Pradesh. Maitreya Project Trust.

(2002). "Roads Blocked during Opposition to Land Acquisition." *Sahara*. October 2. [Hindi]

(2002). "Unrest among Farmers Affected by the Land Acquisition Process of Maitreya Project." *Sahara*. September 11. [Hindi]

(2003). "Memorandum of Understanding." Lucknow, Department of Culture—Uttar Pradesh. Maitreya Project Trust.

(2004). "Demonstration and *Tehsil* Surrounded to Oppose Maitreya Project." *Aaj*. September 10. [Hindi]

(2004). "Farmers Demonstrate against Maitreya, Burn Effigy." *Dainik Jagran*. September 10. [Hindi]

(2004). "Maitreya Project, Kushinagar." Report. Lucknow, Department of Culture—Uttar Pradesh.

(2005). "Murder, Hanging . . . Whatever Happens, We Will Not Give Up Land." *Sahara*. January 16. [Hindi]

(2006). "Announcement of Struggle by Affected Farmers against the Maitreya Project." *Dainik Jagran*. August 14. [Hindi]

(2006). "Farmers Warn of Agitation in Connection with Compensation Amount." *Dainik Jagran*. January 14. [Hindi]

(2006). "Government Wants to Erect Palace on the Fertile Land of the Poor." *Hindustan*. August 18. [Hindi]

(2006). "Human Development Report 2006." www.hdr.undp.org/en/content/human-development-report-2006. Accessed: November 2017.

(2006). "Human Development Report 2006, Uttar Pradesh." http://planning.up.nic. in. Accessed: October 2014.

(2006). "Starvation Deaths of the Poor Are a Blemish on the Face of the Government: Tikait." *Padrauna Nagar.* August 4. [Hindi]

(2007). "Better Tourist Facilities, Not the Maitreya, Will Increase the Importance of Kushinagar" *Dainik Jagran.* April 4. [Hindi]

(2007). "Fast Continues for Removal of Maitreya Project." *Rashtriya Sahara.* February 13. [Hindi]

(2007). "Maitreya Project: Chasm in the Buddhist Monk Ranks." *Dainik Jagran.* February 17. [Hindi]

(2007). "Nandigram Turns Blood Red." March 15. *The Economic Times.* www.eco nomictimes.indiatimes.com. Accessed: December 2017.

(2007). "Red-hand Buddha: 14 Killed in Nandigram Re-entry Bid." *The Telegraph.* March 15.

(2007). "Singhur Flares Up Again." *Tribune News.* www.tribuneindia.com. Accessed: July 2016.

(2008). "Fresh Violence in Nandigram, Two Injured." *Times of India.* May 5 www. timesofindia.indiatimes.com. Accessed: July 2016.

(2008). "India: Urgent Inquiry Needed into Nandigram Violence." Human Rights Watch. Report.

(2008). "The Metogpa Project." http://chris.fynn.googlepages.com/TheMetogpa Project.pdf. Accessed: February 24, 2008.

(2008). "Recent Fire at Instituto Lama Tsong-khapa." Email from CPMT. http:// groups.yahoo.com/group/kadampa. Accessed: January 2009.

(2008). "Tata Pulls Out of Singhur." *Ananda Bazar.*

(2008). "Urgent Need to Address Large Scale Human Rights Abuses during Nandigram 'Recapture.'" Amnesty International. Report.

(2011). Census of India. www.censusindia.gov.in. Accessed: October 2014.

(2012). "What Will Happen to Maya's Pet Projects?" *Times of India.* March 7. www. timesofindia.indiatimes.com. Accessed: April 15, 2017.

(2013). "Akhilesh Yadav to Lay Foundation for 200 ft Buddha Statue, Park." *India Today.* December 12. http://indiatoday.intoday.in. Accessed: April 25, 2017.

(2014). "Letter from Lama Zopa Rinpoche." FPMT website. http://fpmt.org/ wp-content/uploads/projects/other/maitreya/LZR-letter-2-MPs-0214.pdf? x33127. Accessed: April 18, 2017.

(2014). "An Update from Kushinagar." *Mandala.* April–June: 18.

(2016). "Govt Grants Land, Buddha to Stand Tall in Kushinagar." *Times of India.* August 21. www.timesofindia.indiatimes.com. Accessed: August 21, 2016.

(2016). "Maitreya Project History: A Quick Recap." www.mbpkushinagar.org. Accessed: August 30, 2016.

(2016). "Rajnath Promises Buddha Statue in Kushinagar." *Hindustan Times.* April 25. www.hindustantimes.com. Accessed: April 15, 2017.

(2017). "Tsatsa Studio—Center for Tibetan Sacred Art." www.tsatsastudio.org. Accessed: June 19, 2017.

(2017). "Tsum Monastic Communities." http://kopanmonastery.com/about-kopan/ affiliated-communities/tsum-monastic-communities. Accessed: April 18, 2017.

Authored Sources

Ahmad, Asam. 2015. "A Note on Call-out Culture." *Briarpatch Magazine*. March/April. www.briarpatchmagazine.com. Accessed: May 24, 2017.

Ahmad, Faraz. 2007. "No Forcible Eviction for SEZs: Minister." *Hindustan Times*. June 17. www.hindustantimes.com. Accessed: December 2007.

Appadurai, Arjun, ed. 1986. *The Social Life of Things: Commodities in Cultural Perspective*. Cambridge: Cambridge University Press.

——. 1996. *Modernity at Large: Cultural Dimensions on Globalization*. Minneapolis: University of Minnesota Press.

——. 2001. *Globalization*. Durham, NC: Duke University Press.

Arthur, Chris. 1997. "Maitreya, the Buddhist Messiah." In *The Coming Deliverer: Millennial Themes in World Religions*, edited by F. Bowie and C. Deacy, 43–59. Cardiff: University of Wales Press.

Asad, Talal. 1993. *Genealogies of Religion: Discipline and Reasons of Power in Christianity and Islam*. Baltimore, MD: Johns Hopkins University Press.

Baker, Nick. 2016. "Fire, Brimstone and Human Kebabs: Inside the World's Second Largest Statue." *Myanmar Times*. July 21. www.mmtimes.com. Accessed: June 7, 2017.

Banerjee, Sumanta. 2007. "Into Thin Air." *Hindustan Times*. July 10. www.sacw.net/article341.html. Accessed: November 22, 2017.

Banerjee, Nirmalya. 2007. "Red Terror Continues in Nandigram's Bylanes." *Times of India*. November 15. www.timesofindia.indiatimes.com. Accessed: November 24, 2017.

Bano, Arjumand. 2016. "Government Grants Land, Buddha to Stand Tall in Kushinagar." *Times of India*. August 21. www.timesofindia.indiatimes.com. Accessed August 21, 2016.

Barnett, Tony. 1977. *The Gezira Scheme: An Illusion of Development*. London: Frank Cass.

Bartholomew, Ian. 2001. "Massive Buddha Taking Shape in Taiwan: The Maitreya Project Aims to Erect a 152m Bronze Buddha in India That It Hopes Will Stand for 1,000 Years." *Taipei Times*. www.taipeitimes.com. Accessed: January 2009.

Batchelor, Stephen. 1994. *The Awakening of the West: The Encounter of Buddhism and Western Culture*. Berkeley, CA: Parallax Press.

Baudrillard, Jean. 1994. *Simulacra and Simulation*. Ann Arbor: University of Michigan Press.

——. 2008. *The System of Objects*. New Delhi: Navayana Publishing.

Baumann, Martin. 2001. "Global Buddhism: Developmental Periods, Regional Histories, and a New Analytical Perspective." *Journal of Global Buddhism* 2:1–43.

Bechert, Heinz. 1984. "Buddhist Revival in East and West." In *The World of Buddhism: Buddhist Monk and Nuns in Society and Culture*, edited by Heinz Bechert and Richard Gombrich, 273–85. New York: Facts on File.

Becker, Catherine. 2015. *Shifting Stones, Shaping the Past: Buddhist Sculpture from the Stupas of Andhra Pradesh*. Oxford: Oxford University Press.

Becker, Ernest. 1973. *The Denial of Death*. New York: The Free Press.

Beckett, Samuel. 1954. *Waiting for Godot: A Tragicomedy in Two Acts*. New York: Grove Press.

Behar, Ruth. 1996. *A Vulnerable Observer: Anthropology That Breaks Your Heart*. Boston: Beacon Press.

Benjamin, Walter. 1968. *Illuminations*. New York: Schocken Books.

Bentor, Yael. 1996. *Consecration of Images and Stūpas in Indo-Tibetan Tantric Buddhism*. Leiden: E. J. Brill.

Bertels, Marcel. 1996. "Lama Zopa Rinpoche Puts a Smile on Maitreya Buddha's Face." *Mandala*. November/December: 11.

Berzin, Alexander. 2000. *Relating to a Spiritual Teacher: Building a Healthy Relationship*. Ithaca, NY: Snow Lion Publications.

Bhushan, Nalini, and Abraham Zablocki. 2009. "Introduction: Authenticity in the Context of Transformation." In *TransBuddhism: Transmission, Translation, Transformation*, edited by Nalini Bhushan, Jay L. Garfield, and Abraham Zablocki, 1–20. Amherst: University of Massachusetts Press.

Blackburn, Anne M. 2003. "Localizing Lineage: Importing Higher Ordination in Theravādin South and Southeast Asia." In *Constituting Communities: Theravada Buddhism and the Religious Cultures of South and Southeast Asia*, edited by J. C. Holt, J. N. Kinnard and J. S. Walters, 131–150. Albany: State University of New York Press.

Boucher, Daniel. 2002. "Sūtra on the Merit of Bathing the Buddha." In *Religions of Asia in Practice*, edited by Donald S. Lopez Jr., 206–215. Princeton, NJ: Princeton University Press.

Bourdieu, Pierre. 1977. *Outline of a Theory of Practice*. Cambridge: Cambridge University Press.

——. 1988. *Homo Academicus*. Stanford: Stanford University Press.

——. 1990. "The Scholastic Point of View." *Cultural Anthropology* 5(4): 380–391.

Boyer, Dominic. 2003. "The Medium of Foucault in Anthropology." *Minnesota Review* 58–60 (Fall): 265–272.

——. 2005. *Spirit and System: Knowledge, Media and Dialecticism in Modern German Intellectual Culture*. Chicago: University of Chicago Press.

Butterfield, Stephen T. 1994. *The Double Mirror: A Skeptical Journey into Buddhist Tantra*. Berkeley: North Atlantic Books.

Capper, Daniel. 2002. *Guru Devotion and the American Buddhist Experience*. Lewiston, NY: Edwin Mellen Press.

Chambers, Robert. 1983. *Rural Development: Putting the Last First*. Harlow: Longman.

Chappell, David. W., ed. 2003. *Socially Engaged Spirituality: Essays in Honor of Sulak Sivaraksa on His 70th Birthday*. Bangkok: Sathirakoses-Nagapradipa Foundation.

Chaudhari, S. N. 1985. "Concepts, Experience and Problems in Community Participation and Involvement," In *Rural Poor: Their Hopes and Aspirations*, edited by M. S. Mishra. Calcutta: Indian Institute of Management.

Cheah, Joseph. 2011. *Race and Religion in American Buddhism: White Supremacy and Immigrant Adaptation*. New York: Oxford University Press.

Clifford, James, and George Marcus, eds. 1986. *Writing Culture: The Poetics and Politics of Ethnography*. Berkeley: University of California Press.

Coleman, James William. 2001. *The New Buddhism: The Western Transformation of an Ancient Tradition*. Oxford: Oxford University Press.

Collins, Steven. 1998. *Nirvana and Other Buddhist Felicities: Utopias of the Pali Imaginaire*. Cambridge: Cambridge University Press.

Colony, Merry. 1997. "Malaysian Feng-shui Masters and Taiwanese Architects and Technicians Work on Maitreya Project in Bodhgaya." *Mandala*. May/June: 12.

———. 1998. "The Blessings of Chenrezig Himself: The Guarantee of Future Success." *Mandala*. March/April: 38.

Comaroff, Jean. 1985. *Body of Power, Spirit of Resistance: The Culture and History of a South African People*. Chicago: University of Chicago Press.

Coomaraswamy, Ananda K. 1956. *Medieval Sinhalese Art*. New York: Pantheon Books.

Copeman, J. 2005/6. "Blood, Blessings and Technology in India." *Cambridge Anthropology* 25(3): 39–51.

Courtin, Robina, and Tenzin Zopa, eds. 2003. *The Thousand Buddha Relic Stupa: Commemorating the Great Mahasiddha Geshe Lama Konchok*. Nepal: Tenzin Zopa.

Cousens, Di. 2007. "The Maitreya Project." http://www.bodhgayanews.net/kushi nagar.htm?. Accessed: December 2007.

Cozort, Daniel. 2003. "The Making of the Western Lama." In *Buddhism in the Modern World: Adaptations of an Ancient Tradition*, edited by Steven Heine and Charles S. Prebish, 221–248. New York: Oxford University Press.

Crapanzano, Vincent. 1980. *Tuhami: Portrait of a Moroccan*. Chicago: University of Chicago Press.

———. 1985. *Waiting: The Whites of South Africa*. New York: Random House.

———. 2004. *Imaginative Horizons: An Essay in Literary-Philosophical Anthropology*. Chicago: University of Chicago Press.

Crook, Tony. 2007. *Anthropological Knowledge, Secrecy, and Bolivip, Papua New Guinea: Exchanging Skin*. New York: Oxford University Press.

Deloria, Vine, Jr. 1969. *Custer Died for Your Sins: An Indian Manifesto*. Norman: University of Oklahoma Press.

Diehl, Keila. 2002. *Echoes from Dharamsala: Music in the Life of a Tibetan Refugee Community*. Berkeley: University of California Press.

Diemberger, Hildegard. 2005 "Female Oracles in Modern Tibet." In *Women of Tibet*, edited by Janet Gyatso and Hanna Havnevik, 113–168. New York: Columbia University Press.

Dorje, Lama Sherab. 1998. "The Unique Teachings of Tibetan Buddhist Meditation and Its Future in the West." In *Buddhism in America*, edited by B. D. Hotchkiss, 36–53. Rutland, VT: Charles E. Tuttle.

Doyle, Tara. 2012. "Why Cause Unnecessary Confusion? Re-inscribing the Mahabodhi Temple's Holy Places." In *Cross-Disciplinary Perspectives on a Contested Buddhist Site: Bodh Gaya Jataka*, edited by David Geary, Matthew R. Sayers, and Abhishek Singh Amar, 119–138. New York: Routledge.

Dreyfus, Georges. 1998. "The Shuk-den Affair: History and Nature of a Quarrel." *Journal of the International Association of Buddhist Studies* 21(2): 227–270.

———. 2003. *The Sound of Two Hands Clapping: The Education of a Tibetan Buddhist Monk*. Berkeley: University of California Press.

Dreze, Jean, Meera Samson, and Satyajit Singh, eds. 1997. *The Dam & the Nation: Displacement and Resettlement in the Narmada Valley*. New Delhi: Oxford University Press.

D'Souza, Dilip. 2002. *The Narmada Dammed: An Inquiry into the Politics of Development.* New Delhi: Penguin Books.

Eade, John, and Michael J. Sallnow. 1991. "Introduction," In *Contesting the Sacred: The Anthropology of Christian Pilgrimage,* edited by John Eade and Michael J. Sallnow, 1–29. London: Routledge.

Eck, Diana. 1982. *Banaras: City of Light.* New York: Alfred A. Knopf.

Ellington, Ter. 1998. "Arrow and Mirror: Interactive Consciousness, Ethnography, and the Tibetan State Oracle's Trance." *Anthropology and Humanism* 23(1): 51–76.

Eppsteiner, Fred, ed. 1985. *The Path of Compassion: Writings on Socially Engaged Buddhism.* Berkeley, CA: Parallax Press.

Escobar, Arturo. 1995. *Encountering Development: The Making and Unmaking of the Third World.* Princeton, NJ: Princeton University Press.

Falcone, Jessica. 2001. "Buddhist Development Strategies in India: A Modern Twist on an Ancient Doctrine of Compassion." MA Thesis, George Washington University.

——. 2007a. "Questioning the Maitreya Project: What Would the Buddha Do?" *Wild River Review.* www.wildriverreview.com. Accessed: December 2007.

——. 2007b. "Questioning the Maitreya Project: What Would the Buddha Do? The Debate Continues. . . ." *Wild River Review.* www.wildriverreview.com. Accessed: March 2008.

——. 2010a. "'I Spy . . .': The (Im)possibilities of Ethical Participant Observation with Antagonists, Religious Extremists, and Other Tough Nuts." *Michigan Discussions in Anthropology* 18(1): 243–282.

——. 2010b. "A Meditation on Meditation: The Horizons of Meditative Thinking in Tibetan Monasticism and American Anthropology." *Michigan Discussions in Anthropology* 18(1): 402–441.

——. 2011. "The Buddhist Lama and the Indian Farmer: Negotiating Modernity and Tradition in the Development Plans for Kushinagar, India." In *Inequality in a Globalizing World: Perspectives, Processes, and Experiences,* edited by Sangeeta Parashar and Yong Wang, 107–117. Dubuque, IA: Kendall-Hunt Publishing.

——. 2012a. "Maitreya or the Love of Buddhism: The Non-event of Bodh Gaya's Giant Statue." In *Cross-Disciplinary Perspectives on a Contested Buddhist Site: Bodh Gaya Jataka,* edited by David Geary, Matthew R. Sayers, and Abhishek Singh Amar, 152–171. New York: Routledge.

——. 2012b. "Putting the 'Fun' in Fundamentalism: Religious Extremism and the Split Self in Hindu Summer Camps in Washington D.C." *Ethos* 40(2): 164–195.

——. 2013. "The *Hau* of Theory: The Kept-Gift of Theory Itself in American Anthropology." *Anthropology and Humanism* 38(2): 122–145.

——. 2016. "Dance Steps, Nationalist Movement: How Hindu Extremists Claimed Garba-raas." *Anthropology Now* 8(3): 50–61.

——. 2017. "A Transnational Tulku: The Multiple Lives of FPMT's Spanish-born Lama Ösel." *Revue d'Etudes Tibetaines* 38 (February): 220–240.

Falcone, Jessica, and Tsering Wangchuk. 2008. "'We're Not Home': Tibetan Refugees in India in the Twenty-First Century." *India Review* 7(3): 164–199.

Faure, Bernard. 2004. *Double Exposure: Cutting across Buddhist and Western Discourses.* Stanford: Stanford University Press.

Feng, Xiao. 2005. "Giant Buddhist Statue Enshrined in Hainan." *China Daily*. April 16. www.chinadaily.com.cn. Accessed: June 7, 2017.

Ferguson, James. 1994. *The Anti-Politics Machine: "Development," Depoliticization, and Bureaucratic Power in Lesotho*. Minneapolis: University of Minnesota Press.

Feuerstein, Georg. 1990. *Holy Madness: The Shock Tactics and Radical Teachings of Crazy-Wise Adepts, Holy Fools and Rascal Gurus*. New York: Paragon House.

Fields, Rick. 1992. *How the Swans Came to the Lake*. 3rd ed. Boston: Shambhala.

——. 1998. "Divided Dharma: White Buddhists, Ethnic Buddhists and Racism. In *The Faces of Buddhism in America*, edited by Charles S. Prebish and Kenneth K. Tanaka, 196–206. Berkeley: University of California Press.

Finn, Janet L. 1998. *Tracing the Veins: Of Copper, Culture and Community from Butte to Chuquicamata*. Berkeley: University of California Press.

Fish, Jefferson. 2012. *The Myth of Race*. Montclair, NJ: Argo-Navis.

Foucault, Michel. 1979. *Discipline and Punish: The Birth of the Prison*. New York: Vintage Books.

Fortun, Kim. 2001. *Advocacy after Bhopal: Environmentalism, Disaster, New Global Orders*. Chicago: University of Chicago Press.

FPMT. n.d. "Selection of Verses for Offering Robes." Pamphlet.

——. 2008a. "Foundation Membership." www.fpmt.org. Accessed: December 2008.

——. 2008b. "Foundation Membership FAQ." www.fpmt.org. Accessed: December 2008.

——. 2008c. "The FPMT Puja Fund." www.fpmt.org. Accessed: December 2008.

——. 2008d. "Lama Tsongkhapa Teachers Fund." www.fpmt.org. Accessed: December 2008.

——. 2008e. "Sera Je Food Fund." www.fpmt.org. Accessed December 2008.

——. 2009a. "Center Frequently Asked Questions." www.fpmt.org. Accessed: January 2009.

——. 2009b. "Osel." www.fpmt.org. Accessed: December 2009.

——. 2010. "Friends of FPMT." www.fpmt.org. Accessed: April 2010.

——. 2017a. "The Buddhas Revolution: An FPMT Documentary." www.fpmt.org. Accessed: April 2017.

——. 2017b. "FPMT Board of Directors: Members of the Board." www.fpmt.org. Accessed: April 2017.

——. 2017c. "Resident Teachers at FPMT Centers." www.fpmt.org. Accessed: April 2017.

Fuchs, Dale. 2009. "Boy Chosen by Dalai Lama Turns Back on Buddhist Order." *Guardian*. May 31. www.guardian.co.uk. Accessed: October 2009.

Gardner, Katy, and David Lewis. 1996. *Anthropology, Development and the Post-Modern Challenge*. Sterling, VA: Pluto Press.

Gatter, Linda. 2001. "Maitreya Project: A Ray of Hope at the Site of the Buddha's Birth." *Turning Wheel* Summer: 28–31.

——. 2007a. "Maitreya Project to Proceed Only if All Stakeholders Give Consent." *Buddhist Channel*. www.buddhistchannel.tv. Accessed: September 2007.

——. 2007b. "What Would the Buddha Do? The Maitreya Project Replies." *Wild River Review*. www.wildriverreview.com. Accessed: December 2007.

——. 2008. "Maitreya Project: Setting the Record Straight." *Mandala*. February/March: 30–33.

Gaya Forum of Village Republics. 1999a. "Cover Letter." July 24. http://www.bodh gayanews.net/statue/statue01.htm. Accessed: April 2010.

———. 1999b. "Letter to Maitreya Project." May 28. http://www.bodhgayanews.net/ statue/statue01.htm. Accessed: April 2010.

Geary, David. 2012. "World Heritage in the shadow of zamindari." In *Cross-Disciplinary Perspectives on a Contested Buddhist Site: Bodh Gaya Jataka*, edited by David Geary, Matthew R. Sayers, and Abhishek Singh Amar, 141–152. New York: Routledge.

Geary, Patrick. 1986. "Sacred Commodities: The Circulation of Medieval Relics," In *The Social Life of Things: Commodities in Cultural Perspective*, edited by Arjun Appadurai, 169–194. Cambridge: Cambridge University Press.

Geertz, Clifford. 1988. *Works and Lives: The Anthropologist as Author*. Stanford: Stanford University Press.

Gell, Alfred. 1998. *Art and Agency: An Anthropological Theory*. New York: Oxford University Press.

Gethin, Rupert. 1998. *The Foundations of Buddhism*. Oxford: Oxford University Press.

Gombrich, Richard, and Gananath Obeyesekere. 1988. *Buddhism Transformed: Religious Change in Sri Lanka*. Princeton, NJ: Princeton University Press.

Goonatilake, Susantha. 1999. "De-Westernizing Futures Studies." In *Rescuing All Our Futures: The Future of Future Studies*, edited by Ziauddin Sardar, 72–81. Westport, CT: Praeger Press.

Gregory, Peter. 2001. "Describing the Elephant: Buddhism in America." *Religion and American Culture: A Journal of Interpretation* 11: 233–263.

Grodzins Gold, Ann. 1988. *Fruitful Journeys: The Ways of Rajasthani Pilgrims*. Berkeley: University of California Press.

Guha-Thakurta, Tapati. 2004. *Monuments, Objects, Histories: Institutions of Art in Colonial and Postcolonial India*. Delhi: Permanent Black.

Gupta, Akhil. 1997. "The Song of the Nonaligned World: Transnational Identities and the Reinscription of Space in Late Capitalism." In *Culture, Power, Place: Explorations in Critical Anthropology*, edited by Akhil Gupta and James Ferguson, 179–199. Durham, NC: Duke University Press.

———. 1998. *Postcolonial Developments: Agriculture in the Making of Modern India*. Durham, NC: Duke University Press.

———. 2013. "Messy Bureaucracies." *HAU: Journal of Ethnographic Theory* 3(3): 435–40.

Gusterson, Hugh. 1996. *Nuclear Rites: A Weapons Laboratory at the End of the Cold War*. Berkeley: University of California Press.

Guyer, Jane I. 2007. "Prophecy and the Near Future: Thoughts on Macroeconomic, Evangelical and Punctuated Time." *American Ethnologist* 34(3): 409–421.

Gyatso, Tenzin. 2000. *The Meaning of Life: Buddhist Perspectives on Cause and Effect*. Boston: Wisdom Publications.

Harvey, David. 1989. *The Condition of Postmodernity: An Enquiry into the Origins of Cultural Change*. Oxford: Basil Blackwell.

Havnevik, Hanna. 2002. "A Tibetan Female State Oracle: Religion and Secular Culture in Tibet." In *Tibetan Studies II: Proceedings of the Ninth Seminar of the International Association of Tibetan Studies*, edited by H. Blezer, 259–289. Leiden: E. J. Brill.

Holland, Jeremy, and James Blackburn, eds. 1998. *Whose Voice?: Participatory Research and Policy Change*. London: Intermediate Technology Publications.

Holt, John Clifford. 1993. *Anagatavamsa Desana: The Sermon of the Chronicle-To-Be*. Delhi: Motilal Banarsidass Publishers.

Hori, G. Victor Sogen. 1998. "Japanese Zen in America: Americanizing the Face in the Mirror." In *The Faces of Buddhism in America*, edited by Charles S. Prebish and Kenneth K. Tanaka, 49–78. Berkeley: University of California Press.

Hubbard, Jaime. 2006. "Putting Buddhist Ideas into Social Practice for Peace and Justice: The Truth of the Conventional." In *Buddhist Exploration of Peace and Justice*, edited by C. Mun and R. S. Green, 151–172. Honolulu: Blue Pine.

Huber, Toni. 1999. *The Cult of Pure Crystal Mountain*. New York: Oxford University Press.

——. 2008. *The Holy Land Reborn: Pilgrimage & the Reinvention of Buddhist India*. Chicago: University of Chicago Press.

Hull, Matthew. 2012. *Government of Paper: The Materiality of Bureaucracy in Urban Pakistan*. Berkeley: University of California Press.

Hunt-Perry, Patricia, and Lyn Fine. 2000. "All Buddhism Is Engaged: Thich Nhat Hanh and the Order of Interbeing." In *Engaged Buddhism in the West*, edited by Christopher S. Queen, 35–66. Boston: Wisdom Publications.

Inada, Kenneth K., and Nolan P. Jacobson. 1984. *Buddhism and American Thinkers*. Albany: State University of New York Press.

Jain, Kajri. 2016. "Post-reform India's Automotive-Iconic-Cement Assemblages: Uneven Globality, Territorial Spectacle and Iconic Exhibition Value." *Identities* 23(3): 327–344.

Jaini, Padmanabh S. 1988. "Stages in the Bodhisattva Career of the Tathâgatha Maitreya." In *Maitreya, the Future Buddha*, edited by Alan Sponberg and Helen Hardacre, 54-90. Cambridge: Cambridge University Press.

Jay, Ruby. 1982. *A Crack in the Mirror: Reflexive Perspectives in Anthropology*. Philadelphia: University of Pennsylvania Press.

Jenkins, Jolyon. 2012. "The Reluctant Lama." *BBC News*. September 28. Accessed: September 2012.

Junker, Kirk. 1999. "How the Future Is Cloned." In *Rescuing All Our Futures: The Future of Future Studies*, edited by Ziauddin Sardar, 19–35. Westport, CT: Praeger Press.

Kay, David N. 2004. *Tibetan and Zen Buddhism in Britain: Transplantation, Development and Adaptation*. New York: Routledge Curzon.

Kedge, Peter. 1998. "Gratitude for the 'Tremendous Goodwill and Support.'" *Mandala*. March/April: 40–41.

——. 2005a. "Maitreya Project, Latest Update, December 2005." www.maitreyaproject.org. Accessed: September 2009.

——. 2005b. "Maitreya Project, Latest Update, January 2005." www.maitreyaproject.org. Accessed: September 2009.

——. 2006. "Maitreya Project, Latest Update, August 2006." www.maitreyaproject.org. Accessed: September 2009.

——. 2007a. "Maitreya Project, Latest Update, November 2007." www.maitreyaproject.org. Accessed: December 2008.

——. 2007b. "The Maitreya Project, Latest Update, September 2007." www.maitrey aproject.org. Accessed: March 2008.

——. 2007c. "Maitreya Project Structure and Financial Summaries." www.maitrey aproject.org. Maitreya Project International. Accessed: March 2008.

Keown, Damien. 2006. "Buddhism: Morality Without Ethics?" In *Buddhist Studies from India to America: Essays in Honor of Charles S. Prebish*, edited by Damien Keown, 45–55. New York: Routledge.

King, Sallie B. 2005. *Being Benevolence: The Social Ethics of Engaged Buddhism*. Honolulu: University of Hawai'i Press.

Kitagawa, Joseph M. 1981. "The Career of Maitreya, with Special Reference to Japan." *History of Religions* 21(2): 107–125.

——. 1988. "The Many Faces of Maitreya." In *Maitreya, the Future Buddha*, edited by Alan Sponberg and Helen Hardacre, 7–22. Cambridge: Cambridge University Press.

Klima, Alan. 2002. *The Funeral Casino: Meditation, Massacre, and Exchange with the Dead in Thailand*. Princeton, NJ: Princeton University Press.

Kongtrul, Jamgon. 1999. *The Teacher–Student Relationship*. Translated by Ron Garry. Ithaca, NY: Snow Lion Publications.

Kopytoff, Igor. 1986. "The Cultural Biography of Things: Commoditization as Process." In *The Social Life of Things: Commodities in Cultural Perspective*, edited by Arjun Appadurai, 64–94. Cambridge: Cambridge University Press.

Kotler, Arnold, ed. 1996. *Engaged Buddhist Reader: Ten Years of Engaged Buddhist Publishing*. Berkeley, CA: Parallax Press.

Kraft, Kenneth. 1999. *The Wheel of Engaged Buddhism: A New Map of the Path*. New York: Weatherhill.

——. 2000. "New Voices in Engaged Buddhist Studies." In *Engaged Buddhism in the West*, edited by Christopher S. Queen, 485–511. Boston, Wisdom Publications.

Landaw, Jonathan. 1982. "Introduction to the First Edition." In *Wisdom Energy: Basic Buddhist Teachings*, by Lama Yeshe and Lama Thubten Zopa Rinpoche, 1–10. New Delhi: Wisdom Publications & Timeless Books.

Latouche, Serge. 1997. "Paradoxical Growth." In *The Post-Development Reader*, edited by M. Rahnema and V. Bawtree, 135–142. Atlantic Highlands, NJ: Zed Books.

Latour, Bruno. 1996. *Aramis or the Love of Technology*. Cambridge: Cambridge University Press.

Layman, Emma McCloy. 1976. *Buddhism in America*. Chicago: Nelson-Hall.

Lief, J. 1998. "Cultivating Loving-Kindness through the Slogans of Atisha." In *Buddhism in America*, edited by B. D. Hotchkiss, 7–23. Rutland, VT: Charles E. Tuttle.

Lowe, Lisa. 1996. *Immigrant Acts: On Asian American Cultural Politics*. Durham, NC: Duke University Press.

Loy, David R. 1997. "The Religion of the Market." *Journal of the American Academy of Religion* 65(2): 275–290.

Lutgendorf, Philip. 1994. "My Hanuman Is Bigger Than Yours." *History of Religions* 33(3): 211–245.

Mackenzie, Vicki. 1988. *Reincarnation: The Boy Lama*. London: Bloomsbury.

——. 1995. *Reborn in the West: The Reincarnation Masters*. New York: Marlowe.

Marcus, George. 1995. "Ethnography in/of the World System: The Emergence of Multi-sited Ethnography." *Annual Review of Anthropology* 24:95–117.

Masco, Joseph. 2005. "A Notebook on Desert Modernism: From the Nevada Test Site to Liberace's Two-Hundred-Pound Suit." In *Histories of the Future*, edited by Daniel Rosenberg and Susan Harding, 19–49. Durham, NC: Duke University Press.

Maurer, Bill. 2003. "Uncanny Exchanges: The Possibilities of Failure of 'Making Change' with Alternative Monetary Forms." *Environment and Planning D: Society and Space* 21(3): 317–340.

Mauss, Marcel. 1966. *The Gift: Forms and Functions of Exchange in Archaic Societies.* London: Cohen & West.

McAra, Sally. 2007. *Land of Beautiful Vision: Making a Buddhist Sacred Place in New Zealand.* Honolulu: University of Hawai'i Press.

McDonald, Kathleen. 1984. *How to Meditate: A Practical Guide.* Boston: Wisdom Publications.

McLellan, Janet. 1999. *Many Petals of the Lotus: Five Asian Buddhist Communities in Toronto.* Toronto: University of Toronto Press.

McLeod, Jaime. 2007. "Proponents of the Maitreya Project Heartless, Arrogant." *Buddhist Channel.* www.buddhistchannel.tv. Accessed: September 2007.

McMahan, David L. 2008. *The Making of Buddhist Modernism.* New York: Oxford University Press.

Meddegama, Udaya. 1993. *Anagatavamsa Desana: The Sermon of the Chronicle-to-Be.* Delhi: Motilal Banarsidass Publishers.

Miller, Daniel, ed. 2005. *Materiality.* Durham, NC: Duke University Press.

Miyazaki, Hirokazu. 2003. "The Temporalities of the Market." *American Anthropologist* 105(2): 255–265.

Mohan Mathur, Hari, ed. 2001. *Resettling Displaced People: Policy and Practice in India.* New Delhi: Routledge.

Mohan Mathur, Hari, and David Mardsen, eds. 1998. *Development Projects & Impoverishment Risks: Resettling Project-Affected People in India.* New Delhi: Oxford University Press.

MPI. 2000. "Maitreya Project, Latest Update, October 2000." www.maitreyaproject. org. Accessed: December 2009.

——. 2001a. "Maitreya Project, Latest Update, June 2001." www.maitreyaproject. org. Accessed: September 2009.

——. 2001b. "Maitreya Project, Latest Update, November 2001." www.maitreyapro ject.org. Accessed: September 2009.

——. 2003. "Maitreya Project, Latest Update, May 2003." www.maitreyaproject.org. Accessed: September 2009.

——. 2004a. *Maitreya Project.* DVD, Maitreya Project International.

——. 2004b. "Maitreya Project, Latest Update, August 2004." www.maitreyaproject. org. Accessed: September 2009.

——. 2004c. "Maitreya Project, Latest Update, December 2004." www.maitreyapro ject.org. Accessed: September 2009.

——. 2005. "Maitreya Project," www.maitreyaproject.org. Accessed: September 2005.

——. 2007a. "Maitreya Project, Latest Update, June 2007." www.maitreyaproject. org. Accessed: September 2009.

——. 2007b. "Project Partners: Delcam," www.maitreyaproject.org. Accessed: December 2007.

——. 2007c. "Summary of Receipts & Payments, 1990–2006." www.maitreyaproject.org. Accessed: February 2008.

——. 2007d. "Summary of Receipts & Payments, 2006." www.maitreyaproject.org. Accessed: February 2008.

——. 2008a. "Funding Proposal Maitreya Healthcare Project." www.maitreyaproject.org. Accessed: September 2009.

——. 2008b. "Maitreya Project, Latest Update, October 2008." www.maitreyaproject.org. Accessed: November 2008.

——. 2009. "Maitreya Project, Latest Update, September 2009." www.maitreyaproject.org. Accessed: September 2009.

——. 2010. "Maitreya Project, Latest Update, April 2010." www.maitreyaproject.org. Accessed: April 2011.

——. 2012. "Announcement by Lama Zopa Rinpoche." www.maitreyaproject.org. Accessed: August 2013.

Mullin, Glenn H., ed. 1998. *Living in the Face of Death: The Tibetan Tradition.* Ithaca, NY: Snow Lion Publishers.

Myers, Fred R. 1986. *Pintupi Country, Pintupi Self: Sentiment, Place, and Politics among Western Desert Aborigines.* Washington, DC: Smithsonian Institution Press.

——, ed. 2001. *The Empire of Things: Regimes of Value and Material Culture.* Santa Fe, NM: School of American Research Press.

Nattier, Jan. 1988. "The Meanings of the Maitreya Myth: A Typological Analysis." In *Maitreya, the Future Buddha,* edited by Alan Sponberg and Helen Hardacre, 23–47. Cambridge: Cambridge University Press.

——. 1998. "Who Is a Buddhist? Charting the Landscape of Buddhist America." In *The Faces of Buddhism in America,* edited by Charles S. Prebish and Kenneth K. Tanaka, 183–195. Berkeley: University of California Press.

Nelson, Niki, and Susan Wright. 1997. *Power and Participatory Development.* London: Intermediate Technology Publications.

Numrich, Paul David. 1996. *Old Wisdom in the New World: Americanization in Two Immigrant Theravada Buddhist Temples.* Knoxville: University of Tennessee Press.

Ohnuma, Reiko. 2005. "Gift." In *Critical Terms for the Study of Buddhism,* edited by Donald S. Lopez, 103–123. Chicago: University of Chicago Press.

Ondaatje, Michael. 2000. *Anil's Ghost.* New York: Vintage International.

Ong, Aihwa. 1987. *Spirits of Resistance and Capitalist Discipline.* Albany: State University of New York Press.

——. 2003. *Buddha is Hiding: Refugees, Citizenship, the New America.* Berkeley: University of California Press.

Pandey, Geeta. 2008. "Dying of Hunger in Indian State." *BBC News.* March 5. www.bbc.co.uk. Accessed: March 2008.

Parkum, Virginia Cohn, and J. Anthony Stultz. 2000. "The Angulimala Lineage: Buddhist Prison Ministries." In *Engaged Buddhism in the West,* edited by Christopher S. Queen, 347–371. Boston: Wisdom Publications.

Parry, Jonathan P. 1994. *Death in Banaras.* Cambridge: Cambridge University Press.

Pattnaik, Soumyajit. 2007. "Knot Right: SEZs Affect Marriage." *Hindustan Times.* June 5. www.hindustantimes.com. Accessed: December 2007.

Pepper, Daniel. 2007a. "Indian Farmers Oppose Giant Buddha Statue." *Christian Science Monitor*. September 10. www.csmonitor.com. Accessed: December 2007.

———. 2007b. "Villagers Fight Plan for Giant Buddha." *Washington Times*. September 20. www.washingtontimes.com. Accessed: September 2007.

Pierce, Lori Ann. 2000. *"Constructing American* Buddhisms: Discourses of Race and Religion in Territorial Hawai'i." Ph.D. Dissertation. University of Hawai'i.

Pontones, Diego. 2009. "Osel's Awakening: A Kid against His Destiny." *Babylon Magazine* 5:57–73.

Powers, John. 1995. *Introduction to Tibetan Buddhism*. Ithaca, NY: Snow Lion Publications.

Prakash, Satya. 2007. "SC Asks Centre, States, to Explain the Misuse of Act." *Hindustan Times*. May 20. www.hindustantimes.com. Accessed: October 2007.

Prebish, Charles S. 1993. "Two Buddhisms Reconsidered." *Buddhist Studies Review* 10(2): 187–206.

———. 1998. "Introduction." In *The Faces of Buddhism in America*, edited by Charles S. Prebish and Kenneth K. Tanaka, 1–10. Berkeley: University of California Press.

Puri, Bharati. 2006. *Engaged Buddhism: The Dalai Lama's Worldview*. New Delhi: Oxford University Press.

Pye, Michael. 1978. *Skilful Means: A Concept in Mahayana Buddhism*. London: Duckworth.

Queen, Christopher S. 2000. "Introduction: A New Buddhism." In *Engaged Buddhism in the West*, edited by Christopher S. Queen, 1–31. Boston: Wisdom Publications.

Queen, Christopher S., and Sallie B. King, eds. 1996. *Engaged Buddhism: Buddhist Liberation Movements in Asia*. Albany: State University of New York Press.

Rabinow, Paul. 1977. *Reflections on Fieldwork in Morocco*. Berkeley: University of California Press.

Rabten, Geshe. 1974. *The Preliminary Practices*. Dharamsala: Library of Tibetan Works and Archives.

Ray, Himanshu. 2012. "From Multi-religious Sites to Mono-religious Monuments in South Asia: The Colonial Legacy of Heritage Management." In *The Routledge Handbook of Heritage in Asia*, edited by Patrick Daly and Tim Winter, 68–84. London: Routledge.

Ricoeur, Paul. 1986. *Lectures on Ideology and Utopia*. New York: Columbia University Press.

Rinpoche, Gyatrul. 1999. "Introduction." In *The Teacher-Student Relationship*, by Jamgon Kongtrul, 11–17. Ithaca, NY: Snow Lion Publications.

Rinpoche, Lama Thubten Zopa. 1998. "Foreword." In *The Bliss of Inner Fire: Heart Practice of the Six Yogas of Naropa*, by Lama Thubten Yeshe, vii–xx. Somerville, MA: Wisdom Publications.

———. 2004. "Dedication Prayers for Special Occasions." Dictated to Holly Ansett. Edited by Kendall Magnussen. Pamphlet. Published by FPMT Education Services.

———. 2006. "Benefits of Having Many Holy Objects." *Tashi Delek: Newsletter of Amitabha Buddhist Center Singapore*. July/August: 6–7.

———. 2006b. "Extensive Offering Practice." Booklet. Kopan Edition. Published by FPMT, Inc.

——. 2008. *How Things Exist: Teachings on Emptiness*. Boston: Lama Yeshe Wisdom Archive.

——. 2014. "Maitreya Buddha: Bringing Loving Kindness to the World." *Mandala*. April–June: 18–19.

Rinpoche, Patrul. 1994. *The Words of My Perfect Teacher*. San Francisco: HarperCollins Publishers.

Robbins, Thomas and Susan J. Palmer. 1997. "Patterns of Contemporary Apocalypticism." In *Millennium, Messiahs, and Mayhem: Contemporary Apocalyptic Movements*, edited by Thomas Robbins and Susan J. Palmer. New York: Routledge.

Robinson, Richard H., and Willard L. Johnson. 1977. *The Buddhist Religion*. Belmont, CA: Wadsworth Publishing.

Rocha, Cristina. 2006. *Zen in Brazil: The Quest for Cosmopolitan Modernity*. Honolulu: University of Hawai'i Press.

Rodriguez, Jason. 2012. "NGOs, Corruption, and Reciprocity in the Land of Buddha's Enlightenment." In *Cross-Disciplinary Perspectives on a Contested Buddhist Site: Bodh Gaya Jataka*, edited by David Geary, Matthew R. Sayers, and Abhishek Singh Amar, 189–201. New York: Routledge.

Rose, Linda. 1998. "The Coming of Maitreya." *Mandala*. March/April: 32–37.

Rosenberg, Daniel, and Susan Harding, eds. 2005. *Histories of the Future*. Durham, NC: Duke University Press.

Sachs, Wolfgang, ed. 1992. *The Development Dictionary: A Guide to Knowledge as Power*. London: Zed.

Sardar, Ziauddin, ed. 1999. *Rescuing All Our Futures: The Future of Future Studies*. Westport, CT: Praeger Press.

Scheper-Hughes, Nancy. 1995. "The Primacy of the Ethical: Propositions for a Militant Anthropology." *Current Anthropology* 36 (3): 409–440.

Schopen, Gregory. 1991. "Monks and the Relic Cult in the Mahaparinirvanasutta: An Old Misunderstanding in Regard to Monastic Buddhism." In *From Benares to Beijing: Essays on Buddhism and Chinese Religion in Honor of Prof. Jan Yunhua*, edited by K. Shinohara and Gregory Schopen, 187–201. Oakville: Mosaic Press.

——. 1997. *Bones, Stones and Buddhist Monks*. Honolulu: University of Hawai'i Press.

Scott, James C. 1985. *Weapons of the Weak: Everyday Forms of Peasant Resistance*. New Haven: Yale University Press.

Seager, Richard Hughes. 1999. *Buddhism in America*. New York: Columbia University Press.

Setty, E. D. 1991. *Rural Development: Problems and Prospects*. New Delhi: Inter-India Publications.

Shah, Pankaj. 2016. "BSP: Maya Will Not Embrace Buddhism Now." *Times of India*. April 16. http://timesofindia.indiatimes.com/city/lucknow. Accessed: April 2017.

Sharma, Aradhana, and Akhil Gupta. 2006. "Introduction: Rethinking Theories of the State in the Age of Globalization." In *The Anthropology of the State*, edited by A. Sharma and A. Gupta, 1–41. Oxford: Blackwell.

Shiva, Vandana. 1988. *Staying Alive: Women, Ecology and Development*. London: Zed Books.

Singh, Ram. 2007. "A New Law for the Land." *The Indian Express*. June 7. www.indianexpress.com. Accessed: April 2010.

Snellgrove, David. 1987. *Indo-Tibetan Buddhism: Indian Buddhists and Their Tibetan Successors*. Boston: Shambhala.

Sopa, Geshe Lhundup. 1983. *Lectures on Tibetan Religious Culture*. Dharamsala: Library of Tibetan Works and Archives.

Sponberg, Alan. 1988. "Introduction." In *Maitreya, the Future Buddha*, edited by Alan Sponberg and Helen Hardacre: 1–4. Cambridge: Cambridge University Press.

Spooner, Brian. 1986. "Weavers and Dealers: The Authenticity of an Oriental Carpet." In *The Social Life of Things: Commodities in Cultural Perspective*, edited by Arjun Appadurai, 195–235. Cambridge: Cambridge University Press.

Stephen, Ann. 1980. "Margaret Preston's Second Coming." *Art Network* 2:14–15.

Stoler, Ann Laura. 2002. "Developing Historical Negatives: Race and the (Modernist) Visions of a Colonial State." In *From the Margins: Historical Anthropology and its Futures*, edited by Brian K. Axel, 156–185. Durham, NC: Duke University Press.

Strong, John S. 2004. *Relics of the Buddha*. Princeton, NJ: Princeton University Press.

———. 2008. *The Experience of Buddhism: Sources and Interpretations*. Belmont, CA: Wadsworth/Thomson Learning.

Swearer, Donald K. 2004. *Becoming the Buddha: The Ritual of Image Consecration in Thailand*. Princeton, NJ: Princeton University Press.

Szondi, Peter. 1986. "Hope in the Past: On Walter Benjamin." In *On Textual Understandings and Other Essays*, 145–159. Minneapolis: University of Minnesota Press.

Tambiah, Stanley J. 1984. *The Buddhist Saints of the Forest and the Cult of Amulets: A Study in Charisma, Hagiography, Sectarianism and Millennial Buddhism*. Cambridge: Cambridge University Press.

———. 1992. *Buddhism Betrayed? Religion, Politics and Violence in Sri Lanka*. Chicago: University of Chicago Press.

Tanaka, Kenneth K. 1998. "Epilogue: The Colors and Contours of American Buddhism." In *The Faces of Buddhism in America*, edited by Charles S. Prebish and Kenneth K. Tanaka, 287–298. Berkeley: University of California Press.

Taussig, Michael. 1980. *The Devil and Commodity Fetishism in South America*. Chapel Hill: University of North Carolina Press.

Thomas, Nicholas. 1991. *Entangled Objects: Exchange, Material Culture, and Colonialism in the Pacific*. Cambridge, MA: Harvard University Press.

Titmuss, Christopher. 2001. "The Unhappy Prince and the Maitreya Statue Project." *Turning Wheel* Summer: 31–34.

Trainor, Kevin. 1997. *Relics, Ritual, and Representation in Buddhism*. Cambridge: Cambridge University Press.

Trainor, Kevin, and David Germano, eds. 2004. *Embodying the Dharma: Buddhist Relic Veneration in Asia*. Albany: State University of New York Press.

Trawick, Margaret. 2007. *Enemy Lines: Warfare, Childhood, and Play in Batticaloa*. Berkeley: University of California Press.

Tsing, Anna Lowenhaupt. 2005. *Friction: An Ethnography of Global Connection*. Princeton, NJ: Princeton University Press.

Turner, Terence S. 1993. "The Role of Indigenous Peoples in the Environmental Crisis: The Example of the Kayapo of the Brazilian Amazon." *Perspectives in Biology and Medicine* 36(3): 526–545.

Tweed, Thomas A. 1999. "Night-Stand Buddhists and Other Creatures: Sympathizers, Adherents and the Study of Religion." In *American Buddhism: Methods and Findings in Recent Scholarship*, edited by D. R. Williams and Christopher S. Queen, 71–90. Richmond: Curzon Press.

——. 2002. "Who Is a Buddhist? Night-Stand Buddhists and Other Creatures." In *Westward Dharma: Buddhism Beyond Asia*, edited by Charles S. Prebish and Martin Baumann, 17–33. Berkeley: University of California Press.

——. 2006. *Crossing and Dwelling: A Theory of Religion*. Cambridge, MA: Harvard University Press.

——. 2011. "Theory and Method in the Study of Buddhism: Toward 'Translocative' Analysis." *Journal of Global Buddhism* 12:17–32.

Tworkov, Helen. 1991. "Many Is More." *Tricycle* 1(2): 4.

Tyler, Stephen A. 1986. "Post-modern Ethnography: From Document of the Occult to Occult Document." In *Writing Culture: The Poetics and Politics of Ethnography*, edited by James Clifford and George Marcus, 122–140. Berkeley: University of California Press.

Wangmo, Jamyang. 2005. *The Lawudo Lama: Stories of Reincarnation from the Mount Everest Region*. Boston: Wisdom Publications.

Wayman, Alex. 1987. "The Guru in Buddhism." *Studia Missionalia* 36:195–213.

Weber, Max. 1968. *On Charisma and Institution Building*. Chicago: University of Chicago Press.

Weigman, Robin. 2000. "Feminism's Apocalyptic Futures." *New Literary History* 31(4): 805–825.

Weiner, Annette. 1985. "Inalienable Wealth." *American Ethnologist* 12(2): 210–227.

Willford, Andrew. 2006. *Cage of Freedom: Tamil Identity and the Ethnic Fetish in Malaysia*. Ann Arbor: University of Michigan Press.

Williams, Brackette F. 1989. "A Class Act: Anthropology and the Race to Nation Across Ethnic Terrain." *Annual Review of Anthropology*.18: 401–444.

Williams, Paul, and Anthony Tribe. 2000. *Buddhist Thought: A Complete Introduction to the Indian Tradition*. New York: Routledge.

Willis, Jan. 2001. *Dreaming Me: From Baptist to Buddhist, One Woman's Spiritual Journey*. New York: Riverhead Books.

Wilson, Jeff. 2012. *Dixie Dharma: Inside a Buddhist Temple in the American South*. Durham, NC: University of North Carolina Press.

Wolf, Eric. 2002. "The Virgin of Guadalupe: A Mexican National Symbol." In *A Reader in the Anthropology of Religion*, edited by M. Lambek, 168–174. Malden, MA: Blackwell.

Yeshe, Lama Thubten. 1998. *The Bliss of Inner Fire: Heart Practice of the Six Yogas of Naropa*. Somerville, MA: Wisdom Publications.

——. 2008. *Universal Love: The Yoga Method of Buddha Maitreya*. Boston: Lama Yeshe Wisdom Archive.

Zablocki, Abraham. 2008. "After Protestant Buddhism: Beyond the Modern/Traditional Binary in the Anthropology of Contemporary Buddhism." Conference Paper. Delivered at the American Academy of Religion Meetings in Chicago.

——. 2009. "Transnational Tulkus: The Globalization of the Tibetan Buddhist Tulku." In *TransBuddhism: Transmission, Translation, Transformation*, edited by Nalini Bhushan, Jay L. Garfield, and Abraham Zablocki, 43–54. Amherst: University of Massachusetts Press.

Zopa, Tenzin. 2003. "A Brief History of the Winter Jang Debate Session, Sera-je Buddhist Study Center." www.fpmt.org. Accessed: April 2010.

✿ INDEX

CPSIA information can be obtained
at www.ICGtesting.com
Printed in the USA
LVHW101613030822
725086LV00002B/197

9 781501 723483